WHISTLEBLOWING AND ORGANIZATIONAL SOCIAL RESPONSIBILITY

Corporate Social Responsibility Series

Series Editor:
Professor David Crowther, London Metropolitan University, UK

This series aims to provide high quality research books on all aspects of corporate social responsibility including: business ethics, corporate governance and accountability, globalization, civil protests, regulation, responsible marketing and social reporting.

The series is interdisciplinary in scope and global in application and is an essential forum for everyone with an interest in this area.

Also in the series

Repoliticizing Management: A Theory of Corporate Legitimacy
Conor Cradden
ISBN 0 7546 4497 9

Making Ecopreneurs: Developing Sustainable Entrepreneurship
Edited by Michael Schaper
ISBN 0 7546 4491 X

Corporate Social Responsibility in the Mining Industries
Natalia Yakovleva
ISBN 0 7546 4268 2

Ethical Boundaries of Capitalism
Edited by Daniel Daianu and Radu Vranceanu
ISBN 0 7546 4395 6

Human Values in Management
Edited by Ananda Das Gupta
ISBN 0 7546 4275 5

Nonprofit Trusteeship in Different Contexts
Rikki Abzug and Jeffrey S. Simonoff
ISBN 0 7546 3016 1

Corporate Social Performance: A Stakeholder Approach
Stuart Cooper
ISBN 0 7546 4174 0

Whistleblowing and Organizational Social Responsibility
A Global Assessment

WIM VANDEKERCKHOVE
Ghent University, Belgium

ASHGATE

Published by
Ashgate Publishing Limited
Gower House
Croft Road
Aldershot
Hampshire GU11 3HR
England

Ashgate Publishing Company
Suite 420
101 Cherry Street
Burlington, VT 05401-4405
USA

Ashgate website: http://www.ashgate.com

British Library Cataloguing in Publication Data
Vandekerckhove, Wim
    Whistleblowing and organizational social responsibility : a
    global assessment. - (Corporate social responsibility
    series)
    1. Whistle blowing 2.Social responsibility of business
    I.Title
    174.4

Library of Congress Cataloging-in-Publication Data
Vandekerckhove, Wim.
    Whistleblowing and organizational social responsibility : a global assessment / by
Wim Vandekerckhove.
        p. cm. -- (Corporate social responsibility series)
    Includes bibliographical references and index.
    ISBN 0-7546-4750-1
    1. Business ethics. 2. Whistle blowing. I. Title. II. Series.

    HF5387.V36 2006
    174'.4--dc22

2006009526

ISBN-10: 0 7546 4750 1
ISBN-13: 978 0 7546 4750 3

Printed and bound in Great Britain by Antony Rowe Ltd, Chippenham, Wiltshire.

Contents

List of Figures   *vii*
List of Tables   *ix*
Preface   *x*
Acknowledgements   *xi*

Introduction   1

1   Developing Research Questions   7
     Whistleblowing in an Organizational Context   7
     Whistleblowing Policies and this Research   19
     Possible Definitions of Whistleblowing   21
     Limitations of this Research   25
     Data Collection   27

2   Developing the Framework for an Ethical Assessment   29
     Normative Legitimation and Meaning-giving   29
     Niklas Luhmann   31
     Max Weber – *Verstehende Soziologie*   37
     A Foucauldian Perspective – and Some Deleuze   49
     Alain Touraine   59
     The Individual, the Organization and the Semantic   67

3   Possible Legitimation of Whistleblowing Policies   73
     Introduction   73
     Globalization Semantic   75
     Whistleblowing as a Human Right   92
     Whistleblowing and Organizational Social Responsibility   101
     Whistleblowing and Responsibility – Accountability   108
     Whistleblowing and Integrity   116
     Whistleblowing and Loyalty   124
     Whistleblowing and Efficiency   134
     Organizational Inefficiency   136
     Drawing Up the Screening Grid   142
     Actor, Subject and Recipient Element   145

4   Screening Whistleblowing Policies   163
     United States   163
     Australia   187
     New Zealand   206

United Kingdom   210
South Africa   221
Japan   231
Belgium   236
Whistleblowing Legislations Passing Through Parliaments   243
Others   263
Intergovernmental Bodies and Whistleblowing Policies   270

5   Towards what Legitimation of Whistleblowing?   279
     Tendencies in the Legitimation of Whistleblowing Policies   279
     How Ethical are these Tendencies?   295
     Lobbying for Ethical Whistleblowing Policies   307
     Suggestions for Future Research   314

References   *317*

Index   *339*

List of Figures

2.1   Linking Luhmann, Weber, Foucault and Touraine   30
2.2   Inserting the institutional level in the enterprise   63
2.3   Touraine's double and interrelated use of the term 'political'   65
2.4   IOS-diagram   70
3.1   Globalization semantic (primary concepts)   73
3.2   Freeman's 1984 'hub' model   93
3.3   Freeman and Evan's 1990 shift in perspective   93
3.4   Rowley's 1997 network perspective   93
3.5   Globalization semantic (human rights)   101
3.6   Globalization semantic (OSR-network)   107
3.7   Globalization semantic (OSR-stakeholder)   109
3.8   Globalization semantic (responsibility)   112
3.9   Globalization semantic (accountability)   116
3.10   Globalization semantic (integrity)   124
3.11   Globalization semantic (loyalty)   134
3.12   Globalization semantic (efficiency)   142
3.13   Human rights construct in IOS-diagram   156
3.14   OSR-network construct in IOS-diagram   157
3.15   OSR-stakeholder construct in IOS-diagram   157
3.16   Responsibility construct in IOS-diagram   158
3.17   Accountability construct in IOS-diagram   159
3.18   Integrity construct in IOS-diagram   160
3.19   Rational loyalty construct in IOS-diagram   161
3.20   Efficiency construct in IOS-diagram   161
4.1   Evolution of legitimation lines (US)   186
4.2   Evolution of legitimation lines (Australia)   207
4.3   Evolution of argumentation lines (New Zealand)   212
4.4   Evolution of legitimation lines (UK)   223
4.5   Evolution of legitimation lines (South Africa)   233
4.6   Evolution of legitimation lines (Japan)   237
4.7   Evolution of legitimation lines (Belgium)   242
4.8   Evolution of legitimation lines (the Netherlands)   252
4.9   Evolution of legitimation lines (Ireland)   254
4.10   Evolution of legitimation lines (Canada)   260
4.11   Evolution of legitimation lines (India)   264
4.12   Evolution of legitimation lines (Germany)   267
4.13   Evolution of legitimation lines (Switzerland)   269
4.14   Evolution of legitimation lines (intergovernmental bodies)   276
5.1   IOS-diagram of legitimation constructs with high usage   301

5.2   IOS-diagram of legitimation constructs with low usage   302
5.3   Whistleblowing 1970–2000 – from dilemma to paradox   313

List of Tables

1.1   Number of publications on whistleblowing in academic journals   12
1.2   Matrix of possible whistleblowing definitions   24
3.1   Possible normative legitimation main lines of argument   143
3.2   Grounding ethical theories of the legitimation constructs   146
3.3   Actor, subject and recipient elements derived from the
      legitimation constructs   153
3.4   Screening grid   154
4.1   Whistleblowing elements specified in US policies   185
4.2   Early 1990s recommendations (Australia)   190
4.3   Australian state legislation on whistleblowing   197
4.4   New Zealand Bills and Act   211
4.5   Subsequent UK whistleblowing Bills   222
4.6   South Africa Bills and Act   232
4.7   Whistleblowing policy in Japan   238
4.8   Flemish whistleblowing legislation (Belgium)   241
4.9   Whistleblowing policies proposed in the Netherlands   251
4.10 Whistleblowing policies proposed in Ireland   255
4.11 Whistleblowing policies proposed in Canada   259
4.12 Whistleblowing policies proposed in India   265
4.13 Whistleblowing policies developing in Switzerland   268
5.1   Clarification of the distinction subjectivation/subjectaffirmation   300
5.2   Distinction subjectivation/subjectaffirmation and IOS-
      movements   300
5.3   IOS-movements of current legitimation tendencies   301
5.4   Subjectaffirming movements in the legitimation constructs   308
5.5   Lobbying positions for more ethical whistleblowing policies   311

Preface

Developing and carrying out the research and writing the book have been very fulfilling experiences for me. Many people have helped me in conducting the research and writing the book. A special word of thanks goes out to M.S. Ronald Commers, for his comments, support, and guidance on the research, for his amazing erudition, but also for his trust and loyalty towards me the past years. I would also like to thank Melanie Verstappen, amongst many things for the very keen writing scheme she came up with for me.

Thanks goes out also to the European Business Ethics Network (EBEN), the Social Responsibility Research Network (SRRN), and Asian-Pacific Researchers in Organization Studies (APROS) for allowing me to present earlier drafts of chapters as papers at their conferences. A word of thanks must certainly also go out to Robin Van den Hende at Public Concern at Work, who was very generous in providing me with documents I needed for the research on the UK. Many other people have helped me with valuable comments on ideas or drafts: David Frenkel, Werner Cornelis, Koen Raes, Luc Van Liedekerke, Heidi von Weltzien-Hoivik, Nikolay Dentchev, Rit Vanden Bergh, Tom Viaene, An Verlinden, Herman Siebens, Suzan Langenberg, Jos Leys, Guillaume Eliet, Yvan Biefnot, Luk Bouckaert, Eric Vanhaute, Freddy Mortier.

Last but certainly not least, I thank my family for their consideration in hectic times.

Wim Vandekerckhove

Acknowledgements

The section 'Whistleblowing and Loyalty' in Chapter 3 was previously published in the *Journal of Business Ethics* 53:1–2, 225–33 '(with kind permission of Springer Science and Business Media).

Introduction

What are 'good reasons' to protect whistleblowers? The first answer that comes to you when going through the numerous case studies is that because whistleblowers disclose information in the public interest, they deserve to be protected against organizational retaliations. As I will be showing in this book, the early literature on whistleblowing gives you the same answer but also points at a dilemma in disclosing information: the public has a right to know but organizations require loyalty and secrecy. That was the conflict between 'society' and 'organization' that the whistleblowing activism of Ralph Nader in the early 1970s addressed. Nader challenged the norm of the 'organization man', which required employees to have an undivided loyalty to their employers. It is that conflict, between the public interest and the interests of the organization, which fires any discussion about an appropriate policy towards whistleblowing and whistleblowers. This book is about those discussions and how they have changed in the past 30 years.

The overall shift that has taken place – and of which the appearance of whistleblowing as an issue was one of the earliest signals – is that organizations have become less 'black boxes' that generate welfare for society's well-being. Organization and society are looked upon today as having a direct interdependent relationship. As the quest for efficiency has set the tone and even citizens have become customers, the distinction between private versus public sector organization has become blurred. Today, business, non-profit organizations as well as government agencies are expected to explicitly address their relation with the societies they operate in. They need to be clear on their Organizational Social Responsibility, whether they are corporations or charities.

This book, and the research it is based on, is very timely. When I had the idea for this book the first time, in 1998, the US, Australia and the UK had legislation specifically aimed at protecting whistleblowers. Meanwhile, new whistleblowing policies have been legislated in the US, Australia, South Africa, New Zealand, Japan, Belgium and initiatives towards legislation have been undertaken in Ireland, the Netherlands, India, and Canada. Clearly, we are experiencing a momentum of whistleblowing legislation all over the world. Different parts of that world and different cultures might discuss the issue in different terms, but having to deal with the issue seems to have become a global thing. There is no way to avoid the discussion. Whistleblower protection is coming!

And so, this is an excellent time to reflect upon the 'good reasons' to protect whistleblowers and how these 'good reasons' might be put into policy. This book does just that and it is unique in doing so. The research it is based on inquires into how whistleblowing policies are legitimated. How are they advocated and what reasons are considered as 'good' ones to pass laws protecting whistleblowers? This kind of research has not been done before. While there is literature comparing whistleblowing legislation, the focus is on the effectiveness of a particular aspect of a scheme, not on the way in which these policies are legitimated and hence not on the ethics of whistleblowing policies.

What is of concern in this book is the ethics of whistleblowing policies, with the kind of whistleblowing these policies protect and their implications for the relation between the organization, the individual and society, hence the ethical inquiry. To do that, I screen whistleblowing policies on three elements that make up the conditions for offering protection to the whistleblower: 1) the actor element (who can blow the whistle); 2) the subject element (about what can the whistle be blown); and 3) the recipient element (to whom must the whistle be blown). Part of this book develops the framework to perform such a screening. The period covered in this research (1970–2005) is also the time-span in which what we today call 'globalization' has risen, has 'defeated' the cold war constellation, has promised us everything but has also gained massive critique from the end of the 1990s on. That globalization of a private capital oriented economy entails a strong normative discourse. A discourse is a specific set of concepts used to describe a reality but which immediately also entails norms and goals about reality. Likewise, the discourse of globalization puts forward an image of societal goals, of what is possible, desirable and necessary. Hence, researching 'good reasons' to protect whistleblowers cannot be carried out without putting it into the context of globalization.

Thus, this book is a story about two evolutions in discourse. The first concerns whistleblowing. Whereas in the early 1970s the discourse on whistleblowing raised a dilemma and posed a problem – the conflict between society and organization – by 2005 a large number of whistleblowing policies have developed that succeeded in legitimating whistleblowing. The second evolution in discourse concerns globalization. From the discontent with labour discipline at the end of the 1960s grew ideas about individuation and identity. These became picked up and mobilized in restructuring the world and hence the local as well as the global production relationships. By the 1990s a 'globalization semantic' had developed. The term 'semantic' denotes words gaining their meaning through their connections to other words. Thus, a semantic is a network of words that refer to one another in a specific way and it is that specific way that turns the words into concepts, or words-with-meaning. A semantic too, just like a discourse, is descriptive as well as normative, but discourse emphasizes power whereas semantic emphasizes words within a referring network of other words. Nevertheless, it is through words-with-meaning that we make sense of what we experience, that we render reality a meaning and that our actions become meaningful. The 'globalization semantic' that has developed is a semantic network of words such as 'flexibility', 'competition', 'decentralization', 'uncertainty', 'governance', 'network', and 'stakeholder'. The framework to perform the screening that is developed in this book connects both evolutions.

Rather than assuming these semantic shifts took place along a predetermined master-plan, Niklas Luhmann's evolutionary view on the dynamics of the semantic seemed much more plausible. In Luhmann's view, semantic evolution takes place through endogenous processes of variation, selection and stabilization. We constantly produce conceptual variation. But the whole of variations is under selection pressure, of which the stabilizing potential of a particular variation is the criteria. Stabilization points at the need for humans to make sense of experiences of reality, hence to the continuation in meaning-making. In that evolutionary process, Luhmann links ideas and meaning with societal structures, but says the question which of the two are primordial is unanswerable – of importance is that both evolve together.

However, Luhmann's approach is not a 'plug-and-play' theory. Therefore, in order to outline a methodology for this research, I look for inspiration in the work of others. Max Weber's method of interpretation through idealtypes appears adequate because this was the way Weber arrived at non-nomothetic causal explanation. And because whistleblowing, more specifically the retaliation against whistleblowers is an issue of power, I also look at Weber's writings on power. Another perspective that showed potential for my research was the Foucauldian perspective of the power-knowledge-norms triad. Whistleblowing entailed a power issue, but also involved a knowledge issue in the sense that what whistleblowers do, is to disclose information. My fascination with the way whistleblowing is legitimated then also makes the normative aspect of the Foucauldian perspective appropriate. My inquiry into the ethics of whistleblowing policies is thus also an inquiry into what kind of individual subject was being produced through these policies. In connection to Michel Foucault, I also glance at Gilles Deleuze's thinking, specifically the notions of rhizome and lines of flight. It seems that these notions fit well in an approach that takes seriously the semantic, endogenous variation of meaning, unplanned shifts in meaning, self-reference, and dominant meanings exercising selection pressure on variations in terms of stabilization. *If* the whistleblowing advocated in the early 1970s was an attempt to escape the dominant norm of 'organization man' but as time went by whistleblowers started to get protection through legitimate whistleblowing policies, *then* it was very likely that the whistleblowing-public interest-'line of flight' had broken off into different kinds of whistleblowing-'lines of flight'. Finally, I look at Alain Touraine's institutional level in the organizational process to make the notion of 'legitimate organization' clear. What I draw from Touraine is that the conflict between society and organization – a conflict the 1970s discourse on whistleblowing emphasized – must not be overemphasized, but instead we can regard organizations as political actors in the sense that they try to impose on society a concept of society, of societal goals and of societal evolution. Thus, the conflict between society and organization is not so much a conflict between the public interest and organizational goals, but rather a conflict between the individual and the organization over the definition of the public interest.

The framework used for screening the whistleblowing policies, is a heuristic device based on the theoretical approaches I just mentioned. It starts from the 'globalization semantic', which I describe in the book in a self-referring way.

The words in that semantic gain their meaning through mutual reference to each other. That 'globalization semantic' can then be used to generate ways in which the protection of whistleblowers can be legitimated today. The possible ways of doing so make up the idealtypes of legitimating whistleblowing policies.

But the assessment of whistleblowing policies carried out in this book is not only descriptive. The policies are evaluated as well. In other words, the research question is not just 'what are the current trends in legitimating whistleblowing policies?' but also 'how ethical are these tendencies?'

As whistleblowing is about an individual disclosing organizational practices and thus involves the categories of the individual and the organization, the ethical criteria involve these categories. The ethical problem in whistleblowing is that whistleblowers get retaliated against by the organization, even when blowing the whistle was the justified thing to do. This points at a specific relationship between the individual and the organization – see the dilemma of the public interest and the 'organization man'. What whistleblowing policies do, is to protect whistleblowers from such retaliation *if* the whistleblowing meets the conditions set out by the policy. Now, if whistleblowing policies are part of organizational practice, then this too must imply a specific relationship between the individual and the organization.

That is where I situate the ethical criteria. The relation between the individual and the organization is a power relation. My criteria make that power relation ethically relevant. The end of the 1960s and the early 1970s were marked by a surge of criticism of the organizational domination over the individual. The advocacy of whistleblowing can be seen as an exponent of that protest. The question with regard to current trends in whistleblowing policies is whether these policies protect the individual from organizational dominance, or whether the normative discourse of globalization has turned whistleblowing into a mechanism of organizational dominance. I call the first *subjectaffirmation* and the latter *subjectivation*.

The idealtypes of legitimation of whistleblowing policies must be constructed within the globalization semantic. Within each idealtype, subjectivating and/or subjectaffirming movements must be identified. Then, whistleblowing legislation, proposals and discussions can be screened using the framework of idealtypes. To the extent that idealtypes are matched, current tendencies can be identified. The ethical evaluation can be made by looking at the extent to which idealtypes and movements within idealtypes are not found in the whistleblowing policies.

Here lies another contribution of this research. It draws up legitimation for whistleblowing policies based on the concepts used to describe organizations and organizing in the context of globalization. Hence, it makes explicit the normative implications of a descriptive activity. The research shows that not every possible legitimation is used today.

Also, it is often argued that globalization is double in the sense that it opens possibilities but also poses threats. This research makes that very concrete. It points out in detail what the subjectivating and subjectaffirming movements are within each possible legitimation of whistleblowing policies. It shows the double possibilities of globalization with regard to whistleblowing, and it also shows which direction we are heading.

Thus, the methodology of this research is able to screen a social phenomenon within its proper context, and to evaluate that screening without getting stuck in ethical relativism.

The findings of this research show a clear tendency in favour of particular kinds of legitimation. They also show some possible legitimation not used today. In general, the subjectivating legitimation possibilities seem more successful and within these legitimation constructs, the subjectivating movements are dominant. Therefore, the conclusion is that current trends in whistleblowing policies entail the ethical risk of subjectivation, of organizational domination over the individual and hence of institutionalizing the employee. In that sense, the advocacy of whistleblowing has experienced a backlash. From an exponent of the protest against labour discipline it seems to have turned into a disciplinary apparatus itself.

The recommendations given at the end of the final chapter are also an important contribution of this research. They are recommendations on how to amend whistleblowing policies in order to avoid the ethical risk of subjectivation. The recommendations too are very concrete, because they are drawn from the same methodological framework as the screening.

In the proceeding chapters of this book, the steps I have just outlined are taken up and worked out in detail. Chapter 1 develops the research questions. The origins and the evolution of the concept of whistleblowing in an organizational context are discussed through a literature review. I also address what the growing attention for whistleblowing might mean and how this research approaches whistleblowing policies. In the literature, there is consensus that whistleblowing is a dissenting voice. However, the consensus is lost when it comes to delineating whistleblowing in an organizational context. Therefore, still in Chapter 2, I offer an overview of possible delineation of whistleblowing. Finally, I point at the limitations of this research and clarify what data was used.

Chapter 2 develops the methodology. It is here that I develop an operationalization of Luhmann's evolutionary approach to semantic dynamic, by looking at the works of Weber, Foucault, some Deleuze, and Touraine. At the end of Chapter 2, I line out the work plan for this research, and I make a first pointer with regard to the ethical criteria.

In Chapter 3, I construct the idealtypes of legitimation of whistleblowing policies. First, I describe the globalization semantic through the mutually referring concepts of flexibility, decentralization, governance, network and stakeholder. It is within that globalization semantic then, that I draw up eight idealtypical legitimation constructs: 1) whistleblowing as a human right: 2) whistleblowing from an OSR-network perspective; and 3) from an OSR-stakeholder perspective; 4) whistleblowing and responsibility; 5) whistleblowing and accountability; 6) whistleblowing and integrity; 7) whistleblowing and loyalty; 8) whistleblowing and organizational efficiency. At the end of Chapter 4, I draw up the screening grid, consisting of rationales of the idealtypical constructs, dominant ethical theory of the constructs, and the derived actor, subject and recipient elements. I also identify subjectivating and subjectaffirming movements within each idealtypical construct.

Chapter 4 contains the screening of the whistleblowing policies laid down in legislation and the law proposals, and the kind of whistleblowing advocated in the discussions. I do this for the US, Australia, New Zealand, the UK, South Africa, Japan, Belgium, the Netherlands, Ireland, Canada, India, Germany, Switzerland, and for intergovernmental bodies such as the OECD, the European Commission, and the Council of Europe. For each of these, I draw out how the legitimation of whistleblowing policies has evolved, using the set of idealtypes as a heuristic tool.

Chapter 5 then, starts by identifying tendencies in the legitimation of whistleblowing policies, based on the screening performed in Chapter 4. Common constructs are pointed out, as well as combinations of constructs, absence of particular possible constructs and patterns of evolution in legitimation between 1970 and 2005. Then, I take a closer look at the ethical criteria and evaluate the identified tendencies. Finally, from that evaluation, lobbying positions are derived for realizing more ethical whistleblowing policies and suggestions are made for future research.

Chapter 1
Developing Research Questions

Whistleblowing in an Organizational Context

Origins

Whistleblowing in an organizational context has relatively recently rendered 'to whistle' or 'to blow the whistle' an extra meaning. The 1961 edition of the Oxford English Dictionary does not mention 'whistleblowing' or 'whistleblower'. But it does mention a meaning of 'to whistle' as 'to speak, tell, or utter secretly, to "whisper"; to give secret information, turn informer'. The 1976 edition of Webster's Third New International Dictionary of the English Language doesn't mention 'whistleblowing' or 'whistleblower' either, but does list a meaning of 'to whistle' as 'to squeal [...] to signal or summon by or as if by whistling' which is often used with 'up' as in 'whistling up the law'. However, a 1986 supplement to the Oxford English Dictionary does mention 'whistleblowing' as 'to blow the whistle on (a person or thing): to ring an activity to a sharp conclusion, as if by the blast of a whistle; now usually by informing on (a person) or exposing (an irregularity or crime)'. Under 'whistle call – whistle-blower' it says 'chiefly U.S., one who "blows the whistle" on a person or activity, especially within an organization'.

The first usages of whistleblowing in an organizational context I have found were an editorial and a letter to the editor, both in the journal *Computer* and both in an issue from 1971. In an ed-op under the name 'The Forum of Social Implications', Hartmann (1971) is very negative towards whistleblowing. He asks: 'why should a professional belittle his own gremium when it appears that his whistle blowing [...] only enhances the power and prestige of an outsider at the expenses of his own profession and himself' and states that 'it is unethical to "badmouth" professional colleagues outside of the given profession'.

Some months later, Smith (1971) responds in a letter to the same journal, agreeing that whistleblowing might not be 'the optimum solution', but at the same time denouncing the attitude of Hartmann, arguing that a profession is in a very bad state when shortcomings, mistakes and problems are hidden instead of responsibly admitting them and trying to alter them. He also notes that if whistle-blowing cannot be tolerated because it would benefit another profession, then this is a mode of thought dominated by inter-professional bickering and paranoia, whilst the then current trend was inter-disciplinary opening and cooperation.

I have also come across a quote from James Roche, then chairman of the board of General Motors, who, also in 1971, warned against whistleblowing:

Some critics are now busy eroding another support of free enterprise – the loyalty of a management team, with its unifying values of cooperative work. Some of the enemies of business now encourage an employee to be disloyal to the enterprise. They want to create suspicion and disharmony, and pry into the proprietary interests of the business. However this is labelled – industrial espionage, *whistle blowing*, or professional responsibility – it is another tactic for spreading disunity and creating conflict (Roche 1971, quoted in Walters 1975, emphasis added).

However, all literature[1] on whistleblowing traces whistleblowing in an organizational context to 1972[2] when, at a conference on professional responsibility, consumer advocate Ralph Nader defined whistleblowing as:

an act of a man or woman who, believing that the public interest overrides the interest of the organization he serves, blows the whistle that the organization is involved in corrupt, illegal, fraudulent or harmful activity (Nader 1972, vii).

Nader defined the whistleblower as a pro-social person, whilst the general attitude at that time towards whistleblowing was rather hostile. Ravishankar (2003) mentions an arbitrator in a case from 1972 – the same year as Nader's legitimating definition – who told the employee that 'you cannot bite the hand that feeds you and insist on staying on for the banquet'.

Now, what both views on whistleblowing share is, that whistleblowing is contrasted to organizational loyalty, and is seen as a breach of that loyalty. That breach is the disclosure of information. Hence, the sound from the whistle carries information which is supposed to be confidential. What is important is that the use of whistleblowing in an organizational context marks a quarrel about how people in organizations should behave with regard to the relation between organization and society. On the one side there is the position that employees should have undivided loyalty to their employers. According to Ravishankar (2003), this is characteristic of corporate America's norm of the 'organization man' of the 1950s and 1960s. Consider a Nixon White House memorandum on Ernest Fitzgerald, who blew the whistle in 1968 on an air transport fraud of $2 billion: 'Fitzgerald is no doubt a top-notch expert, but he must be given very low marks on loyalty; and loyalty is the name of the game' (quoted in Ravishankar

---

[1]   Reference to Nader et al. (1972) was made, for example, in Walters (1975); Stewart (1980); Elliston (1982a); Near and Jensen (1983); Dozier and Miceli (1985); Jensen (1987); Johnson and Kraft (1990); Near et al. (1993a); Perry (1998); Miceli et al. (1999). Some of them also mention a book by two editors of Washington Monthly, Peters and Branch, which is also from 1972, but Walters (1975) is clear that Nader et al. (1972) is 'the first published and still the best general treatment [...]', but also mentions a book by Fitzgerald (1972), which is an autobiographical case-report of whistleblowing on fraud on the part of the Pentagon and defence contractors.

[2]   Nader must have raised the issue already in 1971 as a 'call for responsibility' and an 'encouragement to blow the whistle' at some gatherings and meetings, because Hartmann (1971) refers to newspaper articles from 1971 reporting on Nader's activism.

2003). Walters (1975) names Lawrence, Leavitt and Presthus as organization theorists who also support the proposition of absolute loyalty.[3] On the other side of the quarrel stand those who acknowledge situations in which the public interest takes priority over organizational loyalty. Apart from activists like Nader, an organization theorist taking this latter stance is Kerr (1964, quoted in Walters 1975), who advocates plural loyalties as a guarantee against totalitarianism. The idea is that employees in a free society should not be obligated to restrict their loyalty to only one institution or cause. Kerr takes position against a society where people see their pattern of activities set for them by a single external institution rather than work with divided loyalties and set their own pattern of activities.

It seems to me that this is the societal context in which the origin of the usage of whistleblowing in an organizational setting has to be situated. Hardt and Negri (2001, 261–74) see a crisis of capitalist production in the late 1960s, resulting mainly from an intense workers attack directed at disciplinary regimes of labour. The refusal of work in general and a refusal of factory work in specific is itself an effect – or a produced subjectivity – of the ideology of modernization, creating new desires the established relations of production could not manage.[4] Hardt and Negri (2001) see the 1970s as the decomposition of Fordism.[5] The crisis of late 1960s had opened two paths to respond to the social struggles. The first was automation and computerization of production. This took Taylorist[6]

---

[3]   The organization theorists Walters (1975) lists as taking the loyalty stand are from the 'organization man' era (1950s and 1960s). Lawrence (1958) writes that 'we would want one sentiment to be dominant in all employees from top to bottom, namely a complete loyalty to the organizational purpose', Leavitt (1965) sees an 'ideal organization [which] has loyal employees who see no conflicts between personal goals and organizational purposes' and Presthus (1962) regrets but admits that 'organizational logic ... has been essentially authoritarian' (all quoted in Walters 1975).

[4]   Hardt and Negri see the sudden increase in the costs of raw materials, energy, and certain agricultural commodities in the 1960s and 1970s as a symptom of these new desires.

[5]   Fordism – going back to Henry Ford (1863–1947), founder of Ford Motor Company – signifies a phase of economic and social history in which the production method of the moving assembly line manufacturing was introduced (1913) and stood central in the organization of labour. Along with that production method came the mass production and consumption of affordable luxury products – in the case of Ford this were automobiles.

[6]   Taylorism is a management style named after Frederic Winslow Taylor (1856–1915), and designates a detailed division of labour along the principle of 'scientific management', which entails the decoupling of the labour process from the skills of the workers. Traditional knowledge of craftsmen is chased out of the labour process through rules and formulae, developed by management and handed down to the workers. This means that all 'brain work' is removed from the work floor and centred in the planning department. It also means that workers can not decide themselves how to go about their tasks. Instead, management prescribes in great detail how and how fast the tasks must be performed. Workers are no

and Fordist mechanisms to its limits in the sense that these could no longer control the dynamic of productive and social forces. The second path however was the one that according to Hardt and Negri constitutes a paradigm shift in employment relations. It implied responding to the new production of subjectivity. In a sense this was a struggle over the mode of life, and it led to the development of immaterial labour. But that new production of subjectivity in my view also cracked the 'organization man' ethos and emphasized the legitimacy of extra-organizational life and hence public interest. That new production of subjectivity was an assault on the disciplinary regime up till the 1960s. And it forced a change in the quality of labour organization, because the refusal of that disciplinary regime was accompanied by a re-evaluation of the social value of the whole set of productive activities:

> The prospect of getting a job that guarantees regular and stable work for eight hours a day, fifty weeks a year, for an entire working life, the prospect of entering the normalized regime of the social factory, which had been a dream for many of their parents, now appeared as a kind of death. The mass refusal of the disciplinary regime, which took a variety of forms, was not only a negative expression but also a moment of creation [...] (Hardt and Negri 2001, 273–74).

In this sense, Ralph Nader's whistleblowing definition of 1972 was one such variety of the refusal of the disciplinary regime, and a moment of creation. But even at that moment in time when the term 'whistleblowing' appeared in an organizational context, some authors tagged it as a political exponent of social change. Peters and Branch (1972, mentioned in Walters 1975) saw whistleblowing as a new development in the history of American reform movements. And the analysis of Vogel (1974) shows a shift during the late 1960s and early 1970s away from protest aimed at government actions towards protest against corporations, as business became more and more a direct target of public demands. Vogel notes advocating whistleblowing as one of the tactics of anti-corporate activity to put pressure on corporations.

Hence, whistleblowing in an organizational context appears in a politico-ethical usage. It designated a practice of resistance to organizational authority, and of unsealing boundaries of accountability for activities of and within organizations. But why use the word 'whistleblowing' for such a practice? For Miceli and Near (1992, 15) 'the analogy is to an official on a playing field, such as a football referee, who can blow the whistle to stop action'. As I see it, that analogy falls short, because the whistleblower is someone who indeed blows the whistle to stop action, but typically lacks the power and authority to do so – unlike

---

longer craftsmen nor professionals, but mere performers of routine tasks. Taylor called this form of management 'scientific' because the labour division and the detailing and pacing of tasks was based on time and motion study to find the 'one best method', meaning without unnecessary movements. Taylorism is linked with Fordism in the sense that both are historically associated with mass production methods in manufacturing factories.

a football referee – and therefore must appeal to someone or some institution who is able to stop and change the action. Another analogy is to the police officer summoning public to help apprehend a criminal. This one does point at a lack of power, but still misses the fact that whistleblowers are not supposed to blow the whistle, at least not within the mindset contra-posing whistleblowing and loyalty. Interesting enough about these analogies is that they show whistleblowing as necessary to align organizations with society. If the general attitude towards whistleblowing is changing, then possibly the mental opening created by these analogies plays a role.[7]

Evolution

Even though whistleblowing in an organizational context[8] originated as an activist and hence politico-ethical concept, the momentum it gained in academic literature has also led to a de-activation of the concept.

My review of the evolution in coverage of the whistleblowing issue in academic literature is based on a search for 'whistleblowing' and 'whistle blowing' in title, abstract or keywords in the following databases: current contents, sociological abstracts, science citation index expanded, social science citation index, arts and humanities citation index. The few books on whistleblowing I have included in the following review are or have been, in my view, significant to the evolution of research on whistleblowing.

The number of publications for each year my search came up with are shown in Table 1.1. The 'A' column shows the number of articles, while the 'B' column stands for the number of editorials, book reviews and letters (letters were counted per issue, so five letters in one issue counts as 1; 1+ for 1977 means one article plus the special issue of *Bureaucrat*).

The academic literature on whistleblowing kicks off in 1973, with a book review of Nader et al. (1972) in *Social Work* (Orlin 1973). The first article in a law journal dates from 1974 and is an overview of accountants' duties in relation to whistleblowing (Isbell 1974). From the same year is Vogel's already mentioned article on the politicization of the corporation. Publications on whistleblowing in law journals and in journals on politics and social issues will remain constant but very scarce, with more book reviews than articles. Also, management journals join in pretty early, starting with Walters (1975) with an article in *Harvard Business Review*. The article files under the section 'Thinking Ahead' and warns companies

---

[7]   I see a more neutral analogy of the Oxford English Dictionary meaning of 'whistle-blowing' as 'to bring an activity to a sharp conclusion, as if by the blast of a whistle', in 'to whistle off or to whistle down the brakes', a saying in railroad engineering to instruct the brakeman by means of the locomotive whistle (see *A Dictionary of Americanisms*, University of Chicago Press 1966).

[8]   From now on I will use 'whistleblowing' instead of 'whistleblowing in an organizational context'.

Table 1.1   Number of publications on whistleblowing in academic journals

Year	A	B
1971	–	2
1973	–	1
1974	2	–
1975	1	1
1977	1+	–
1979	1	–
1980	3	7
1981	1	3
1982	2	7
1983	2	6
1984	1	3
1985	6	6
1986	2	4
1987	2	5
1988	3	5
1989	5	3
1990	3	1
1991	11	5
1992	8	3
1993	9	3
1994	10	2
1995	11	4
1996	11	7
1997	2	1
1998	18	12
2000	9	5
2001	10	5
2002	13	3

to be on guard for the growing tendency of courts 'saying that matters traditionally considered an organization's own business may be the public's as well'. Court rulings at that time seem to take the US first amendment argument of free speech seriously, especially for government personnel. The tone of the article is that the future might very well bring laws protecting whistleblowers in private companies and installing whistleblowing as an exemption from the employment at will doctrine. An article from 1977 (Conway 1977) reviews that possibility. Overall, there seems to be a higher attention for whistleblowing from public management journals – starting with a special issue of *Bureaucrat* from 1977 which focuses on whistleblowing in terms of government accountability – than from management journals aimed at private sector organizations.

The issue of whistleblowing gains momentum in the academic literature from the 1980s on, but the growth in publications is mainly due to book reviews and editorials. The issue is particularly present in journals on engineering, information technology (computers) and scientific research. The 1980s also show whistleblowing studied from a sociological and psychological perspective. Sociological research on whistleblowing might have been triggered by the publication of a study by Anderson et al. (1980) of whistleblowing during the development of the Bay Area Rapid Transit system – BART – in California. The authors see the then available publications on whistleblowing consisting of 'brief descriptive accounts of specific incidents that are either journalistic or highly partisan in form' (Anderson et al. 1980, 16). Their book offers extensive descriptions of whistleblowing incidents at BART, but also sees the need to place the issue in the context of organization theory. They set out a set of research questions that seem to have been picked up by other scholars from the 1980s on. Anderson and his colleagues stated the need to 'identify the organizational conditions – authority structure, lines of communication, opportunities to participate in decision-making – that give rise to initial acts of disagreement with, or concern about, some organizational practice' (Anderson et al. 1980, 5). The most important authors in research on whistleblowing from a psychological perspective are Miceli and Near, who publish frequently on individual characteristics of whistleblowers from 1984 on.[9] Glazer and Glazer (1989) is also to be situated in that field with their six-year study on employees blowing the whistle on their employers, researching the role of their belief system in their decision to blow the whistle and in coping with retaliation. Important to note is that, even though sociological and psychological research on whistleblowing keeps the politico-ethical undertone of power struggles within organizations and the public interest aspect of whistleblowing, the emphasis of the research is not on whistleblowing as a politico-ethical relevant practice, but rather on the whistleblower – personal characteristics of whistleblowers (their belief system, their organizational position) – and on the act of whistleblowing – predicting whistleblowing and finding out what the determinants of organizations with a high risk of whistleblowing are.[10] Except for articles in law journals from the second half of the 1980s researching the effects of whistleblowing statutes and legislation,[11] publications on whistleblowing protection are practically absent from the 1980s,[12] but are more present in the first half of the 1990s and stem mainly

---

[9]　See Miceli and Near (1984; 1985; 1989; 1991; 2002); Near and Miceli (1985; 1996); Dozier and Miceli (1985); Miceli (1988).

[10]　For research on personal characteristics of whistleblowers, see footnote 9 and Near et al. (1993a; 1993b); Keenan (1995); Glazer and Glazer (1986). For research on organizational characteristics, see, for example, Keenan (1983); Rothschild and Miethe (1992; 1999); Barnett (1992).

[11]　Rongine (1985); Dworkin and Near (1987); Parker (1988); Rosecrance (1988); Massengill and Petersen (1989).

[12]　An exception is Near (1989), which is an editorial.

from journals on nursing, medicine, engineering and auditing.[13] It is only from 1998 onwards that the politico-ethical question with regard to whistleblowing is raised again in academic literature other than political journals.

Dworkin and Callahan (1998) argue that during the 1990s two conflicting trends have occurred. On the one hand, whistleblowers have gained more protection from retaliation through expanded legislation. But on the other hand, employers have increased the use of secrecy clauses to prevent information leaking out of the organization, which has resulted in more court cases in which judges were asked to enforce secrecy agreements against whistleblowers. Even though the motive for the disclosure, the identity of the information recipient, the seriousness of the wrongdoing and the strength of the evidence can safeguard a whistleblower from secrecy agreements being used to retaliate against them, Dworkin and Callahan claim employers have gained extra protection through such agreements, one important protection being that they can require that employees first report wrongdoing internally.

Perry (1998) charges the literature on whistleblowing with the unproblematic reproduction of the Enlightment ideal, i.e. combining individual autonomy and social rationality. Analyses of whistleblowing tell a story of moral man against immoral organization. The problem is that the empirical content of these studies contrasts with their narrative form. Whistleblowers are celebrated in these studies, but at the same time it is shown how bleak their fate is. Retaliation in terms of job loss and the disastrous consequences on the health and family life of whistleblowers is a constant. In effect, Perry argues, potential whistleblowers are cautioned against going public by the very same authors who commend the integrity of those who do. Perry calls for an alternative interpretation of whistleblowing practices as tracers of shifts and realignments within and between discursive and institutional structures, an approach which is more contextual and less axiomatically heroic. Such an approach sees whistleblowing as a signal of the state of social organization. Shifting relationships between business and state mean inter-institutional blurring and boundary crossing. This is also associated with realignments in control and legitimation. Patterns of reward change and it is communication control which becomes functionally indispensable in uncoupling the production of conduct from the rhetoric of justification. In other words, there is a dualism between legitimating principles and operational practices of an organization. This is an uneasy co-existence which needs ritualized and

---

[13]   Arnold and Ponemon (1991); Feliu (1991); Frader (1992); De Maria (1992); Doyall and Cannell (1993); Barnett et al. (1993); Ponemon (1994); Vinten (1994); Hooks et al. (1994); Hipel et al. (1995). Also see the book edited by Hunt (1994) which deals exclusively with whistleblowing in the UK health care sector (NHS – National Health Service). A clear exception is Vinten (1994), a book strongly in favour of internal whistleblowing channels and even referring to them as 'institutionalization of whistleblowing' or 'whistleblowing as a safety net', a terminology popping up again after 2000 (see Kaptein 2002; Callahan 2002; Vandekerckhove and Commers 2004).

ceremonial activity to keep it stable. Whistleblowing then, points at a failure of the attempt to stabilize that dualism. However, whistleblowers are truth tellers (cognitive) who become whistleblowers (moral) because they need to speak in the narrative and dramatic conventions which the media produce. The text of the whistleblower becomes dissent through the process of media definition. In this sense too, whistleblowing is the product of inter-institutional realignments and discursive shifts.

Jubb (1999) comes to terms with the different ways in which whistleblowing has been defined over the years in academic literature. Without explicitly mentioning Nader, Jubb re-introduces the politico-ethical definition of whistleblowing emphasizing dissent and the ethical dilemma of conflicting loyalties.

Vandekerckhove and Commers (2000) put whistleblowing in the context of loss of democratic control over society due to globalization and see whistleblowing laws and channels as candidates for a new guarantee for democracy and well being of society.

O'Connor (2001) identifies whistleblowing as a form of resistance used by female scholars within the Irish academic community to raise awareness of gender inequality, but then argues that raising the awareness is not enough to resolve the problem.

Riesenberg (2001) reviews the Securities Exchange Act enacted by US Congress in 1995,[14] which requires the reporting by independent auditors of illegal acts. He argues that the scope of those requirements is ambiguous, but concludes that an examination of the statutory language and legislative history of the act shows it is but a modest statute with limited significance.

Buchholz and Rosenthal (2002) elaborate on the moral dilemma arising from a market economy in which the corporation is the primary institution through which new technologies are introduced. Because corporations are primarily interested in economic goals, they cannot – or do not – ask adequate questions about the safety of a particular technology. Hence, concerns of engineers and technicians clash with managers' eagerness to favour organizational economic interests. Buchholz and Rosenthal argue that technology creates a moral situation which should provide the context for decision-making. Tensions within that context can be seen as a structural problem inherent in the capitalistic system, but they can also be seen as an organizational problem that requires facilitation of whistleblowing.

Grant (2002) puts whistleblowers on a pedestal, arguing that the moral sensitivity involved in whistleblowing approaches religious proportions in terms of courage, determination and sacrifice.

These publications are examples of the re-emphasis on whistleblowing as a politico-ethical concept from the end of the 1990s onwards. It coincides with the rise of the anti-globalization activism and mass protests. But the politico-ethical

---

[14] More specifically, Riesenberg reviews Section 10A of the Securities and Exchange Act enacted by US Congress in 1995.

question also reappeared in a different tone. Internal whistleblowing channels were 'in' again, and although the first half of the 1990s had seen some publications on internal disclosure policies,[15] the tone of the articles from the end of the 1990s onwards on internal whistleblowing channels is less politically protesting, less conflicting, but more morally laden in a legitimating sense.

The article of Benson and Ross (1998) is almost a corporate advertisement. The authors argue that the commitment of the management of Sundstrand is exemplary, and one of the reasons is that internal whistleblowing is encouraged and protected.

Gunsalus (1998) focuses on systemic elements for cultivating an ethical environment in organizations and argues that handling complaints and grievances at their earliest stages is important and that internal whistleblowing channels should be supported.

Gordon and Miyake (2001) review codes of conduct to get insight into corporate approaches to anti-bribery commitments and compliance management. Although the language and concepts used to describe bribery and corruption is very diverse, the authors regard the bribery codes as evidence of an emerging consensus on managerial approaches to combating bribery and an internal whistleblowing channel is one of those management tools.

Kaptein (2002) argues for an 'ethics helpdesk' characterized by low barriers, positive approach and simple procedures. Such a helpdesk can be seen as an internal whistleblowing channel, because it increases the chances of detecting unethical conduct which enable management to take adequate and timely measures.

Callahan et al. (2002) argue that establishing internal whistleblowing procedures is a way for corporations to improve efficiency and employee morale. The best way to do so, according to the authors, is through implementation of the BMI-model – Business as Mediating Institution – which offers beneficial aspects of both contractarian and communitarian forms of corporate governance. Their BMI-model with its internal whistleblowing channels is legitimized by linking it with the concepts of empowerment and shared values.

De Maria (1999) describes this promotion of new ethics regimes as an 'ethical meltdown', because those promoting them sound more like management consultants than like impartial critics of practice. Interesting is that De Maria regards whistleblowing as the 'test case' of how seriously the ethics movement in management is.

So, whereas in the early 1970s whistleblowing was a politico-ethical concept pointing at a conflict between organization and society, what we see in the last group of publications I described, is that intra-organizational whistleblowing policies are presented as a politico-ethical concept able to eliminate conflict between organization and society, between the interests of private capital and

---

[15] Dworkin and Callahan (1991); Barnett et al. (1993); Hooks (1994); Ponemon (1994); Rothschild (1994).

the public interest. What does this mean? Does it signify the ideological backlash of an activist concept, 30 years after its appearance? The renewed activist undertone in Perry (1998), Vandekerckhove and Commers (2000), O'Connor (2001), Riesenberg (2001) and Grant (2002) would then be a mere convulsion before the final recuperation. Or does it point at a genuine adaptation of business to public demands?

The research I will present here examines this matter further. To do that I must consider at length the kinds of legitimation whistleblowing policies are given. I will not touch upon the vast research on psychological characteristics of the individuals who blow the whistle, nor will I go into the sociological research on organizational power. Because it is not the 'act of whistleblowing' which needs to be documented in order to answer the question of 'legitimation of whistleblowing policies'. In other words, I am not out to find out more about whistleblowing. What the most recent literature on whistleblowing policies calls for is a contextualization of the apparently welcoming attitude of organizations towards whistleblowing. In this respect, Ravishankar (2003) distinguishes an evolution from corporate America's 'organization man' norm where 'loyalty to the company was the ruling norm, to the present time when public outrage about corporate misconduct has created a more auspicious climate for whistleblowing'. So, in order to research the place of whistleblowing in today's society, there is no point in trying to infer *the* definition or *the* ethics of whistleblowing. Far more crucial is to find out what kinds of whistleblowing our society and organizations are hoping for and what they come up with to answer those hopes. What is demanded and what is delivered?

Meaning

Indeed, the attention for whistleblowing among the public, media, government institutions and business managers seems to be both growing and turning into a positive attitude. Hollywood has celebrated whistleblowing in popular culture through movies like 'Serpico', 'Silkwood', 'Erin Brockovich' and most recently 'The Insider'. And certainly the December 2002 issue of Time made 'whistleblowing' part of Western standard vocabulary. In that issue, Time presented the persons of the year 2002, three women who had 'blown the whistle' on their organization: Cynthia Cooper of WorldCom, Coleen Rowley of the FBI and Sherron Watkins of Enron. They were portrayed as highly intelligent, as very serious about their job and the societal goals of their organization, as people acting with integrity, and as family people.[16] A telephone poll among adult Americans, taken for *Time*/CNN in December 2002, shows 59 per cent thinks whistleblowers are heroes and only 18 per cent regarding them as traitors. At the same time, also European

---

[16] Portraying someone as a family person is legitimating, certainly in a US context. It shows that person – and therefore what that person is saying or doing or has done – is not a marginal figure, but very much at the centre of society.

and other governments are holding commissions on whistleblowing and are developing legislation to protect whistleblowers, or have done so recently. And perhaps business managers have come to see whistleblowing is something they will have to deal with.

What could the growing attention for whistleblowing mean? I see two possibilities: the first is that whistleblowing is an action done more often, the second is that whistleblowers have become attractive as a source of information.

In the first case, the question remains why there would be more whistleblowing than before. There is no research comparing the prevalence of whistleblowing over the past decades. So there might be more whistleblowing or there might be just as much as before. In principle, there might even be less, but then explaining the growing attention for it would be hard. But if whistleblowing is an action done more often, it might be: 1) because it has become possible to do so; or 2) because there is a bigger need to do it. That there is a bigger need would mean that there is more organizational wrongdoing. That it has become possible to do so could again mean a couple of things. There might be attitudinal changes that would make people more willing to blow the whistle, or there might be organizational changes such as different structures of labour division, different control mechanisms, a different situation in terms of labour market. Of course, these possibilities do not exclude each other and could even be connected to each other.

If whistleblowing is not done more often than before, then the reason for the growing attention for the issue might be that whistleblowers have become attractive as a source of information. The question is then, attractive to whom? They might be attractive as a source of information for consumers. That would mean a change in consumers' attitude. Note that using the term 'whistleblower' in an organizational context is traced back to consumer advocate Ralph Nader. But whistleblowers might also be attractive as a source of information to the media.[17] This option suggests the media either sees the information received from whistleblowers leaking information to the media as relevant and legitimate information, or in other words, the media regards reporting whistleblowing information as their role in society. Note how consumer interests and media interests blend well here. A third way to understand the attractiveness of whistleblowers is to look at

---

[17] Van Es and Smit (2003) describe a case from three perspectives: the whistleblower, the organization and the media. They warn that whistleblowers have to be aware of the media logic and that they should ask themselves 'if they are prepared to mould their story in a suitable media format' (Van Es and Smit 2003, 150). Perry (1998) argues that whistleblowers – specifically within scientific and technological settings – see themselves as truth tellers, as just doing their job, and are turned into moral actors when tagged as whistleblowers by the media. The stories of *Time*'s 3 Whistleblower-Persons of the Year 2002 seem to confirm this. Cooper, Rowley and Watkins became public figures because the internal memo's they had sent up the power ladder somehow leaked, not because they themselves decided to become whistleblowers.

it from the perspective of semantics. If the term 'whistleblowing' shows up in an organizational context from the 1970s on, but the practice of disclosing dissenting and accusing information is not new, then a change in context must have occurred which allowed tagging that practice as 'whistleblowing'. A growing attention for whistleblowing then means a rising popularity of the term, implying a context favouring the usage of the term.

The point I am trying to make is that whichever way the growing attention for whistleblowing is interpreted, it points at a changed societal context in which social actors – business, media, consumers, employees, governments – operate. The overall term to tag this change is globalization.[18] The term is very broad in scope. It designates the totality of demands, barriers, risks and opportunities that come along with an intensified – in breadth and in depth – domination of private capital over society. Privatization and opening of markets – in geographical scope as well as in the commodification of life-aspects – are direct exponents of such a domination, and result in organizational changes.[19] In this sense, my research will need to find out whether or not whistleblowing policies are one of those organizational changes.

Whistleblowing Policies and this Research

The whole issue of whistleblowing policies first came about in the US, as is the case with reviews of the effectiveness of those policies. However, other countries have passed whistleblowing legislation during the 1990s and into the 2000s – Australia, New Zealand, the UK, South Africa, Japan, Belgium – or are developing legislation – the Netherlands, Ireland, Canada, India, Germany, Switzerland.

---

[18] While globalization is often identified with the massive privatization and deregulation policies of the 1980s, the shifts that prepared the reigns of Reagan and Thatcher must be dated at the end of the 1960s and the beginnings of the 1970s. I already wrote that Hardt and Negri (2001, 261–74) see those shifts setting in at the end of the 1960s. By that time, the ideology of modernization had produced a new subjectivity and hence created new desires unmanageable through the established relations of production. Hardt and Negri see the sudden increase in the costs of raw materials, energy, and certain agricultural commodities in the 1960s and 1970s as a symptom of these new desires. An attempt to answer the crisis was to abandon the Bretton Woods system of maintaining the gold standard as a guarantee for the dollar. This happened in 1971. Note that the G7's first gathering was in 1973. There certainly is a consensus that the elimination of capital controls has triggered globalization. But interesting in this sense is that globalization seems to be something that was not new in the early 1970s, but a process of increased integration of international markets which was merely interrupted from 1914 to 1970 (Bordo 2002). Hence, my dating of a change in societal context in which organizations operate – globalization – shortly before Nader's first known definition of whistleblowing in an organizational context in 1972.

[19] The assumption here is of course that organizations only exist to the extent that they are adapted to the environment in which they are functioning.

Intergovernmental bodies have stated to show interest in whistleblowing policies around the end of the 1990s – e.g. the OECD, the European Commission and the Council of Europe.

Whistleblowing policies are the institutionalization of whistleblowing. To the extent that whistleblowing is done and dealt with through a stable and standardized interaction process of which the procedures are knowable to all participants, whistleblowing is an institution. In this sense, policy documents and legislation should be seen as attempts to institutionalize whistleblowing. They are not expressions of an acquired consensus on the modalities of how whistle-blowing should be done and be dealt with, but rather expressions of a growing consensus on the issue. The research presented here inquires into the nature of that consensus.

If 'institution' designates a set of internalized norms with regard to a practice, so that it can be said that these are taken for granted or are seen as 'normal', then institutionalization designates an 'on the way towards', a 'normalization'. In the case of whistleblowing and taking into consideration where it comes from – i.e. breaking with the ethos of the 'organization man' — to develop and adopt policies and legislation, which implicates finding support for it, and to see a positive attitude towards whistleblowing, must indicate an 'on the way towards' a normalization of whistleblowing. In other words, there must be, in the overall belief system of the public and the respective belief systems pertaining to government officials and business people, normative steppingstones for whistle-blowing policies. The research presented here tries to identify those normative stepping stones.

Hence the aim of this book is to make an assessment of the way whistleblowing is being institutionalized. The assessment I make aims both at understanding the evolution in legitimating the protection of whistleblowers, as well as making an ethical evaluation of that evolution. Thus, the assessment is both an assessment of the ethics of whistleblowing – how is it being legitimated – as well as an ethical assessment – how ethical are whistleblowing policies.

By looking at whistleblowing policies and their development process, my research is an analytical examination of the institutionalization of whistle-blowing in the sense that it is an inquiry into the meaning and justifications of whistleblowing policies. So, my research is first of all an assessment of the ethics of whistleblowing policies. I have argued that the concept of whistleblowing originated as a politico-ethical concept and that very recently, this politico-ethical content has been re-emphasized. Hence, any organizational response, whether barely or highly institutionalized is necessarily value-laden.

But at the same time the assessment itself is ethical as well, and not just an assessment of a particular mobilization of ethics. The analytical examination I am about to undertake is not just a description of the way whistleblowing is institutionalized, but will also include an evaluation of that process.

The literature review I presented earlier shows that such an assessment has not been done yet. However, given the most recent re-sacralization and heroification of whistleblowers, such an assessment seems to be needed, or as I wrote earlier, it is crucial to find out what kinds of whistleblowing our society and organizations are hoping for and what they come up with to answer those hopes.

To carry out the task I have just put myself to, I will need to review whistle-blowing policies and legislations and look for what exactly they are trying to 'fix' and why. The policy documents resulting from discussions and decisions within governmental and intergovernmental bodies can shed light on how whistleblowing is perceived, what problems it raises, what problems whistleblowing protection might solve and just how this should be done.

The politico-ethical concept of whistleblowing involves the categories of organization, individual and society. Originally, the politico-ethical message was that individuals, by 'blowing the whistle' could warn society of organizational practices harmful to society. However, I suspect the politico-ethical message speaking from some early twenty-first century literature to be that whistleblowing, performed by individuals but protected and encouraged through whistleblowing policies, is able to eliminate conflict between organization and society, between the interests of private capital (organization) and the public interest (society).[20] To find out whether that holds and to what extent, these three questions will guide my assessment of whistleblowing policies:

- What are the organizational/societal possibilities for whistleblowing?
- What are the organizational/societal necessities for whistleblowing?
- Do possibilities and necessities correspond?

Assessing whistleblowing policies through these questions implicates that justifications of whistleblowing protection and encouragement as given in policy documents will have to be placed in the context of current discourses of organization and society. In the next two chapters I will develop a hermeneutic to undertake such a contextualization and assessment. The next chapter covers the theoretical framework for the systematic interpretation of the collected data on whistleblowing policies. In Chapter 3 then, I draw up the concrete referents for that interpretation, resulting in a grid against which the collected data will be screened. But before I get there, the remaining sections will set out the research process, specifying possible definitions of whistleblowing, pointing out some limitations to this research – what whistleblowing policies will be looked at – and specifying the data collection for the research.

Possible Definitions of Whistleblowing

As my review of the evolution of academic attention for whistleblowing shows, the concept of whistleblowing has proliferated in meaning. As Miceli and Near

---

[20] I wrote that De Maria (1999) described this as an 'ethical meltdown'.

(1992) point out, usage of the term is 'probably as confounded as its original source'. Peter Jubb (1999) reviewed a number of definitions[21] of the term 'whistle-blowing' in order to arrive at a restrictive, but general purpose definition of the term. According to Jubb, this is necessary because of the risk that whistleblowing becomes interchangeable with informing, whilst Jubb insists that whistleblowing is a special case of socially useful informing. More precisely, what is distinguishing about whistleblowing is that the disclosure of information is an indictment and the disclosure qualifies as an act of dissent. To say that whistleblowing is a dissenting act means that it is 'a chosen action, not one done under oath or under some kind of duress such as threats' (Jubb 1999, 79–80). Whistleblowing is indicting in the sense that it identifies a wrongdoing and accuses and challenges a person or an organization. I think the underlying assumption is very important, namely that the whistleblowers have to make indicting disclosures because they have no authority over those whom they report on and they lack the power to cause change otherwise.

The definition Jubb comes up with is:

> Whistleblowing is a deliberate non-obligatory act of disclosure, which gets onto public record and is made by a person who has or had privileged access to data or information of an organization, about non-trivial illegality or other wrongdoing whether actual, suspected or anticipated which implicates and is under the control of that organization, to an external entity having potential to rectify the wrongdoing (Jubb 1999, 78).

This definition is very instructive in the sense that it contains six elements and is able to generate a number of definitions by altering the elements' descriptive component and qualifiers. The six elements are: action, outcome, actor, subject, target and recipient. Jubb's definition does not contain the motivation of the whistleblower as an element, but he does discuss it and considers it a highly contentious issue.[22] His argument to leave it out rests on his aim to develop a

---

[21] Jubb regards the definitions of whistleblowing in Bowie and Duska (1990); Chambers (1995); Chiasson et al. (1995); Courtemanche (1988); De Maria (1994); Elliston et al. (1985); Miceli and Near (1992) as a representative selection of whistleblowing definitions. While there are other definitions in the literature (see Chalk and von Hippel 1979; De George 1980; Bok 1980; Dworkin and Near 1987; Jensen 1987; Glazer and Glazer 1989; Vinten 1994), I find Jubb's claim that his selection is representative acceptable because he points out the different purposes and disciplinary focus the selected definitions were intended to suit. Whether or not Jubb's definition is a good one will be of less importance to my research than the structure of his definition.

[22] Five out of seven definitions in Jubb's sample can tell us something about motive as an element in a whistleblowing definition. Chiasson et al. (1995) and Courtemanche (1988) are the ones not mentioning it. Out of the five who mention motive, three include it in their definition. De Maria (1994) is explicit about the moral motive for whistleblowing, whilst Bowie and Duska (1990) and Chambers (1995) implicitly suggest it. Chambers does so in regarding whistleblowing as disclosure in the public interest, Bowie and Duska

restrictive definition for whistleblowing. To state that a proper motive would be required to classify an act of disclosure as whistleblowing, would render the definition more problematic, because motives may be mixed, misrepresented and very hard if not impossible to decipher.

Another core dispute in defining whistleblowing is whether or not it only designates external disclosure. Does internal disclosure qualify as whistleblowing? Chiasson et al. (1995) explicitly say it does. Miceli and Near (1992) argue that empirically there is a conceptual distinction to be made between internal and external disclosure, because internal disclosure commonly precedes external disclosure. Moreover, both internal and external disclosures of organizational wrongdoing come down to a dissent being voiced by an insider aimed at rectifying organizational wrongdoing. However, I think there are more distinctions to be made than just internal/external. Internal disclosure can follow conventional hierarchical lines of authority or they can thwart those lines. External disclosures can be made to an entity with an identified role for handling complaints or disclosures, or it can be made to the media. Both these external disclosures get – like Jubb calls it – 'onto public record', which means they are not known to the general public, but the information is 'accessible without too many bureaucratic obstacles' (Jubb 1999, 90).

So, Jubb's six elements plus a seventh one – motive – make up the matrix of possible definitions of whistleblowing (Table 1.2), hence the full scope of what whistleblowing policies can aim at. In the next section, I limit the scope of whistleblowing policies to be looked at in this research. The seven elements of the matrix are:

- *act* → the act of whistleblowing is always a disclosure, but that disclosure can be intended or not, authorized or not, obligatory or not in terms of professional status or organizational function;
- *motive* → is the whistleblowing done out of altruism, to further the public interest without personal benefits, or with a rather egoist motive, because of personal benefits, regardless of whether this furthers the public interest or not;
- *subject* → the disclosure regarded as whistleblowing can be about illegalities, immoral acts, specific contraventions or other wrongdoing, and in all cases these can be either trivial or non-trivial, and they can be actual, past or potential;
- *target* → who gets targeted by the disclosure? The subject of the disclosure can either be occurring in the organization, it can be outside but in control of

---

suggest moral motive in summing up about what a disclosure is made: unnecessary harm, violations of human rights. It is Elliston et al. (1985) and Miceli and Near (1992) who explicitly exclude it from their definition because of research reasons, more precisely the impossibility of measuring motive.

Table 1.2   Matrix of possible whistleblowing definitions

Element	Descriptor	Qualifier
Act	Disclosure	Intended/unintended
		Authorized/unauthorized
		Obligatory/non-obligatory
		Role prescribed/not role prescribed
Outcome	On public record	Anonymous/identified
	Not on public record	Anonymous/identified
Actor	Employee	Internal auditor
		Ethics officer
		Other
	Organization member	Past/present
	Person with privileged access to organization's data or information	Past/present
Motive	Altruism	Further the public interest without personal benefits
	Egoism	Further the public interest with personal benefits
		Because of personal benefits furthering the public interest
Subject	Illegality	Trivial/non-trivial
		Actual/past/potential
	Immoral acts	Trivial/non-trivial
		Actual/past/potential
	Specific contraventions (e.g. code of conduct)	Trivial/non-trivial
		Actual/past/potential
	Wrongdoing	Trivial/non-trivial
		Actual/past/potential
Target	Occurs in the organization	
	In control of organization or involving organization	
	Involving a member of the organization	In function/out of function
Recipient	Internal authorities	Following formalized or conventional lines of communication
		By-passing formalized or conventional lines of communication
	External authorities	
	Media	

the organization, or the disclosure can target a member of the organization, whether in function or in private life;

*   *recipient* → to whom the disclosure is made can vary between internal authorities, external authorities or the media, and in the case of internal authorities, the disclosure can either follow or by-pass formalized or conventional lines of communication.

Limitations of this Research

I wrote that whistleblowing policies are the institutionalization of whistleblowing, as they set out procedures and norms explicitly aimed at individuals disclosing information on perceived organizational malpractices. But what do these policies do? They allow or encourage such disclosures to be made according to the procedures and norms set out in the policy. How do they do that? By offering individuals who disclose according to the policy – legitimate whistleblowers – protection. Exactly what they protect varies, but in general, they protect legitimate whistleblowers against being dismissed, demoted, or otherwise retaliated against because they blew the whistle. Whistleblowing policies laid down in legislation sometimes offer compensation or damages to legitimate whistleblowers who have been retaliated against despite the policy.

First Limitation – Actor, Subject, Recipient

This research will not look into the kind of protection offered by whistleblowing policies. The aim of this research is to try to answer the question whether or not whistleblowing policies resolve the conflict between organization and society, in terms of what kind of whistleblowing is put forward by the respective policies as legitimate. This requires looking at how whistleblowing policies stipulate who can disclose (actor), about what (subject) and to whom (recipient), not at amounts rewarded or protection offered. Therefore, as the focus of this research is to find out what kind of whistleblowing is regarded as legitimate, of main interest in screening whistleblowing policies will be the actor, subject and recipient elements inherent in these policies.

Second Limitation – Policies Explicitly Aimed at Whistleblowing

The act of making allegations about organizational practices perceived as malpractices is not new. In retrospect, whistleblowing has been compared with earlier forms of making such allegations under the name of 'civil disobedience' (Elliston 1982a; Grant 2002). However, coining such allegations as 'whistle-blowing' is new since the 1970s, emphasizing organizational members disclosing information rather than 'any' citizen making allegations. It is the legitimation of the concept of whistleblowing this research is concerned with. Hence, this research is limited to legitimation attempts of policies explicitly aimed at whistle-blowing.

Third Limitation – Not Role-Prescribed Disclosures

Some professions include in their professional standards the prescription to disclose particular information on organizations they do work for or are employed by (for example lawyers, auditors, some banking functions). Although these provisions aim at clarifying loyalties of those professionals (Davis 2002, 44), they are institutionalizing particular organizational functions into professions rather than institutionalizing whistleblowing. It would be interesting to research how disclosure policies have been developed in professional standards and what the particular role is of including such policies for the professionalization of specific organizational functions, but this lies beyond the scope of this research. Therefore, this research will not consider role-prescribed whistleblowing.

Fourth Limitation – Whistleblowing Policies Through Legislation

One way to find out whether or nor whistleblowing has backlashed from an activist concept into a managerial tool, would be to count the number of corporations and other organizations that have installed internal whistleblowing procedures for their organization since the emerging of the concept in the early 1970s. To do so would constitute quantitative research on the matter. The research here presented however, has a qualitative concern, more precisely: what kind of whistleblowing is regarded as legitimate? As I have pictured the rise of the whistleblowing concept as one of the phenomena of globalization, of relevance is, if and how the discourse of globalization has rendered whistleblowing a specific legitimate content. Given this qualitative outlook, three research set-ups are possible:

1 to research a limited number of organizations who have installed whistle-blowing policies, looking for attitudes with regard to whistleblowing;
2 limit the research to legitimation of whistleblowing as put forward by whistle-blowing policies laid down in legislation;
3 research a limited number of geo-political contexts (countries or regions) comparing legitimation as put forward by legislation with organizational attitudes towards whistleblowing.

Given the absence of research into the legitimation of whistleblowing, I opt for the second set up. By doing this, I will be able to identify the tendency at global level in legitimating whistleblowing. Future research on the issue, taking set-up 1) or 3) might thus benefit from such an identified global tendency to compare their findings with.

However, there is another reason why I will focus on whistleblowing policies laid down in legislation. My research question was inspired by a suspicion that whistleblowing activism might have backlashed into a managerial tool. Now, if whistleblowing legislation is developing – which is the case – and whistleblowing activism has from the outset been a call for legislation on the matter – which is the case – then my research question can best be answered by looking into whistleblowing policies laid down in legislation to find out how much activism is left.

Data Collection

Tracing legitimation of whistleblowing through whistleblowing policies laid down in legislation implies two types of data that can be used: whistleblowing legislation and discussions leading up to whistleblowing legislation.

Material of the first type will be found in: texts of the Acts stipulating a whistleblowing policy, and reviews of whistleblowing legislation by academics and NGOs.

Material of the second type will be found in: texts of legislative Bills, reports of parliamentary readings and discussions on the Bills, reports from official commissions looking into the feasibility and desirability of whistleblowing policies, academic research on whistleblowing (in books and journals as well as conference papers), and position papers from NGOs.

These two types of data will be collected for: countries with whistleblowing legislation, countries where lobbying for whistleblowing policies is taking place or has already resulted in Bills, and intergovernmental bodies recommending whistleblowing policies.

Chapter 2

Developing the Framework for an Ethical Assessment

Normative Legitimation and Meaning-giving

In Chapter 1 I wrote that my research wants to find out if and to what extent whistleblowing policies are one of the organizational changes resulting from globalization. I also wrote that to do this, I will make an ethical assessment of the whistleblowing policies developing or recently developed. Such an ethical assessment consists of comparing possibilities and necessities. But how exactly I am going to do that, is something I will discuss in this chapter.

Throughout this chapter, it is important to keep the following in mind. In Chapter 1, I wrote that the concept of whistleblowing involves the categories of individual, organization and society. How whistleblowing makes those three categories relate to each other seems to have shifted. And it is the current status – how these categories relate today – which I am researching by assessing the normative legitimation of whistleblowing policies. I also wrote that a whistle-blowing policy is an attempt to institutionalize whistleblowing. So:

whistleblowing policy

=

institutionalization of:
people blowing the whistle (individual)
→ on organizations operating within (organization)
→ the context of globalization of private capital oriented economy (society)

To research normative legitimation of whistleblowing policies means to look at the ways in which those policies are justified. These justifications are attempts to formulate an answer to questions and problems each of the three categories face. More precisely, the three categories relate to each other through these questions and problems. The normative legitimation of whistleblowing policies are attempts to give meaning to those relations. This meaning-giving is lingual. The normative legitimation is done through 'words-with-meaning'.

That is the starting point of my hermeneutic, a systematic way of interpreting the collected data on whistleblowing policies. It is from that assumption that I will develop the tools to undertake the research. In the next section, I will look at what Niklas Luhmann has to say about the assumption I start from.

However, Luhmann's view on networks of 'words-with-meaning' – or semantic – is definitely not a 'plug-and-play' theory. To find out how Luhmann's insights on the dynamics of semantics might be operationalized for an assessment of normative legitimation for whistleblowing policies, I will look to other authors and try to develop a work plan by rephrasing Luhmann's view, inspired by aspects of the work of Weber, Foucault and Touraine. Figure 2.1 gives an idea of what aspects of the work will serve as inspiration for rephrasing Luhmann's view into a work plan for this research.

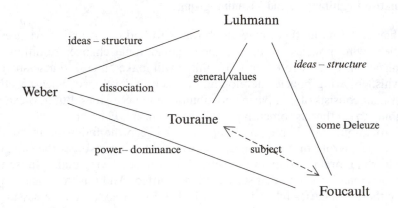

Figure 2.1   Linking Luhmann, Weber, Foucault and Touraine

After that, I argue that both Luhmann and Weber try to describe the interdependence of ideas and structure. I also point out to what extent my operationalization of what Luhmann calls variation and selection is a kind of Weber's *Verstehende Soziologie*. In the same section, I pay attention to some of Weber's insights into power and dominance, which is the bridge to describing a Foucauldian perspective. But to fully read Luhmann's view on semantic through the Foucauldian concept of discourse and visa versa, I need to add some Deleuze to account for Luhmann's variation mechanisms. And, starting from the mutual presupposition Weber and Touraine have about the dissociation between the individual and the organization, I find in the section on Touraine that his notion of the institutional level in organizations and the role of general values link back to Luhmann's semantic. However, Touraine's call for the affirmation of the subject seems to run counter a Foucauldian perspective. At the end of this chapter then, I write out the full work plan and tools for the assessment of normative legitimation of whistleblowing policies.

Niklas Luhmann

In *Gesellschaftsstruktur und Semantik*, Luhmann (1980) discusses an important issue in the sociology of knowledge, more precisely that of changes in the sets of ideas and concepts that accompany the transition to modern society. For Luhmann, meaning-giving regards the complex of signification of the natural and social reality, which always also has to do with feelings and sensitivities, with evaluation, denouncing and approval. The signification is always lingual, always done through 'words-with-meaning'. Luhmann's starting point is that human experience and action are meaningful, and that these experiences and actions are accessible only through that meaning. More precisely, the meaning of an actual event can only be considered in the form of the references to other possibilities. Hence, every meaning guarantees that future experience and action will fit the present. This implies that every meaning presents reality as punctuated with other possibilities, and that every meaning puts the relation of the present to those other possibilities under selection pressure. Thus, there is a surplus of possibilities because of all the possibilities, only this or another contingency will be actualized, thematically intended and acted upon (Luhmann 1980, 17–18). Meaning is only real in what is happening now. It is always present, always now, always current. There is no meaning without reference to what is lived and experienced today.

Luhmann looks at the meaning-giving structure in relation to a social history and calls this a semantic. It is a lingual, and thus a cognitive whole of meaning and signification, within the framework of a historical process of social differentiation (Commers 1995). This is important in the work of Luhmann. He explicitly rejects the idea that culture as a semantic-symbolical complex could be a differentiating action system in itself. Culture does not go through an independent evolution, compatible with different kinds of structures of society. In other words, ideas do not vary independently from, but rather in relation to the structure of society – using or utilizing those ideas (Luhmann 1980, 17). In researching that relation, Luhmann makes it clear that an 'idea-causality' is not his concern (Luhmann 1980, *vorwort*). He writes that this distinguishes him from Max Weber, who did have an 'idea-causality' in mind. Actually, I doubt it whether Weber really had this in mind. In the introduction of *Economy and Society*, Guenther Roth[1] writes that Weber went against the 'isms' of his time, e.g. Social Darwinism and Marxism, but that an 'idea-causality' was not his goal. Weber rejected all mono-causal theories,

---

[1]   See Weber 1968, xxix. Mathieu Lemmen (1990, 18) makes the same assessment of Weber's intentions, but does it with regard to *Die protestantische Ethik*. According to Lemmen, this work is clearly a rejection of the Marxist notion that religion is merely a reflection of technologically determined social relations of production. Weber denies that the Reformation could be deduced as a historical necessity of certain economical changes. However, states Lemmen, Weber also rejected the thesis that the spirit of capitalism can be understood exclusively in terms of influence from the Reformation, as idiot and dogmatic.

both the materialistic as well as the idealistic, and the mechanistic as well as the organistic. I would therefore say that Luhmann, not in contrast to but rather just like Weber, wants to specify the interdependence of ideas and structures of society. Luhmann works from the suspicion that in the historical process not the content of ideas but rather the contingence of ideas can be causal. In other words, there is no downward causation in the sense of ideas finding their way from culture into heads and through hands onwards into things. Rather, it is the possibility of being otherwise which stimulates activities from which a systematizable content follows (Luhmann 1980, *vorwort*, 220). Hence, for Luhmann, a semantic is never stable. Reflection on and theorizing about changes in semantic are the tasks Luhmann sets himself in the sociology of knowledge.[2]

I already wrote that for Luhmann, meaning is always related to actual experience. Meaning is therefore always acted-out-meaning. Luhmann speaks of *gepflegter Semantik* – a cared-for-semantic – and describes it as an 'in the heads of people individualized reality'. It is not a series of independent transcendent ideas, but rather a self-inciting, auto-moving critical mass, in which every element only exists to the extent that it is connected to or referring to the other elements. A cared-for-semantic is a semantic network (Luhmann 1980, 18), a complex whole with broad differentiation, with historical overlaps, with continuous reactions to itself, with sensibilities for nuances, with progressive as well as conservative ideas and with an uncalculatable potential for individually raised innovations, partly resonating and partly left untouched (Luhmann 1980, *vorwort*).

Two concepts are of importance in Luhmann's work: complexity and system differentiation. Moreover, these concepts are interconnected. A system is complex when not every element can be connected to every other element. In other words, in a complex system, relating the elements occurs selectively. A system is differentiated when it repeats its structure within itself and hence creates subsystems within itself. Repeating the structure within itself implies that the system differentiates within itself between system and – internal – environment (*Umwelt*) (Luhmann 1980, 21). In his last work, *Organisation und Entscheidung*,[3] Luhmann sees such a differentiation as underlying the notion of organization. Society as a system draws within itself a border through which appears on the one side ever more complex organizations and on the other side something which these organizations regard as environment (*Umwelt*) (Luhmann 2000, 383).

Luhmann understands the interconnection of complexity and system differentiation as follows: the maximum complexity a social system can

---

[2]   In this sense, Luhmann develops a semantic on changes in semantic. It is a meta-semantic, which is a historico-political semantic. Luhmann is aware of the problem of self-reference here: talking about a semantic always takes place within a semantic, or, to specify the interrelation of structure of society and ideas, one always uses ideas – concepts – which themselves are interrelated with the structure of society from which one is talking.

[3]   Luhmann had finished the manuscript before his death in 1998, but it was only published in 2000.

acquire, depends on its form of differentiation.[4] Hence it is the primary form of differentiation which offers the action system more or less space for different kinds of action. In other words, depending on the way a first layer of subsystems is organized, more or less selective, more or less contingent action-wholes appear for the actors. And with that varies the incitement to conscious meaning-giving and to the construction of a semantic which sorts out, aggregates and keeps accessible all experience of meaning.

The existing world can be experienced only through a cared-for-semantic, which for Luhmann – as I emphasized earlier – evolves in connection to changes in structure of society. More precisely, the changes in the complexity of the social system – and the contingency of her operation – accompany changes in semantic (Luhmann 1980, 15). Important in Luhmann's evolutionary perspective is that changes in the level of complexity are a side effect of structural changes, i.e. of changes in the form of differentiation.[5] Whenever the complexity changes, the semantic needs to adapt in order that reality would remain accessible for experience and action. Hence, complexity is an intervening variable which mediates in evolutionary changes in structure and transformations of semantic. The implication is this: society does not evolve in the direction of an anticipated situation which one wants to realize; but rather, pictures of the future arise based on the experience of the changes that are taking place, and these pictures can have an influence (Luhmann 1980, 21).

Let me recapitulate and then move on. Luhmann uses an evolutionary perspective on the sociology of knowledge, in which the evolution of ideas presupposes an evolving social coherence – an empirical corpus – with interdependencies and independencies, specific interconnected meaning – cared-for-semantic. Such a semantic is a network of actualized meaning and of meaning which lies in the reference horizon of that actualized meaning. The dynamic of such a semantic is an interplay of variation mechanisms, selection mechanisms and stabilization mechanisms.

---

 [4] In their reading of Luhmann, Mortier and Raes (1992, 245–57) emphasize the complexity reducing function of a semantic.

 [5] Luhmann sees an evolution in the structure of society from segmental differentiation, to a stratificatory differentiation and then further to a functional differentiation (Luhmann 1980, 25–34). In a segmental differentiated society, every subsystem regards the innersocietal environment (*innergesellschaftlige Umwelt*) as a collection of identical or resembling systems. In the stratificatory differentiated society, the organization principle lies in an unequal layering of society, but every layer shows a segmental differentiation. The functional differentiated society is a social form which according to Luhmann has only once existed, namely in the modern society of Europe, and is therefore without any historical parallels. In his *Gesellschaftstruktur und Semantik*, which bears the subtitle *Studien zur Wissenssoziologie der modernen Gesellschaft*, Luhmann develops insights into the semantic transformations occurring with the transition – Luhmann speaks of a transitional semantic – from a stratificatory to a functional differentiated society, and he does that by studying the conceptual shifts within anthropology.

Luhmann states the variation mechanism is endogenous (Luhmann 1980, 47). It is the semantic itself which provokes variation. But, there appears to be a mechanism at play which guarantees a variation that is considerable yet structurally adapted. The variations are always variations to a semantic tradition; always variations arizing from that semantic. Now, for a semantic component to drag along and to support other semantic components, mediating operations are needed which at the same time co-steer the variation process. Cognitive inconsistencies and problems – especially unsolvable problems – are the motor of those operations. Knowledge, writes Luhmann (1980, 47), can only be systematized and kept together through the formulation of problems. Variation can exist in a deviation of the core of words or a new combination of cores of words. It can also rest on misunderstandings or planned misuse. But in any way, variation is part of a cared-for-semantic.

We continuously produce deviations and variations on the semantic tradition, but these variations are usually without consequences, because of selection mechanisms and stabilization mechanisms. The selection aims itself in its procession on a ready and standing by stock of 'types', and on what can be stabilized through reference to well known patterns (Luhmann 1980, 18). At stake is always keeping the world accessible for experience, communication and action. This comes down to a 'clearing' of meaning and signification from doubts and perplexity; a normalization of restlessness and discomfort. This 'clearing' is always lingual, always semantical, through old and new networks of 'words-with-meaning' (Commers 1995). Luhmann uses the word typifying (*typisieren*) – resulting in a stock of 'types' – designating that meaning is generalized according to the needs of a time/object/social context. It comes down to a particular way and measure of abstractions and details, of 'same' and 'different', which concepts signify and give meaning through the ordering of those concepts.

Luhmann refers to Karel Weick's concept of *enactment* (Luhmann 1980, 18; 2000, 35). I consider this reference important for the hermeneutic I am trying to develop here. Karel Weick is an organization psychologist who, in his research from the 1960s on, focuses on cognitive dynamics within organizations. Based on cognitive dissonance theory, Weick develops his own perspective on meaning-giving. Weick does not have a clearly delineated definition of the 'enactment' concept. He reformulates his perspective according to the organizational sub-problem he is researching.[6] Because of that, it is a perspective rather than a theory. In Weick's perspective, giving meaning is a complex of both proactive as well as retroactive meaning-giving: 'Organizations talk in order to discover what they are saying, act in order to discover what they are doing' (Weick 2001, 191). A second constant in Weick's perspective is that meaning-giving always

[6]   I am referring to Weick (2001), which is a collection of reworked articles published by Weick between 1977 and 1999. These articles are all elaborations of his *The Social Psychology of Organizing* from 1969, the work to which Luhmann is referring in his *Gesellschaftstruktur und Semantik*.

runs through cyclic processes of enactment, selection and retention (Weick 2001, 189, 193). Here, enactment refers to the arrangement of the continuous stream of experience into blocs of data. The selection process refines that arrangement and connects the blocs of data, making them into information, through which an 'enacted environment' arises. This is an environment which is momentary knowable and understandable. In a next cycle, this knowledge becomes 'retained enacted wisdom', which can limit possible new enactment. However, the possible limits stemming from retained enacted wisdom can not be seen as determinant, because Weick writes that in the enactment, the arrangements – Weick uses the word 'bracketing' – happen arbitrarily (Weick 2001, 190).

In my opinion, Weick remains unclear here. But if we are to link the perspectives of Weick and Luhmann, then we should regard 'enactment' as the pinning down of the variation function, which makes the processing of ambiguity within the system possible. As I see it, the importance of Weick's perspective lies in the blurring of the distinction between organization and environment. The environment is always an enacted environment, partly created by the organization rather than discovered. In Weick's perspective, the organization is not reacting to its environment. Rather, there is a process of meaning-giving to what one is already doing. For Weick, as for Luhmann, meaning is both active as well as reactive. But Weick never talks about forms of differentiation or structures of society. And Weick's analysis seems less functionalistic than Luhmann's. However, Weick does not seem to succeed in explaining how new semantic turns arise. One moment, enactment is arbitrary, the next moment it is limited by 'retained enacted wisdom'.[7] Weick describes meaning-giving as the infrastructure of organizational inertia (Weick 2001, 176). With this he means that action delivers proof of meaning which is already at work. Hence, although it would be wrong to call Weick's perspective deterministic, it can not be denied that his research focuses on organizational meaning-giving as a self-fulfilling prophecy. In contrast, Luhmann's research question to which he puts his semantic analysis at work, is to what role a certain factor – in Luhmann's case the anthropology of an era – plays as variation mechanism, as selection mechanism, as stabilization mechanism, and, how that factor contributes to a stronger differentiation without however losing the possibilities of cooperation.

But my research is not a case-study illustrating Luhmann's insights into the sociology of knowledge. Luhmann's research question in *Gesellschaftstruktur und Semantik* is different from mine in a number of ways. First of all, Luhmann studied a bit more than a century within the period seventeenth–eighteenth century. I am just taking a picture at a given moment: three decades at the turning

---

[7]   See the quotation: 'If enactment is described as pure trial, as random activity, as indiscriminating bracketing, as generating raw data, and as loosely coupled actions, as well as activity that may be constrained by previous enactment, then the subtle mixture of chaos and order that seems to characterize this initial process has been captured' (Weick 2001, 194).

of twenty-first century. This is related to a second difference. Luhmann's research is a case-study of his evolutionary perspective on the sociology of knowledge. He describes a transitional semantic, and points at a transition from stratificatory to functional differentiated society. Such is not my aim. I do not regard the present as transitory to yet another form of differentiation. Neither does Luhmann. He writes that the growing attention for networks is indeed appearing jointly with the faster and more clear-cut possibilities of structural changes within the own and the other systems, but this only makes more visible what already was the case, namely that for organizations, the environment is not just the market or public opinion, but rather separate systems (Luhmann 2000, 410) – or functional differentiation.

Nevertheless, my research topic and question can be rephrased within the Luhmannian framework. How? Well, it is research into what the role is of the discussion on whistleblowing and the incitements to the institutionalization of whistleblowing, within the cared-for organizational semantic as variation mechanism, selection mechanism and stabilization mechanism.

In Chapter 1, I wrote that Jubb's proposition about whistleblowing is that there is always an underlying dissent to it. In Luhmann's perspective, every dissent is a variation in and from the cared-for-semantic. The incitements to institutionalize whistleblowing could be described as stabilization mechanisms. But all this is also subject to a selection mechanism which makes the possibilities that cannot stabilize, appear as not opportune. Therefore:

- the question whether or not institutionalization of whistleblowing is a selectable possibility, can be answered by checking its compatibility with the current organizational semantic.

The first thing to do then, is to develop a grid to screen the whistleblowing policies. There are also variations in the normative legitimation for whistleblowing policies. I will need to 'collect' those variations and order them. The variations are possibilities, some might be selectable, others not. But it will be in comparing the possible variations in the organizational semantic, with the particular ones used in whistleblowing policies, that I will be able to say something about how whistle-blowing policies work as the selection mechanism and the stabilization mechanism. To do this, I will need a tool to position the attempts to institutionalize whistle-blowing in relation to each other and to the correlate of structure and semantic. I will develop that hermeneutic tool in Chapter 3. It will serve as an instrument to see just what forms of whistleblowing are being institutionalized. In the next sections I will set out the theoretical framework for that hermeneutic tool.

To a certain extent, the work plan I have just set myself – look for possibilities and then see which ones are acted on – is a kind of Weber's *Verstehende Soziologie*. In the next section I will point out to what extent exactly and also look at what Weber has written that could be useful to the whistleblowing case.

Max Weber – *Verstehende Soziologie*

Max Weber developed a sociological approach emphasizing a distinction between the normative and the empirical. In this sense, Weber's work is a reaction to that of Rudolf Stammler,[8] a neo-Kantian, who claimed that the relation between the legal and the economical order was not a causal relation but rather a relation of form

---

[8]   Rudolf Stammler (1856–1938) is considered to be one of the most influential legal philosophers of the early twentieth century. Stammler – a neo-Kantian – distinguished between the concept of law, which is the embodiment of pure reason, and the idea of law, which is 'the realm of purposes realized by violition'. Unlike Kant, for whom practical reason was not a matter of intellectual perception, Stammler sought to formulate a universally valid idea of justice on pure reason. By dong so, Stammler tried to save the notion of natural law. Social phenomena needed to be regulated from an external standpoint, more precisely, by the norms of law. Hence, for Stammler, law is before the state and external regulation of human interaction is the necessary prerequisite of social life which has a specific goal. Weber's critique of Stammler, especially the critique on the contrast between convention and law, somehow becomes close to that of early Soviet law scholars. Stuchka, in the early days after the October Revolution had described the nature of law as a system of relationships which answers to the interests of the dominant class and which safeguards that class with organized force. Pashukanis, one of the most influential Soviet law scholars – and the number one Soviet jurist of the 1920s and early 1930s – pointed out that Stuchka's definition implied that law is just another form of social relationship. Pashukanis argued that not every social relationship assumes a legal character. The fundamental principle of legal regulation is opposed private interests. There is one social relationship that inevitably reflects in the form of law, and that is the relationship between commodity owners. Therefore, it is not in naked power that the origin of law is to be sought, but in the existence of private property and the equivalent exchange of commodities. In this sense, law does not come before the state. Weber saw this structural similarity as well: the strictly rational organization of work could only develop in an bureaucratic state with rational laws where the behaviour of the legal system is predictable. He even pointed out that in a system in which formally 'equal' parties are at play – which the notion of equivalent exchange of commodities presupposes – like the employment relation, starting with a formally 'voluntary acceptance' of the conditions set by the employer, the relationships are only *formally* equal. Weber however, pierced through the notions of 'formal equality', 'voluntary acceptance' and 'consensus' not in terms of class struggle but in terms of dominance by monopoly and dominance by authority. There is however, another point at which Weber was working 'against Stammler'. It concerns the distinction between the natural and the social sciences. Stammler argued that if both are to generate general theories about cause and effect, then the social sciences can only be based on historical materialism. However, Stammler thought historical materialism to be incomplete and poor. But Weber did integrate interpretation and explanation of social phenomena. True, he did not regard a nomological explication to be appropriate for historical events. Rather, what is to be known about a historical outcome in retrospect is what causes can be identified as having 'favoured' it to a significant degree. Hence, for Weber, causal analysis of social phenomena is possible, in the sense that it explains why the course of historical development ultimately produced the explanandum rather than some other outcome.

and content. Weber refused such a position. His critique (Weber 1968, 325–33) was aimed at: 1) the confusion between the normative and the empirical validity of an order; 2) the confusion between the regularity of an action resulting from a normative orientation and merely factual regularity; and 3) the claim that there is a contrast between convention and law, and that this contrast can be expressed in terms of free will – as if conventions do not entail coercion. Hence, it is also a critique against the view that law and convention are forms of behaviour in contrast to the content of behaviour.[9]

Weber's distinction between the normative and the empirical is the crux of his *Verstehende Soziologie*. He – just as Luhmann later – approaches experience and action from meaning-giving and signification. Understanding experience and action can only be done by looking at the specific meaning-giving and signification. However, Weber's *Verstehende Soziologie* does not consist of a semantic analysis. What Weber does is to develop 'idealtypes' (*Idealtypen*). These are normative. Explaining and understanding action then, is possible by looking at the extent to which this action differs from the idealtypes, which is the empirical aspect. Thus, Weber's method consists of two steps. The first is the construction of purely rational courses of action – idealtypes. These constructions show how a rational course of action would look like, given the goals of the actors and an adequate knowledge of circumstances. The merit of the constructed idealtypes is that they are easy to understand and are averse to ambiguity. The second step in his method is then to compare the factual course of action with the idealtypes, which makes the factual action understandable and explainable as to what irrational factors such as affects or mistakes – and I would add deceit – influence the factual action (Weber 1968, 6). It is important to note that nowhere in reality one will encounter a course of action which is fully in line with an idealtype (Weber 1968, 59). Empirical phenomena can never be an idealtype; they can only more or less approximate a constructed idealtype. More precisely, Weber constructed sets of idealtypes, forming a continuum on which concrete actions can be posited.

It would be a mistake to characterize Weber's work as normative.[10] But it would be just as big a mistake to pass by the fact that Weber points out the influence of the normative on the empirical. Even though Weber regarded idealtypes as merely methodological instruments (Weber 1968, 6), they do have validity in reality. For example, the reason why Weber regarded Taylor's system of *Scientific Management* as triumphant is exactly because it organizes labour on the basis of an idealtype of

---

[9]   This is also the analysis MacIntyre makes of Weber's work. However, underlying MacIntyre's 'cure for society' is the rejection of Weber's distinctions (MacIntyre 1981).

[10]   To do this would be analogue to the confusion of Darwin's evolution theory with Social Darwinism. It seems to me that MacIntyre's rejection in *After Virtue* of the insights Weber offers, can only be defended from such a confusion. I acknowledge the reality of the confusion, in the sense that the confusion was and still is made, but I somehow reproach MacIntyre for not correcting it. Furthermore, it might be relevant to know that Weber argued against the principles of Social Darwinism (see Weber 1968, xxix).

mechanization. Indeed, it is an instrumental rationality – *Zweckrationalität* – but it is linked with a founding value rationality – *Wertrationalität*. The value rationality is always at work in a normative way through the instrumental rationality.[11]

Let me make clear just how I see the work plan I have set myself as 'a kind of Weber's *Verstehende Soziologie*'. The hermeneutic I am developing here in this chapter will also consist of two steps. The first will be to list, given the organizational semantic, the possible variations regarding normative legitimation of whistleblowing policies. But to list those possibilities, I will need to construct them. These constructions can be seen as idealtypes in two ways: 1) I will construct them within the limits set by the value rationality of the organizational semantic; and 2) I do not expect to find the actual normative legitimation used in recent or in developing whistleblowing policies as matching idealtypes. Rather – and here too my hermeneutic is 'a kind of' Weber's method – the validity of the assessment lies in the extent to which the normative legitimation given to whistleblowing policies resembles particular idealtypical constructs *and not* the other constructed idealtypes.

In addition to these two steps and as indicated earlier, my assessment of normative legitimation of whistleblowing policies will also include a third step: an ethical evaluation of current tendencies in the normative legitimation of whistle-blowing policies. As will become clear at the end of this chapter (and further on in Chapter 5 where I will carry out that ethical evaluation), this third step builds further on the first two, in the sense that my ethical evaluation will be based on which of the idealtypical constructs do not appear in the current legitimation tendencies.

But there is also an important aspect in which my work plan might be problematic with regard to Weber's aspirations. The importance of Weber's work and method lies in its integration of interpretation *and* explanation of historical events and processes (Ringer 1997). The research I am presenting here certainly is an interpretation of how the protection of whistleblowing has been legitimated over the last 30 years. And, in addition to Weber's method, my ethical evaluation of that historical evolution will be very explicit. But what might be problematic with regard to Weber's method, is my explanation of that historical event. Weber did not regard a nomological explication as appropriate for historical events. Nevertheless, he is to be regarded as a causalist in the sense that it is important to know, in retrospect rather than in prediction, what 'causes' – i.e. decisions, actions, circumstances, texts – can be identified as having 'favoured' a historical outcome to a more or less significant degree (Ringer 1997, 69). In the research I am presenting here, and in line with Luhmann's evolutionary view on the dynamic of semantics, the causal elements for explaining the historical event of normative legitimation of whistleblowing policies over the past 30 years, will be the current

---

[11] Weber's *Die protestantische Ethiek und der Geist des Kapitalismus* can be seen as an example of this. Another, it would seem to me more direct example – because it does not have the religious connotation – is the excursus in *Economy and Society* on the superiority of the status stimulation compared to physical coercion (Weber 1968, 967–8).

organizational semantic – or globalization semantic as I will name and describe it in Chapter 3. Hence, the explanation of why current tendencies in normative legitimation resemble more certain specific idealtypical constructs rather than other possible constructs is already given in Luhmann's evolutionary approach: the current tendencies in legitimation are those variations that are able to stabilize the organizational semantic. But, as I have argued in at the beginning of this chapter and will further argue in Chapter 3, whistleblowing in an organizational context as an issue appears at the same time as the organizational semantic starts to shift into the globalization semantic. The only way to avoid a tautological explanation therefore is to find out what that stabilization consists of, or in other words, how do the current tendencies in normative legitimation of whistleblowing policies deal with the conflict between organization and society?

What I have discussed so far constitutes the first reason why I'm devoting a section to Weber: meaning-giving is normative and makes reality accessible, but is never unambiguous. Or, in Weber's terms, idealtypes have validity in reality, but the explanation for and the understanding of action – which is what matters – can be found where reality differs from the idealtypes. Or, in the words Ringer (1997) has formulated Weber's method in,[12] understanding and explaining action is possible only by finding out why the real course of action has followed one particular path and not the other possible paths.

But there is another reason why I am paying attention to Weber's work. Power and dominance are central concepts in Weber's work. When talking about whistleblowing and its institutionalization, power and dominance are important concepts with regard to the relations between the individual, the organization and society. In the remainder of this section, I will point out some of Weber's insights on those themes.

Social action is subjective meaningful action, oriented on the behaviour of others.[13] Normative regulated action is a form of social action. Opposite to that is purely statistically frequent action, those forms of behaviour that are not social in the sense that the action is not subjectively meaningful oriented on the behaviour of others.[14] The subjective meaningfulness can consist of an instrumental rationality. In this case, action is based on the assumption that one can expect

---

[12]   Ringer (1997) describes Weber's model as a dynamic model of alternate historical sequences or paths. Ringer's book also puts the work of Weber into its German historical and intellectual context.

[13]   Weber used the term *Gemeinschaftshandeln*, which he later replaced by *Soziales Handeln*.

[14]   For this kind of action, Weber used the term *Massenhandeln*. In an essay from 1913 (and reprinted as Appendix I in Weber 1968), he gives the following example: when two cyclists collide without the intention to do so – it is an accident – then this is not social action because it is not subjectively meaningful action. It becomes social action when they try to avoid the collision, when they argue after the collision, or when they peacefully settle the matter through negotiation.

subjectively meaningful action from others. But the subjective meaningfulness of an action can also be based on the 'value' of an act. In that case, the behaviour is not oriented on expectations, but on values.

In any way, social action is individual behaviour which – historically observable or theoretically possible or probable – stands in relation to the factual or anticipated potential behaviour of other individuals. Thus, for Weber, it is individual people who act, not groups or society. However, individual people can act collectively, and those who act together form groups. These groups continue to exist on the condition that they have a constitution in the sense that their order is accepted by their members – and to a certain extent also by outsiders – through consensus, for whatever reason. A belief in the legitimacy of the order is not necessary. Accepting the constitution can have other reasons.

Weber calls acting together in a group *Gesellschaftshandeln*. He characterizes it as rational regulated action and claims that it: 1) is meaningfully oriented on rules – common declarations or unilateral demands and orders – which 2) rationally originated in view of expected behaviour of the associates (*Vergesellschaftete*) and to the extent that 3) the meaningful orientation is instrumentally rational from the side of the actor. Weber's idealtype of association (*Vergesellschaftung*) is the voluntary association (*Zweckverein*). It is a continuing association in which all participants rationally agree on the statute which defines goals and means of the association, and has general rules and a staff of its own.[15]

Now, interesting are the moderations Weber makes concerning voluntary association. For one, there might be dominance (*Herrschaft*) at play. Weber contrasts dominance with power (*Macht*) (Weber 1968, 53–4). Power is the probability that, within a social relation, an actor will be in the position to carry out his own will, despite resistance and regardless of the basis of that probability. Dominance then is formulated categorically as that situation in which the manifested will of the dominator or dominators – order or demand – is meant to influence the behaviour of an other or others – the dominated – and indeed influences that behaviour in a way that their behaviour appears as if the dominated have made the content of the manifested will the maxim of their behaviour. In Luhmann's terms, this comes close to a cared-for semantic, described as the 'in the heads of people individualized reality'. Domination is when an order is carried out by a given group of people for the sake of the specific content of that order. This situation can be arrived at through discipline, which is the probability that a command is immediately and automatically carried out in stereotype forms.[16]

---

[15] An opposite idealtype is that of the occasional association (*Gelegenheitsvergesell-schaftung*). Here, the association rests on an ad hoc agreement. There are no general rules and no staff, only a rational plan. Weber gives the example of the occasional association which carries out a murder as quick revenge. Hence, this type of association is not continuing.

[16] Luhmann would use the word *problemlos*, meaning: without hindsight to what is perceived, hence openly. My translation of 'ohne Rücksicht auf den, der es wahrnimmt, also öffentlich' (Luhmann 2000, 422).

Discipline then regards the forming of habits, or the standardization of behaviour. Weber states that it is dominance which makes amorphous and interrupted social action transform into continuing association.

Another moderation Weber makes concerning voluntary association, and which I already mentioned earlier on, regards consensus (*Einverständnis*). We can speak of consensus when the expectations with regard to the behaviour of others is realistic because of the objective probability that others will accept those expectations for themselves, even when there is no explicit agreement to do so. The reason for accepting those expectations is not important when consensus is concerned. Hence, for Weber, consensus does not mean that those pending consensus are happy about it. They can act according to consensus out of fear for the consequences of acting alternatively. In this sense, fear can result in an unwanted yet formally 'free' agreement.

For a third moderation, it is important to come back to Weber's critique on Stammler. Rudolf Stammler made a distinction between convention and legal norm based on whether or not an individual followed the norm out of free will. Weber responds that to base that distinction on free will makes no sense. He argued that it is incorrect to say that following conventional norms – for example social etiquette – is not imposed upon the individual and that not complying to those norms simply results in a free and voluntary removal from a voluntary association. Weber sees proof for this in the fact that there are associations that have done away with legal sanctions, i.e. they have conceived their legal norms as conventional ones. Not because they are convinced that all those whom they want to comply will do so out of free will. No, Weber states these associations have done so based on the assumption that social disapproval of breaching norms, together with indirect consequences will be a sufficient sanction functioning as a deterrent to non-compliance. It is in this sense that Weber argues that conventions too are supported by both psychological as well as – at least an indirect – physical coercion. It is only with regard to the structure of the coercion that the legal order differs from the conventional. The conventional order has no specialized personnel for the implementation of coercive power.

According to Weber, the development of conventions consists of the transformation of merely factual regularity of action into binding norms, and it is especially psychological coercion which is the drive behind that transformation. Therefore, the development of conventions is the transformation of statistically frequent action (*Massenhandeln*) into consensus oriented action (*Einverständnishandeln*). But it is a transformation which is vague. On the one hand, the statistical regularity of an action leads to the appearance of moral and legal beliefs with a corresponding content. On the other hand, the threat of physical and psychological coercion imposes a certain kind of action, thereby producing habit and hence regularity of action. In Weick's terms, by doing what ones does, justifications are produced for what one is doing. It should be clear that habit, convention or consensus and legal norm make up one continuum. And according to Weber's *Verstehende Soziologie* this implies that facts from reality can only be interpreted by placing them on that continuum.[17]

The definition of dominance I gave earlier is dominance in its pure form, as a special form of power. Elsewhere (Weber 1968, 941–8), Weber writes that dominance, in general, is one of the most important elements of social action.[18] It seems to me that Weber held the opinion that every sphere of social action was to a large extent influenced by structures of dominance, in the sense that the structures of dominance and the way they unfold are decisive for the form of social action and the orientation of that action on goals. The control over economic goods – economic power – for instance, is, according to Weber, both a result of dominance as well as one of the most important instruments of dominance. On the one hand, a group reaches a position of economic power in society through the position of dominance in other domains – language for example. On the other hand, dominance quite often uses economic power as its foundation and maintenance. Weber writes that nearly all economic organizations entail a structure of dominance, and most of the time that structure is both a factor of economic importance as well as a result of economic conditions.

Weber describes two types of dominance – two structures of dominance: 1) dominance by virtue of authority – pure dominance as the power to command and the duty to obey; and 2) dominance by virtue of constellation of interests, more specific that of a monopoly.

Big credit banks serve as an example of dominance by market monopoly. These banks dominate the capital market, precisely because they are that big and have a position of quasi-monopoly. The dominance lies in the fact that the credit banks can impose conditions on credit takers.[19] However, they make no authority claim nor do they demand obedience. Every party pursues their own

---

[17] Weber extends his idealtypical distinction between consensus and legal norm to the field of associations. He states that in the organization (*Verband*), organized action is oriented on consensus, not on rational rules. More precisely, it is a consensual action in which 1) membership of the group is awarded by consensus, without rational agreement of the participant, 2) an effective consensual order is imposed by certain people – those in power – despite the absence of rationally formulated rules, and moreover, 3) those persons are prepared to use physical and psychological coercion against those breaching consensus. In contrast, compulsory associations (*Anstallten*) are groups in which 1) membership depends on objective criteria regardless of the expressed will of those concerned, and 2) rationally formulated rules and a coercive apparatus co-determine individual action.

[18] Weber gives two examples in the field of language: the authorization of a dialect into the status of an official language, and the use and influence of language in schools, the official school-language. These examples, together with Weber's remark that the position of economical power in society is linked with a position of dominance in other spheres of social action, resonate through the work of Bourdieu, who saw clusters of social, cultural and financial capital.

[19] Note that banks also impose conditions on those giving the credit – people who put their money in the bank. Weber does not mention that dominance.

interests. The bank realizes her interests when the dominated persons – acting formally 'free' – also pursue their own interests.

Dominance by virtue of constellation of interests, based on a position of monopoly, can gradually transform into a dominance by virtue of authority. In order to have more control over a credit taker – keeping the payback on schedule, guaranteeing paybacks will be delivered – the bank will demand, as a condition to give credit, that someone from the bank takes a seat in the board of directors of the credit taker and hence gets decision power over the credit taker. This can further evolve to rules and explicit controls by specialized agencies. Here, Weber gives a number of examples in which he – again – expresses moderations regarding 'freeness' of relations. He names the dominance of breweries over pubs, of the Standard Oil Company over gas sellers and of coal producers over coal sellers. He names the dependency of door-to-door salesmen and the totally authoritarian regulation of the labour of the sweatshop worker. But he also names the secretary, the engineer, the office worker and the shop floor worker. All are subjected to a discipline, even though their employment is a creation of the labour market with formally 'equal' parties, and even though the employment relation starts by a formally 'voluntary acceptance' of the conditions set by the employer. Indeed, all are subjected to a discipline, and the transition of the so called voluntary authority relations to the involuntary ones – for example slavery – is but a gradual one.[20] And it is exactly because of this merely gradual difference that Weber focused on dominance as authoritarian power to command as the idealtype of dominance.

Every dominance expresses itself in and functions through an administration. But at the same time every administration presupposes dominance, because administration needs someone in power (Weber 1968, 948). Characteristic for the specific arrangements for dominance, is that there is always a circle of people who are habituated to obey orders and who have a personal interest in the continuation of dominance, by means of their own participation and the resulting advantages (Weber 1968, 952–4). That circle of people has distributed amongst themselves the functions necessary to continue the dominance. They are always standby to execute those functions.[21] *This, writes Weber, is what is meant by 'organization'.*

Luhmann does not define the organization in terms of power or dominance, but as autopoietic systems: 'An organization is a system which produces itself as an

---

[20]   Weber hereby points out that the voluntary association (*Zweckverein*) is an idealtype, not a category. The *Verstehende Soziologie* does not work with categories to which a social action either belongs or does not belong.

[21]   Leaders who claim and carry out the power to command but were not given that power by others, are masters. The circle of people on standby – who are available for the master – are the apparatus. The sociological character of the structure of dominance is determined by: the kind of relation between master and apparatus, the kind of relation between master-apparatus on the one hand and the dominated on the other, and the specific organizational structure, i.e. the specific way in which the power to command is distributed.

organization' (Luhmann 2000, 45).[22] His aim is then to define the way in which this takes place. One of the crucial elements in this is 'decision making' (*Entscheidung*). The basic unit of an autopoietic system takes the form of an event, differentiating between 'before' and 'afterwards'. This means, that organizations can only be analysed as autopoietic systems when the analysis is based on the distinction between 'before' and 'afterwards'. Luhmann calls these events 'decisions'. As this distinction emphasizes discontinuity, it is continuity which needs to be explained. In this sense, Luhmann's organization theory stands in contrast to process theory. Luhmann's organization theory argues that every decision overshadows every next decision. What gets decided are only pointers for a repetition of selection. Also, Luhmann contrasts his theory to action theory, although I think 'contrast' is too strong a statement, given the similar assumption both theories hold. True, action theory ties action to perceptions (intentions, goals) of other actions, while the events shown by autopoiesis theory – such as communications – produce an abundance of possibilities, from which in a next phase one can be selected. This implies that what gets selected is not necessarily anticipated, because a decision is usually taken in hindsight of a previous decision (Luhmann 2000, 45–6). But Luhmann seems to apply his evolutionary perspective on semantics and system/ environment differentiation to organizations. The crux of that perspective was – very similar to Weber's basic assumption – that action and reality are only accessible through meaning-giving and signification. Tying actions to perceptions of other actions seems to me to be the same as understanding actions by looking at the meaning of the other actions the analysed actions are reactions to. If we replace 'actions' by 'decisions' or 'events'[23] then Luhmann's theory seems to differ from action theory in two ways. First, Luhmann stretches out the time-dimension. More precisely, action theory can deal with quasi-simultaneous actions, while Luhmann's autopoiesis theory needs a more long term diachronic account. Secondly, Luhmann's theory concerns a self-driven, endogenous trajectory of events, while action theory allows for exogenous influence.

Another important insight Weber raises is that the continuation of any dominance is always in great need of self-justification, and does so by referring to the principles of her legitimation, or, the expression of the validity of her power to command. That expression can be in the form of a reference to a system of rational rules. Here again, Luhmann links with Weber. In *Organisation und Entscheidung* (Luhmann 2000, 421–2), Luhmann writes that organizations make self-descriptions, centralizing and bundling constantly occurring self-references, and having the function of making clear that it is always the same 'self', that it is always about a system which is identical to itself. And this self-description serves the system – the organization – as an official thought culture (*offizielle*

---

[22] My translation of 'Eine Organisation ist ein System, das sich selbst als Organisation erzeugt'.

[23] At most, decisions and events can be distinguished from actions as 'de-subjectificated' actions, something I will come back to in the section on Foucault.

Gedenkkultur), which can be communicated. More precisely, these communications are the organizations identity. Luhmann writes that organizations have no bodies, but they have text (Luhmann 2000, 422). Weick too has a similar view on the matter. He states that organizations are 'built, maintained, and activated through the medium of communication' (Weick 2001, 136). And depending on the interpretation of it, communication can either strengthen the organization or make it more tenuous. [24] But what shapes the interpretation process is shared language, authority relationships that assign rights of interpretation, norms of communication, and the communication itself.

For Weber, compliance to those rational rules will be a generally binding norm only if such a compliance is claimed by the one appointed by those rules to make such a claim. In other words, the bearer of power is legitimated by a system of rational norms, and this system legitimizes power to the extent that this power is exercized conform those rational norms. Thus, one obeys the norm, not the person. However, the legitimation of the power to command can also rest on personal authority, which can either be traditional or charismatic. [25]

Weber situates charisma on the level of satisfaction of needs that transcend the sphere of daily economic routines (Weber 1968, 1111). Charisma refers to a claim of authority, based on extraordinary personal characteristics of supernatural gifts. Charisma is self-determined, for it stands or falls with the belief of those to whom the claim is made. If those to which the claimant feels called do not recognise him as such, his claim expires. That is why Weber calls charismatic authority unstable. Precisely because of that instability, charismatic authority transforms itself; it routinizes itself into a legal or traditional form. [26]

Now, the disappearance of charisma also means the diminishing of the importance of individual action. The most irresistible force here is that of 'rational discipline'. The content of discipline is the consistently rationalized, methodologically prepared and meticulous execution of the received order, in which every personal criticism is unconditionally suspended, and the actor is ready to carry out the command exclusively and without defect. Moreover the behaviour under command is uniform. The effect of this uniformity stems from its quality as social action within a mass structure. Those who comply do not necessarily do this simultaneously, and they are not necessarily a big mass. Nor

---

[24] Weick illustrates this by showing how KLM is constituted by its speech acts, and how misunderstanding lead to a collision at take off – known as the 1977 Tenerife Disaster (Weick 2001, 125–47).

[25] With regard to dominance by virtue of authoritarian power to command, the causal chain from command to factual compliance can vary. Analogue to the three types of legitimation, Weber distinguishes three forms of psychological influence: persuasion by rational argument, inspiration and empathy.

[26] I have documented the routinization of charisma in two new religious movements in Vandekerckhove (1998).

do they need to be united in a specific place. Decisive for discipline is that the compliance of a plurality of people is rationally uniform.

Discipline is – just as bureaucracy, according to Weber her most rational offspring – impersonal. Discipline drills in favour of habitually routinized skills, in stead of heroic ecstasy, loyalty, or spiritual enthusiasm for a leader and a personal devotion or cult of honour. To the extend that discipline claims ethical motives, it presupposes a kind of duty and consciousness: 'men of conscience versus men of honour' (Weber 1968, 1150). It serves the rationally calculated optimum of physical and psychological preparedness of the uniformly conditioned mass. In Luhmann's terms this – again – comes close to a cared-for semantic, described as the 'in the heads of people individualized reality'.

Even though enthusiasm and unreserved devotion can play a role in discipline, just as other emotional means, Weber sees as the sociologically decisive points of discipline:

- that everything is rationally calculated, and certainly the apparently imponderable and irrational emotional factors, calculable – in principle at least – in the same way as the 'yields of coal and iron deposits' (Weber 1968, 1150);
- that the devotion is impersonal, oriented towards a goal, a common cause, a rationally intended goal, and not a person as such, although personal devotion is possible in the case of a fascinating leader.

I wrote that Weber regards bureaucracy as the rational offspring of discipline. In other words, it is the idealtype of a rationally regulated association within the structure of dominance. Weber describes the entrance into a bureaucratic apparatus – office holding or *Kontor* – as a profession, but with the connotation of vocation (*Beruf*) (Weber 1968, 958). This finds its expression in the description of the idealtype. First, a prescribed formation is required, which takes fulltime work capacity for a long period. Next, prescribed special exams are a condition for the employment, for the appointment of the *Kontor*. Moreover, the position of the *Kontor*-holder has the character of a duty, which in turn characterizes the relations as follows: legally and factual, holding *Kontor* is not regarded as ownership of a source of income, to be exploited in return for delivering services. Rather, taking up *Kontor* is regarded as accepting a specific duty of loyalty to the goal of the *Kontor* (*Amtstreue*) as return for a secured existence. It is decisive for loyalty to a *Kontor* that, in the pure type, this is not a relation to a person – as is the case for the vassal or the disciple – but is a dedication to impersonal and functional goals.[27]

---

[27] However, these goals are rendered an ideological halo from cultural values (state, church, community, party, company, …) that seem a surrogate for inner-worldly or outer-worldly masters.

So, both discipline and bureaucracy have an essentially impersonal nature. They are functionally oriented and operationalize this functionality not by means of the whip, but by means of authoritative dominance. Indeed, Weber saw a fully rational basis for the discipline in the capitalistic factory. That basis was an adequate measurement to calculate the optimal profitability of any individual worker, just as could be done for any material means of production. Taylor's *Scientific Management* is the completion of the potential of mechanization and disciplining of a factory unit through rational conditioning and training of work performances. Weber saw this kind of rationalization as a universal phenomenon reducing more and more the importance of charisma and of individual differentiated behaviour.[28]

Whether that analysis can still be drawn today remains to be seen. Of course, Weber was writing in the heydays of Taylorism in the United States. In Europe too, Taylorism gained ground and remained an exponent of the organizational semantic until the 1960s. As I wrote in the previous chapter, it is around that time that Hardt and Negri (2001) situate a first major crisis of capitalism and with it the shifting away from Taylorism and Fordism. Luhmann (2000, 14–15) links Taylor's study of the organization of labour historically with mass markets for standardized products remaining the same for a long period. He adds that the introduction of micro-electronics in the production process has altered the viability of those products – and hence of Taylorist labour organization.

But the subject of my research is the current institutionalization of whistleblowing. I am not studying the first half of the twentieth century – if I was doing that, then Weber's admiration for Taylor's *Scientific Management* would be able to give me a valid assessment grid – nor am I researching the shifts in organizational semantic during the 1960s and 1970s. I am researching the current organizational

---

[28]   See Weber 1968, 1155–6: 'No special proof is necessary to show that military discipline is the ideal model for the modern capitalist factory, as it was for the ancient plantation. However, organizational discipline in the factory has a completely rational basis. With the help of suitable methods of measurement, the optimum profitability of the individual worker is calculated like that of any material means of production. On this basis, the American system of "scientific management" triumphantly proceeds with its rational conditioning and training of work performances, thus drawing the ultimate conclusions from the mechanization and discipline of the plant. The psycho-physical apparatus of man is completely adjusted to the demands of the outer world, the tools, the machines –in short, it is functionalized, and the individual is shorn of his natural rhythm as determined by his organism; in line with the demands of the work procedure, he is attuned to a new rhythm through the functional specialization of muscles and through the creation of an optimal economy of physical effort. This whole process of rationalization, in the factory as elsewhere, and especially in the bureaucratic state machine, parallels the centralization of the material implements of organization in the hands of the master. Thus, discipline inexorably takes over ever larger areas as the satisfaction of political and economic needs is increasingly rationalized. This universal phenomenon more and more restricts the importance of charisma and of individually differentiated conduct.'

momentum. Hence, not only will I have to describe the current organizational semantic – instead of taking Weber's analysis, I will also have to seek how the *oeuvre* of Max Weber might be actualized in order to analyse today's relations between the individual, the organization and society.

Describing the current organizational semantic is something I will do at the start of the next chapter. In the remainder of this chapter, I will find out how Weber's work might be adequately actualized in order to complete my hermeneutic to assess the normative legitimation of whistleblowing policies. In the next section I will show how a Foucauldian perspective might deliver us insights into how a semantic operates in organizations. After that, I will look at the work of Alain Touraine for a more up to date analysis of the relations between individual, organization and society.

A Foucauldian Perspective – and Some Deleuze

That the work of Michel Foucault can be seen as an actualization of Max Weber's insights, is not a mere personal interpretation. Hamilton (1985) writes that although Foucault was answering different questions[29] than Weber, Foucault's work can be read as a number of essays on the development of specific rationalities in a number of central spheres of modern society. Clegg (1989) too argues that Foucault's perspective on the industrial society and disciplinary control are latently present in the work of Weber. Barker and Cheney (1994) see Foucault's concept of discipline as a logical offspring of Weber's perception of growing rationalization of society, even though Foucault – unlike Weber – had a deep aversion to theoretical generalizations. For Barker and Cheney, Foucault's work represents a searching exploration for extreme tendencies of modernism. More precisely, it was an attempt to point out the micro-techniques of power at work, rationalizing and normalizing not only individuals but also collective, organized entities. And according to Hardt and Negri (2001, 88–89), both Max Weber and Michel Foucault have described the administrative mechanisms at work in the modern sovereignty. Both describe the transformation of command to function as the sociological figures of power. Both describe how the disciplinary coincides with the administrative.

McHoul and Grace (1995, vii–xi) and O'leary (2002, 9) see three periods in the work of Foucault. A first runs up to *L'archéologie du savoir* from 1969. Here, Foucault apparently focussed on epistemological questions, and calls units of knowledge *discours*. During a second period, ending with *La volonté du savoir*

---

[29]   On the difference in outlook: '[...] Foucault's analysis of the underlying models of organization of thought bears heavily upon the relations of power and knowledge through which human beings are transformed into subjects, whilst Weber's could be said to be concerned with the domination of means-end rationality over social life' (Hamilton 1985, 8).

from 1976, Foucault dealt with the more political questions regarding control, management and surveillance. His attention was aimed not so much on discourse and knowledge, but rather on the body and its surveillance. Foucault's third period then supposedly focussed on the subject. However, McHoul and Grace themselves acknowledge the arbitrariness of such a differentiation into periods. Political questions and questions concerning the subject are already implicitly present in his so-called first period. In *Les mots et les choses* from 1966, Foucault shows that human sciences were only conceivable by taking over models from biology, economics and philology. What happened was that sets of concepts[30] from those specific domains were taken up within the common volume of the human sciences. These concepts make the concept of 'human sciences' possible, by allowing a specific study domain: man as subject. So, what Foucault focuses on seems to be an unsuitable criteria to base a division into periods on. More accurate arguments to do that might rest in how Foucault thought about power. According to Lambrechts (1980, 262), from *Surveiller et punir* (Foucault 1975) onwards, Foucault denounced a merely repressive vision of power in favour of the view that power is primarily productive and only repressive in its limit.

Of course, Foucault's analysis of the appearance of human sciences along the lines of sets of concepts taken over from already existing domains, is analogue to what Luhmann calls generalization. Certain words-with-meaning become relatively independent from a specific situation, and can be used to signify and give meaning to diverse experiences. Hence, what Luhmann calls *Semantik*, Foucault would call *discours*.

In the previous section, I wrote that Weber's work was interesting for two reasons. The first was that Weber saw meaning-giving as normative and as making reality accessible, but never unambiguous. The second was that power and dominance are central concepts in his work. It is precisely these two aspects I will be looking for in Foucault's work. An exegesis of Foucault is certainly not my aim and would be beside the point for this research, but a limited interpretation of Foucault's work will give valuable insights into the two aspects I am interested in.

Even though Foucault is regarded by many[31] as a structuralist, a static historian, a determinist and a fatalist with regard to the subject, and most of all an anti-humanist, I choose a somewhat moderate reading of Foucault. In that alternative reading, Foucault is not in search of a systematic course of history, but wants to show the internal dynamic through which changes and fractions arise (Lambrechts 1980, 18).[32] With regard to the theme of the subject, some authors – amongst others Deleuze – have protested against a reductionist

---

[30] Three sets of concepts played an important role: *functions-normes* (biology), *conflit-règle* (economy), and *signification-système* (philology) (Foucault 1966, 369).

[31] See the discussions about Foucault described in Lambrechts (1980).

[32] Apparently, Foucault himself said that already in *Les mots et les choses* (1966) he wanted to describe transformations (Brochier 1969, cited in Lambrechts 1980, 36).

lecture of Foucault, arguing it is not subject-negation, but rather the denial of subject-centrism which Foucault is pointing at (Lambrechts 1980, 11). Note that Luhmann also introduces a decentralization, where the individual is subjected to a system of words-with-meaning through which we perceive the world and act in it. Even in Weber's writing on discipline and rationalization of society, such a decentralization is already looming. True, Luhmann leaves a certain possibility for the individual to pick up several possible variations. But the Foucauldian perspective too is not absolutely deterministic, fatalistic or pessimistic, as if a diffuse cynicism would be our fate. Foucault sees himself as an optimist (Boeser 1977, cited in Lambrechts 1980, 293). Resistance can never be totally silenced. Power is essentially dynamic and is unthinkable without counter-power. The right strategy for resistance can be found through a right analysis of power relations (Lambrechts 1980, 293–4). In *Le souci de soi-même*, Foucault (1995) talks about a *being before the law*. Man is empty handed before the law. Both autonomous subjectivity as well as heteronomous legitimation are possible and it is precisely this category carrying with it the possibility of resistance. But to think that category, we need an ethic in which we, as subjects, stand in relation to the law. Foucault's aim is to increase our freedom, starting from the specific way in which we are determined by historical forces. These forces have made us the kind of individuals that we are, and particularly modern Western techniques of subjectivation fix individuals to their identities in a constraining way. The task of ethics, for Foucault, is to allow us to open up a space between us and the identity imposed on us. Ethics is then a care for the self, a set of techniques for self-transformation (O'Leary 2002, 31, 154).

And what about Foucault's anti-humanism? Hardt and Negri (2001, 88–92) note that at the end of his life, Foucault raised the question of humanism after the death of Man, or, the question of an anti-humanistic humanism. However, they see no break in the work of Foucault and are even convinced – based on the fact that Foucault himself insisted on the continuity within his work – that Foucault would agree with them. But an anti-humanistic humanism, what do Hardt and Negri – and Foucault – mean by that? They make a link between the anti-humanistic project of Foucault and Spinoza's struggle. Spinoza refused to attribute to human nature any law that was different from the laws of nature in general. To separate Man from nature, implies that Man does not exist. This is the death of Man. Humanism after the death of Man – anti-humanistic humanism – refers to a continuing constitutive project to create and re-create ourselves and our world.[33]

The reason why Foucault's insights can help me develop the hermeneutic for my research is his analysis of power. In his work, Foucault concentrated on pointing out and tracing the historically rooted power relations in organizations and institutions. Looking back, this was already the case in his so-called first

---

[33] Note that Ronald Commers makes a similar distinction between two forms of humanism (see Commers 1991).

phase, in which he undertook conceptual – epistemic – research. His *archéologie du savoir* was always just as much an *archéologie du pouvoir.*

The Foucauldian perspective I will use to develop the hermeneutic for this research, is based on the lecture of Foucault's work by Hardt and Negri (2001), Lambrechts (1980), Du Gay (1996), and Barker and Cheney (1994) who wrote about Foucault's triad of power, knowledge and rules of right, and how that triad was at work in organizations. From that Foucauldian perspective, power is never the possession of a certain class or group who would have acquired that power. In this sense, Foucault stands in contrast to Weber, who wrote about administrations with someone 'in power' and about 'bearers of power'. But from a Foucauldian perspective, analysing power is not done by asking 'Who?' but rather 'How?'. This implies that power is not monolithic. Power is never exercized from a singular point onto its environment. Power can not be perceived within a dualistic scheme of active and passive – of those exercizing power and those undergoing power. From a Foucauldian perspective, there is no Power written large, there are only power relations.

Another important element in the Foucauldian perspective is that power is not merely repressive. On the contrary, power is first of all productive. It makes things possible. Power produces things, pleasure, discourse and knowledge. However, power relations are a condition for all that – one can not make sense of something like things, pleasure, discourse and knowledge outside of power relations – just as much as power is an effect of these – to experience certain pleasures, to engage in certain discourses and to mobilize certain knowledge will put us in respective power relations. It is the interrelation of power and knowledge – *pouvoir/savoir* – which is central to the Foucauldian perspective. They are entangled: *pouvoir/ savoir* is always also *savoir/pouvoir.*[34]

But a third element is just so important: moral norms. These are also produced by the power/knowledge bond. But at the same time, it is this element which sets the power relations in motion. Moral norms identify, create, define and limit power and knowledge between and amidst people in action within organizations. They form the contours of authority, the formal limitations of power, driving life within a social system: 'C'est à condition de masquer une part importante de lui-même que le pouvoir est tolerable' (Foucault 1976, 112). Power is only bearably when it succeeds in hiding itself. It is the moral norms – Barker and

---

[34] Consider this passage from an interview with Foucault: '... j'ai l'impression qu'il existe, j'ai essayé de faire apparaître, une perpétuelle articulation du pouvoir sur le savoir et du savoir sur le pouvoir. Il ne faut pas se contenter de dire que le pouvoir a besoin de telle ou telle découverte, de telle ou telle forme de savoir, mais qu'excercer le pouvoir crée des objets de savoir, les fait émerger, accumule des informations, les utilise. On ne peut rien comprendre au savoir économique si l'on ne sait pas comment s'exerçait, dans sa quotidienneté, le pouvoir, et le pouvoir économique. L'exercice du pouvoir crée, perpétuellement du savoir et inversement, le savoir entraîne des effets de pouvoir' (Grisoni 1976, 171–2).

Cheney (1994) speak of 'rules of right' – that hide power and hence determine the limits of its legitimacy.

Together with Commers, I have used such a Foucauldian perspective for understanding downward workplace mobbing (Vandekerckhove and Commers 2003). The term workplace mobbing is used to describe phenomena of repeated aggression by individuals to harm others with whom they work. Research on the prevalence of workplace mobbing showed that downward mobbing – mobbing by a superior against a subordinate – is the most prevalent. From a Foucauldian perspective, downward workplace mobbing appears as overt power, as power which has lost its legitimation and has become coercion. Forms of knowledge produced in today's organization include quality norms (ISO standards), organizational decentralization and responsibilization of teams, quality circles, and personality profiling. These instruments of evaluation, classifying and ordering produce the data (knowledge) through which the organization can be rationally remodelled and adjusted (power). This organizational discourse, this power/knowledge bond calls forth concepts like excellence, risk, adventure, creativity and responsibility. But the moral norms, the rules of right as delineating the power/knowledge bond, as that aspect of discourse which controls power – in other words, which masks a certain manifestation of power and therefore makes that power bearable – are the normative implications and conditions of those concepts through which we describe work: excellence, risk, creativity and responsibility imply and require empowerment and autonomy. It is the failure to implement these normative implications and conditions into the power relations which is responsible for perceiving those relations as downward workplace mobbing.

Barker and Cheney (1994) use the Foucauldian perspective for a case-study of a company who shifted its management culture from a traditional, hierarchical management to self-managing teams. According to Barker and Cheney, this boils down to installing a system of multilateral micro-control amongst equals. The changes in power relations were huge. Under self-management, a team member was accountable not to one person – the manager – but to the whole team. Barker and Cheney note that the new disciplinary discourse which came along with the change in management structure, became so much part of their thinking and acting, that the discourse entailed a wilful individual subjectivation to the organization's power relations. This became clear when the attendance-related discipline was looked at. Before, employees were obliged to register arrival and leaving using a time clock, which meant their attendance was controlled by the manager. Coming in five or ten minutes late was no big deal. But with the shift to self-managing teams, the time clock registration was abandoned and team members began to apply and to expect from each other to identify with value-laden premises to one another's activities: 'being a good team member requires demonstrating personal responsibility and commitment to the team' (Barker and Cheney 1994, 34). Coming in late became a very big deal. Team members were very wilful in confronting and punishing a team member that came in late, with the result that that team member 'wanted' to become a better team member – or, wanted to behave according to the discipline. The teams had built their own collective panopticon.[35]

What Barker and Cheney argue is, that the intricate interaction of power, knowledge and rules of right – discipline through discourse, or in Luhmann's terms a cared-for semantic – operates on the level of organizational activity and works in four ways (Barker and Cheney 1994):

• discipline entails unobtrusive methods of gaining wilful individual subjectivation to the organization's power relationships;
• discipline is collaboratively generated and reinforced;
• discipline is embedded in the social relations of the organization and its actors;
• disciplinary mechanisms are the most potent when they are associated with or grounded in highly motivating values that appeal to the organization's actors.

This implies that an assessment of the normative legitimation for whistleblowing policies must also look to what extent the institutionalization of whistleblowing is a disciplinary mechanism – or, to what extent it is subjectivating. The work plan I have set myself still seems suitable for that, because it consists of putting the whistleblowing policies into a semantic context, or, from a Foucauldian perspective, it looks at the discourse of whistleblowing policies and tries to find out what kinds of knowledge, power and rules of right are involved. Comparing those findings with the possible power-knowledge-norms constellations, ought to shed some light on the methods of gaining wilful individual subjectivation to the organization, on how discipline is collaboratively generated and reinforced, and how it is embedded in the social relations of the organization and its actors.

But does the Foucauldian perspective leave room for several 'possible power-knowledge-norms constellations'? At the beginning of this section, I denied that Foucault's work was absolutely deterministic or fatalistic. But the opening in the Foucauldian perspective to think of dissent, resistance, or the possibility of an alternative seem to me to lie in the difference Foucault makes between power and dominance – *pouvoir* and *dominance* (Foucault 1995), and which is quite similar to the distinction Weber made. Power refers to the influence people exert on each other in and through relations. Wherever people are involved with one another, wherever people associate with one another, there is coordination and leadership. Hence, to exert power or to undergo power is both unavoidable as well as a vital

---

[35]   It makes Barker and Cheney conclude that '[when] we, for example, ask that organizations of many types move into the realm of specifying values and ethics, we should be careful for what we wish. Organizations may indeed respond to that request in such a way that reduces personal latitude while being in another sense more moral and more concerned with the individual's interest' (Barker and Cheney 1994, 39).

part of life. But this does not mean that power stands in direct opposition to freedom (Chan 2000, 1064–8). One has to be free to take part in power. How is that? Foucault emphasizes 'power to' in contrast to 'power over' – positive freedom in contrast to negative freedom. If power is thought as the antitheses of freedom, then power is always imposed – it takes the form of external constraints – and only negative freedom is thinkable, for in that case, one can only be free when one is 'free from' power. In contrast, 'power to' or being free to partake in power – hence 'freedom to' – presupposes the freeing of internal limits to the kinds of action the actor is capable of undertaking.[36] Freedom from a Foucauldian perspective then, is the possibility of resistance against the authority of forces that limits our self-representation. Where there is no such possibility, Foucault does not speak of power but of domination. Power can pervert and backlash into domination. Thus, for Foucault, domination is a special form of power. It is power in its limit, or in a Weberian sense, domination is the pure type of power. It is 'freedom to', or resistance that distinguishes power from dominance. Foucault's resistance – his care for the self – is reflecting on the genealogy of how we became who we are, how we ended up being subjectivated the way we are, and then revalue the values, norms, kinds of knowledge and power relations at play. In this sense, there is room for other 'possible power-knowledge-norms constellations'.

To say there is room for those possible constellations is one thing, but how can I know what those possible constellations are? The answer lies in adding to the Foucauldian perspective I have just set out, some Gilles Deleuze.

Deleuze and Foucault had a mutual admiration for each others work and have had a mutual influence upon each other, the extent of which is difficult to disentangle (Goodchild 1996, 131). To a large extent, what I've described as the Foucauldian perspective is a Deleuzean reading of Foucault (see Hardt and Negri 2001, 28–29; Goodchild 1996, 131–5; Bogue 1993, 130–32). However, the work of Deleuze differs from that of Foucault in the emphasis Deleuze puts on desire instead of power, and on the primacy of lines of flight instead of resistance (Bogue 1993, 106; Goodchild 1996, 135).

Deleuze wrote together with Félix Guattari for a while.[37] The thoughts and concepts developed during that period are therefore Deleuzeguattarian thoughts and concepts. However, I will in the following pages write 'Deleuze' and 'Deleuzean' for the simple reason that scholars on that work do so too, and finding out what the difference might be between Deleuzean thought and Deleuzeguattarian thought is not the aim of this research. My concern with

---

[36] According to Patton (1994, 354), constraints upon freedom from a Foucauldian perspective can be regarded as structure of affects making up a particular kind of person and determining the kinds of decisions the person is capable to make, or as the internal features of person's intellectual and moral constitution – Luhmann's cared-for semantic – which limits the kinds of actions the person is capable to undertake.

[37] Deleuze wrote together with Guattari from 1972 untill 1980: *l'Anti-Oedipe* (1972), *Kafka* (1975), *Mille plateaux* (1980).

Deleuze's or Deleuze-Guattari's work is merely looking for inspiration to grasp Luhmann's variation mechanism.

Deleuze's concept of 'desire' does not refer to an attraction between bodies or people, but designates a social relation as an event that could not have been anticipated. In this sense, it is a pure social relation, because it escapes a particular power constellation – the Foucauldian power-knowledge-norms constellation. Every power constellation is an arrangement of desire, a pinning down of desire and as such a repression of desire.

What Deleuze means by this, and how this can shed a light on Luhmann's view on the dynamic of a semantic and thus on the hermeneutic for this research, can become clear through the concepts of rhizome, lines of flight, and deterritorialization and reterritorialization.

Deleuze contrasts rhizome-thinking to tree-thinking. The tree is an image of a way of thinking, an apparatus which makes thought produce correct ideas (Deleuze and Parnet 1991, 48–9). A tree has an origin, a core and centre, it is a binary machine, with its continuous branching off. Tree-thinking arranges thought into an order around a centre, structures thought into a system of points and positions dividing the possible into a hierarchical system of categories. A power constellation always takes the form of tree-thinking. Rhizome-thinking however, thinks in lines. Ideas are not static points, but movements on lines, crossing each other, splitting up, running into dead ends and suddenly breaking into a different direction. The image of a rhizome is that of grass. It is a net-structure on the surface, without a one single origin deep into the ground. In rhizome-thinking, concepts shape other concepts in mutual and reciprocal presupposition. There are no longer any transcendent, hidden or fixed presuppositions (Goodchild 1996, 57).

From my exposés on Luhmann and Foucault, what Deleuze calls tree-thinking is familiar with what Foucault calls domination. Rhizome-thinking then allows for Luhmann's variation. In the rhizome, the smallest unit is not a word or concept, but a coupling. Expressions are the products of couplings (Deleuze and Parnet 1991, 85). Coupling of words express meaning, but what is expressed is an attribute of things. In Luhmann's terms it reads that meaning is always related to actual experience. For Deleuze events only emerge within words, but that which emerges pertains to things (Bogue 1993, 72). So both Luhmann as well as Deleuze see the world accessible only through words-with-meaning, or coupled words; couplings between words and couplings of meaning and events. For Deleuze, meaning and events form a single surface. For Luhmann they form a semantic. Deleuze's version of Luhmann's variation then, lies in Deleuze's view that meaning is a collection of virtual infinitives, each referring to a set of possible other meanings which may be actualized in language. For Luhmann, a semantic is a network of actualized meaning and of meaning which lies in the reference horizon of that actualized meaning. The variation process – reference horizon of actualized meaning – is driven by cognitive inconsistencies and problems. Knowledge could only be systematized and kept together through the formulation of problems. Deleuze sees problems as establishing the field of possible solutions. Problems are structures, but they are virtual structures, not actual ones. But to say they are virtual does not mean that they are vague. Rather, they are distributions of singular points, they are possibilities, they are a set of possible couplings, each designating a possible actualization or embodiment. In Luhmann's terms, they are variations under a selection pressure. Those that will get selected are those that can have a stabilizing effect on our experience and meaning-giving. For Deleuze, an idea has a virtual and an actual part – possible variations and selected variations.

I wrote that in Luhmann's view, the variation mechanism is endogenous, that it is the semantic itself which provokes variation. It seems to me that for Deleuze too, variation is generated from within the rhizome. According to Deleuze, we make up new couplings from the couplings that have produced us. It is only amidst the existing couplings that new couplings can be made (Deleuze and Parnet 1991, 85–7). But by making a coupling, that which is coupled changes.[38] Making a new coupling is creating a 'line of flight'. This is always an experiment, because we never know in advance which direction a line is going to take. A 'line of flight' is to be understood within the image of the rhizome-thinking. It is an as yet unexisting line. In this sense, a line of flight is a deterritorialization. Let me try to explain this as follows. Words and events are a set of couplings. They refer to each other and get their meaning from that. We express, the objects-as-expressed, through those couplings. Deleuze would say that words and events show a specific territorialization. When I make a new coupling, that which I am coupling changes. It has to, since words, events, meaning are nothing but couplings, nothing but mutual and reciprocal references. Changing couplings changes meaning, changes expressions and hence objects-as-expressed. This is what is meant by deterritorialization, or line of flight. But of course, every deterritorialization implies a reterritorialization. The line of flight is an as yet unexisting line being drawn, but she will surely encounter already existing lines, or other lines of flight. When two lines meet, two things can happen: conjugation or connection. In conjugation, the line of flight is reterritorialized upon the line which it encounters – Luhmann's *typisieren*. But a connection involves a mutual deterritorialization. What does this mean? In Luhmann's terms, a variation might be stabilized – conjugation, or, a variation can incite further variation – connection. When there is only conjugation, or when no lines of flight are being created, we find ourselves in what Guattari calls a 'black hole' and what Deleuze calls 'a white wall' (Deleuze and Parnet 1991, 77). Thought is pinned down on dominant meanings. This is a Foucauldian situation of dominance, a Weberian *Herrschaft*, and a Luhmannian cared-for semantic. A dominant discourse determines what is thinkable (Foucauldian perspective), an 'in the heads of

---

[38] The coupling refers to an *and*-relation. Other relations between elements (or, on, between, …) leave the elements untouched, but the *and*-relation changes the relating elements. More precisely, each of the elements will also and immediately express the other.

people individualized reality' determines what is, what can be and what should be (Luhmann's cared-for semantic). Likewise, a majoritarian language is a language pinned down on dominant meanings – a black hole/white wall. Through reflection, dominant meanings – mutual and reciprocal presuppositions – mask themselves as necessities. Everyone knows them and can understand them (Goodchild 1996, 54). Therefore, these dominant presuppositions have the tendency to propagate themselves. In Luhmann's terms it would read that selected variations serve as basis for future selections.

So, if from a Foucauldian perspective, a semantic can be thought of as a discourse, as a constellation of power-knowledge-norms, the Foucauldian perspective needs Deleuze's rhizome and lines of flight to account for Luhmann's variation.

Coming back to the work plan I've set myself, how would it read from a 'Foucauldian-with-some-Deleuze perspective'? It would say that in the early 1970s, the concept of whistleblowing appears as a line of flight, creating a new coupling of labour, organization and society. This new coupling can be seen as a deterritorialization – Hardt and Negri's analysis of the 1970s and the decomposition of Fordism. During the 1980s and early 1990s, the line of whistleblowing appears to have crossed the lines of psychological and sociological research on organizational life, and appears to be reterritorializing at the end of the 1990s, beginnings of 2000. The aim of this research is to find out just how whistleblowing is being reterritorialized. What I will be doing in this research is to find out what the idea of whistleblowing is, what is virtual and what is actual. The work plan then looks like this: 1) construct conjugations and connections of the line of whistleblowing with current organizational lines; 2) look at normative legitimation for whistleblowing policies to find out which of the possible constructs are actualized. This would be a Deleuzean reframing of the work plan.

The Foucauldian perspective however tells me to express the possible constructs in terms of power-knowledge-norms constellations. I wrote that my assessment of whistleblowing policies would entail both a descriptive as well as an ethical evaluative aspect. Expressing the possible constructs in terms of power-knowledge-norms constellations is to point out the subjectivating forces of whistleblowing policies, or, finding out what the disciplining turn might be of the legitimation of these policies as a method of gaining wilful individual subjectivation to the orgnization's power relationships. The extent to which whistle-blowing policies can be – through their legitimation – described as subjectivating, will be the basis for the ethical evaluation. Even though, as I have argued, Foucault does not *only* point at subjectivation, Deleuze's or Guattari's notion of 'black hole' points at the unethical limit of subjectivation. The 'black hole' leaves no possibility for escaping a particular meaning-making of reality. No line of flight, no new coupling can escape dominant meaning. If this turns out to be the case for whistleblowing, it would mean that the line of whistleblowing as a line of flight breaking up or escaping the discipline of work, has turned into a micro-fascism, meaning that it is enforcing that which it was escaping from. If whistleblowing policies are subjectivating, they are enclosing the individual into the organizational discipline through motivating values that appeal to the organization's actors. The organizational discipline from which the whistleblowing-activism was supposed to be an escape, has then re-entered on a micro-level, through the wilful individual subjectivation to the organization's power relationships.

But the ethical evaluation also requires an opposite movement to that of subjectivation. I will call this subjectaffirmation. In its limit, subjectaffirmation is the ethical position of the individual with regard to the organization's power relationships. To the extent that whistleblowing policies are subjectaffirming, they will block the enclosure of the individual into the organizational discipline. Thus, the hermeneutic of this research, instructing the assessment of normative legitimation of whistleblowing policies, must also include a way to discern which movement – subjectivating or subjectaffirmation – is the strongest one in the current whistleblowing policies. In the next section, I will show that Touraine's dissociation between the individual and the organization leads up to the notion of subjectaffirmation.

Alain Touraine

It is Touraine himself who links his work to that of Weber.[39] What they share is an orientation which first of all consists of being attentive of the dissociation between the individual and society, and secondly of taking that dissociation as the starting point for their work. Both Weber and Touraine feel uncomfortable with functionalism, just as with historical-materialism and other all-encompassing theories.[40] Moreover, Touraine's action-sociology was inspired by Weber's impetus

---

[39] See the next passage from an interview with Alain Touraine in Atalaia: '... le Sujet est la volonté de l'individu d'être un acteur. J'entends par acteur celui ou celle qui modifie son environnement plus qu'il n'est déterminé par lui. Vous avez raison de suggérer qu'il existe une opposition entre une analyse en termes de Sujet et une analyse en termes de société. Depuis que la tradition, la loi divine ou l'association des deux ne semblent plus à la majorité suffisantes pour légitimer le Bien et le Mal, c'est à l'utilité sociale que nous avons fait surtout appel en opposant le normal et le pathologique, l'utile et le nuisible. La force de l'utilitarisme sous toutes ses formes a été d'affirmer la convergence de l'utilité personnelle et de l'utilité collective. On trouve encore des traces importantes de cette pensée dans la Théorie de la justice de Rawls. J'appartiens à une école de pensée opposée, celle qui croit, depuis Nietzsche et Freud, à la dissociation croissante de l'individu et de la société, du plaisir et de la loi. Ceux qui pensent ainsi cherchent le moyen de dépasser cette opposition et de construire un Sujet capable de bâtir un projet de vie original. Il est vrai qu'on peut hésiter à appeler encore sociologique une telle pensée mais j'observe que les maîtres de la sociologie classique, Durkheim, Weber ou Simmel sont partis de cette dissociation entre l'individu et la société' (Touraine et al. 1995).

[40] However, this doesn't mean they totally reject those theories, see Roth (1968, lxiii–lxiv), Lammers (1994, 115) and Knöbl (1999, 405).

to a sociology in which meaningful action is central (Lammers 1994, 115). But, while Weber – in dealing with dynamics – constructed idealtypes in order to describe behaviour in terms of its deviation from those types, Touraine emphasizes – also in dealing with dynamics – conflict, crisis and change. Man is not merely product, but just as much producer of social processes and forms of community. Societal life is permeated by a process of rationalization – Weber's *Entzauberung der Welt*, taking oneself and nature at hand within the framework of a goal oriented strife. That rationalization takes place through organization and leads to bureaucracy. But – using a metaphor – this becomes an obstacle instead of a vehicle. In realizing his freedom, man makes himself to a certain extent always un-free. Still, Touraine is not a pessimist. Knöbl (1999, 404) characterizes his work as a radical undermining of conventional thought within the categories of social order, as a swiping away of the idea of a unified society, and as emphasizing the freedom and the possibilities of human action.

But also the centrality of power and dominance in Weber's work – the second reason why I paid attention to his work – can be found in that of Touraine.[41] With the appearance of a social rationalization and hence the formation of big mechanized enterprises, the effectiveness of an enterprise became to a large extent dependent on her efficiency as an organization.[42] Touraine sees this view on the enterprise weakened by two opposed rather than complementary directions. First, the study of the behaviour of workers shows that workers take a position opposed to rather than amidst the enterprise. The wish to participate is restricted by the defence of self-interest. Thus, the enterprise has a game to play. She does not control the conditions of her actions and has to take decisions in function of the shifts that could be caused by her partners – or stakeholders. In the limit, the enterprise no longer appears as a collective, but rather as a system of relations between external and internal demand. The enterprise becomes an instrument of negotiation and choice without stable content, without a system of norms of its own, without roles or statutes defining the conditions of the equilibrium in a relatively stable way.[43]

---

[41] The exposé on power and dominance in Touraine's work is based on 'L'entreprise: pouvoir, institution et organisation', the third chapter of Touraine's *La société post-industrielle* (Touraine 1969, 189–260).

[42] The implication of this is, as Weber argued, that the administration of work determined to an ever larger extent the results of fabrication. This opened a new field of research, more precisely that of the reactions of workers towards labour. It is here that Taylors *Scientific Management* has to be situated. The opening of that field of research marked the development of techniques to reduce slowdown – *freinage* designating the slowing down of the labour pace by the workers. One of those techniques was the instalment of coloured blocks as an evaluation of the worker, but visible to all. After Taylor – and surely because of his work – attention was paid to collective sentiments and labour norms. These needed to be taken into account, not to respect them or to answer them untouched, but rather as an obstacle to overcome. I hereby would like to draw to the attention of the reader that Weber ended with Taylor, while Touraine starts off with Taylor.

[43] The current stakeholder theory of the firm seems to be based on this limit.

Secondly, the enterprise can be thought of as a political entity. In an entrepreneurial capitalism, the model of development is based on risk, profit and market. These describe a certain state of economical and social organization, but not of the internal values of that organization. While growth is mainly defined by the capacity to mobilize means for long-term programmes aimed at creation and development, the organization as a whole seems to be subjected to development objectives pertaining to society. The large organization carries in it the model of rationalization which orients social activity. Now, the more one regards the enterprise as a community, the more emphasis is put on conflicts of power – conflicts regarding the social control of that model of rationalization. It is here that the enterprise can be defined as the relationship of rationalization and politics.

Let me go through that again. The organization organizes rationally. This means that she not only adjusts her means to her goals and to a continuous change in her environment, but also that she strains herself to realize rational goals. But, she can only realize those goals by defending her self-interest. And this defence manifests itself both on the level of means as on the level of goals. This is the starting point of Touraine's sociology of the enterprise, which he formulates as follows: the enterprise is a private institution serving a social function; the rationality of the enterprise is driven by a private political system.[44] Touraine stipulates that the enterprise is a private institution so far as she is not a bureaucratic system in a Weberian sense,[45] but the enterprise is no longer an institution when the director or the workers can not find the connection between

---

[44] My translation of 'Tel est le point de départ d'une sociologie de l'entreprise, institution privée remplissant une fonction sociale; intention de rationalité gérée par un système politique privée' (Touraine 1969, 196).

[45] This claim about the enterprise diverts from an older conception of organizations which, according to Touraine, stemmed from Weber's view on bureaucracy. According to Touraine, an organization which is exposed to continuous change, can not work that way. It is no longer the rule, but rather the goal that commands. And neither is it the department or the division, but rather the project which constitutes the fundamental unit of action. Moreover, change or adjustment becomes easier when the enterprise has: 1) a more pragmatic vision and is more void of principles and rules, and 2) is concerned with adapting its elements to one another in an arrangement which is always limited and temporary. Hence, the mechanistic conceptualization of the enterprise is replaced by the image of a market of influences, in which the equilibrium is unstable and thus adjustable. Nevertheless, the enterprise is still an organization, with a centre of decision making and boundaries, and imposing a loyalty upon its members. More precisely, it is a loyalty allowing to pursue strategies within strict limits. But it is the flexibility of forms of organization which demands more powerful mechanisms for social integration. When clear and stable rules – objective beacons – are lost, all members of the organization must be oriented towards her integration. They must all interiorize her values and norms and gain an *esprit de maison*. This implies intervening in attitudes and intentions (see Barker and Cheney's example of discipline in contemporary organization from a Foucauldian perspective). Hence, the enterprise is both pragmatic and integrative (Touraine 1969, 230).

defending self-interest and striving for goals that are regarded as legitimate by society. The aim of a sociology of the enterprise then, is to research how these goals are aimed for through private labour relations. Hence, the object of a sociology of the enterprise consists of the relations between strategy, equilibrium and politics of enterprises.[46]

For a sociology of the enterprise, one does not need to look at the whole of production nor at the internal system of social relations. Rather, it is the contradicting visions diverse groups have on societal values that are crucial. Every actor refers to general values, but always does so through the contradiction between defending self-interest and opposition to other interests. But the field of action – the field of contradicting visions – has no unit of its own. What I mean is that it is not organized around norms and values in a Parsonian sense. Even though norms and values are just as central in Touraine's view as in Parsons', Parsons assumed that norms and values were transcendent to social relations. Touraine deems such an assumption idealistic and rejects it. Touraine's view emphasizes human action as creating values, rather than action realizing pre-existent values. Hence, action can not be defined as a mere reaction to a situation in which already existing values are involved. It is the action itself which creates these values. This is why action is always creation, innovation and meaning-giving.[47] If I was to rephrase this in Luhmannian terms, it would read that human action is creating semantic variation. However, Touraine's view is less subjectivating than that of Luhmann and certainly than that of Foucault. I will come back to that later on in this section.

Touraine analysed the transformation of 'the' enterprise – or, the evolution of the conceptualization of the enterprise – as a progressive appearance of organizational and institutional mediation between economic power and professional activity. In that transformation, he discerns three phases. In the first phase, the power of capital directly operates on labour and results in the accumulation of capital. In a second phase, the organization of labour appears and with that the concept of 'organization'. Economic power operates on labour through the organization. But the organization has a certain autonomy allowing it to wield a number of concepts like statute, role, stratification, authority, integration. The director of the enterprise is no longer merely capitalist, he is manager as well. He governs, runs, coordinates, integrates and maintains.

---

[46] Touraine argues that the industrial psycho-sociology – the study of workers' attitudes towards labour – researches determinants of the relations between three levels of workers' behaviour on the one hand – behaviour in function of self-interest, statute and role within the organization – and the conflict of power in which they are involved on the other. However, the concepts of industrial psycho-sociology – work satisfaction, moral climate – have no scientific justification and try – according to Touraine, in vain – to mask ideological choices (Touraine 1969, 199).

[47] Knöbl (1999, 406) writes that Touraine's sociology is not a sociology of values, but rather a sociology of value creation.

In the third phase, economic power distances itself further from direct domination on productive labour. No longer are only the accumulation of capital and management capacity determining growth. More and more, this is done by the whole of actions directly aimed at growth and at new forms of production and efficiency of economic systems. The directors of economic production take part in those actions. The enterprise is no longer merely a unit of production or an organization, she is also an autonomous centre of decision making. What's more, the enterprise also has to calculate her own interests, both with regard to other units of decision as well as with regard to continuous changes in the conditions of her activity. In other words, an institutional level is inserted (see Figure 2.2).

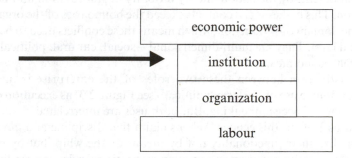

Figure 2.2   Inserting the institutional level in the enterprise

In this sense, the enterprise defines itself as a political control system of technical and economical rationality. Her institutional system can then be defined as the system which forms the social control of economic development. The pivot of the institutional level is the *legitimate organization*. This means that the principle of legitimation is to be situated within the relation between production and social use. Technocrats defend the power of the production system and oppose it to the needs of the consumers. They argue against those needs or distort them, and the image of the society they refer to is that of a society of continuous growth – in every sense of the word – which automatically will bring an improvement of the social existence.[48] The workers in their turn, define themselves no longer by their profession or their qualification, but rather by their professional status, by their

---

[48]   This is a double technocratic pretension: that they know what those needs are and that the production system they are defending is an optimal fulfilment of those needs. However, choosing 'the system that fulfils our needs best' seems to amount to choosing for aeroplanes at night instead of good sleep, choosing for highways instead of open green space, and choosing to deliver weapons instead of relieve hunger. Touraine shows that the technocratic argument hides a contradiction between politics of power and fulfilment of needs.

worklife and their career. These are private principles taking a parallel place with regard to what the strength of the enterprise is for the directors.

The enterprise as an institution[49] is the place where social forces negotiate and arrive at defining the rules and the form of their opposition, and thereby the institutionalization of their conflict (Touraine 1969, 223). Because the enterprise situates itself more and more on the institutional level, the enterprise has an autonomous system of economical decisions and of social negotiations at its disposal. Yet at the same time, the enterprise is an element of a power system, and hence of social conflicts exceeding her, because of the fact that economic development is no longer vaguely determined by accumulation of capital and organization of paid work, but also and to an ever larger extent by research and development, by formation and by mobility of information and factors of production. This makes social conflicts exceed the boundaries of the organization and of the domain of production, which means these conflicts need to be situated at a global level. They are multi-dimensional – social, cultural, political – rather than purely economical.

The distinction between these two roles of the enterprise is marked by Touraine's double use of the term 'political' (see Figure 2.3) as execution of power and as system of decision making. But both uses are interrelated.

As far as I see it, this echoes Weber's claim that discipline and bureaucracy operationalize their functionality not by means of the whip, but by means of authoritative dominance, gearing compliance to rational rules as a binding norm. The system of rational norms is political in the sense that it is the power that defines the field of collective action and – in Weber's terms – legitimizes the bearer of power. But it is also political in the sense that decisions are interactions within that field and – again in Weber's terms – legitimize power to the extent that power is exercized conform those rational norms.

Touraine's analysis can also be seen as pointing at what from a Foucauldian perspective is called discipline through discourse, or the power-knowledge-norms constellation. I wrote that the norms set the power relations – the power-knowledge bond – in motion. The concepts of society, and surely of the goals of society and of societal evolution are normative concepts and as such they identify, define and limit power. They make certain knowledge appear as necessary to realise the goals of society. Hence, power generates knowledge on the basis of which the decisions will be taken. In this way, the generated knowledge constrains the

---

[49]   Apparently, this was first noted by Berle and Means in their 1932 publication of *The Modern Corporation and Private Property*. Berle and Means wrote that because of the separation of ownership and control in the public corporation, stockholders ought to be regarded as passive recipients of capital returns rather than active owners. This implied that the traditional logic of property no longer applied. Coupled with increasing corporate size, Berle and Means claimed that the corporation had 'ceased to be a private business device and had become an institution' (Berle and Means 1932, quoted in Kelly 2001, 70).

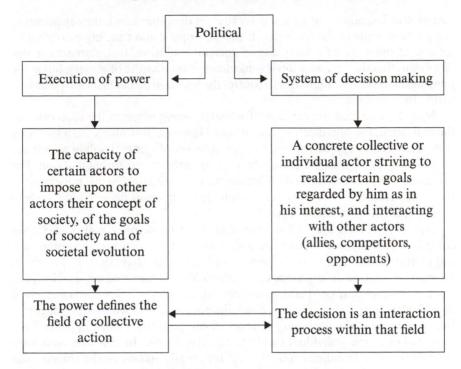

Figure 2.3   Touraine's double and interrelated use of the term 'political'

possible decisions and thereby reinforce power and the concepts of society, goals
of society and societal evolution.

A rephrasing in Luhmann's terms is also possible. The political as the power
defining the field of collective action, is the cared-for semantic, established
through networks of words-with-meaning which give content to the concepts
of society, of the goals of society and of the societal evolution. The political as
the interaction process within that field of collective action then, designates an
interaction process using a cared-for semantic, or in other words, the interaction
process creates variation – negotiation is generating variation – but the power
defining the field of collective action – or interaction – functions as the selection
mechanism, ensuring that selected variations will fit the present accessibility of
the world and actions through words-with-meaning.

What are the implications of Touraine's view for the hermeneutic I am
developing in this chapter? Approaching Touraine's claims about the organization
as an institution from my interpretations of Luhmann and the Foucauldian
perspective, Touraine seems to say that on the one hand, the organization
functions as a legitimate organization in the sense that its decisions are products
of interaction and negotiation of actors defending their self-interest but who are
able to connect their self-interest with striving for goals regarded as legitimate by

society. But Touraine also seems to say that on the other hand, the organization is a political actor in the sense that it tries to impose upon society a concept of society, of the goals of society and of societal evolution. In Luhmann's terms, this means that the organization is subjected to the semantic of society, but at the same time, the organization tries to control the selection mechanism for variations within the semantic.

Now, I wrote that the concept of whistleblowing involves the categories of the individual, the organization and society. However, Touraine's analysis shows that society can only be regarded as the domain of general values which are referred to when interacting and where values are created through action. For the assessment of the normative legitimation of whistleblowing policies, it is therefore more sound to work with 'individual-organization-semantic' instead of 'individual-organization-society'.

However, Touraine's view contains another aspect which deserves consideration. Earlier in this section, I wrote that Touraine's view is less subjectivating than that of Luhmann and certainly than that of Foucault. Touraine states that decisions are interactions of self-interested actors. However, from a Foucauldian perspective, subjectivation determines what is perceived as self-interest and thus, perceived self-interest is in line with power-interests. But, as I wrote at the beginning of this section, Touraine's starting point is the dissociation of the individual (subject) and the system. In *Pourrons-nous vivre ensemble* (1997), Touraine explicitly calls for an affirmation of the subject. The idea that the individual fully coincides with the system's rationality, is an idea of modernism. That correspondence was arrived at through the constitutional state. However, Touraine regards the present time as a time of de-modernization (Touraine 1997, 44–5). This de-modernization is a dissociation of two universes: the universe of technology and markets on the one hand, and the universe of cultures on the other – in other words, the universe of instrumental rationality and the universe of collective memory, with two new ideologies: neo-liberalism and communitarianism. Now, the subject can only be affirmed by a double severance – *double dégagement* (Touraine 1997, 100–3). The subject only forms itself by rejecting both instrumentality and identity, both the market and the community. This double movement can only be carried out by a personal subject and requires 1) the solitary courage – *le courage solitaire* – denunciating powers, and 2) the force of collective action – protecting the rights of the individual and allowing the subject its double severance.

This is Touraine's call for an affirmation of the subject. He acknowledges that this call has strong moral connotations. And in this sense he understands Foucault's hostility towards the theme of the human subject. What's more, Touraine regards the critique on the moralization of the workers class through religious principles as a conservative summon to self-control, aimed at subjecting workers to social norms, as a necessary critique (Touraine 1997, 117). But only on the condition that this critique does not replace an affirmation of the subject. This critique can not replace attempts of liberation nor attempts to construct the subject beyond production and beyond culture. Touraine blames Foucault for not understanding that.

Foucault seems to say we are suffering from integration – coincidence of individual and rationality – while Touraine argues that we are suffering from des-integration – the rift between economy and society. Surely, these are claims highly relevant to the issue of whistleblowing. But they are claims to be taken back up after the assessment of the normative legitimation of whistleblowing policies is done. It is with the results of the assessment that I might be able to say whether or not whistleblowing policies – in the way they are being developed – are more Foucauldian or more Tourainean. I will therefore now proceed to the next section where the assessment grid will be drawn up. Touraine's call for the affirmation of the subject will be further discussed in Chapter 5.

The Individual, the Organization and the Semantic

I wrote that whistleblowing involves the categories of the individual, the organization and society. I also wrote that these categories relate to each other through questions and problems. Whistleblowing is an example of such a problem. Answering the problem is an attempt to stabilize a crisis of the relation of the three categories. The development of whistleblowing policies are the formulation of such answers. I also wrote that whistleblowing policies are an attempt to institutionalize whistleblowing.Let me go over that again.

Whistleblowing is:

* individuals blowing the whistle on;
* organizations operating within;
* the context of globalization of private capital oriented economy.

The institutionalization of whistleblowing then, is:

* the process of stabilizing a set of procedures and norms about;
* individuals blowing the whistle on;
* organizations operating within;
* the context of globalization of private capital oriented economy.

The aim of this research is to make an assessment of normative legitimation of whistleblowing policies, or in other words, to make an assessment of the justifications for the set of procedures and norms about whistleblowing. These justifications are always lingual, always take place through words-with-meaning – a semantic. Thus, where whistleblowing involves the individual, the organization and society, the institutionalization of whistleblowing involves the individual, the organization and the semantic. I remind the reader that a semantic is a network of actualized meaning and of meaning which lies in the reference horizon of that actualized meaning, and that it designates an interplay of variation, selection and stabilization. In this regard, I wrote that whether or not whistleblowing can be institutionalized depends on whether or not a whistle-blowing policy, with its particular normative legitimation, is a selectable variation within the semantic at stake.

Now, with Touraine, I argued that the organization contains an institutional level in which the pivot was the notion of legitimate organization. And the principle of legitimacy was to be situated within the relation between production and social use. If this was all that was to it, it would imply that I would have to maintain the categories of the individual, the organization and society. However, I showed that Touraine argues that because of the appearance and importance of the institutional level, the organization becomes political in the two senses of the word: 1) the organization as the locus of interactions and decisions within a particular field of collective action, but also 2) the organization as the power to define that field of collective action, in the sense that it imposes concepts of society, of goals of society and of societal evolution.

Hence, the category of society should be replaced by 'semantic' as the interplay of variation, selection and stabilization of words-with-meaning, that signify and give meaning to experience and action. The semantic at stake here – the network of words-with-meaning through which normative legitimation for whistleblowing policies is generated – is the semantic signifying the organizations operating within the context of globalization of private capital oriented economy.

Therefore, I need to rephrase the research questions I formulated at the end of the Chapter 1. There, I wrote that the three questions guiding the assessment of whistleblowing policies would be:

Q1 → What are the organizational/societal possibilities for whistleblowing?
Q2 → What are the organizational/societal necessities for whistleblowing?
Q3 → Do possibilities and necessities correspond?

From the linked interpretation of Luhmann/Weber/Foucault-Deleuze/Touraine throughout the previous sections, I can rephrase those questions into two research questions:

RQ1 → How can whistleblowing be described as a variation within the current semantic?
RQ2 (Q2 and Q3) → Which variations do not get selected?

The rephrasing into two questions (RQ1 and RQ2) mirror the work plan I have set myself earlier in this chapter, and indeed show that this work plan is 'a kind of *Verstehende Soziologie*'. For, RQ1 implies the construction of, given the semantic, possible variations regarding normative legitimation of whistleblowing policies. With Deleuze – in the Foucauldian perspective – I argued that such constructions can be made by generating new couplings within the semantic – the rhizome.

Such constructions consist of letting the line of whistleblowing cross existing lines within the rhizome. This means that the concept of whistleblowing will gain content through its position and links within the network of words-with-meaning. These constructions then, are all possible variations, they all are (see Q1) organizational/societal possibilities for whistleblowing.

RQ2 then is the second step in my 'kind of *Verstehende Soziologie*', where the actual course of action is compared – and insight into it is gained – with those possibilities. In Deleuze's terms, dominant meanings mask themselves as necessities. In Luhmann's terms it reads that past selected variations – the current semantic – serves as a basis or limits current selections. Therefore, the forms of normative legitimation actually being used in justifying whistleblowing policies – or, in other words, the way whistleblowing is being institutionalized – will point out which of the possible variations are – see Q2 – the organizational/societal necessities for whistleblowing.

Immediately, and this is why RQ2 entails Q2 and Q3, it will also be clear which possible variations are not 'necessary' variations, or, which variations do not get selected. Based upon that, I will be able to make an ethical evaluation of the current tendency in whistleblowing policies. In Chapter 1 I phrased the need for such an evaluation as finding out whether or not whistleblowing policies are presented as a politico-ethical concept able to eliminate conflict between organization and society. I also wrote that the assessment of normative legitimation of whistleblowing policies can tell us whether the institutionalization of whistleblowing is subjectivating or subjectaffirming, or, enclosing the individual into the organization or rather emphasizing a dissociation between individual and organization.

In order to make that ethical evaluation based on the assessment, I will need to set out the possible variations in a diagram consisting of the individual, the organization and the semantic (see Figure 2.4). The possible variations are then variations within the current semantic, but instigated or embodied by and between the individual and the organization.

What do I mean by this? How do I operate this diagram?

- The individual does not fully coincide with the organizational subject (Touraine, Weber) as identified within the framework of – drawing its identity from – organizational discourse.
- Possible semantic constructions of whistleblowing policies – possible variations – will either emphasize this difference or will try to enclose the individual within the organizational discourse (Foucault).
- Any variation implies all three domains: I, O, S: two domains relate through the third.
- Depending on whether they emphasize difference or enclosure, the constructed possibilities will move through the diagram in a particular direction;

How?

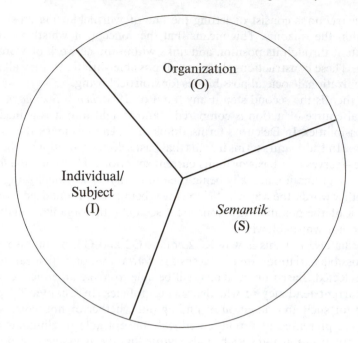

Figure 2.4   IOS-diagram

- Given the presupposed power play (Foucault) what can hypothetically be regarded as the beneficiary of the variation – who or what might use it to promote or defend what? Who is instigating whistleblowing into the power play? It can be any social actor, using the semantic – giving arguments[50] – to discuss or justify actions, to negotiate, to coordinate, to manage or to protest, thereby creating variation.
- However, I will limit the number of identifiable instigators to two: individual and organization.
- If the organization is the instigator, creating a variation with the purpose of enclosing the individual, then this movement will be OS-I;
- If the individual is the instigator, then this movement will be IS-O;
- SO-I and SI-O movements signify variations as unintended consequence of other intended variations (OS-I or IS-O). They are not instigated by the organization nor by the individual, but are a side effect of particular variations,

---

[50] An argument is either: 1) mentioning a norm on which there is full consensus – however, this is really an argument but rather an admonition; 2) applying a norm to a new field – broadening the scope of the norm; or 3) changing implications of norm through deduction from other consented norms – an argument in the line of 'if you subscribe to proposition A and B, consistency requires you to subscribe to C as well'.

enclosing discourse on the individual (SO-I) or emphasize a difference (S-IO).

- This leaves me with the IOS and OIS movements, which are logically impossible. The assessment of normative legitimation is built on the assumption that all signification of reality and actions takes place through semantic, through words-with-meaning. In this sense, there is no possibility for the individual to create a semantic variation through the organization (IOS) nor for the organization to create a semantic variation through the individual (OIS). All normative legitimation is generated through semantic (OS-I and IS-O) or is an indirect effect of such generating (SO-I and S-IO).

I now have all the tools to undertake the assessment of normative legitimation of whistleblowing policies. In Chapter 3, I will answer RQ1 – how can whistleblowing be described as a variation within the current semantic. I will first describe which concepts make up the focal points of the network of words-with-meaning – or the semantic of organizations operating within the context of globalization. The remaining sections of Chapter 3 will then consist of variations within that semantic regarding the meaningful conceptualizations of whistleblowing. Every section will be dedicated to a different conceptualization of whistleblowing by describing its content in terms of links with other concepts within the semantic. In this sense, every section will generate a possible normative legitimation for whistleblowing policies.

At the end of Chapter 3, a grid will be drawn up which will be used in Chapter 4 to screen whistleblowing policies for their normative legitimation. Also at the end of Chapter 3, I will identify subjectivating and subjectaffirming movements within each legitimation construct. This will serve the ethical evaluation in Chapter 5.

Chapter 4 will then look at actual normative legitimation for whistleblowing policies recently developed or under development. These will be screened against the grid consisting of possible normative legitimation for whistleblowing policies to be constructed throughout Chapter 3.

Chapter 5 then, will start with an overview of the tendencies in normative legitimation of whistleblowing policies, as they appear from the screening in Chapter 4. Building on that, Chapter 5 will also answer RQ2 – which variations do not get selected. To do this I will – as I noted there – develop further the issue of Touraine's affirmation of the subject, and use the diagram of 'individual – organization – semantic' and the positions the possible and necessary (actualized) variations take within that diagram. This will make up the ethical evaluation of the current tendency of institutionalizing whistleblowing. Finally, some recommendations will be made for future lobbying for ethical whistleblowing policies.

Chapter 3

Possible Legitimation of Whistleblowing Policies

Introduction

In this chapter I construct the possible normative legitimation of whistleblowing policies. The previous chapter argued that this had to be constructed within the relevant semantic. I wrote that the semantic at stake in this research is the semantic signifying and rendering meaning to the organizational context of globalization of private capital oriented economy. But before I connect the concept of whistleblowing with concepts that are part of the globalization semantic, I need to point at three central[1] concepts within that semantic and two paradigmatic perspectives on organizations, linked to the globalization semantic. Hence, the globalization semantic can be visualized as in Figure 3.1. The three concepts and how they render each other content – flexibility, decentralization, governance – are described in the first section. In the two sections after that, I will discuss respectively the network perspective and stakeholder theory.

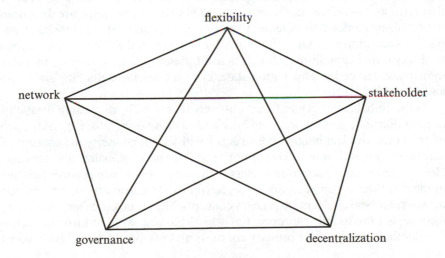

Figure 3.1 Globalization semantic (primary concepts)

---

[1]   In Deleuze's terms, there is nothing central about a 'central concept'. Rather, the semantic rhizome shows a high density around particular nodes (concepts).

It is these concepts and perspectives that I deem crucial in the globalization semantic, as enabling us to make sense and give meaning to realities and activities in and of organizations within a context of globalization. The reader will notice I do not make a distinction between public organizations, private business organizations and NGOs. There are reasons for this. First, most of the conceptual variation and selection with regard to these concepts has been generated focussing on private business organizations. Second, characteristic of the globalization process is the grown influence of private business organizations over public organizations. And third, what seems to have happened is that the process of globalization has rendered the idea of 'organizing' – or the power/knowledge/norms triad on 'organizing' – a set of concepts used in public sector organization discourses and in NGO discourses just as much as in private business organization discourses.

Do I claim that the concepts and perspective I am about to discuss are representational for today's organizational practice? Are organizations really flexible? If there is decentralization now, does that mean that there is no longer any centralization? Is governance really new? I claim no such things, and research shows it is wise not to claim such things.[2] Even though the globalization concepts might sound revolutionary, they did not cause a revolution in organizing. Rather, they are pointers at how organizing is becoming, how organizing is thought of, evaluated, justified, and experienced. The globalization semantic should be seen as functionally normative. Globalization certainly constitutes a crisis in how individuals relate to one another through the organization of work, both regionally and internationally. The globalization semantic is an attempt to stabilize that crisis and in this sense, the concepts making up the semantic are directions in organizing conform the attempt to stabilize the crisis of the categories of our previous commitments. Or, as Lash and Urry wrote on the shift from organized to disorganized capitalism: 'All that is solid about organized capitalism, class, industry, cities, collectivity, nation-state, even the world, melts into air' (Lash and Urry 1987, 312).

Is the globalization semantic exhaustively described by discussing flexibility, decentralization, governance, networks and stakeholders? No, it is not. Each of the normative legitimation constructs I will set out connects the concept of whistleblowing with another concept to be situated in the globalization semantic. However, every construction also refers to the concepts and perspectives I discuss in the first three sections. In this sense, flexibility, decentralization, governance, networks and stakeholders are primary concepts. Moreover, the other – secondary – concepts I use to link the concept of whistleblowing with, in turn connect to one another through these primary concepts and perspectives. In this chapter I

---

2   Van Hootegem (2000), Gaudin (2002), Gallie et al. (1998), Burke and Cooper (2000), Apostel and Walry (1997) point out that despite changed rhetoric of organizational shifts, previous forms of organizing persist, although these are made sense of and given meaning through a different semantic.

construct normative legitimation constructs for whistleblowing policies around the concepts of human rights, organizational social responsibility, responsibility and accountability, integrity, loyalty and efficiency.

In the final section of this chapter, I draw up the grid against which recent or developing whistleblowing policies will be screened in Chapter 4. First, I summarize the legitimation constructs and their relevant secondary concepts in Table 3.1. Then I point out the dominant ethical theory to each possible normative legitimation (Table 3.2). After that, I specify the actor, subject and recipient elements as they can be derived from the legitimation constructs (Table 3.3). The screening grid (Table 3.4) to be used in Chapter 4 then, is a combination of those three tables. Finally, in preparation for Chapter 5, where the screening will be evaluated, I will also place each constructed normative legitimation within the diagram of organizational enclosure and emphasizing individuality I presented in Chapter 2.

Globalization Semantic

Flexibility, Decentralization, Governance

What concepts compose the globalization semantic? One of its key concepts is *flexibility*. Dahrendorf (1998) writes that flexibility is the inescapable condition of globalization. For organizations then, globalization is signified by the pressure for more flexibility. But what does that mean? According to Sennett (1998) the concept of flexibility originally designated the capability of a tree or a branch to bend with the wind without breaking. If the branch is flexible enough to bend under stormy winds without breaking, it can survive storms and stay alive.

With regard to organizations then, a flexible organization is an organization that has a specific structure which allows it to adjust to inevitable and changing forces, operating under and in the name of the market. 'Free market', 'global market', 'open market': what these terms designate is the removal of rigidities with regard to market access and scope. This does not imply an overall abandoning of rules, but rather multiple sets of rules and norms in which organizations operate or with which they compete. A company can produce different elements of a product in different countries and regions of the world, each with a distinct set of norms about behaviour, leadership, work time – for example the importance of fastening in some regions of the world – and a distinct set of labour laws – or the absence of such laws. Or, a company can produce and sell its products or services within the same country or region of the world, but will have to compete with companies who produce elsewhere – resulting in a competition related to product quality and pricing – or who sell elsewhere – resulting in a competition related to work force or raw materials.

Boltanski and Chiapello (1999) have argued that the uncertainty of the market is being transposed on the workers through the flexibilization of the organization of work. In a paper on atypical forms of employment, Roma (1999) distinguishes between four types of flexibility. Quantitative flexibility refers to organizing in such a way as to determine the quantity of labour employed as a function of the fluctuation of the market and of the demand for goods and services, through subcontracting and reducing the size of the organization. Functional flexibility is the ability of an organization to obtain optimal productivity from employees by introducing new methods into productive models, for example rotating jobs, delegating responsibility to individuals or groups, face-to-face consultation, or teamwork. Also, innovation is regarded as a form of flexibility in the productive process, resulting from the introduction of new technologies, for example new products, information technology, through automation or through the installation of new plants. Finally, contract flexibility aims at reducing the dependency of the organizational productivity on regular jobs, especially with regard to working hours, by regulating employment through part-time and short-term contracts.

On an organizational level, the growing use of temporary workers instead of regular workers means more flexible organizations. They might employ just as many people as before, but can reduce their workforce at times of low demand, without having to negotiate with trade unions or pay extra months wages. Flexibility of this kind has also been tagged the 'leaner organization', where temporary workers are not considered full members of the organization. This leads to two kinds of employees: core and periphery employees (Apostel and Walry 1997, 304; Rosenblatt and Schaeffer 2000, 141). Workers who are functionally flexible, that is, whom the organization can re-deploy quickly and smoothly between tasks, are granted job security. But workers who are relatively more replaceable and rigid are deprived of job security.

I described the flexibility driving 'forces' as inevitable and changing. I have called them inevitable because they are used to justify actions in a specific way. To take well known examples: production units are moved from one country to another and people loose there jobs because of increased price competition – 'that's just the way it is and there's nothing you can do about it' or what has become known as the TINA-tendency (There Is No Alternative).[3] And I have called these forces changing, because organizations are flexible to the extent that they are ready and able to adjust to changes in quantity and quality of demand, changes in technology, in reward schemes, in work time, in work pressure, in bosses, brands and corporate logos. The central role which the concept of flexibility plays in the globalization semantic is dual. First, if it points at an ability of the organization to adapt to external change, then it has the connotation of maintaining an organizational status quo. Second, if flexibility is regarded as an organizational virtue, then it designates the ability of the organization to produce internal change to reposition itself with regard to the environment. In

---

[3]	TINA – There Is No Alternative, came up in a scenario-planning session at Royal Dutch/Shell in the mid 1990s. It designated the trio of globalization-liberalization-technology as an unavoidable power-group in the late 1990s.

this latter sense, the flexible organization facilitates creativity and innovation while maintaining coordination, focus and control (Volberda 1998, cited in Koornhof 1998). In any way, the following seems to be utterly important: the concept of flexibility can only play a central role in the survival and success of organizations if there is also an assumption that organizations function in a changing environment. Koornhof (1998) develops a definition of organizational flexibility that reads:

> Flexibility is the process of being aware, responsive, willing and able to take action to reposition the resources and functions of the organization in a manner consistent with the evolving vision, strategies and goals of management as they respond proactively or reactively to new information on foreseen and unforeseen change in the organization and its environment (Koornhof 1998, 138).

Koornhof comes to this encompassing definition after reviewing definitions of flexibility from operating, financial, strategic, marketing and behavioural perspectives. It is important to notice the definition is based on an open system perspective of a dynamic relationship between the organization and its environment.

It is here that a second central concept of the current globalization semantic comes in, namely *decentralization*. In an open system perspective, organizing becomes highly complex. Complexity within the organizational semantic refers to the myriad of factors relevant to planning and to the numerous information units to be processed in order to take a decision. One could argue that an increased environmental complexity – or at least such a perception – turns organizations into more complex systems. Internally, organizations are faced with increased complexity due to flexibilization (project specific arrangements in terms of speed and labour), scale shifts (mergers but also outsourcing), internationalization (operating different tasks in different norms-and-rules contexts), heightened competition (a still imperfect yet increased openness of markets) (Dahrendorf 1998, Forrester 1996). But, how does that internal organizational complexity manifest itself? The complex organization can be described as an organization without one central point of decision making. In this sense, the complex organization is the contrary of a Weberian bureaucracy. Touraine (1969, 108) and Castells (1996, 171) have also juxtaposed in this sense. Guéhenno (1999) writes that it is no longer the case that the top of the enterprise hierarchy makes big decisions which are then carried out, but rather that because of information technology, decisions have to be taken fast. And since the risk of taking a wrong decision increases not only with the amount of relevant information but also with the speed at which the decision is taken, organizations try to neutralize that risk by not taking one big decision, but instead take many small decisions in a decentralized way.

This internal decentralization process is referred to as a flattening of organizations. Less hierarchical levels imply that employees at a lower level are given more discretionary power, for example by responsibilization of employees or by introducing team work through self-managing teams. In this way, certain management levels can be deleted, or, need not to be expanded when mergers occur. Flattening of organizations equals decentralization, for the following reason. Less hierarchical levels means that the scope of activities a manager overviews has increased, with the result that groups, when compared to managers, might possess much richer information on the production process, on work behaviours, on performance, on product or service quality (see Liden et al. 2001). Hence these groups are in a better position to make decisions. Management's task is then to coordinate interactions between decision-making groups.

The concept of flexibility and its assumption of a changing organizational environment, linked with the concept of complexity and its organizational exponent of external and internal decentralization, get their decisive meaning through their semantic link with the notion of uncertainty. Changes within the environment can be characterized as either incremental, discontinuous, foreseen or unforeseen. Changes are complex in the sense that they are unpredictable. And, decentralization does not only take place within organizations, but is also a process at societal level. Privatization can be described as society delegating responsibilities to companies and private organizations.[4] In this sense, Kaptein

---

4   Clifton et al. (2003, 92) define privatization as 'any movement toward a market-driven economy – or any movement that diminishes public ownership and control and increases private ownership and control'. They also write that privatization has been driven by the increasing globalization. Decades of rapid growth in international trade and investment has resulted in the need for nations to be competitive in international trade in order to be able to create jobs, raise real wages, and generate wealth. Hence, privatization is often the only effective method for raising investment capital. The privatization wave gained momentum in the mid 1980s in the UK, New Zealand and Latin America, and rushed over Western Europe, Asia and Central Europe during the 1990s (Clifton et al. 2003, 84, 92). With the rapid implementation of privatization policies world-wide came a rhetoric of more efficiency brought about by privatization, liberalization and deregulation policies. High expectations were raised as to what the market would be able to do in terms of quality and efficiency. However, market efficiency relies on two basic assumptions: private ownership and competitive market. Clifton et al. (2003, 87) claim most privatization policies have over-emphasized private ownership as a condition for efficiency, at the expense of establishing a competitive market, assuming that profit-maximizing behaviour of the new owners would automatically and necessarily increase efficiency. However, if competition is lacking, what is created is a private unregulated monopoly, which is very likely to result in higher prices and not in innovation or efficiency. Privatized monopolies create huge rents. Regulatory and competitive reforms are vital if rent-seeking and its corruption effects are to be countered (TI 2000). Clifton et al. (2003, 87, 139–40) see this as a reason for the increased social dissatisfaction with privatized utilities. Hence the claim that privatization is a delegation of responsibilities from society to private organizations. Even though privatization policies were not concerned with that aspect in the past, they are today. The satisfactory provision of public services for citizens and users is one of the key contemporary issues at the level of intergovernmental organizations such as the UN and the EU.

and Wempe (1998) have argued that the internal decentralization process is an organization's answer to an increased environmental complexity generated by a societal decentralization process. Decentralization as the giving up of central decision making, as the impossibility of efficient central planning also carries with it the notion of uncertainty. Because of the perception of uncertainty as irreducible, the policy approach – both at societal as well as at organizational level – shifts from 'government' to *governance* – the third central concept in the globalization semantic.[5]

What is governance? Gaudin (2002) contrasts it with government. The concept of government is constituted through its links with notions of certainty, controllability, centrality of the state in interventions, economy, exchange, negotiations, labour law, health care, pensions. Government stands for the possibility and desirability of scientific management. However, Gaudin argues, we live in an era of uncertainty, where economic planning is more complex. The state moves away from the centre of public action because – due to the perception of uncertainty and complexity – the state looses its legitimation to act. Governance refers to that phenomenon and in that sense it is a concept of the 1990s.[6] Societal

---

[5]   I already mentioned this shift in Vandekerckhove and Commers (2000), where it was argued that because of this shift, anti-corruption becomes a priority issue. The article then reviews a number of anti-corruption measures, including whistleblowing policies.

[6]   Gaudin regards Rosenau and Czempiel (1991) and Kooiman (1993) as anticipating publications. Nevertheless, Gaudin is aware that *govern*, *government* and *governance* share the same etymological base, referring to *to lead*, *to guide*, *to steer*. It designates both the choice of goals as well as the continuous adaptations to reach those goals in a changing context. In that sense, it is a dialectic of voluntarism and pragmatism. Gaudin points out that during the middle ages, the three words had the same meaning and were used interchangeably. Later, the meaning of the term *government* is pinned down to designate the idea of hierarchical power, vertical and top down directed relations of obedience. Another perspective is then that of the science of government. Here, practical knowledge is generated regarding the collection and management of taxes, of organizing justice in relation to observations from society, and drawing up an inventory of persons and goods. It was also a knowledge of bookkeeping and of organizing exchange. That knowledge corresponded with trade, for it were the merchants who developed that knowledge. Later, nation-states – Great Britain and France – are to stimulate that knowledge and reflection, making it evolve into the field of economy before its diversification. But, Gaudin argues, this practical knowledge – knowledge stemming from and needed for action, for praxis – is not found at universities, where political philosophy and law are studied. At least in Europe. The US, as a new country was different because it was characterized by pragmatism. This is, according to Gaudin, the reason why this kind of knowledge did find its way into universities in the US. And it is also there that pragmatism finds it way into philosophy. John Dewey was to make the first methodological analyses of public policy in the 1930s. It is also Dewey who, with regard to the pragmatic management of organizations, in specific private company organizations, uses the term *governance*. From then on the meaning of governance is slowly pinned down. It is in the mid 1970s that governance gains popularity in the sociology of organization through Marge and Olsen (1976) who use the term governance

decentralization partly took place through privatization – Gaudin calls it a neo-liberal mobilization to save our welfare through a slimming cure for the state – but also through a change in orientation of public management: from government to governance, which means that public management becomes management of collaborations between public and private organizations – private companies and NGOs. Along with that coupling, with that blurring of the institutional borders between public and private organization, came the need to use a common language. That language is the language of governance.[7] It aims at efficiency and effectiveness, and is sensitive for legitimacy.

Gaudin distinguishes three levels at which the concept of governance is meaningful. The first is the most direct level in the sense that governance is a direct appeal to the realism of negotiation. International agreements are more decisive for growth than national or regional organization. At a second level, governance gains a moral connotation. Governance is a call for responsibility at every organizational level, in order to guarantee effectiveness. The third level is idealistic. Governance is the principle of a new global humanism in a worldwide political order. Governance enters as the new hope, filling a political vacuum brought about by the collapse of the big utopias.

If we are to organize and manage in a world characterized by uncertainty, by perplexity, by doubt, by the perception that what is to come will be unexpected and unpredictable, then pragmatism is to be our organizing principle. This means that solutions are progressive in the sense that they are always provisional and can be placed in a succession of trial and error. Governance is not taking the golden path to utopia but taking the experiment to find out the next step.

The three concepts – flexibility, decentralization, governance – are interrelated and are constitutive for each others meaning. Of course, more concepts are linked with these three, and in the remainder of this chapter more of those will be taken up to develop semantic constructions of normative legitimation for whistleblowing policies. However, before I start out to do that, there are two other central concepts in the globalization semantic I need to point out. The concepts are *network* and *stakeholder*, and their relevance lies in the way they are needed to let us see and 'act' flexibility, decentralization and governance.

The Network Perspective

Organization theory has not stayed untouched by postmodern philosophy. The influence resulted in a changed vision on autonomy and coherence of

---

to describe the way in which decisions are taken in very complex organizations and in situation characterized by limited rationality. From the 1990s on, the term governance dominates the analysis of public policy (it is spread by organizations such as the IMF, the World Bank, the EU, the European Central Bank, the WTO, the UN).

[7]   New Public Management is the term used to denote the change to governance centred policy within the public sector (see Van Hooland 2003; Maesschalck et al. 2002).

organizations, a changed vision on representation and information, and a changed vision on borders and power. Apostel and Walry (1997) regard the work of Gilles Deleuze[8] as a crucial inspiration for postmodern organization theory, taken there by Stewart Clegg, Robert Cooper and Gibson Burrell at the end of the 1980s.[9]

Because meaning is regarded as an interpretation which always implies reinterpretations from the viewpoints of different social roles, and because individuals have a fluctuating set of social roles from which they interpret, coherency and autonomy as an independent identity is no longer possible. Not at the level of the individual subject, nor at the level of the group or the organization.

This also implies that the image an organization constructs of its environment becomes vague and incoherent. The construction of an image of the environment takes place by gathering information. Through selection of what is to be regarded as relevant information, a representation is constructed, which is a reduction of complexity, enabling control at distance. Postmodern organization theory does not regard representation as having any truth-value. Rather, representation is viewed as functional for internal self-production. Organizations are considered as living organisms, searching their environment for elements to reproduce themselves – organizations as autopoetic systems. Postmodern about this is not the functionalistic view on representation, but rather that the notion of organization as an autopoetic system emphasizes process over structure. Secondly, the locus of rationality shifts from the global to the local. It is not the organizational system as a whole which is rational, but rather every element within the system that has and acts its own rationality. This means that when emphasizing structure, one emphasizes global rationality, fixing distances between elements within the system. Hence, structures are static. But when emphasizing process, one allows rationality at the level of the elements within a system. The system then, is the set of relations between elements, but without fixed distances. Hence, processes are dynamic. Third, power is also spread over the entire system, and is no longer positioned solely at the top. Note that already Weber had pointed out that those having power only have power as long as those under power recognize the validity of the power – a validity based on either charisma, tradition or law. Foucault however takes it much further, stating power is never held by any group or class, and in this sense power is not binary. Power is not about those holding power versus those under power. Power is not a pattern of activity – passivity. Rather, power is relational and built on consensus[10] through communication. Of course, 'modern'

---

8   Especially Deleuze's rhizome-approach has been taken up. However, one will find Foucault quoted more often, and especially his approach to power.

9   Clegg seems to be the most enthousiastic one where appropriateness of postmodern thinking for organization theory is concerned. Cooper and Burrell take a more moderate stance.

10   I consider Weber's view on *consensus* very important. For Weber, consensus did not imply a categorical willing.

organization theory also included communication. However, postmodern organization theory attaches a far greater importance to communication – on its imperfectness, its multi-directionality and its power aspects. Hence, a changed view on organizational power emphasizes interdependence and mutual constitution of an organizational system by its elements. Gaudin (2002) speaks of polycentric power, Mraović (2004) of networks of power. Interdependence, relational power, dynamic processes … Deleuze's image of rhizome or network fits better than that of a tree-diagram. Hence, postmodern organization theory takes a network perspective.

Taking a network perspective on an organization implies focussing on the interactions between organizational departments, between individuals within organizational departments, and between organizations. A central concern from the network perspective is how the pattern of interactions among these multiple actors affects the behaviour of members of the network. The overall pattern of interactions makes up the network structure,[11] which is seen as providing opportunities for and constraints on specific actions. It is important to note that what is at stake in a network perspective is the overall pattern of relations, not the dyadic interactions. It is sets of simultaneous relations and interactions which link an element with other elements within a system that can give us insights and knowledge about behaviour. Dyadic interaction based perspectives on organizations make abstractions that are untenable when approaching organizations in terms of process, relational power and communication – like a network perspective does.

Neoclassical economic theory regards one-time, two-party transactions to be the norm. A network perspective allows for different types of transactions to exist simultaneously – inter-organizational, intra-organizational – and hence is able to consider repeated, multi-party transactions.

Agency theory conceives of organizations as a nexus of contracts. The behaviour of an organization is like the behaviour of a market. However – and here is why agency theory differs from the network perspective – agency theory focuses on bilateral interactions between principle and agent, thereby excluding multilateral interrelationships within the nexus of contracts and confining its analysis to behaviour of selfishly rational individuals within dyadic interactions. It is the agent-manager who, in the interest of the principal-owner, organizes and closes contracts with other actors. Agency theory is concerned with the problem of how to ensure the agent will close those other contracts in the interest – maximizing the welfare of – the principal. It aims at avoiding agent opportunism – the agent maximizing his or her own welfare – or managerial discretion in favour of goals

---

[11]   Structure here is not the static, one directional, fixed distances version, but rather structure in terms of densities (how many connections are there, how frequent, and how can they be characterized), trends (time-dimension) and processes (what interactions are presupposed in other interactions).

or interest other than those of the principal.[12] An assumption is that the agent-manager is situated at the centre of the nexus of contracts and thus is the only one of the participating actors who enters into a contractual relationship with all other participating groups, and that he is the only one with direct control over the decision-making apparatus of the organization (Hill and Jones 1992). A network perspective does not assume the centrality and exclusive relationships of the agent-manager within the nexus of contracts.

Governance is action by means of networks, through relations and collaborations that are not pre-determined by a transcendent rationality but that have to be reinvented every time. It implies less central commands and less hierarchy, but more procedures for dialogue and collaboration and mutual adaptation. Generally, speaking of a 'network economy'[13] means that also informal channels of communication, persuasion and adaptation are taken into consideration and are valued as important for the proper functioning of an organization.

In this sense too, the network is a form of organizing that stands in contrast to Weber's bureaucracy. The idealtype of bureaucracy is the rational organizing based on impersonal rules; in the limit there is only the formal organization – the organization as perfectly represented in the organizational diagram. In this sense, the rise of bureaucracy is the decline of charisma as basis for authority. In contrast, the network organization praises informal organizational aspects and counts on them for its functioning. Hence, the network organization is a re-mystification of how organizations function. The network organization is the form of organization for an era of complexity, of flexibility, of uncertainty and thus of an opaque world. In complex organizations, or in situations of polycentric power, it is more difficult to point out how a particular decision came about or how a particular collective action – an organizational action – started through a chain of decisions. Hence, with the notions of complexity and governance comes the appraisal for concepts like transparency and accountability.

Castells (1996) writes about the network enterprise as 'that specific form of enterprise whose system of means is constituted by the intersection of segments of autonomous systems of goals' (Castells 1996, 171).[14] The network enterprise

---

[12] Milton Friedman's claim that corporate philanthropy is theft stems from this approach.

[13] Acknowledging the economical importance of SMEs for a region's welfare, the popularity of outsourcing, service focused economy, are exponents of a 'network economy' perspective.

[14] Manuel Castells was a student of Alain Touraine, who, already in 1969 wrote that the governance of the contemporary enterprise consists of combining ever more complex strategies of more and more actors who's capacity to influence is growing. My translation of 'la gestion de l'entreprise consiste de plus en plus à combiner les stratégies de plus en plus complexes d'acteurs de plus en plus nombreux et dont s'accroît la capacité d'influence' (Touraine 1969, 229).

is a new organizational form, emerging with and characteristic of the global economy, or – how Castells calls it – the informational economy, because it is able to fulfil the needs of organizations in terms of flexibility, innovation and learning. Components of the network are both autonomous and dependent with regard to the network, they can simultaneously be part of other networks. But it is precisely being part of a network or not and the dynamics of each network with regard to others that determine dominance and action. This networking logic shapes production, power, knowledge, culture. Hence, Castells speaks of the pre-eminence of social morphology over social action. The new social morphology is that of information technologies, as information is the raw material upon which technologies work – not the other way round – and the enormous span of the effects these technologies have, as information forms an integral part of every human activity.

Wicks et al. (1994) have distinguished two sets of metaphors for what business organizations are, how they relate to other actors and what success means. A first – masculine, as they call it – set is made up of the following metaphors:

- corporations are autonomous entities;
- companies should enact and control their environment;
- the metaphors of conflict and competition best describe how firms should be managed;
- strategy formulation should be objective;
- power and authority should be embedded in strict hierarchies.

They regard this set as inadequate for business organizations facing diverse challenges in an increasingly complex and global marketplace. Instead, they draw up an alternative – feminist – set of metaphors more suitable for today's organizational context. Although they do not refer to it as the set of metaphors making up a network perspective, they do incorporate the influences of postmodern organizational theory I pointed at earlier on. Hence, I consider Wicks et al. their feminist set of metaphors to be the network metaphors:

- corporations are webs of relations among stakeholders;
- corporations should 'thrive on chaos' and environmental change;
- the metaphors of communication and collective action best describe how firms should be managed;
- strategy as solidarity;
- hierarchy is replaced by radical decentralization and empowerment.

Defining the basic identity of a corporation as independent of its environment – corporations as autonomous entities – implies seeing interactions of corporations as atoms colliding with other atoms in a mechanistic process. However, if we think of corporations as webs of relations, we acknowledge identities to be embedded in context and interactions to be more organic than mechanic. Also, perceiving corporations as able to control their environment implies that corporations are able to seek and find a measure of control over external forces and competitors, which they then dominate as a way to restore order and make their corporation flourish. If, on the other hand, corporations are designed to cope with unpredictability and constant change, then interdependency and the necessity for cooperation due to growing turbulence needs to be emphasized. This means that communication and collective action are the key metaphors for organizations rather than conflict and competition.

The claim that good strategy is constructed in an objective and disinterested way, reflects a deep suspicion of emotions, experience and attachment. The normative implication of this is that non-owner participants are not seen as having a legitimate voice in the corporation. What Wicks et al. do here is to contrast an ethic of rationally applied principles, with a relational ethic of care. The latter challenges the idea that so called objective decisions are really neutral and disinterested. Rather:

> [so called objective decisions] merely distance us from the responsibility of choice and mask the reality that the actual motivation is the pursuit of profit for those who have power in the organization (Wicks et al. 1994, 489).

Should strategy be seen as solidarity, it would imply that a dialogue would be set up among multiple actors, in order to expand the scope of possibilities for looking at and making sense of a situation. Instead of closing the corporation off from its outside, strategy as solidarity taps into the creative process of different impressions of a situation and what is at stake.

The respective sets of metaphors culminate in distinct views on how power and authority are to be distributed in the organization. The first set – which Wicks et al. (1994) have called the masculine set – leads to a strong impetus for hierarchy. It is hierarchy which 'helps to simplify, organize and structure the organization by defining roles, duties, and functions clearly' (Wicks et al. 1994, 482). Contrary to that, the second – feminist – set of metaphors steers away from hierarchy. It sees decentralization, team structures and worker empowerment as leading to a more meaningful work experience. In reinforcing attitudes which promote worker involvement, trust is increased and added commitment and productivity is brought about.

Besides the moral attractiveness of the second set of metaphors which make up the network perspective, businesses also experience a need to improve their responsiveness and their adaptability. In an unpredictable, rapidly changing global economy, adopting a network perspective is highly relevant for corporations.

Stakeholder Theory

The term 'stakeholder' appeared in management discourse in 1962 (Andriof et al. 2002, 12) or 1963 (Freeman 1997, 602). In an internal memo at the Stanford Research Institute, Robert Stewart used the term as a generalization of the notion of stockholder in the sense that stakeholders were defined as 'those groups without whose support the organization would cease to exist'. The implication was that executives had to understand the needs and concerns of stakeholder groups in order to formulate corporate objectives that would receive the support necessary for the continued survival of the firm. This approach served mainly as an information function for the corporate planning process.

However, in the same period, Eric Rhenman – a Swedish management theorist – used the concept to argue for more democracy in industrial organizations, defining stakeholders as 'individuals or groups dependent on the company for the realization of their personal goals and on whom the company is dependent for its existence' (Rhenman 1965, 25). Rhenman's work was very influential in Scandinavia, and is to be considered as foundational for the 'Swedish model' (Tengblad 2001). Rhenman considered the owners of a company as one stakeholder amongst others. The implication was that managers gained independence, because it was their task to achieve a balance of interests between different stakeholders. This runs against agency theory, where the manager (agent) has a fiduciary duty towards the shareholders (principal) to act solely on their behalf. A consequence of this Swedish stakeholder perspective of the firm was that companies became more management controlled.[15]

Most texts on stakeholder theory see Freeman as the one who rephrased Stewart's (Stanford Research Institute) concept of stakeholder into its current usage and popularity with his book *Strategic Management: A Stakeholder Approach* from 1984. However, it is my opinion that Rhenman is responsible for the current content of the stakeholder concept. Freeman's merit then is to be the promo-person of the concept within the strategic management and business ethics field. Compared to Stewart's stakeholder-concept, Rhenman's is bi-lateral, for Rhenman takes both the organization's existence and the stakeholder goals into account. In this sense, Freeman's definition of stakeholders as 'any group or individual who can affect or is affected by the achievement of the firm's objectives' (Freeman 1984, 46) is only a widening of Rhenman's, but does not constitute a change in perspective. The widening consists in not specifying what kind of influence the organization and stakeholders have on each other but only

---

[15] Tengblad (2001) describes these shifts from a historical perspective, showing the power going back and forth between more liberal and more socialist views. Rhenman's stakeholder perspective had already restricted the reign of ownership, but a second social movement would, during the 1970s, argue for more direct influence for workers on shop-floor level. Tengblad argues that the Swedish stakeholder model was actually 'a social movement in which representatives for the labour movement, the State and the business community mobilized resources for the creation of a centralized and negotiation-oriented control over the economy' (Tengblad 2001, 10). The model was based on central agreements, often on industry level. Of course, this was more or less the case for most of the Western European countries. And in this sense, it is what Touraine described as the insertion of an institutional level.

that they influence or affect each other. Freeman does not take the existence of an organization into account, but rather the dependency of an organization upon some groups or individuals – stakeholders – for the achievement of the organization's objectives. Like Rhenman's stakeholder notion, it is bilateral because it also recognizes the effects of organizational activity on other people and groups.

By saying Freeman is the promo-person of the stakeholder concept, I by no means want to minimize the importance of his work. Freeman constructed an approach to stakeholder management by providing a theoretical basis for the understanding of the stakeholder concept and thereby paved the way for future research. But what exactly was Freeman's contribution? He developed a three level framework for stakeholder analysis – rational, process and transactional. The rational level consists of identifying those groups who have a stake and of understanding the nature between the stakeholders and the organization. This is then visualized by drawing up a stakeholder map (Figure 3.2). The process level of stakeholder analysis looks at how the standard operating procedures of an organization reflect the relations between stakeholders and organization. Finally, the transactional level concerns the set of transactions among stakeholders and organization – for example, marketing activities, consumer complaint mechanisms, union negotiations, paying dividends to shareholders, social reporting. The merit of Freeman's work is that he places stakeholder management at the centre of organizational strategy, thereby integrating the importance of internal and external environment of an organization in a systemic way.

Nevertheless, Freeman's work was only picked up in the early 1990s.[16] To phrase it in Luhmann's terms, Freeman created a variation of the stakeholder concept which remained latent until it became selectable and indeed got selected when the field of business ethics gained momentum in the 1990s. Stakeholder thinking allowed the firm to be perceived as an open system rather than as a closed system with the only concern being the satisfaction of shareholders (Andriof et al. 2002, 11). In a closed system perspective, the firm is regarded as distinct from society. This pinned down the whole discussion about corporate social responsibility on the format of business *and* society. From the 1990s on however, the concepts of corporate responsibility and corporate citizenship come

---

[16] One more reason to argue in this way is the fact that the stakeholder concept had been taken back up by others prior to Freeman: for example Ackoff in 1974, and Mason and Mitroff in 1981. Their idea of an open system necessarily involved complex and interwoven interactions between the elements in a system, including human elements. They used the stakeholder concept to identify assumptions underlying human behaviour in corporate settings. They also recognized the potential conflicts between stakeholders in terms of interests, and paid attention to possible resolution of conflicting interests through dialectical processes. In that regard, the work of these people has been picked up to further develop Freeman's ideas – for example with regard to the dynamics of stakeholders or the network perspective on stakeholder theory.

to the foreground, taking up Freeman's integrative view that responsibilities are integral to corporate practices (Andriof and Waddock 2002, 23). Hence, it can be argued that Freeman's stakeholder concept was selectable because it stabilized the field of business ethics – it thereby remained able to make reality comprehensible – by turning 'business *and* society' into 'business *in* society' through two shifts: 1) from a reactive attitude towards societal claims to proactive engagement with stakeholders; and 2) by recognition of power relations and interdependencies between firm and stakeholders.

But it is also Freeman's merit – and this explains why I have called him the promo-person of the stakeholder concept – that he has actively kept the concept selectable throughout the 1990s by re-emphasizing and deepening out certain aspects of his work from 1984 in defence against his critics.

A first well known critique came around in 1991 with Goodpaster's formulation of the 'stakeholder paradox' (Goodpaster 1991). Goodpaster reproaches Freeman for viewing stakeholders other than shareholders as instrumental. He argues that even though Freeman's stakeholder definition is symmetric, Freeman only regards 'those affected by the company' as stakeholders because they might one day be in a position to affect the company. Hence, what Freeman means by stakeholders is those groups or individuals who can actually or potentially affect the company (Goodpaster 1991, 59). But Freeman's strategic view of stakeholders is no shift away from the primacy of the shareholder. Therefore, concludes Goodpaster, it is not ethical. He then contrasts Freeman's strategic view with what he calls a multi-fiduciary stakeholder approach, in which a management team processes information from the stakeholders, not in function of the fiduciary duty towards shareholders, but by giving the same care to the interests of employees, customers, local communities and shareholders (Goodpaster 1991, 61). It is multi-fiduciary because all stakeholders are treated by management as having equally important interests.[17] This is the way ethics can be introduced into business decisions: by expanding the list of those in whose trust corporate management must manage. So, Goodpaster argues that if the stakeholder approach is to introduce ethics into management, it is not through Freeman's approach but rather through a multi-fiduciary approach. But at the same time, for managers to have more than one fiduciary duty is incompatible with moral convictions and legal constitution of the corporation. Hence the stakeholder paradox: 'It seems essential, yet in some ways illegitimate, to orient corporate decisions by ethical values that go beyond strategic stakeholder considerations to multi-fiduciary ones' (Goodpaster 1991, 63). What Goodpaster actually argues is 1) that agency theory with a single principal is unethical, but at the same time that 2) agency theory with multiple principal is unethical as well because it runs counter moral convictions and accepted ideas

---

[17]   This multi-fiduciary stakeholder approach is actually what Rhenman proposed in 1964. At the end of Freeman 1984, Freeman contemplates on whether a stakeholder democracy would be possible – whether or not such a theory of management could be constructed.

about how corporations function.[18] Goodpaster's proposal to solve the paradox consists of fully recognizing the fiduciary duty of managers to shareholders, but emphasizing that this duty must be carried out whilst respecting moral obligations to third parties surrounding any fiduciary relationship. The moral obligations Goodpaster has in mind are the duties not to harm or to coerce and the duties not to lie, cheat or steal. Moreover, these duties are not hypothetical, as in the strategic model where they are instrumental to the realization of the firm's objectives, rather, these duties are categorical. How does this operate? First, the moral obligations Goodpaster mentions are the moral obligations referred to in regulations and legislation constraining profit driven business. Second, neither principal nor agent can claim moral immunity from the basic obligations that apply to any human being toward other members of the community (Goodpaster 1991, 68).

Carson (1993) has argued that Goodpaster's proposal to solve the stakeholder paradox is nothing more than a version of Milton Friedman's view of corporate social responsibility. The principle behind Goodpaster's solution of the paradox is to promote the interests of the shareholders whilst refraining from harming, coercing, cheating or lying to stakeholders. But, argues Carson (1993, 173), because Goodpaster puts the foundation of those moral obligations for managers in the universality of these duties – they are moral obligations for any human being – the principle is equivalent to the principle of promoting the interests of shareholders whilst refraining from harming, coercing, cheating or lying to anyone. And, formulated this way, it comes very close to how Friedman described the social responsibilities of corporations. Milton Friedman is often quoted as saying that the only social responsibility of business is to increase its profit.[19] However, what is most often forgotten is that Friedman had put that

---

[18]   Goodpaster further argues it runs counter the basis of capitalism: property rights. Multi-fiduciary management means converting the private corporation into a public institution. In a way, that is just what Rhenman proposed and what the Swedish model did. In another way, to only regard shareholders' property rights is to disregard community property (air, forests, water) and employee property (labour force). But Goodpaster proposes to let those rights be protected by law and morally significant non-fiduciary obligations. In a critique of agency theory, Crowther (2004, 48) argues that: 1) in actual fact fiduciary duty does not limit managers to a narrow shareholder approach but merely requires the manager to have an open and honest relationship with the shareholder and not gain illegitimately from their office, and 2) when in the past, in US courts, shareholders have challenged the actions of managers as being too generous to other stakeholder groups – Friedman's stealing – then the courts have generally upheld 'the right of management to manage'. Thus, concludes Crowther (2004, 48), 'the tension between fiduciary responsibility and the responsibility to other stakeholder groups, the so-called stakeholder paradox [...] is not as apparent as is often assumed'.

[19]   The quote is: 'there is one and only one social responsibility to business – to use its resources and engage in activities designed to increase its profits'. However, the rest of the sentence is most often left unquoted, but it reads: 'so long as it stays within the rules of the game, which is to say, engages in open and free competition without deception or

into context. The duty to maximize profit has to be carried out within the rules of the game, which state that: 1) there is also a duty to engage in open and free competition: 2) a duty to refrain from deception and fraud; and 3) a duty to obey the law (Friedman 1963, 133; 1972, 178). Hence, there is nothing new about Goodpaster's proposal to solve the paradox.[20]

A second critique on Freeman concerned the different uses of stakeholder theory. Donaldson and Preston (1995) have distinguished between three versions of the stakeholder theory: descriptive, instrumental and normative. Others have turned this into a critique (for example Jones and Wicks 1999) saying these versions are used incompatible and that convergence between them is necessary.

How does Freeman respond to those critiques? First, prior to Goodpaster's article, Freeman was aware that he might have overemphasized an instrumental justification of stakeholder theory for strategic management. To correct that, he published in 1988, together with Evan, a more deontological argumentation for stakeholder theory (Evan and Freeman 1988). They argue that the stakeholder approach allows the theory of the firm to be reconceptualized along Kantian lines, in the sense that it allows managers to consider stakeholders as ends in themselves, rather than as mere means to the firm's ends. In defence against the critique that his stakeholder theory would be instrumentally motivated, he refers to that 'compensatory' article from 1988 (Freeman 1994).

---

fraud' (Friedman 1963, 133, but mostly quoted from an article in the *New York Times* of 13 September 1970).

[20]   Carson then proceeds to formulate his own proposal of the stakeholder paradox. He argues that business executives have prima facie positive duties to promote the interest of all stakeholders. But the duties to some stakeholders are more important than those to other stakeholders. What needs to be done then is justify why different weights are assigned to the interests of different stakeholders. Carson actually proposes to solve the paradox by drawing up a stakeholder matrix. In a sense this idea has been picked up by people writing about the dynamics of stakeholders. Mitchell et al. (1997) for example developed a theory of stakeholder identification and salience through the construction of a typology of stakeholder groups. The typology is based on whether or not stakeholders possess one or more of three relationship attributes: power, legitimacy and urgency. The typology is normative because it stipulates which stakeholder groups managers *should* pay attention to. The typology is also dynamic because stakeholder attributes are not regarded as a steady state, but rather as variable. Powerful stakeholders are those who have or can gain access to coercive, instrumental or symbolic means enabling them to impose their will in the relationship. Legitimate stakeholders are those who bear a recognized – a socially constructed recognition – voluntary or involuntary risk with regard to an organization's activities. The urgency attribute then, makes the typology dynamic, and is based on 1) time sensitivity as the degree to which managerial delay in attending to the claim or relationship is unacceptable to the stakeholder, and 2) criticality, designating the importance of the claim or the relationship to the stakeholder (Mitchell et al. 1997, 867). Based on whether or not groups or individuals posses one or more of these attributes, Mitchell et al. (1997, 872) then theorize about which type of stakeholder will be most salient to managers.

Second, Freeman refutes the Goodpaster's stakeholder paradox because it is built on what Freeman calls the 'Separation Thesis', which says that: 'The discourse of business and the discourse of ethics can be separated so that sentences like, "x is a business decision" have no moral content, and "x is a moral decision" have no business content' (Freeman 1994, 412). Goodpaster's paradox is a clear example of the Separation Thesis, since he says we need but can not have both the strategic stakeholder approach – business without ethics – and the multi-fiduciary stakeholder approach – ethics without business. Freeman states that 'the whole point of the stakeholder approach is to deny the Separation Thesis' (Freeman 1994, 412). The stakeholder approach is a heuristic emphasizing that there is always a context to business theory, and that this context is moral in nature.[21]

In the same sense, Freeman argues that one can not discuss business, organizations, stockholders or stakeholders without engaging in discourse which is at the same time normative, descriptive and instrumental.[22] Hence, Freeman denies the need to integrate the three versions of stakeholder theory by pointing at the error of separating them (Freeman 1999).

The discussions amongst scholars[23] actually show to be impetuses for the stakeholder concept, with each reformulation or defence constituting a new or stronger semantic link. Another strong impetus for the stakeholder concept was the connection Rowley (1997) made between the network perspective and the stakeholder concept. Rowley recognizes the popularity of the stakeholder concept in the business and society literature, and sees a reason for this popularity in the emphasis the concept puts on how organizations function with respect to the relationships and influences within its environment. He further states that the development of stakeholder theory has concentrated on identifying and classifying stakeholders. However, research into the field has always concentrated on dyadic relationships between stakeholders and the organization. What Rowley does is to move beyond the dyadic interaction perspective and use the concepts from social network analysis to consider multiple, interdependent and simultaneous interactions in stakeholder environments. Focussing on individual stakeholder relationships might be appropriate for classifying types of stakeholders,[24] but in order to explain organizational behaviour, an analysis of the structural characteristics of stakeholder environments is needed. Each organization faces

---

[21] Moreover, '[it] is only by recognizing the moral presuppositions of business theory, refining them, testing them by living differently, and revizing them that we can invent and reinvent better ways to live. All of this is just Dewey updated for business' (Freeman 1994, 413).

[22] The article by Donaldson and Preston pointing out the three versions of stakeholder theory – descriptive, instrumental and normative – was published in 1995 in *The Academy of Management Review*. However, an earlier version of the article – as a 'Ciber occasional paper' dated January 1994 – is mentioned and responded to in Freeman 1994.

[23] The 'critiques' on Freeman are some examples of such discussions.

[24] One such example is Mitchel et al. (1997), see footnote 20.

a different set of stakeholders. Organizations respond to the interaction of multiple influences from the entire stakeholder set rather than to each stakeholder individually (Rowley 1997, 890).

A first expansion of Freeman's 1984 'hub'-model (Figure 3.2) was suggested by Freeman himself, together with Evan (Freeman and Evan 1990, cited in Rowley 1997). More precisely, they suggested that a stakeholder environment consists of a series of multilateral contracts among stakeholders (Figure 3.3). The second shift Rowley proposes, is that the focal organization is but one of the focal points in a stakeholder environment, and is not necessarily situated at the centre of the network. In other words, in a network perspective, each stakeholder of a focal organization has its own set of stakeholders (Figure 3.4).

The reason why the network perspective connects so well with the stakeholder concept, is that both view an organization in terms of relationships with its environment, whereby the environment is conceptualized as a set of social actors. The difference however is that previous authors on stakeholder theory have only regarded dyadic interactions, whilst Rowley introduces – with the network perspective – a possibility to examine systems of dyadic interactions, or interaction of interactions. Such an examination takes place along the concepts of density and centrality. The network density is the number of ties in the network, compared with the total number of possible ties. A higher network density then facilitates communication and the diffusion of norms, values and shared information. Centrality of an actor in the network is the extent to which the actor is an intermediary between its stakeholders. A more central position within the network implies a more powerful organization in terms of resistance to stakeholder pressure.

In a network perspective, the stakeholder concept connects very well with the globalization semantic I mentioned earlier on. Recent literature has linked the stakeholder concept to the concepts of uncertainty, dialogue, partnerships and complexity by taking a network perspective (Andriof and Waddock 2002; Crane and Livesey 2003; Welcomer et al. 2003; Cohen 2003; Johnson-Cramer et al. 2003; Vandekerckhove and Dentchev 2005).

Whistleblowing as a Human Right

What is common to all possible definitions of whistleblowing, is that whistle-blowing is always about individuals disclosing information. Why, how, about what and to whom might differ according to the chosen definition, but there is always a communication going on. The whistleblower 'speaks' – although he or she sometimes writes – information. That information can be warnings of risky practices, accusations of illegalities or undue diligence, or expression of concern. But the whistleblower speaks out a judgement of a situation.

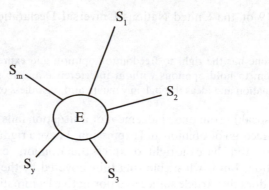

Figure 3.2   Freeman's 1984 'hub' model

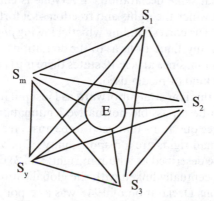

Figure 3.3   Freeman and Evan's 1990 shift in perspective

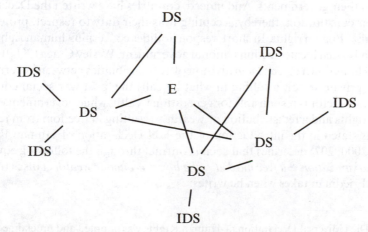

Figure 3.4   Rowley's 1997 network perspective

Article 19 of the United Nations Universal Declaration of Human Rights[25] says:

> Everyone has the right to freedom of opinion and expression; this right includes freedom to hold opinions without interference and to seek, receive and impart information and ideas through any media and regardless of frontiers.

Clearly, speaking out one's judgement of a situation falls under what is called the right to freedom of opinion and expression. I have a right to make the judgement – opinion – and I have the right to express that opinion – expression and imparting information. But is whistleblowing fully covered by the human right of article 19? And does that article suffice as a normative legitimation for a whistleblowing policy? I can answer now that *if* whistleblowing is indeed covered by article 19, then this justifies a whistleblower protection. It even necessitates such protection, given article 28 of that same declaration: 'Everyone is entitled to a social and international order in which the rights and freedoms set forth in this Declaration can be fully realized'. The corresponding whistleblowing *policy* then, would have to contain very few, if any, limitations as to the conditions of expression and the spreading of information, since article 19 states there is to be no interference and no limitations on the kind of media used.

However, none of this is as straightforward as I just put it. For 'whistleblowing as a human right' to be a possible normative legitimation for whistleblowing policies, there are three questions that need to be answered affirmatively: 1) can it be argued that human rights are a responsibility of private organizations; 2) can whistleblowing be described as a human right; and 3) can whistleblowing as a human right be conceptually linked with the globalization semantic?

The United Nations Declaration of 1948 was a response to the atrocities of and prior to the second world war, and was addressed to national governments. In this sense, its aim was to identify inalienable rights to individuals which they can claim on their governments. And indeed, countries have written the Declaration into their constitution, thereby accepting it as their duty to respect, protect and even realize human rights. In short, responsibilities concerning human rights have historically been located within national government. Wesley Cragg (2000) argues that this boils down to a *de facto* division of responsibilities between governments and the private sector, resulting in what he calls the 'post war social contract'. The private sector is responsible for generating wealth, while government ensures human rights and a redistribution of wealth – resulting in freedom from fear and want (as stated in the introduction of the UN Declaration of Human Rights). Cragg (2000, 207) describes that social contract through the following equation: *profit maximization + a free market + the law = economic wealth*. This is the view Milton Friedman takes when he writes:

---

[25]   The Universal Declaration of Human Rights was adopted and proclaimed by the United Nations General Assembly resolution 217 A (III) of 10 December 1948.

there is one and only one social responsibility to business – to use its resources and engage in activities designed to increase its profits, so long as it stays within the rules of the game, which is to say, engages in open and free competition, without deception or fraud (Friedman 1963, 133).

It is also the perspective of 'business *and* society'. However, earlier on I wrote that the stakeholder thinking denotes a shift in perspective from 'business *and* society' to 'business *in* society'. But that would imply a change in social contract between the private sector and the government. Cragg argues in the same way. The incidence of scandals involving private sector employees and senior management acting in function of profit maximization, within a judicial vacuum or abroad in a state of ethical confusion, and resulting in huge damages to both societies and the organizations they work for,[26] is a first reason to question the strict division of responsibilities. A second reason Cragg sees is the increased corporate power. Driving that power is corporate mobility. It has rendered multinational corporations a remarkable freedom to choose the legal systems in which to deploy their operations. This freedom boils down to a search for the most favourable legal environment, to be more precise the one that puts the fewest possible regulatory constraints on the buying, employing, producing, selling and marketing. In this sense, globalization has put national governments in 'regulatory competition' with each other (Cragg 2000, 209). The result is a weakening of the variable 'law' within the social contract equation, which makes the social contract to be experienced as if it read *free markets + profit maximization = economic wealth*. Cragg points out that free markets and profit maximization without powerful law, amounts to *the virtue of greed*, and sees this reflected in the corporate practice of the 1980s. As such, the post war social contract is no longer tenable, for 'greed is the enemy not the driving force of a free market economy' (Cragg 2000, 211). Hence, a new social contract is needed, which does not divide responsibilities, but stresses the shared responsibilities of business, governments and civil society in ensuring 'freedom from fear and want' (Cragg 2000; Bouckaert 2004).

A second argumentation is possible, showing that the responsibility for human rights is not restricted to national government. If, as I wrote, the responsibility for human rights is the duty to respect, protect and realize human rights, and if that responsibility is confined to national governments, then the implicit assumptions are that: 1) national governments are the sole perpetrators of human rights (therefore the duty to respect); 2) national governments alone are able to ensure individuals can claim their human rights (therefore the duty to protect); and 3) only national governments have the means to realize societal conditions allowing individuals to enjoy their human rights (therefore the duty to realize). Within the context of globalization, none of these assumptions hold. First, even though the UN Declaration of Human Rights was aimed at national governments and was

---

[26] Cragg names the Lockheed scandal, the Bhopal disaster and the Barings Bank collapse.

a response to the human rights abuses by governments prior to and during the second world war, it has become increasingly clear that transnational corporations are also perpetrating human rights.[27] Therefore, the duty to respect human rights has also become an issue for transnational corporations. Second, private business can be efficient in protecting human rights by sending out clear messages to their employees, suppliers and subcontractors that certain practices will not be tolerated – e.g. discrimination or child labour. Also, NGOs as private organizations have come to play a major role in reporting about and campaigning for human rights. Clearly, they themselves see it as their responsibility to protect human rights. And third, as Mary Robinson argues, 'business corporations, offering something all governments want – the prize of foreign currency and investment – have an extra bargaining chip in their pockets' (Robinson 1998, 15). Even though reality may show Robinson's view to be a mere potential of private business decisions to weigh positively – in the sense of persuading governments to impose laws rather than to abandon regulation – on regulation, the fact that they indeed have that potential induces on them that responsibility. Moreover, instead of asking business to fulfil the role of government or to persuade governments to fulfil their role in a certain way, private business can at least in part realize situations in which people can enjoy their human rights. For example, in countries where labour unions are not a stable part of the institutional landscape, corporations can encourage their workers to organize their representation.[28] Besides that, NGOs can play a role in promoting literacy, entrepreneurial skills or offering micro-loans.[29] Thus, the responsibility for human rights does not lie only in national governments, rather it is also an issue for private business and private organizations such as NGOs. Together with governments, these organizations share the responsibility for respecting, protecting and realizing human rights.

And now for the second obstacle. Crucial to the Declaration of Human Rights is that the rights can not be interpreted separately. A right can not be claimed (by a person, group or state) if exercising that right would imply the violation of the rights of others (Article 30). Moreover, the UN Declaration also stipulates in Article 29 that one has 'duties to the community in which alone the free and full development of his personality is possible', and that the exercise of

---

[27] See AI (1998), Christian Aid (2004) and Bendell et al. (2004) reports for cases of business companies' responsibility for human rights. See also Van de Ven (2004), arguing for business responsibilities for human rights from a Levinas viewpoint. See also Van de Ven (2005) and the reader edited by Rory Sullivan (2003) for essays on duties for and abilities of business organizations with regard to human rights.

[28] See for example the Unilever 2002 Social Review (Unilever 2002, 14), showing the percentage of Unilever employees in trades union membership, against the national average of workforce in trades union membership. They are on national average for Canada, USA and the Netherlands, but are significantly above national average for Indonesia (77 per cent to just 3 per cent).

[29] See for example the micro-credit programme of the Integra Foundation.

the rights and freedoms is subject to limitations necessary for the public order and the general welfare in a democratic society.[30] This means that human rights need to be interpreted in terms of scope and applicability. Of course, this makes the claimed absoluteness and universality of human rights come under tension. However, Tom Campbell (2002) argues that these claims are 'a way of getting at a more substantive matter, namely the claimed universal value of human existence, or what may be called the idea of equal human worth'. In that sense, the reference point in any interpretation of scope and applicability of human rights is the equal worth of human beings, a value which is closely tied to the idea of human dignity

---

[30] It is interesting to see how reformulations of the UN Declaration of Human Rights have specified the limitations to the right to freedom of expression and information.

The European Convention on Human Rights (1950), article 10 states: 'Everyone has the right to freedom of expression. This right shall include freedom to hold opinions and to receive and impart information and ideas without interference by public authority and regardless of frontiers'. And the limitations: 'This article shall not prevent States from requiring the licensing of broadcasting, television or cinema enterprises'. And more important: 'The exercise of these freedoms, since it carries with it duties and responsibilities, may be subject to such formalities, conditions, restrictions or penalties as are prescribed by law and are necessary in a democratic society, in the interests of national security, territorial integrity or public safety, for the prevention of disorder or crime, for the protection of health or morals, for the protection of the reputation or the rights of others, for preventing the disclosure of information received in confidence, or for maintaining the authority and impartiality of the judiciary'.

The American Convention on Human Rights 'Pact of San Jose, Costa Rica' (1969), article 13 states: 'Everyone has the right to freedom of thought and expression. This right includes freedom to seek, receive, and impart information and ideas of all kinds, regardless of frontiers, either orally, in writing, in print, in the form of art, or through any other medium of one's choice'. With the limitations: 'The exercise of the right provided for in the foregoing paragraph shall not be subject to prior censorship but shall be subject to subsequent imposition of liability, which shall be expressly established by law to the extent necessary to ensure: a) respect for the rights or reputations of others; or b) the protection of national security, public order, or public health or morals'. However: 'The right of expression may not be restricted by indirect methods or means, such as the abuse of government or private controls over newsprint, radio broadcasting frequencies, or equipment used in the dissemination of information, or by any other means tending to impede the communication and circulation of ideas and opinions'.

The Universal Islamic Declaration of Human Rights (1981), article 12 states: 'Every person has the right to express his thoughts and beliefs so long as he remains within the limits prescribed by the Law. No one, however, is entitled to disseminate falsehood or to circulate reports which may outrage public decency, or to indulge in slander, innuendo or to cast defamatory aspersions on other persons'. And further: 'Pursuit of knowledge and search after truth is not only a right but a duty of every Muslim. It is the right and duty of every Muslim to protest and strive (within the limits set out by the Law) against oppression even if it involves challenging the highest authority in the state. There shall be no bar on the dissemination of information provided it does not endanger the security of the society or the state and is confined within the limits imposed by the Law'.

and the Kantian conception of people being ends in themselves. The human rights discourse then is emphasising the high moral status of any human being, and 'a human right is held to be a right that protects or furthers human dignity in very important ways' (Campbell 2002). Hence, a right can be identified as a human right, even if it is subject to many qualifications. A right can also be identified as a human right regardless of whether it is considered as an intrinsic right – a right to do or have things that are worthwhile in themselves, like the right to life – or as an instrumental right – the value of the right then lies in the causal relationship to intrinsic rights and the value of the instrumental right varies with its effectiveness in protecting or furthering intrinsic rights.

Campbell mentions three 'free speech rationales', or three ways to argue for workplace free speech as a human right: 1) the argument for truth; 2) the argument for self-expression; and 3) the argument for democracy. The argument for truth is an instrumental argument. The existence and spread of true belief in society or community is the intrinsic good to which free speech rights are the mechanism. In an organization too, knowledge is valuable. 'True beliefs' are intrinsically good there as well, but at the same time they are also the instrumental mechanism for efficiency. Hence, workplace free speech is an instrumental right, promoting truth and efficiency.

The argument for self-expression shows workplace free speech as an intrinsic right. As Campbell puts it:

> If self-expression is an important human need and is essential to the flourishing of the individuals as moral, rational and creative beings, then we have something that is clearly universal, intrinsic and important. Further, to prevent such self-expressive activity may be deemed a violation of a person's humanity, [...] which denies them dignity and suppresses their individuality.

Hence, protecting workplace free speech is necessary in order to respect human dignity and moral worth.

The third argument is again instrumental. It is a rather traditional argument for the role of political free speech in democracy. How does this apply to organizations? First, there's the possibility of valuing industrial democracy. Second, we can regard the traditional political free speech rights as a way of protecting the individual interests against officialdom – expression of grievances and the role of speech and information in making demands and influencing decisions. These interests are to be protected in a democratic system, and can also apply for the private organization even though no elections are held. But we can also view democracy as a process of dialogue and a way to reach consensus on matters of common concern. This too is applicable to private organizations. Hence workplace free speech rights become valuable in ensuring everyone is treated as a source of ideas and information, and in establishing the consensual idea.

Finally, how are human rights to be linked with what I've called the globalization semantic? The strongest link is through the stakeholder concept. Rhenman had introduced his definition of stakeholders in arguing for more democracy in industrial organizations. The definition recognized the dependence of certain individuals or groups on the organization for the realization of their personal goals. In this sense, workplace free speech rights as a human right can be linked with the stakeholder concept through the argument for self-expression, but also through the argument for democracy. If one is dependent on an organization for the realization of personal goals, then it seems necessary to be able to speak freely about those personal goals and their dependence on the organization and its functioning. If there is such a dependence, then it is necessary to protect the interests of realizing personal goals. Hence the need for a stakeholder approach to guarantee the possibility of self-expression.

I wrote that Freeman broadened the stakeholder definition. He thereby tempered the mutual dependence to a mutual influence. This albeit consequentialist outlook was compensated by Freeman himself. He wrote a deontological argumentation for stakeholder theory. Stakeholders needed to be considered as ends in themselves. Here, all the arguments of human dignity, equal worth, and Kantian autonomy set in. Freeman even uses the term 'stakeholder democracy' to describe a situation where all relevant stakeholders participate and have an equal voice in the decision making process. Hence, through the argument for democracy, human rights can be linked with stakeholder thinking.

So, all three questions raised at the beginning of this section have been answered:

1 it can indeed be argued that human rights are a responsibility of private organizations;
2 yes, whistleblowing can be described as a human right – as workplace free speech; and
3 whistleblowing as a human right can be conceptually linked with the globalization semantic through the stakeholder concept, using the arguments for self-expression and democracy.

But how would a whistleblowing policy, justifying itself by reference to human rights look like? Whistleblowing as workplace free speech refers to the right to freedom of opinion and expression, a right including, according to article 19 of the UN Declaration, the freedom to seek, receive and impart information and ideas through any media. But here comes the difficulty. Does it make sense and is it defendable to distinguish between the expression of opinion and receiving and imparting information? We could argue that within the sphere of business competition, secrecy of information is constitutive for the general welfare of a democratic society. Because, the value of information for a business is not in having it, but in having it exclusively. Accepting this would imply that we acknowledge the freedom of opinion and of expressing that opinion, but not the right to receive and impart freely information about business operations. However, just what we acknowledge then, especially with regard to whistleblowing becomes very thin. Let's suppose the situation where it is a right to have and to express an opinion, but not information about business operations. And suppose, within that situation, I am working for a company producing cars. But I am also an environmentalist. Therefore, I have the right to hold the opinion that cars are very polluting and to express that opinion. Indeed, a very silly situation: someone working at a car company campaigning against cars. However, if I also had the right to impart information, I could argue that the company I work for was not using all the environmentally friendly technology it had in-house. That would make more sense. A second example. I am still working for that car company. During the designing and planning, something had been overlooked which had shown to be a safety danger during testing. However, due to time pressure, the car went into production as it was.[31] If I had only the right to have an opinion and to express it, but not the right to impart information, then the only thing I could do is to say that the company I work for makes bad cars. But I could not give more information. Of course, it still makes sense to say that the company makes bad cars. But for others to find out why the cars are bad will take unnecessary efforts and time, and in that way it is a poor expression of my opinion. Hence, it does not seem to make sense to distinguish between opinion and information, because to express an opinion in an a way which makes sense and is effective, requires the expression of an opinion to be built on information. Thus, a whistleblowing policy legitimating itself by referring to expression of opinion as a human right, must also acknowledge the right to seek, receive and impart information.

How would that kind of whistleblowing policy look on our definitions-grid (Table 1.2)? Well, five have just argued that it needs to be an informed opinion, so it would have to be an intended disclosure. Next, with regard to outcome, there are no intrinsic reasons why it would be necessary to get the disclosure onto public record. However, it might be necessary in order to better protect the whistleblower. The policy would allow for whistleblowing with the widest actor element, because we all have the same rights – equal human worth. As far as motive is concerned, egoism seems to be out of the question, since we can not claim a right if it is to deny another's right. The subject and target of the disclosure are unlimited, because I am not to be told about what I can have an opinion or not. But there is something to be said about the recipient element of the human rights whistleblowing policy. On the one hand, freedom of expression implies the freedom to choose the media through which to express the informed opinion. On the other hand, it might be damaging to the public order and the general welfare of a democratic society to spread the opinion that someone in an organization or some organization is to blame for this or that. The damage could lie in the opinion being based on unchecked information, or, making accusations through the newspapers might make a fair trial impossible. Hence, the policy dilemma is that it is necessary but too risky to allow just any recipient. A way around this is to identify a sequential order within the possible recipients – for example first internal, then government, then media. And as we will see in the next chapter,

---

[31]   I am of course referring to the Ford Pinto case.

some whistleblowing policies have indeed done so. One of the questions I will be answering in that chapter is whether or not these whistleblowing policies are legitimating themselves by referring to human rights. In this section I have shown that they can do so either by explicitly referring to human rights or freedom of expression (the argument for self-expression), but they can also do it by referring to the argument for democracy or the argument for truth. I have also argued that it can still be legitimated as a human right even if it is a qualified right. Still, with regard to some elements (actor, subject, target), it will have to be very wide to use human rights as a legitimation for the policy.

The human rights legitimation construct, as it gains its content through linking the primary concepts of the globalization semantic is visualized in Figure 3.5. In developing the construct, I considered the three rationales of whistleblowing as a human right to free speech: truth, self-expression and democracy. The existence and spread of true belief (knowledge) within a network of stakeholders is valuable. Grounding decentralization is the recognition of human dignity and autonomy, which makes self-expression valuable. Democracy is the governance process keeping decentralized stakeholders together. Moreover, from a network perspective, human rights is a governance issue rather than a government issue.

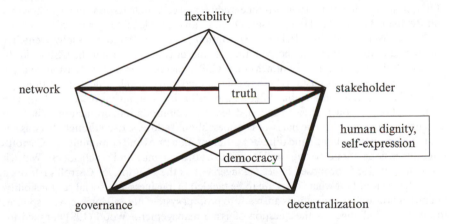

Figure 3.5   Globalization semantic (human rights)

Whistleblowing and Organizational Social Responsibility

A second possible normative legitimation for whistleblowing can be constructed through the currently immense popular concept of Corporate Social Responsibility (CSR). In this section, I will construct such a legitimation in two ways. A short look at where the concept comes from and how it is talked about now, will show it is interlarded with references to stakeholder thinking and the network perspective. The first normative legitimation I will construct hooks whistleblowing policies with the network perspective as a conceptual constituency of CSR. The second construction I will offer here, starts from the link with the stakeholder concept. Earlier in this chapter I argued that stakeholder theory has made our outlook shift from 'business and society' to 'business in society'. This makes reflection about the purpose of business organizations appropriate. It is this line of thought which I will connect to whistleblowing.

The concept 'Corporate Social Responsibility' first arose in the early 1950s (Matten et al. 2003).[32] But the origin doesn't really seem important. The idea that corporations and their managers-owners had social responsibilities is far older, and if it hasn't always been around then certainly from the industrial revolution.[33] What seems to be more important is the debate starting in the 1970s and the production of conceptual variation: corporate social performance (CSP), corporate social responsibility (CSR1), corporate social responsiveness (CSR2), corporate citizenship (CC).[34] Even today, conference discussions quite often get

---

[32]   Nikolay Dentchev (2004) mentions Bowen as the 'father of Corporate Social Responsibility', who published his book *Social Responsibilities of the Businessman* in 1953.

[33]   See for example Stuttard (1992), who describes Robert Owen and the development of 'Owenism' as a lesson for today's business ethics and corporate responsibilities. Crowther and Rayman-Bacchus (2004) also name Owen as an example of early age CSR.

[34]   See Weber and Wasieleski (2003), Matten et al. (2003) and especially Dentchev (2004) of a clear overview of the evolution of and in concepts within the CSR-field. In 1979, Carroll proposed a three dimensional CSR concept. The first dimension held the kinds of responsibilities business hold to society (economic, legal, ethical, discretionary). A second dimension contains the different modes business organizations can adopt with regard to those responsibilities (reaction, defence, accommodation, pro-action). The third dimension consisted of the social issues business should address. Even though this was left unanswered – issues change and differ for different industries and communities – Carroll's three dimensional model became well known to both academics and practicioners. Watrick and Cochran (1985) proposed issues management as the solution for Carroll's left open issues dimension. Not what issues are to be tackled by business as a social responsibility, but rather how well organizations are ready to prompt systematic and interactive responses to unexpected changes, is the question of issue management. Wood (1991) argued for different levels of analysis of CSR (institutional, organizational, individual) in order to get a better insight into what responsibility principles were adequate. Against Carroll's 'kinds of responsibilities' dimension, Wood argued that identifying categories does not say something about what motivates people to act. It seemed to Wood that responsibility principles ought to do just that. Therefore, she proposed the principle of managerial discretion at the individual level, the principle of public responsibility at the organizational level, and the principle of legitimacy at the institutional level. But besides principles, Wood also saw processes and outcomes as dimension to CSR. Processes had to integrate environmental assessment, stakeholder management and issues management. Outcomes were social impacts and programmes. Swanson (1995) is to be mentioned for the emphasis on the importance of personal values of managers and employees as to how CSR can be integrated into corporate culture. Finally, Matten et al. (2003) argue for Corporate

stuck in differences between these variations – CSP is better than CSR or the other way round or CC is beyond both – ending the discussion with the idea that people are talking about different things. I certainly do not agree with that. What these discussions cloud is first, that all those concepts emphasize business relating to society, and second, that even though the subsequent rejection of one concept in favour of another coincided with the gradual integration of the stakeholder approach and the network perspective, today all of these concepts are used with reference to the stakeholder concept and the network perspective. Let me explain. Corporate social 'performance' analyses and measures how expectations of society towards business are answered in terms of performance on issues. Corporate social 'responsibility' takes up stakeholder analysis in that it identifies those groups in society to whom business holds responsibilities. Corporate social 'responsiveness' emphasizes the interaction between business and groups in society. And finally, corporate 'citizenship' acknowledges the network perspective in that it moves the business organization out of the centre of the stakeholder map and regards it as a societal player amongst others. If this was all that was to it, the discussions on what term to use would be totally worthwhile, and probably should end up in all of us talking of corporate citizenship. However, these discussions fail to see that when any of these terms are used today, they all tap in to the stakeholder approach and the network perspective.

For example,[35] as I have shown in Vandekerckhove and Commers (2005), the European Commission's framework on Corporate Social Responsibility (2002)

Citizenship as a concept, because it encompasses both the notion of corporation as a citizen and hence forming a community together with other citizens, as well as the notion of corporations compensating or correcting for government failing to be the guarantor of citizenship. They argue that due to globalization, the state's power has been cut back as a provider of social, civil and political rights. Corporations have taken over more or less of that power and hence have a role to play in the promotion and protection of citizenship.

[35] Other examples are:

- Marjorie Kelly (2002) arguing that the next step for CSR is economic democracy.
- The Business Leaders Forum (BLF 2004) prime objective in the Latin America and Caribbean region is 'to change current practice to good practice through: networks of civil society organizations, including non-governmental and community based organizations and academia; evolving intermediary structures and institutions such as business coalitions promoting responsible business practices; providing links and partnerships with established business networks such as chambers of commerce, management development organizations, trade associations, academia serving business executives'.
- Although the Business for Social Responsibility (BSR 2003) reports of the meeting of CSR leaders does not mention networks, it does speak of applying the stakeholder model, being accountable to stakeholders, empowering stakeholders, provide information useful to stakeholders. But they have also issued a publication dealing with engaging with NGOs, and recognize that many find value in dialogue when seeking to enhance CSR.

mentions stakeholder relations and definitely uses a network perspective.[36] The definition of CSR mentions integrating interaction with stakeholders in business operations (EC 2002, 7), puts stakeholder expectations at the heart of business strategies (EC 2002, 7), and acknowledges the potential of CSR to strengthen the symbiotic relationship between enterprises and society (EC 2002, 12). All this clicks with corporations as webs of relations and with seeing stakeholder voice as legitimate. The 'Communication from the Commission' also sees the principle of continuous improvement and innovation at the heart of business strategies (EC 2002, 7, 12, 22), and sees CSR as an element of a new form of governance, helping to respond to fundamental changes (EC 2002, 8). It also touches the issue of risk management (EC 2002, 12). In our opinion, these are all starting points to further develop a European framework on CSR along the metaphors of environmental change as driver for the corporation. The same goes for communication and collaborative action as metaphors that best describe how businesses should be managed. The 'Communication from the Commission' sees the experience of co-operatives in stakeholder dialogue and participative management as a reference for good CSR practice (EC 2002, 13), and states that even though stakeholders might have conflicting interests, a partnership-based approach can be used to build consensus (EC 2002, 22).

Hence, even though the succession of terms makes sense when one takes a diachronic view to point at the increasing conceptual constituency of 'stakeholder' and 'network' in the terms used to talk about relationships between business and society, it makes much less sense when taking the synchronic view of how all these terms are used today, for all of them are now conceptually constituted by reference to 'stakeholder' and 'network'. At the outset of this chapter, I wrote that I will not be making a distinction between public sector organizations, private business organizations and NGOs. Even though one of the reasons I gave was the growing influence of private business organizations (corporations) over public organizations, using the term CSR for non-corporate actors would seem inappropriate. Therefore, I will use the term *Organizational Social Responsibility (OSR)* to denote the CSR-network-stakeholder concept for any kind of organization, whether they are corporate or non-corporate actors.

---

[36]   My argument is based on the usage of network metaphors in the Commissions Communication on CSR (EC 2002). As a first follow-up to that Communication, the Commission held several rounds of multi-stakeholder dialogues at European level throughout 2003 and 2004. In Vandekerckhove and Commers (2005) we argue that if the Commission wants to be consistent with its network perspective, they should be promoting – or even make it mandatory – multi-stakeholder dialogues at the micro-level.

Whistleblowing, OSR and the Network Perspective

The first construct of a normative legitimation for whistleblowing policies through OSR is possible by focussing on the network perspective and by taking that perspective on OSR to its fullest implications.

Calton and Lad (1995) have used the concept 'network governance' to designate a process by which social contract theory could best be understood and implemented within organizational settings. They focus on processes through which trust is being created and maintained within continuing contractual relations. According to Calton and Lad, this is a necessity in order to realize the competitive and ethical potential of network-organizations. Calton and Lad see networks as an emerging alternative to market transactions and hierarchical governance, because 'network relationships overlay [...] simple, dyadic (two-party) market transactions and bilateral relationships within hierarchies' (Calton and Lad 1995, 274).

In fact, they argue two things. First, to perceive social contracting relations in organizations from a network perspective, beats the neoclassical economic theory and the agency theory, for these are dyadic interaction-based contractual theories of the firm, whereas a network perspective is able to integrate repeated, multi-party transactions, potentially conflicting and non-maximizing interest, goals and stakes. Second, for Calton and Lad (1995, 274):

> social contracting within networks is, essentially, an interactive, participant-driven, developmental trust-building process [and this] works to create and sustain a durable, resilient basis for effective and efficient organizational interaction by minimizing the moral hazard of participant opportunism.

Now, Calton and Lad link trust to their concept of network governance, and they write that:

> to the extent that trust is the essential glue and lubricant for long-term, value-creating organizational interactions, effective network governance would seem to hold the key, not only for ethical, socially responsible business performance, but also for business survival in the ever more turbulent competitive environment' (Calton and Lad, 1995: 274).

Calton and Lad name seven propositions about network governance. These propositions are both descriptive as well as normative prescriptive. In their descriptive dimension, they match the network metaphors I mentioned earlier on in this chapter. The prescriptive, normative dimension of their propositions comes down to:

*   a widespread and formal application of a micro social contracting process for defining and addressing collective, network-based problems;

- the right to negotiate should be regarded as the right which drives the interaction and legitimizes the voice of autonomous, interdependent participants;
- unilateral power is a risk within the exchange structure of relational contracts, therefore, the maintenance of trust among network participants requires an equitable resolution of the problem of unequal power within relational contracts.

There is one particular proposition I would like to highlight here: 'The maintenance of trust among network participants requires an equitable resolution of the problem of unequal power within relational contracts' (Calton and Lad 1995, 283). Calton and Lad reproach neoclassical economic theory and agency theory for simply assuming bilateral power in voluntary contracting. Reality shows unilateral power does exist and can come up within the exchange structure of relational contracts, particularly in the form of discretionary authority. It is absolutely necessary for a trust creating and maintaining network governance, to recognize and compensate the existence of power differentials (Calton and Lad 1995, 283–84). Such compensation needs institutional structures that serve the function of monitoring and enforcing the terms of the implicit contract. With Hill and Jones (1992), Calton and Lad propose trade unions, consumer organizations and other special interest groups that have evolved to represent the interests of stakeholders. One of the concrete aims of these institutional structures is to reduce the information asymmetry which exists between managers and stakeholders.

It is exactly here that whistleblowing policies find their legitimacy as an OSR tool within a network perspective. OSR as network governance is a framework of 'preconditions, processes and outcomes' (Calton and Lad 1995, 278) in which the preconditions are multilateral enforceable institutional structures balancing power and information amongst stakeholders. A whistleblowing policy is such an institutional structure.

The OSR-network construct legitimating whistleblowing policies is visualized in Figure 3.6, connecting the primary globalization semantic concepts of network, governance, decentralization and stakeholder. I argued that network governance is trust building to the extent that it is able to create a power balance in interactions within decentralized organizations. Whistleblowing policies are a way of creating such a power balance by identifying what asymmetries of information need to be balanced and how.

Whistleblowing, OSR, Stakeholders and Purpose

A second possible construction uses the references to the stakeholder concept to link OSR with whistleblowing policies. I already argued that stakeholder theory has made our outlook shift from 'business and society' to 'business in society'. This makes reflection about the purpose of business organizations appropriate. It is this line of thought I will connect to whistleblowing.

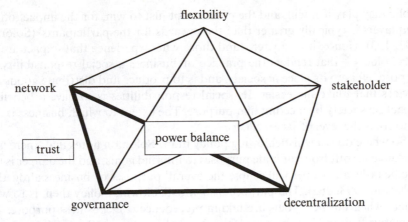

Figure 3.6   Globalization semantic (OSR-network)

Robert Solomon develops an Aristotelian approach to business in *Ethics and Excellence* (1993). He explicitly bases that approach on the stakeholder concept, in that he sees '[the] great virtue of the notion of the stakeholder [...] is its sense of *holism*' (Solomon 1993, 180, emphasis in original). He understands holism as a concern for the whole rather than some of the parts and as an emphasis on the big picture 'rather than the analysis of narrowly circumscribed details such as profits' (Solomon 1993, 180). In that sense, the social responsibilities of corporations are their very point of existence, because the purpose of business is to do what business has always been meant to do – purpose as the Aristotelian notion of *telos* – which is to 'enrich society as well as the pockets of those who are responsible for the enriching' (Solomon 1993, 181). Solomon envisages responsibility and excellence as corporate virtues. Solomon states that excellence is to be measured by its *telos* or purpose and that the excellent corporation entails both cooperation and competition to the extent that they represent a contribution to the larger hole. But excellence is 'not skill for its own sake' (Solomon 1993, 159). Seen like that, market competition is secondary to external requirements and standards that point at the place of business as a practice in the larger whole – society. Solomon distinguishes goals from purposes. Business as a practice has a purpose, and goals are internal to the practice. The purpose of a practice is the reason for engaging in the practice. But the goals are defined and structured by the practice itself. Solomon explains this by giving the example of a football game. The purpose of the game is to kill time, but the goal of the game is to get the ball across a certain line more times than the other team. If in business goals would gain priority over purpose, then business is no longer regarded as a practice but rather as a game.[37] However: 'Business is not an isolated game, which the

---

[37]   Solomon insists that game theory is not just a model for business but an ideology because it is instructive. 'But however enticing the paradoxes of formalism (and they are

public may play if it will, and the point is not just to win, for the impact on the nonplayers is typically greater than the rewards for the participants' (Solomon 1993, 123). Hence, it is impact – and those who experience that impact are the stakeholders – that renders the practice of business a social responsibility. Its purpose refers to its place *in* society, and is to produce and distribute goods and services that make life easier. Its social responsibilities is to have a beneficial impact on society by meeting that purpose. The extent to which business is able to do so, is the level of its excellence.

So where does a whistleblowing policy fit in? Solomon notes that 'there is an unavoidable shift from ultimate purposes to internal goals, and the danger is that specific tasks and duties will eclipse the overall purposes of business altogether' (Solomon 1993, 262). The purpose of a whistleblowing policy then, is to warn society when business goals are taking precedence over business purpose. The normative legitimation for whistleblowing policies here is that society must be warned when the impact of organizational operations will have a negative impact on society and the organization concerned is not at its proper place – or off-track with regard to its *telos*, to bring about general prosperity.

Solomon develops the whole argument about stakeholders, purpose and social responsibility around private business organizations. However, it is easy to extend it to governmental organizations as well as to NGOs. Of course, it seems quite obvious that a governmental organization has the purpose to further the general well being. The same goes for NGOs, still enjoying the image of the 'good guys'. Elsewhere (Vandekerckhove 2003; 2004) I have argued that in their conception phase, NGOs are ethical responses to intolerable situations, but that the danger for goal-blurring and goal-displacement is huge for NGOs. It seems to me that NGOs too should, because of their social responsibilities, institutionalize whistle-blowing.

Figure 3.7 visualizes the OSR-stakeholder construct within the globalization semantic. I argued that decentralization can lead organizational purpose to get out of sight, resulting in a negative impact on stakeholders. It is the stakeholders who – through whistleblowing – can ensure the organization stays focused on purpose.

Whistleblowing and Responsibility – Accountability

In the beginning of this chapter I wrote that complexity had its organizational exponent in decentralization – one of the key concepts of the globalization semantic. I also wrote that there were two decentralization processes at work: an external and an internal one. In the previous sections, a normative legitimation

---

indeed captivating), it is a mistake to think that by solving technical problems in a theory that is already off the mark we will thereby resolve the criticism that it is indeed off the mark' (Solomon 1993, 64).

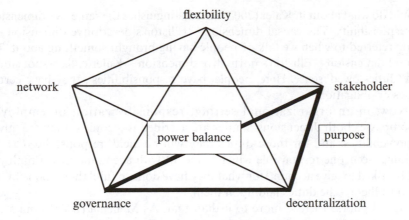

Figure 3.7 Globalization semantic (OSR-stakeholder)

for whistleblowing policies linked to the external, societal decentralization process was constructed around OSR-concepts. Here, in this section, I will construct a normative legitimation taking up the internal decentralization process.

Also, I wrote that organizational decentralization involved giving employees lower in the hierarchy more discretionary power – making the organizational hierarchy appear flatter. Yet, giving more discretionary power to people in an organization implies a responsibilization of those people. If decisions are made in a decentralized way, the organization runs a higher risk than when decisions are taken in a central point at the top and then carried out towards the bottom. The higher risk in decentralized decision making exists in two ways. First, decisions taken by different people might contradict each other. And two, more decision making power might mean more room for opportunism, in taking decisions to further personal interests but harming the organization. The responsibilization of employees is a safeguard to those risks. It is clear that loyalty becomes important here. There is a section further in this chapter that deals with that. Here, I would like to focus on two concepts involved in responsibilization: *responsibility* and *accountability*. There is a tension between the two concepts. They are often used interchangeably, but whenever they are used that way, it is accountability that is meant, for that is the more dominant concept of the two in the organizational discourse. Nevertheless, I will construct a normative legitimation for whistle-blowing policies around both concepts, thereby showing the tension between them.

Responsibility

Elliston (1982b) notes that in an organizational setting, responsibility has two dimensions. The descriptive dimension refers to a causal relationship between one's actions and an outcome, whereas the normative dimensions identifies who should do what about it. Kaler (2002) also distinguishes the same two dimensions to responsibility. The causal dimension – Elliston's descriptive dimension – is being referred to when we talk of people having brought something about. The second dimension – Elliston's normative dimension – Kaler calls responsibility in a 'duties owed' sense. Here, people 'have responsibilities', they have certain duties or obligations.

Now, in an organizational setting, responsibilization of employees encompasses both dimensions. Duties are ascribed to people – they are 'given' responsibilities, and for those duties they will be 'held' responsible. It is this 'holding' someone responsible which is meant with accountability. Employees will be asked to 'give account' for what they have done to fulfil the responsibilities given to them – the duties laid upon them.

But of course there is more to it than that. As Mellema (2003) points out, investigations into recent scandals involving firms such as Enron, Arthur Andersen, and WorldCom have shown the difficulties of identifying particular individuals to blame – responsibility in the causal sense – for particular events. Mellema argues that within the context of highly complex situations – and situations brought about by organizational practices tend to be highly complex – the notion of 'ethical distance' might shed some light on how collective the 'collective responsibility' for organizational outcomes is.[38]

Mellema regards 'ethical distance' as analogous to 'moral distance', but where there is 'moral distance' between one who performs an action and one who forms moral judgments about that action, 'ethical distance' refers to the distance between a moral agent and a state of affairs which has occurred. In the case of organizational crime or scandal, people belonging to the organization might try to distance themselves from that crime or scandalous outcome by arguing that their involvement in the events leading up to the crime or outcome was significantly less extensive than the involvement of others.

Mellema argues that there is an inverse correlation between ethical distance and degrees of responsibility – in Elliston's descriptive sense. He gives several criteria in which to attribute more or less distance and hence responsibility. In general, the more involvement someone has in bringing about an outcome, the less distance there is between that someone and the outcome. As actions increasing

---

[38] I consider Mellema's characterization of ethical distance in terms of moral responsibility as important because it succeeds in steering away from two extremes on the issue of responsibility for organizational outcomes. The first extreme is 'organizational scapegoating', referring to groups or corporations 'pointing the finger of blame at individuals as a means of focusing the responsibility with an individual (scapegoat) even though some responsibility accurately resides with the group' (Wilson 1993, quoted in Bailey 1997). The other, opposite extreme is 'individual scapetribing', referring to individuals 'pointing the finger of blame at organizations (or groups, institutions, and systems) as means of excusing, or ascribing responsibility for, their personally enacted behaviors' (Bailey 1997, 47).

one's involvement in a group context, Mellema mentions planning a strategy for producing the outcome, initiating the sequence of actions which bring it about, and performing actions with the intent that they contribute to it (Mellema 2003, 127). Another criteria is whether or not there are defined institutional roles at play that require certain specific types of behaviour. If there are such roles, and if behaviour according to those roles leads to a scandalous outcome, then the ethical distance is to be considered greater than when such behaviour is pursued free of such institutional constraints. Finally, one's ethical distance from what happens is less if one belongs to a collective bearing responsibility for what happens than if one does not belong to the collective at all.

It is exactly here that a whistleblowing policy functions. Identifying channels and procedures to raise concern about organizational practices – and how these practices are brought about by the discretionary powers of organization members – recasts the notion of ethical distance between organization members and organizational outcomes. In this sense, the normative legitimation for whistleblowing policies is 'effective responsibilization' of employees. How? Whistleblowing policies recognize the complexity in ascribing responsibilities to individuals with regard to organizational outcomes. However, in offering the possibility to raise concern about practices within an organization one does not have the power to alter or to prevent neither by acting or omission, whistleblowing policies decrease the possible ethical distance in organizations in two ways. First, it makes everyone who has knowledge of practices leading to a certain outcome part of the collective responsible for bringing about the outcome. It thereby expands 'collective responsibility' to include witnesses and bystanders. Hence, being able to blow the whistle under a whistleblowing policy makes it impossible to distance oneself from an outcome based on the claim that one knew what was happening but did not have the power to alter or prevent it, nor to distance oneself on the claim that raising concern was not part of the defined institutional role. Those who knew but didn't raise concern are at least to some degree responsible for the outcome. In this sense, whistleblowing policies can be an expansion of normative responsibilities – duties owed – on which causal responsibility can be attributed.

At the same time however, a whistleblowing policy allows individuals to increase their ethical distance from an outcome. Individuals having knowledge of practices leading to a criminal or scandalous organizational outcome and not having the power to alter or prevent those practices, can distance themselves from the practices and the outcome by raising concern. In this sense, whistleblowing policies can allow individuals to shed off causal responsibility by taking up normative responsibility and act out a 'duty owed'. This too is important in a normative legitimation of whistleblowing policies as 'effective responsibilization'. To the extent that the responsibilization of employees is a call upon the moral agency of individuals, there is the assumption of autonomy of the individual – in Kantian terms. However, as Lovell (2002) has shown, the autonomy of an individual is highly vulnerable to contextual factors.[39] These factors are consequences of exercizing autonomy; consequences in terms of employment, remuneration, colleague support, personal reputation. Lovell shows that the experienced dissonance between what responsibilization suggests and allows results in a diminution of autonomy, and hence 'moral agency becomes the victim of autonomy's frailty' (Lovell 2002, 63). Increased decision-making powers suggest heightened levels of autonomy, but both gained power and suggested autonomy will be constrained if they are not backed by an institutional medium such as a whistleblowing policy. These constrains are at least partly self-imposed, but Lovell sees this as a reason to regard the suppression of moral agency more worrying than overt repression, because the suppression is invisible – 'it is not really happening, but it is' (Lovell 2002, 65).

For the visualization within the globalization semantic (Figure 3.8), the responsibility construct can be summarized as follows: flexibility and decentralization call for the responsibilization of individuals, which implies rendering them duties (control through governance) while recognizing their autonomy as stakeholders.

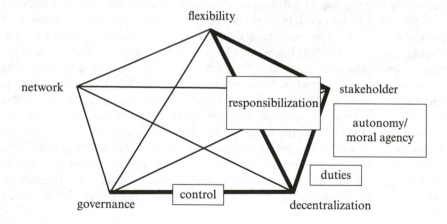

Figure 3.8   Globalization semantic (responsibility)

---

[39]   Lovell's research (2002) consisted of interviewing employees to explore issues within their business lives that had caused them (issues older than four years were left out) or were still causing them ethical discomfort. This means that all cases were real – no hypothetical scenario's were used – as some cases are actually *real time* account of ethical dissonance and the 'travel' between reasoning and action – or how the intention to blow the whistle is self-repressed.

Accountability

Kaler (2002) links responsibility to governance through the concept of accountability.

To be accountable means to provide answers to questions about how well or badly we have carried out our responsibilities. It is giving account of how our causal responsibilities relate to our responsibilities in a 'duties owed' sense. But the account is given to people with legitimate interests. Therefore, accountability is about controlling conduct and preventing misconduct. Kaler distinguishes between 'hard' and 'soft' accountability. Hard accountability is imposed accountability, whilst the soft version is voluntary. But, writes Kaler with regard to soft accountability, 'where, we can ask, is the penal or coercive aspect that will permit it to carry out the controlling function?' (Kaler 2002, 329). There is of course the threat of blame, which can function as a sort of social control, should the answers appear to reveal misconduct or should the answers appear to be fraudulent. Soft accountability is very much the case where social reporting is concerned. However, I am talking about individual accountability in an organizational context. Later I will get back to informative 'soft' accountability in social reporting. Individual accountability in an organizational context is always imposed. It is always a 'hard' form of accountability. This means that the individual who is being held accountable is being vulnerable to punishment by others for what they see as misconduct. Exactly this is where accountability has its fit with corporate governance and governance in general. Governance is a system for directing and controlling, and does so through establishing the structures for decision-making. What these structures point at is that the directing and controlling has a different purpose than serving the interests of those doing the directing and the controlling, and accountability is involved in so far as serving that other purpose is not left to the discretion of those doing the directing and the controlling. If we regard corporate governance from a shareholder point of view – the way it is mostly regarded – then accountability is an issue when there is separation between ownership and control. Management is held accountable by the board which in turn needs to answer to shareholders. In a democratic governance system, the government is held accountable by the parliament which in turn is elected by the public.

However, in an interesting paper on accountability discourses, Miriam Green (2003) has argued that the direction of accountability has been turned around since the 1980s. Responsibilization of employees is a turning around of accountability in the sense that employees are made accountable to power.

She argues that in the 1970s official accounting bodies acknowledged that the disclosure of information to various stakeholders was what accountability was about and that this was essential for democracy. Apparently Keynes and Stone (the 1984 Nobel prizewinner in economics) emphasized the importance of making information about the economy public – 'accounting expressionism' – in order to obtain consensus on the management of economic matters among the public

(Green 2003, 3, citing Suzuki 2003). This democratic ideal was at play for those in corporate bodies as well, where it was a question of those with decision-making powers to propose, explain and justify the use of these powers to those without (Green 2003, 3, citing Medawar 1976). Even though Green takes a critical view on the extent to which the apparent high ideal of accountability was realized up till the 1970s, especially in terms of social accountability, she sees a particular erosion of that ideal taking place from the 1980s onwards. She sees two factors playing an important role: first, the ideology of the free market – and with that the economy of pursuing narrow ends rather than the good of the wider collective, and second the increasing influence of the global market economy over individual and collective lives, who are increasingly powerless to influence the system. Green states that these factors have led to 'an almost complete abrogation of accountability both in practice and also with a changed discourse as to what counts legitimately as accountability' (Green 2003, 5).

Interesting is that Green links this notion of erosion of accountability to changes in organization structure. Decentralization – a flatter hierarchy promising more responsibility, skill and empowerment to employees – tends to produce a management style exercising an even tighter control than under previous structures, with employees being strictly accountable to their managers and very little accountability in the other direction. Decentralized structures leave more decision-making power to lower managers. Like this, they have more autonomy with regard to rules and procedures, giving them more flexibility to adequately cope with complexity – such is, I have argued, the rationale. But of course, as I have argued with Kaler, accountability as a governance concept demands that those given certain responsibilities will have to give account of how they have carried those out.[40] Hence, more autonomy for lower managers with regard to rules and procedures implies more accountability of those managers to their bosses. Green argues that this implies that the subordinates of those managers must follow their instructions at all costs. In this sense, accountability loses all external reference points. Employees are not encouraged to protect consumers or the community. All they need to do is 'satisfy their managers wishes, however whimsical, irrational or incomprehensible they might seem' (Green 2003, 6).

Bureaucratic structures had a stable set of procedures, rules and standards constituting an external reference point against which management instructions could be checked. Decentralized structures do not have that. Whistleblowing policies might compensate for that. But how would the fact that whistleblowing policies were a 'replacement' of the external reference point be a normative legitimation for those whistleblowing policies? First, the external reference point ensured the decision was carried out top-down the way it was decided at the top. In that sense, it was a control instrument. Second, the external reference point function of bureaucratic rules and procedures protected employees from

---

[40]   To a large extent, the responsibilities given to lower managers is in terms of targets to be met, and the question of accountability is whether targets have been met or not.

managerial subjective whims or internal politics.[41] If whistleblowing policies could function as a correction to the power imbalance in decentralized structures, then they would find their normative legitimation there. Third, the external reference point ensured an ethico-political purpose of bureaucratic processes and structures in the sense that they were to ensure fairness, justice and equality. If whistleblowing policies could function that way, they would find their normative legitimation there.

Can whistleblowing policies take over the functions of the bureaucratic external reference point? In a decentralized organizational structure, a whistleblowing policy increases the accountability of lower managers to their bosses, because the subordinates of those lower managers can reveal possible fraudulent 'accounts' on the part of the lower managers. Hence the first function of the external reference point can be taken up by a whistleblowing policy. The second function can also be taken up by a whistleblowing policy, as subordinates are able to disclose the work procedures and risks with which they are demanded to work. Correcting a power imbalance through a whistleblowing policy comes within reach of the third function, ensuring an ethico-political purpose of fairness, justice and equality. This can only be carried out by a whistleblowing policy to the extent that such a policy is able to widen the accountability beyond simply whether or not targets have been reached.

Hence, a whistleblowing policy can find its normative legitimation through its links with the concept of accountability if it allows employees to jump hierarchical steps relatively easy. At all times it must be possible for them to disclose information or raise concern to the board or even the shareholders. This would allow the whistleblowing policy to take up the first function. But for the second and the third to be ensured, there must also be the possibility of external disclosure. The extent to which whistleblowing policies allow external disclosure – regulator, parliament, media – widens accountability and re-turns the direction of accountability. But then, it is a question of collective accountability, which is something I will discuss later. As far as individual accountability is concerned, to base a normative legitimation for whistleblowing policies on, it designates an increasing of the upwards accountability of low managers.

Thus, summing up the accountability construct in order to visualize it within the globalization semantic (Figure 3.9): flexibility and decentralization imply decision-making by autonomous individuals; controlling that decision-making is done through whistleblowing policies, by increasing upwards accountability of line managers and downward accountability by substituting the 'bureaucratic external reference point' – hence a networked governance.

---

[41]   In this sense I have argued that flexibility and decentralization in organizations implies the return of charismatic leadership (Vandekerckhove 2002).

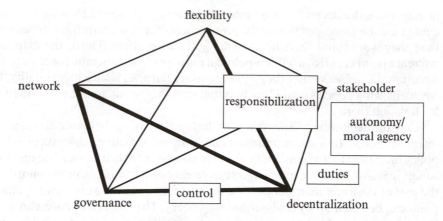

Figure 3.9   Globalization semantic (accountability)

Whistleblowing and Integrity

Integrity is a very popular concept. Integrity is something we want more of, and something we want everybody to have more of: government officials, employees and politicians. Integrity is present in many codes of conduct and mission statements. I see two reasons for its popularity.

The first reason is that, as Solomon points out:

> part of the demand for 'integrity' ... has to do ... with the expectation that [employees] will (on the basis of past experience and accumulated confidence) resist and perhaps straighten out structural distortions in the organization (Solomon 1993, 81–2).

The expectation is that people with integrity will resist opportunism. And in that sense, the demand for integrity is a demand for predictability. People are given more decision-making power, but if the way they will make the decision or even what decisions will be taken are predictable, then the risk of uncertainty is reduced. Clearly, the demand for integrity is symptomatic for the perception of inability to control through structure.

A second reason I see for the popularity of integrity is its connotation of self-regulation. Lynn Sharp Paine (1994) distinguishes two kinds of strategies to implement organizational policies: compliance strategies and integrity strategies. The ethic of compliance strategies is to observe and obey rules and orders. These strategies are based on an anthropological model of humans as autonomous creatures, who's behaviour is guided by material self-interest. Integrity strategies on the other hand, have an ethic of self-regulation based on chosen standards. And the anthropological model assumes that humans are social creatures, not guided merely by material self-interest, but also by values, ideals, friendship, and peers. For De George too, integrity implies self-imposed norms. And this is the reason why integrity is a word which is accepted and used more easily by companies than is the term morality. But these norms must nevertheless be ethically justifiable, and they must be 'proper, and integral to the self-imposed process of forming a whole with a set of positive values' (De George, 1993, 6–7). De George, just like Paine, describes the subject of integrity as autonomous, as acting willingly, but also as forming a whole with values.

So, apparently the term 'integrity' is used referring to self-regulation, autonomy and values. But how do these constitute the concept of integrity, and how can whistleblowing be linked to that?

Robert Meyers (1999) has argued quite extensively on the relation between integrity, autonomy and values. Individual autonomy is the ideal of individual behaviour and is achieved to the extent that one's actions are governed by one's own choices. Personal integrity too is an ideal, requiring people to be true to 'all values that apply to them' (Meyers 1999, 73). Personal integrity requires that persons pay allegiance in their actions both to relative values they happen to have and to whatever values 'should happen to be' (Meyers 1999, 143).[42] Meyers argues that individual autonomy can not be seen independently from personal integrity. First of all they are not independent, for governing your actions by your choices achieves little if those choices themselves are not true to your values. But secondly they should not be independent, for it is by exercising their capacity to individual autonomy – to govern their own actions by their own choices – that people develop a variety of personal concerns. And it is personal integrity which then requires them to take proper account of those concerns. In other words, individual autonomy leads people to value things independently of their commitment to the overall good. Therefore, promoting the overall good implies an equal importance of both individual autonomy and personal integrity.[43] In that sense, individual autonomy and personal integrity are correlative aspects of a more comprehensive ideal of individual behaviour which Meyers calls 'self-governance'. A self-governed person is then:

> not someone who simply performs actions that will reflect her values and commitments as fully and accurately as the circumstances allow; she is someone who also tries to make the circumstances ones in which her values and commitments can be reflected as fully and accurately as possible (Meyers 1999, 144).

---

[42] The whole of Meyers' book is actually an argumentation against value dualism.

[43] This requires restrictions against people inflicting harms on other people that they are not required to bring upon themselves. Otherwise, individual autonomy is assigned a greater importance than personal integrity. Secondly, whenever a prerogative – a principle having the effect of permitting individuals to refrain from bringing about the best available outcome – permits a person to decline from bringing a certain harm upon himself, there should be restrictions in place that forbid other people to inflict that harm upon her. Other wise, personal integrity is assigned a greater importance than individual autonomy (Meyers 1999, 76).

Written law and unwritten conventions, to a large extent shaping the possibilities of action, will be of concern to such a person, but a self-governed person will also enter into negotiations to set and live by rules from which each one of them would benefit.

Solomon argues in a similar vein, contrasting a person with integrity in an organizational setting with 'the opportunist' and 'the chameleon' (Solomon 1993, 168–74). Neither of them is dishonest or hypocrite, nor do they involve inconsistency. The opportunist is true to himself, a self regarded as in hermitage, divided from any sense of community and in this sense the contrary of a self in the midst of others and together with them. The opportunist has no principles relating to the overall good but 'does whatever it takes'. Hence, the opportunist is an ethical hermit merely using others as his instruments. The chameleon's drive is to 'fit in and do whatever seems to please other people'. Solomon describes the organizational chameleon as the typical corporate 'yes-man'. The chameleon's values and actions are consistent with whatever values happen to be in vigour. However, within an organizational setting, this is a fragile consistency, as it depends on the uniformity of other people. Exactly this uniformity is tenuous in today's organization, characterized by flexibility, decentralization, uncertainty and hence contradictory demands and principles. Thus, the opportunist lacks integrity because he is true to a self cut loose from its social situation. And the chameleon lacks integrity because he has no self but only a reflection of the social situation.

Solomon insists on integrity as 'true to self' that is part of a community. So does Meyers. Both refer to integrity as a unity between the personal and the social. And both also refer to integrity as entailing autonomy – as the unity of actions and values. This latter sense of unity is what is heard in popular adagios, defining integrity as 'walking the talk' or 'practice what you preach'. However, that other sense of unity – between the personal and the social – seems just as important to the concept of integrity within an organizational setting. For it is not the loner that is valued in today's organization, but rather the team-player. But what is the content of integrity when it is to be constituted by both senses of unity?

Etymologically, integrity draws on the Latin *integritas* – wholeness, and *integer* – untouched, what has not taken a turn yet, still in abeyance. The latter obviously adds to the concept of integrity the moral connotations of objectivity, impartiality, incorrupt – in a modern sense of the word. The former meaning – wholeness – is opposed to an older meaning of corrupt as fragmented. Late capitalism has left us with fragmented identities, but that does not mean we regard ourselves as corrupt. But we do seem to be convinced that it takes people of integrity to fight corruption – or as I wrote earlier, with Solomon, people of integrity are regarded as able to resist opportunism.

This bears implications for how we can understand integrity to be a sense of 'wholeness' or unity. I see four levels at which we might understand integrity to designate a 'wholeness' or the unities of action/values and personal/social. These four levels are: the functional level, the temporal level, the spatial level, and the interpersonal level. In what follows, I will argue that the first three levels at which we might understand integrity to designate a 'wholeness' are untenable in an organizational context in which meaning-giving is done within the globalization semantic. The fourth level, which is the interpersonal level however renders the concept of integrity as 'wholeness' a meaning consistent with the globalization semantic. It is that understanding of integrity I will then link whistleblowing to.

At the functional level, integrity designates a wholeness of personality throughout the different roles through which an individual functions. It is based on the psychological foundation of a well-integrated personality, referring to a constant identity when being a mother, a friend, a worker, a customer, etc. I am at home who I am at work as in the pub or the play field, in the shower and in bed. However, it is unclear just what that identity might be. Etzioni writes that:

> [people] can, and do, use these multi-memberships (as well as limited, but not trivial, ability to choose one's work and residential communities) to protect themselves from excessive pressure by any one community (Etzioni 1998, xiv).

But then, who or what is the 'self' they are protecting? Is it the mother at work, or the customer as a friend? The worker might be a volunteer at one place but an employee in another, and within the same organization, a single employee might have both subordinates and bosses. All these denote several role-patterns and manifest themselves in different contexts (see Luhmann's functional differentiation). From an organizational perspective, it is not always desirable or efficient to have the mother at work or the friend as a customer. As an individual, we are part of many communities, and carry out different roles with different values in each of them. Hence, the way in which the notion of a well-integrated personality makes sense is as a successful balancing of all our role prescriptions so that the unity of action/value in each of our roles does not imply a fragmentation of that unity in a different role. If Etzioni's words are read that way, I agree – although in that case he should have written it like that – but still, it remains unconvincing in terms of integrity. Let us consider the hypothetical situation that we have the unity of action/values within each role pattern. The unity of personal/social would then be the possibility of a coexistence of all our unities of action/values. But a coexistence is not really a unity, and the sense of wholeness a coexistence entails is but a mere addition.

At the temporal level, integrity refers to a wholeness or unity of action/value and personal/social over a time period. This means that not only are there to be those unities, they are also to be kept constant. I am today who I was yesterday and that is who I will be tomorrow. Integrity at this level implies we cannot change our minds, our convictions nor our values. Of course, to be like that would make us very predictable and as such it would be a small risk giving us more decision-making power. Still, integrity at a temporal level seems irreconcilable with today's organizational context, characterized by constant change, new opportunities, new challenges, and flexibility. Dealing with new situations surely implies approaching the newness of the situation with already acquired value appraisals. Yet dealing with those new situations will just as well entail questioning the appropriateness and maintainability of those value appraisals, and might very well alter them. Moreover, temporal integrity seems to hold an internal contradiction in the required unity between the personal and the social. Even if I were not to change my personal value appraisal, all or some of the relevant others might change theirs. They might do so in such a way that causes a shift in the social value appraisal. Hence, if I am to maintain a unity between the personal and the social, an evolution in social values requires me both to question my personal value appraisal and the social value appraisal. And, such a questioning implies a possibility of change. Thus, although a certain predictability is sought for in the organizational demand for integrity, the organizational context and the personal/social unity itself also demand a continuous questioning of the personal and the social.

The third level at which integrity as wholeness could be thought, is the spatial level. Earlier in this chapter I wrote that flexibility, as one of the key concepts of the globalization semantic, partly referred to the recognition of the existence of geographically spread multiple sets of rules and norms regarding organizing, production, labour, and marketing. The flexible organization incorporates the existence of those different sets into its strategic planning. This is most blatantly the case in transnational organizations. But indirectly – it does regard their own actions but their actions presuppose other organizational actions in different regions – it also holds for SMEs, or for example for the self-employed carpenter and the various price-quality-origins of the wood he or she uses. Hence, integrity at the spatial level can be described as the wholeness of organizational practices across communal boundaries. An organizational practice entails behaviour in function of organizational goals and this behaviour is always carried out within relations. Both aspects of an organizational practice – behaviour and relations – pose a problem for integrity of today's organization, if it is to be understood at the spatial level. Crossing communal borders implies that the same behaviour will not be maintainable, for the simple reason that different regions have different norms and regulation about behaviour. Also, the kind of organizational activity differs according to its geographical presence. Designing a product, producing the product, market the product for consumption, all these different activities are performed in different regions of the world, just as the place of decision making regarding that spread is also located in specific areas, namely, where it is most convenient. This convenience is a trade off between a number of factors such as labour costs, regulative burdens, availability of resources, risks, etc. The point is however that these different organizational activities require different relations. For example, workers require different representation mechanisms than consumers. In this sense, the same relational frame for organizational practices across communal boundaries is not desirable.

Thus, the notion of integrity at spatial level, as a wholeness of organizational practices across boundaries, seems to implode, because the same behaviour across communal boundaries is not acceptable and neither are the same relations across these boundaries desirable.

But are there no ways to resist such an implosion of the notion of integrity at spatial level? Let's see. One could argue that integrity at spatial level can only mean a wholeness of intention of actions across communal boundaries. This would allow and even implicate that the concrete behaviour and relations that embody a particular intention would differ from region to region. The work of Geert Hofstede seems relevant here. Apart from the five dimensional framework for positioning countries (power distance, individualism, uncertainty avoidance, masculinity, and long term orientation), Hofstede's research also provides sets of very concrete 'do's and don'ts' with regard to dress-code, eating, gift giving, communication, etc. But what this does is to emphasize cultural relativism; it is not interested in 'wholeness' but merely offers insights into what 'the Romans' do and why, so that 'when in Rome', one could 'do what the Romans do'.

Another candidate to avoid the implosion of the notion of integrity at spatial level is the 'Integrated Social Contract Theory' (ISCT) developed by Donaldson and Dunfee (1995; 1999). ISCT recognizes the existence of community specific norms, but does not get stuck in cultural relativism. Every community generates norms and rules. These are authentic when they are supported both in attitude as well as in behaviour by a substantial majority of the members of that community. However, ISCT limits the relativism of the 'moral free space' by only taking those norms and rules into consideration which are not only authentic but legitimate as well. Authentic norms are legitimate when they are compatible with what Donaldson and Dunfee call 'hypernorms'. These are principles fundamental for human existence and are reflected in all religious, philosophical and cultural beliefs. Coming back to our problem of integrity at spatial level, or the wholeness of organizational practices across communal boundaries, the ISCT approach implies that behaviour and relations attributed to organizational actions can differ across communities, yet still maintain integrity, as long as the behaviour and relations correspond with legitimate authentic norms and rules within the respective community.

The crux of the matter is not the authenticity of the norms; Hofstede's 'do's and don'ts' can be regarded as an impressive listing of those. Rather, it is the legitimacy of authentic community norms and rules, or, their compatibility with hypernorms which is of crucial importance. And that is the problem, for the weak point in ISCT is precisely the existence and especially the identification of hypernorms. ISCT would have the same problem as we are examining here in identifying what integrity is, and would name honesty and trustworthiness rather than integrity as hypernorm. Integrity at spatial level would thus imply behaviour within relations that manifest honesty and trustworthiness in specific communities. But then there is no longer the need to fill in the concept of integrity, for we could content ourselves with honesty and trustworthiness.

Thus, neither integrity as the wholeness of intention of actions across communal boundaries, nor the ISCT approach can resist the implosion of the notion of integrity at spatial level. Nevertheless, it was this kind of integrity that featured as the central problem to De George's book on integrity in international business (De

George 1993). One of the solutions he proposes in that book is solving dilemmas through ethical displacement. In short, this tells us to look for ways out of a dilemma by taking them to a different level than that at which they appear. The individual employee, conscious about company policies and code of conduct, might find him/herself in a situation in which the local custom or the situational circumstances demand behaviour and relations that pose a dilemma. A good way to deal with this is, according to De George, to take the dilemma to a different level, meaning to talk the dilemma through with colleagues or with one's superior. It is this theme that I will now develop further. I have already examined integrity at the functional, the temporal and the spatial level, but neither of the three levels could give the concept of integrity a meaning that could be constructed consistently within the globalization semantic. Ethical displacement as taking a personal dilemma to another organizational level however, as I will argue now, is able to give integrity a meaning that is tenable. It is integrity at the interpersonal level.

Exactly of what is integrity a wholeness of at this level? What I am referring to is a wholeness of personality throughout the different dimensions of a situation. What are the different dimensions of a situation? First, there's the perception of a situation. Second, there's the acting in a situation. And third, there is the social dimension of a situation – I share a situation with others. How is there to be a wholeness of those dimensions? Stephen Carter (1997) has defined integrity as the wholeness of three steps: 1) discerning what is right and what is wrong; 2) acting on that discernment; and 3) openly stating the connection between acting and discernment. Carter's three steps correspond to what I have called the three dimensions of a situation. It is in perceiving a situation that we will make sense of – and give meaning to – an experience. This implies a discernment of the perceived situation on a continuum between good and bad. Carter's second step, acting on that discernment, ensures the wholeness of the perception and action dimensions. And his third step involves what I have called the social dimension of a situation.

This seems the most fruitful way to think about integrity – a wholeness of discernment, action and speech, or, integrity at the interpersonal level – especially in an organizational context. It fits well with the two reasons I mentioned for the popularity of the concept of integrity. To act according to self-imposed norms, but justified toward others. This contains the two unities of action/value and personal/social. In justifying the norms, reference is made to values. The justification process links the personal to the social value appraisal. I wrote that Meyers states that a self-governed person enters into negotiations with others in order to have an influence over the circumstances in which that person will have to act. He also writes that it is through those negotiations that the distance between personal and social are diminished.[44] Integrity conceptualized as the

---

[44] Meyer argues that 'negotiating with one's fellows and abiding by the results is something that in fact has considerable value for most people. And to the extent that this is true the distance between the demands of self-governance and the demands of morality will naturally be correspondingly diminished' (Meyers 1999, 145).

wholeness of discernment, action and speech – integrity at the situational level – indeed encompasses a sense of self-regulation, carried out by autonomous yet social individuals.

The other reason I gave for the popularity of integrity was that the demand for integrity was a demand for predictability in the sense that it was symptomatic for the perception of inability to control through structure. Does the concept of integrity which I have just developed fit such a demand? I have argued that the high predictability of integrity at the temporal level makes little sense in an organizational setting. It allows no change and fails to encompass interaction and reflection about values. Integrity at the interpersonal level however, leaves enough flexibility for value reflection and changes in value appraisal to cope with new and complex situations, whilst it also allows a certain control in its third situational dimension, namely communicating about the link between action and value. It is through that communication process that control can be exercised. This communication process should be seen as a learning process, in which distances between personal and social value appraisals are diminished.[45] Hence, predictability of decentralized decision-making and of actions within increased discretionary power is achieved through the insurance that one has to communicate about how one manifests the unity between action and values, and the unity between personal and social value appraisal. Integrity at the interpersonal level not only implies 'walking the talk' but also 'talking the walk'.

It is here that whistleblowing can be linked with integrity. Integrity at the interpersonal level favours whistleblowing. If an employee discerns a situation implicating and under the control of the employing organization as wrongdoing, that employee should come forward by communicating that wrongdoing. In fact, in the case of whistleblowing, two dimensions of integrity coincide, more precisely the acting based on the discernment and the speaking about that discernment. In the context of whistleblowing, speaking up is the act part of integrity. And it is here that a whistleblowing policy founded on integrity finds it normative legitimation. Self-regulation and acting according to self-imposed norms are justified to the extent that 1) individual autonomy is assumed, 2) the perceived situation does not allow control through structure, 3) this self-regulation will contribute to the overall good. The conditions 1 and 2 are fulfilled given the organizational context constituted by the globalization semantic. Condition 3 is fulfilled if we conceptualize integrity at the interpersonal level and include a

---

[45] Such a learning process certainly involves dilemma training, but could also be seen as a way to implement codes of conduct and a way to measure the implementation. Nijhof et al. (2003) talk about the process of responsibilization which breaks down into six subprocesses in which dilemmas are being registered and categorized, a code is written from concrete dilemmas that occur in daily business practice, with indicators referring to activities and feedback loops, through registration and monitoring of internal process risks, and transparent and wide communication within the organization.

whistleblowing policy allowing 'speaking up' to coincide with 'acting according to discernment'. Hence, a whistleblowing policy finds it normative legitimation in the concept of integrity in that it justifies self-regulation.

I argued (see Figure 3.10) that the flexibility required of organizations impede a self-regulation within a network. However, this implies that stakeholders act autonomously (discernment and acting) and decentralized. The impossibility to control through structure (law, command) calls for a network governance based on the accountability of autonomous stakeholders (speaking up about discernment and acting).

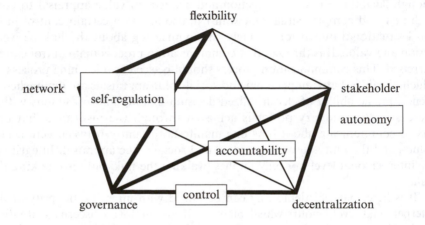

Figure 3.10 Globalization semantic (integrity)

Whistleblowing and Loyalty

In this section, I will construct a normative legitimation for whistleblowing policies on the notion of organizational loyalty. I consider this construction even more crucial than the previous one. The reason is that throughout the literature,[46] whistleblowing has been regarded as conflicting with loyalty. Hence, to create a conceptual constituency for whistleblowing from loyalty is not that straightforward. The way I will go about this task is by looking at what concept of loyalty organizations can maintain, given what I have called the globalization semantic. I will show that the concept of loyalty that is maintainable, is exactly a kind of loyalty making a whistleblowing policy necessary, hence normatively legitimate. The argument of this section is that there is no contradiction between whistleblowing and loyalty, if loyalty is adequately conceptualized.

---

[46] See Duska 1997 but also Jubb 1999.

What do I mean with 'adequately' conceptualizing loyalty? The need for organizational loyalty has certainly not decreased within the context of globalization. I mentioned complexity as an important concept of what I called the globalization semantic. It pointed at the speed at which decisions had to be made as well as at the increased factors to take into account. It also referred to decentralization processes external and internal to the organization. As society increasingly delegates responsibilities to companies and private organizations, the environmental complexity of those companies and organizations also increases. To adequately respond to that complexity, it is necessary to responsibilize employees (see the section on responsibility) – give more discretionary power to employees lower in the hierarchy. This is exactly the reason why organizations need to be able to rely on the loyalty of the employee to the organization, as a form of indirect control. If tasks and duties can no longer efficiently be made explicit in formal contracts and job descriptions, then the boundaries of the 'elbow room' which employees are to be given can only be installed in a symbolic way, by rituals and value statements identifying and promoting the organization as the object of employee loyalty.

But at the same time, because of flexibility, notions of job insecurity and desired job mobility are constraints as to just how organizational loyalty can be obtained. An adequate conceptualization of organizational loyalty takes both the need for and the constraints on loyalty into considerations. Previous attempts to argue beyond the contradiction between loyalty and whistleblowing are not satisfying because they have failed to adequately conceptualize organizational loyalty.

In his classic work *Exit, Voice and Loyalty*, Hirschman (1970) identified three response categories to abnormal behaviour in organizations. Exit is to distance oneself from a problem and is the standard response to dissatisfaction within business organizations. Forms of exit are changing brands or shops as a customer, changing jobs as an employee. Voice is a response category which is rather used to deal with dissatisfaction or disagreement in social or political organizations. Note that for Hirschman, both exit and voice are ways of giving signals urging the organization to change or correct itself. Loyalty then as a response means to stay and keep on functioning in the organization as it is. Important is however, that although Hirschman thought that in the economic domain, 'exit drives out voice' (Hirschman 1970, 120), he did see relations between the three response categories. There is no loyalty if there are no exit options, and if employees or customers could be stimulated to choose the voice option rather than the exit response, this would increase loyalty and result in tighter customer bonds and higher retention of employees.

Duska (1997) writes that 'most business ethicists claim that employees have some obligation to the company or employer, which is usually characterized as an obligation to loyalty. Whistleblowing violates that obligation'. Duska sees whistleblowing as an obligation one has to the public to prevent harm.[47] Moreover, even in situations where it would be morally required to blow the whistle, there is still a violation of the obligation to loyalty. What is Duska's way out of this dilemma?

Apparently Ronald Duska (1990) does not agree with most business ethicists. Duska himself claims that employee loyalty to companies is a category mistake, because companies are not proper objects of loyalty. Hence, within the context of companies, there is no conflict between the duty to loyalty and the duty to blow the whistle simply because there is no duty of loyalty.[48]

In a recent article, John Corvino (2002) has argued against Duska's exclusion of loyalty from business. Duska's objections are 1) that loyalty to business requires granting business the status of a person, and 2) that loyalty depends on ties that demand self-sacrifice without expectation of reward. Since business does not deserve the status of a person, Duska argues, and since employment relations imply a reward for made efforts, there is no such thing as a duty of loyalty to a company. However, Corvino refutes both of Duska's objections, and rightly so. To say that only persons are proper objects of loyalty is something which Duska does not prove or argue. Besides, as Corvino states, companies are without doubt groups of persons. So Duska's first objection does not seem to hold. With regard to his second objection, Corvino argues that the absence of reward is not a prerequisite, since relationships where Duska does see loyalty as appropriate – particularly among teammates in sports, but also relationships between friends and family – always entail some expectation of reward. Thus, Duska's second objection seems untenable.

---

[47] I have constructed a normative legitimation for whistleblowing policies on that argument in section on OSR.

[48] Solomon (1993, 136–44) argues for the recognition of people in business to be regarded – and judged – as professionals. Professionalism emphasizes a sense of social service. Professionals pledge themselves to the public in oaths and in their explicit allegiance to public well being or even the constitution. 'One of the essential features of a profession is the enforced qualifications and competence if its practitioners where the public good is concerned, and any adequate conception of the free market must be construed *within* the frame of this demand' (Solomon 1993, 139, emphasis in original). This becomes interesting when discussing – like I am doing in this section – conflict of loyalties. As Davis mentions briefly, 'professionals – *by definition* – cannot put the welfare of their employer ahead of their profession's standards' (Davis 2002, 44, emphasis in original). Davis (2002, 50–52) too sees those professional standards as rules made explicit to outward society, serving a moral purpose – the profession explicitly acknowledges its role within or function to the 'good society'. Even though the references for behaviour are explicit and legitimate norms, they are self-imposed. However, this doesn't mean they are self-imposed without input or interference from outsiders to the profession, nor that trespassing the rules would be left unsanctioned. It is in this sense that I will propose the concept of 'rational loyalty' further on in this section.

However, with Duska's objections overruled, Corvino does agree with him that there is no conflict of duties between loyalty and whistleblowing. Corvino's way out of the dilemma is that

> while loyalty requires a certain degree of tolerance of shortcomings, it does not require absolute or complete tolerance [... or,] loyalty is a virtue only to the extent that the object of loyalty is good (Corvino 2002, 184).

Duska's solution is unacceptable because 1) his objections to loyalty in business do not hold, and 2) because I have pointed out that business organizations are in need of loyalty. And even though Corvino's answer to the dilemma is interesting because it is a position which allows both loyalty and whistle blowing, it stays too vague. Corvino talks of 'some' tolerance of shortcomings, but it is not clear just how much that is. It appears to us that in an organizational setting, it needs to be clear just how much 'some' is.

The discussion between Duska and Corvino is valuable because it points at an analytical problem which both Duska and Corvino fail to solve in a satisfying way. The problem is the following. I have an obligation to be loyal to my company, which means I have a duty towards object A. But I also have an obligation to prevent harm to my community, which means I have a duty towards object B. Both duties are quite similar, I believe, as both imply preventing harm to and further the well being of the object. Hence it becomes clear that these duties only conflict when the objects of those duties are incompatible. Duska solves the conflict by stating rather explicitly that there is only one appropriate object, the community. The position of Corvino – loyalty is a virtue only to the extent that the object of loyalty is good – on the other hand seems to imply that loyalty only stretches as far as the two objects are the same or are at least compatible with one another.

Although I find Corvino's answer too vague, it does point in a direction favourable for the purpose of this section, namely to make loyalty and whistle-blowing compatible. Duska and Corvino have made it clear that the answer lies in clarifying the object of loyalty in a way that shows to be compatible or even coinciding with the object of whistleblowing.

Loyalty

In the *Encyclopedic Dictionary of Business Ethics*, Sydney Axinn (1997) writes that loyalty refers to a willingness to sacrifice. It carries that notion of sacrifice with it, because a loyal individual designates someone who is willing to act for the benefit of someone or something else. A quick etymological sidestep[49] shows such interpretation is very partial. 'Loyal' is traced back through Old French *loial* and *leial* to Latin *legalis* and *legalem*, with roots *leg-* and *lex-*, which designate law. 'Loyal' hence means what is conform to the law, or that which is of the conditions

---

[49] The etymological sidestep is based on the Oxford English Dictionary, the American Heritage Dictionary, and the Nouveau Dictionnaire Universel (by Maurice Lachatre).

required by the law. In this sense it is said of goods that they are loyal, or legal. However, when it is said of persons, the reference to an explicit object or promise is still there. 'Loyal' then means 'true to obligations', 'faithful to plighted troth', 'faithful or steadfast in allegiance to the sovereign or constituted government'. In that sense it is connected with and sometimes mentioned as a synonym for 'fidelity', which means 'unfailing fulfilment of one's duties and obligations', but also a 'strict adherence to vows or promises'. Also stemming from that Old French *leial* is the English 'leal' which means 'loyal, faithful, honest, true' and also 'true, genuine, real, actual, exact, accurate'. In the light of the realignment of the concept of loyalty, it is important to keep those historical semantic links in mind.

There are however, many contemporary authors on business ethics who refer to and even praise loyalty. Hartman (1996) argues that loyalty contributes to organizational effectiveness, because it preserves the commons. Indeed, not taking loyalty seriously can have bad economic consequences, like a costly competition among organizations for employees, a lowered willingness to make joint or long-term investments that are in the interests of both employer and employee, and the cost of free rider occurrence. Moreover, Hartman (1996, 173) writes that 'loyalty and care for one another's interests are required beyond what any possible rules or contracts, however carefully designed, could specify'. On the nature of loyalty, Hartman states there is 'an emotional basis that requires community support' (Hartman 1996, 173). In this sense, it is the corporate culture which complements moral principles, work rules and evaluation systems in creating loyalty. Firstly because the corporate culture can feed emotions that affect the desires and beliefs of employees. But that affection is not a *conditio sine qua non*:

> Even where affection is lacking, rituals and symbols can help generate the kind of loyalty that causes employees to act in ways that benefit the organization [...] (Hartman 1996, 173).

Loyalty makes an employee further the interests of on organization 1) because it feels right to do so, 2) because he/she is convinced it is the right thing to do, or 3) a combination of 1) and 2). Also, Hartman sees a kind of second-order desire as characteristic of a loyal person, more precisely 1) to be motivated by that which serves the interests of the beneficiary of one's loyalty, and 2) to rationally believe that the beneficiary of loyalty is loyal as well.

The aspect of mutuality is also emphasized by Robert Solomon (1993; 1997). Taking an Aristotelean view, Solomon describes loyalty as an emotion of the self, but an emotion not entirely absorbed in self-interest. Rather:

> [loyalty] is a kind of integrity, not within oneself (conceived of as a self-sufficient, integral whole) but rather with oneself conceived as a part of a larger self, a group, a community, an organization, or institution (Solomon 1993, 220).

For Solomon, loyalty is not an abstract principle but rather:

a question of mutual obligations. What a company can expect from its employees
[...] depends on what employees expect, and have got, from the company (Solomon
1997, 175).

However, Solomon sees that as a new kind of loyalty. An older kind of loyalty
seemed to have been one-sided – employee loyalty to the corporation – and
taken for granted, because jobs were hard to come by and important promotions
came from the inside. But that kind of loyalty withered as corporate mobility
increased and job hopping became a way to improve salary and status. That is
the context which has, according to Solomon, made loyalty to a certain extent
a question of fair exchange. But that does not mean that loyalty is a matter of
financial incentives. These might encourage people to stay, but will not inspire
loyalty. What Solomon seems to emphasize in 'winning' employee loyalty, is
explicitness and exemplarity in standards being set, in expectations, in feedback
and in coaching.

Empirical research confirms Solomon's statement about the deterioration
of an old concept of loyalty. Managers' perception of loyalty is affected by a
redundancy of workforce (Worrall et al. 2000). Of the surveyed organizations
that had carried out a redundancy, 60 per cent of the managers said their loyalty
to the organization had decreased, whereas of the surveyed organizations where
restructuring had not involved redundancy, only 34 per cent reported lower
loyalty. Worrall et al. (2000) put forward a possible explanation for this, namely
that where redundancy is seen as a violation of the psychological contract, this
leads to a reduced sense of obligation to employers.

The notion of psychological contract is important. For Jeurissen (1997), loyalty
is an attitude aimed at an object. It involves a predisposition to act, is durable and
contains an aspect of preference. Moreover, with Parsons, Jeurissen states that
loyalty is a diffuse attitude, which means it is a social role based on the totality of
meanings and values which are attributable to the object of the attitude. Duska
(1990) claims it is an affective attitude. I have mentioned that Hartman sees
emotions and affections as one way to foster loyalty, but that rituals and symbols
can do it just as well. Likewise, Jeurissen focuses on an affectively neutral form of
loyalty, which is partly based on deontological norms and is a loyalty oriented on
a contractual framework and based on agreement. It is a contract which makes
closing of loads of other contracts less costly; it is a relational contract. According
to Calton and Lad (1995), relational contracts define the 'rules of the game' that
govern durable organizational interactions. A corporate mission statement is an
explicit relational contract. So is an employment contract. They define the initial
set of formal rights en duties associated with a relation. However, a lot of the
'rules of the game' are implicit. The implicit relational contracts are enacted over
time within a pattern of interactions. Or in terms of Jeurissen, loyalty is a learned
attitude. Loyalty is always situated within a concrete context of social relations.
It is through those relations that a specific loyalty is learned, which means that
loyalty is not only an attitude towards an object, but also an attitude towards the

relation of the loyal subject to the object of loyalty. And so, as loyalty is bilateral (Jeurissen 1997; Hartman 1996; De George 1993; Solomon 1997; Reichheld 1996), the attitude towards the relation is a shared one. This automatically disqualifies any conceptualization of loyalty which can not be reciprocated on. In other words, a company can only ask from its employees that kind of loyalty which it can also have towards those employees. In this sense, a company can not ask of its employees a loyalty which boils down to sticking with the organization no matter what, simply because that company can not guarantee its employees that the company will stick with them no matter what. The organization in terms of hierarchies, functional positions and physicalities is not an adequate object of loyalty because the organization can not guarantee lifelong employment. What I will do in the next subsection is develop a concept of loyalty that is adequate, or, reconceptualize loyalty in a way that fits current organizational needs.

Out of the etymological roots and literature review, the framework within which loyalty can be rethought is constrained by four criteria:

1   loyalty is an attitude aimed at an object;
2   loyalty has an explicit external referent;
3   loyalty is a learned attitude; and
4   loyalty is bilateral.

Rational Loyalty

Overlooking the discussion between Duska and Corvino, I have argued that a re-conceptualization of loyalty consists of specifying the object of loyalty. In order to do this, I would like to introduce the notion of rational loyalty. The adjective 'rational' is not intended to narrow loyalty down to a calculative attitude. My intention is rather to emphasize a rational deliberation regarding the object of loyalty. In previous sections I showed that there is an interdependence between civil society and business. The concepts of corporate social responsibility, corporate citizenship, the notions of sustainable or ethical investment, consumer activism, and initiatives such as the UN Global Compact, support that. At the same time, organizations increasingly make their goals, their procedures and the values by which they wish to operate explicit and public through mission statements, quality labels and reports. Now, by doing this, these organizations situate themselves within society. They acknowledge being part of society and point out in what way they contribute to society. They do that in an attempt to be regarded by civil society as a legitimate part of society.

It is in this line of thought that I situate the notion of rational loyalty: the object of rational loyalty is not the physical aspects of the company – buildings, executives, boards, hierarchies, colleagues – but the explicit set of mission statement, goals, value statement and code of conduct of the organization which is judged as legitimate.

An organization who makes its missions, goals and values explicit and public – for example by publishing them on the website or in their annual report – makes a statement about what the organization stands for. These statements almost always include a profit for shareholders (if they are publicly traded companies), respecting the law, making quality products, and positive relations towards communities, employees, customers and suppliers. What organizations do here is to describe what their purpose is and they do that in a legitimating way. They try to convince the public that the organization deserves a 'licence to operate'. A counter-example would be a company explicitly stating that its mission is to rip people off, or to be excellent in extortion practices. But we do not see mafia organizations publishing a mission statement saying they are a mafia organization. Even organizations that are set up to kick back huge sums of money by being dishonest and fraudulent to suppliers, customers and employees will have a mission statement which is acceptable to the wider society. Hence, if we conceive of that explicit mission statement as the object of loyalty, then we have an object of loyalty which is compatible or even coinciding with the object of whistleblowing. For, my duty of loyalty to an object which is regarded as legitimate by society can never contradict my duty to blow the whistle in order to prevent harm to and further the well being of society. Any contradiction between those two duties would imply that the object of my duty of loyalty is not a legitimate object.

The adjective 'rational' in rational loyalty indicates the need for the individual to make a deliberation whether or not his/her acts are a contribution to the explicit mission, values and goals of the organization he/she is loyal to. If he/she finds him/herself in a situation where organizational behaviour diverts from its explicit mission, goals and values, then rational loyalty – loyalty to the explicit mission, goals and values – would demand of him/her to blow the whistle. It is important to understand the crucial role of the explicit mission statement. If an organization in terms of hierarchies, functional positions and physicalities behaves different from what its explicit mission statement says, then that organization suffers goal-displacement. Rational loyalty demands an employee to be loyal to the organization identified in and through the explicit mission statement. The employee does not owe any loyalty towards the organization identified through organizational behaviour that runs counter to the kind of behaviour described in its mission statement.

Perhaps I can clarify this even further with an example. The Volvo Group states in its code of conduct that it 'observes neutrality with regard to political parties and candidates'. The code also states that 'neither the names nor the assets of Volvo Group companies shall be used to promote the interests of political parties or candidates' (Volvo 2003, 2). If you are an employee of Volvo, then the organization demanding your loyalty is an organization which observes political neutrality the way it is described in its explicit code of conduct. Should your plant manager allow assets of Volvo to be used in her husband's promo campaign – her husband runs for representative in the city council – then rational loyalty would imply blowing the whistle on that, even if her husband could favour the local Volvo plant should he be elected.

Let's look at another Volvo example. The Volvo Group Mission Statement says Volvo uses its 'expertise to create transport-related products and services of superior quality, safety and environmental care...'. Therefore, any action compromizing the quality of a product is a disloyal action. Any order to act in such a disloyal way is an example of organizational misbehaviour and should that action be carried out, it will result in goal-displacement. A loyal act here would be to blow the whistle, since the organizational setting (specific hierarchies, functional positions and physicalities) demanding the Volvo-employee to compromize on quality, is certainly not the organizational identity (explicit mission, values, goals of Volvo) the employee is loyal to. What's more, to act loyal in such a situation is to do everything possible to correct the organizational misbehaviour and goal-displacement. Speaking up about it is part of the possible acts. Hence, whistle-blowing is a loyal act here.

Does this meet the organizational need for loyalty? I believe it does. If employees are 'steadfast in allegiance' with the missions and goals of an organization, they will exercise their decision-making authority in function of those missions and goals. Rational loyalty allows consistent decentralized decision-making. It merges with Castells' concept of the network enterprise I mentioned in an earlier section as 'that specific form of enterprise whose system of means is constituted by the intersection of segments of autonomous systems of goals' (Castells, 1996, 171) in the sense that rational loyalty allows autonomous systems of goals to willingly intersect as means to the object of that loyalty.

And does the concept of rational loyalty appear within the constraints mentioned at the end of the previous subsection? The first constraint was that loyalty is an attitude aimed at an object. I stated that the object of rational loyalty is the explicit set of mission statement, goals, value statement and code of conduct of an organization. But what about the attitude? It is an attitude of acting in the interest of the object. And so rational loyalty implies a deliberation whether or not a possible or ordered act is in the interest of the object of rational loyalty.

The second constraint I identified through looking at the etymology was that loyalty always needs an explicit external referent. The explicit referent of rational loyalty is the mission statement, goals, value statement and code of conduct, made explicit and made public in some way.

Third, I noted that loyalty is a learned attitude. More precisely, with Jeurissen, loyalty is a diffuse attitude oriented on a contractual framework and based on agreement. In that sense, it is a relational contract. The notion of rational loyalty then, emphasizes the explicit relational contract. However, there are also implicit 'rules of the game'. Rational loyalty certainly does not exclude those, but instead points at a possibility to deliberately steer the enactment over time of those implicit aspects of a relational contract. Rational loyalty calls for explicit learning of loyalty. If loyalty is always situated within a concrete context of social relations, then this concrete context must be addressed to learn loyalty, from one another and through discussion with one another. This learning process certainly involves dilemma training, but could also be seen as a way to implement codes of conduct and measure the implementation. Nijhof and others talk about the process of responsibilization which breaks down into six sub-processes in which dilemmas are being registered and categorized, a code is being written from concrete dilemmas which occur in daily business practice, with indicators referring to activities and feedback loops, through registration and monitoring of internal process risks, and transparent and wide communication within the organization (Nijhof et al. 2003). Hence, this learning process becomes part of the explicit relational contract and thus loyalty is not only the attitude towards the object – explicit missions and goals – but also – as argued in the previous subsection – an attitude towards the relation to the object of loyalty.

It is here that whistleblowing policy comes in. The concept of rational loyalty not only demands whistleblowing from loyal employees but, following from the fourth constraint I identified as the bilaterality of loyalty, also demands loyal organizations to institutionalize whistleblowing. Of course rational loyalty is demanded from all people in the organization, from bottom to top, including top management and the board of directors. But in what sense is rational loyalty bilateral? If rational loyalty demands from an employee or manager to act only so as to realize the object of loyalty – mission, values, goals – then this loyalty has to be reciprocated by protecting those who act in that way. As I have argued, whistleblowing is an act of rational loyalty if it is done to correct organizational misbehaviour or goal-displacement. Thus, rational loyalty implies – as the reciprocating part – institutionalization of whistleblowing. This means setting up a simple and clear set of procedures for employees who want to raise a concern. That is what can be understood by institutionalization of whistleblowing.

One might wonder if rational loyalty is in any way different from 'organizational commitment' or 'value commitment'. 'Organizational commitment' is used to denote what employees are prepared to do for the organization, in terms of effort and flexibility.[50] It seems to denote what has been called the 'zone of indifference', meaning the set of orders acceptable to those getting the orders without questioning the authority giving the orders (Van Hootegem 2000, 51). Value commitment – the extent to which employees see their personal values as matching or similar to the values of the organization – is deemed important as to how wide the zone of indifference will be. Gallie et al. (1998, 234–60) did research on that and found that organizational commitment was reduced where the organization was perceived as not caring for the well-being of its employees. It seems to me that organizational and value commitment are measurable variables to talk about motivation and job satisfaction. Rational loyalty on the other hand denotes the execution of discretionary power in the interest of the organizational values – rather than whether or not there is enough commitment to execute a given

---

[50] See Mowday's 'Organizational Commitment Questionnaire' (Mowday et al. 1979).

order. It also designates the readiness of the organization to attune its practices according to its values.

Let me resume. I have argued that rational loyalty is the kind of loyalty an organization can demand from their employees, because it is the kind of loyalty they can reciprocate on. And as whistleblowing can be an act of rational loyalty, organizations should institutionalize whistleblowing in order to protect employees who blow the whistle as an act of rational loyalty. This institutionalization is what organizations do when they reciprocate on the rational loyalty they demand from their employees.

Visualizing how the rational loyalty construct takes position within the globalization semantic (Figure 3.11), I have argued that rational loyalty calls for both a social responsibility of the organization and a responsibilization of the individual. Both carry the responsibility of staying focused on the purpose as made explicit in the corpus of mission and value statements of the organization. Through that corpus, the organization and the individual indirectly control one another.

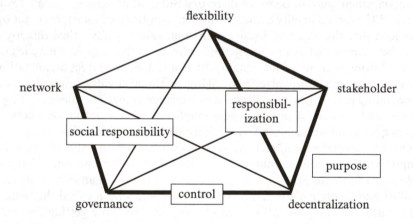

Figure 3.11 Globalization semantic (loyalty)

Whistleblowing and Efficiency

The last normative legitimation I will construct for whistleblowing policies regards whistleblowing as a source of information. Of course, in some of the previous constructs whistleblowing also functioned as a generator of information. And in any case, the definition of whistleblowing pivots around a disclosure of information. And yet, the construct in this section differs from the previous ones, in that here, it is not the disclosure itself which is normatively legitimate, but the goal it serves. Previous constructs showed a whistleblowing which was normatively legitimate: whistleblowing as a human right is a legitimate whistleblowing because human rights are legitimate, whistleblowing as an act under the framework of OSR is legitimate because OSR is legitimate, and the same goes for responsibility, integrity and loyalty. Here however, whistleblowing as a source of information finds its normative legitimation not in being the source of the information, but rather in what the information is used for. The construct I am about to develop concerns a whistleblowing policy as an instrument for organizational efficiency. Hence, the questions to be answered are:

1   how does efficiency link with the globalization semantic?
2   what is the normative legitimation for organizational efficiency?
3   what is the instrumental value of a whistleblowing policy as a source of information?

Efficiency and the Globalization Semantic

> Reaching organizational goals is an indication of *effectiveness*; not wasting resources along the way is an indication of *efficiency* (Petrick and Quinn 1997: 3, emphasis in original).

This description recognizes that one can be effective regardless of whether one is also efficient or not, but to be efficient is the optimal way to be effective in terms of input-output. Hence, efficiency is very central to economic reasoning and refers to organizational processes. What's more, not being efficient has a moral connotation of waste.

William Greider sees efficiency as a capitalistic virtue:

> The great virtue of capitalism – the quality that always confounded socialist critics and defeated rival economic systems – is its ability to yield more from less. Its efficient organization of production strives to produce more goods from less input, whether the input is capital, labour or raw resources (Greider 1997: 45).

Greider actually links efficiency with globalization through examples of organizational shifts in the car industry. I see this as no coincidence. The efficiency of Taylorism was celebrated until the 1960s in the way production was organized at the Ford Motor Company, and to show that globalization undermines Taylorist – or Fordist – efficiency makes the claim that globalization changes the conditions for efficiency a very strong one. Of course, information technology and CAD-CAM technology have created new opportunities to enhance efficiency through organizational (data communication) and production design (automation). But the 'free market'-conditions of globalization demand continuous suppression of costs, including labour costs, as well as the geographical relocation of production elements to capture local advantages – lower wages, lower taxes, less regulation. With regard to costs, it is especially fixed costs that need to be reduced. And the way to do that is by dismantling corporate assets: 'selling plants and properties, shrinking middle-level bureaucracies, converting jobs to temporary status'

(Greider 1997, 47). Hence, within the globalization semantic, to be flexible is to be efficient. This refers to both flexibility with regard to regulation as to flexibility with regard to the organization of labour.

In the public sector, the notion of efficiency grounds the 'new public management' and serves as a legitimation for privatization and public-private partnerships – governance is more efficient than government.[51] It seems decentralization is deemed necessary in order to ensure efficiency. The perception of higher complexity demands decentralization of decision-making and goal-setting, as this allows a narrower goal-description and hence less complex planning. If goals and planning are too complex – because they are too central and thus include too many targets – it is hard to show the efficiency of the activities. It is easier to find out whether small units, autonomously defining their single issue-goal are realizing their goal in an efficient way or not. In that sense, what globalization has changed in terms of conditions of efficiency is that the need to be efficient has to a large extent become the need to prove ones efficiency or at least to appear as efficient.

Organizational Inefficiency

There are two ways in which we can conceive of 'organizational inefficiency'. The first regards that which makes it impossible for organizations to improve their efficiency, the second way regards that what makes organizational processes inefficient.

A possible barrier to process innovation is regulation constricting flexibility in terms of fast changes – hiring/firing people, relocating production, and all sorts of government licensing needed in order to operate. For national governments, there is the pressure not to regulate, because more regulation in one region compared to another one often means impeding the competitiveness of the region.[52] Quite often, the private business sector lobbies against 'overregulation'.[53]

---

[51]   Such has certainly been the argumentation of the IMF and the World Bank in requesting the restructuring of the public sector towards privatization as a condition for loans. Japan's Overseas Economic Cooperation Fund issued a white paper questioning the World Bank's structural adjustment plans (Greider 1997, 277–8), arguing the importance of a 'crucial social subtext: a poor country aspiring to industrialize [...] must do so in ways that shares the economic benefits widely among its citizens, both to maintain political stability and to justify the subsidies and special treatment accorded certain sectors'.

[52]   Of course, when one looks at the issue in terms of competitiveness, they have every reason to lobby against regulation, if the regulation can not be implemented on a global level. If all competitors need to abide by the same rules, the competitive advantage of operating in a particular region falls away.

[53]   This is exactly what happened with regard to the European Commission's position on CSR (see EC 2002 and our comments in Vandekerckhove and Commers 2005). For the European Commission, CSR became an issue when Delors made an appeal to European

The second sort of organizational inefficiency puts private business and public sector organizations at the same side. Here, the inefficiency is caused by a human factor. The organizational processes are designed as very efficient, but they are not carried out the way they are planned or intended. Two such organizational inefficiencies have gotten very high on the agenda of both governments and businesses: fraud and corruption. Fraud is the deliberate misrepresentation in order to obtain an unauthorized benefit, and as such can be considered as an inefficiency in information providing. Corruption on the other hand is an inefficiency in allocation – of goods, of services, of contracts, etc. – in the form of rent-seeking, bribery, cartels.[54]

In one way, state monopolies are being reproached with being corrupt and serving personal interests of power hungry politicians. But in another way, it is exactly in the privatization process that corruption and fraud occurs (Racic 2002; TI 2000, 19–20). In a third way, within private business too, the fear for fraud increases (see for example the annual KPMG or Ernst&Young fraud surveys). It seems that decentralization is necessary to ensure efficiency, but at the same time it increases the risk of inefficiency. Decentralized decision-making and more discretionary power to people lower in the hierarchy increases opportunities for fraud and corruption, because more people are able to cause such inefficiencies and at the same time those able to do it are less likely to get caught. Hence, decentralization calls for new ways of control. It is precisely here that whistle-blowing policies as a source of information come in.

---

business to take part in the fight against social exclusion. At the European Council in Lisbon of March 2000, a special appeal was made to companies' sense of social responsibility regarding practices for lifelong learning, work organization, equal opportunities, social inclusion and sustainable effort. At the same time, a pledge was taken to make Europe the world's most competitive economic area, and the Commission regards CSR as strategic to that goal. In the discussion over whether or not the Green Paper emphasis on CSR as characteristically voluntary actions would be maintained in the Commission's Communication (EC 2002), business argued along the lines of 'competitiveness' and 'no one-size-fits-all solutions'. Hence, the message from the business sector was clearly that social goals must and could be reached by initiatives that do not impede flexibility and competitiveness, or, government should not regulate but rather 'support innovation' or 'highlight best-practice'.

[54] To qualify corruption as an inefficiency in allocation covers both petty corruption and grand corruption. Petty corruption is any kind of administrative corruption, for instance in the case where offering a small bribe speeds up – 'greases' – bureaucratic processes. The inefficiency lies in the undue course of the process, for example going against queuing principles. Grand corruption is irregular influence in judiciary or in lawmaking, for example when a powerful lobby influences court cases or parliamentary voting on law proposals. The inefficiency there lies in the thwarting of political institutions such as democratic representation or impartial judiciary.

Whistleblowing as a Source of Information

Three factors seem important for the occurrence of fraudulent acts within organizations: 1) organizational conditions allowing fraudulent acts (both having the power to do it and weak internal control environment); 2) motivations for committing the fraud (poor liquidity position); 3) ethical attitudes indicating a possible willingness to commit an act of fraud (Loebbecke and Willingham 1988, cited in Hooks et al. 1994). Hooks et al. (1994) argue that the move towards total quality management (TQM) implies an emphasis on process controls. Therefore, auditors too might be placing more weight on the control of environment. As TQM approaches also imply empowerment and decentralization, and come in a time of computerization, Hooks et al. see difficulties for maintaining uniform accounting systems and internal control procedures. Instead, they bring forward the idea of an internal control environment, serving as the linkage between subunits, and being 'in part, an operationalization of organizational culture' (Hooks et al. 1994, 88). As enhancing communication within the organization about fraudulent acts or risks is regarded as improving the internal control environment, Hooks et al. bring whistleblowing forward as a form of such an enhanced – and 'upstream' – communication.

Basically, organizing is becoming too complex to keep everything under control. Moreover, if organizations are getting flatter, this simply means that superiors have more subordinates under them doing different things, being flexible, and having more job control. At a certain point in that shift, the problem of how a manager can know what is going on at the work floor, needs to be answered differently. Whistleblowing policies can be a way to get information about what is going wrong on the work floor. Can be, indeed, on the condition that they work well. Methods used to collect information about inefficiencies are only legitimate to the extent that these methods themselves show to be effective. More precisely, whistleblowing as a source of information is only justified to the extent that it generates accurate and reliable information.

Building on Hook et al. (1994), Ponemon (1994) regards three organizational factors as important for constructing an effective 'upstream' communication. The first is an identified internal channel to do so. The second factor pertains to how well retaliations can be avoided and to the reward structure – financial, honour, promotion – created by the organization for truthful disclosures. The third, and according to Ponemon most important factor however is the 'moral atmosphere' of the organization. The moral atmosphere of an organization is defined as that part of the organization culture that deals with ethical problems and the resolution of moral conflict. A positive moral atmosphere will have people feel free to express and discuss diversity in moral point of views. I think it is Ponemon's most puzzling factor. He writes about the 'moral atmosphere' of an organization as both result of and condition for accurate and reliable disclosures: upstream communication can foster the moral atmosphere of the organization (Ponemon 1994, 118), a negative moral atmosphere will censor or block disclosures (Ponemon 1994, 124). Hence, a negative moral atmosphere tends to make whistleblowing inefficient, but at the same time, it is organizations with a negative moral atmosphere that are most in need of whistleblowing, since it is there that fraud is most likely to occur. Ponemon is aware of this paradox, but gives no answer to it (Ponemon 1994, 125, 128).

A second condition on which the justification of whistleblowing as a source of information depends is the extent to which the whistleblowing policy itself, institutionalizing the disclosure of information, is efficient. Anechiarico and Jacobs (1996) have argued that anti-corruption initiatives – including whistleblowing policies – have made government inefficient. Since the 1970s, ever more practices that are in one way or another undesirable, have been tagged as 'corruptive'. Anechiarico and Jacobs (1996) speak of a 'purity potlach' and the 'overproduction of political scandal'. They argue that along with the proliferation of the corruption concept, since the 1970s, the anti-corruption project has gained a panoptic vision. The term comes from Jeremy Bentham, designing the panopticon as an architecture in which the watcher could see everything – and more important – everyone, without being seen. It was explicitly proposed as a model of an inspection-house, 'a new principle of construction applicable to any sort of establishment in which persons of any description are to be kept under inspection'.[55] Michel Foucault has taken the image of the panopticon as resembling the disciplinary society, in which undetected deviancy is impossible.

It is exactly here that whistleblowing as a source of information finds its legitimacy as countering organizational inefficiency. It is the panoptic vision that makes 'overregulation' unnecessary, as whistleblowing policies will generate information on whether something is going wrong. And in terms of fraud and corruption – practices that are only possible to the extent that they are hidden or invisible – the panoptic vision will scare off potential fraudulent or corrupt people and hence prevent organizational inefficiency. Moreover, any wrongdoing or malpractice will be detected at a very early stage, only requiring minimal action to rectify the damage. Such is the legitimation for whistleblowing policies as a source of information.

However, Anechiarico and Jacobs (1996) argue that the contribution of whistleblowing to detecting corruption is not measurable. On the other hand, the negative effects on public administration are clear. It undermines the disciplinary authority of agency heads and supervisors over their subordinates (Anechiarico and Jacobs 1996, 63). Also, the investigations following a whistleblowing can paralyse a whole department, as the agency head refuses to act for fear of triggering criticism while investigations are on – a case is cited where the investigations took six years (Anechiarico and Jacobs 1996, 68).

---

[55] The quote is part of the title of Bentham's bundling of letters of 1787. He saw this model as relevant in particular for 'penitentiary houses, prisons, houses of industry, poor-houses, lazarettos, manufactories, hospitals, and mad-houses'.

Coupled with whistleblowing policy as a panopticon – every one is both a potential trespasser and an investigator – is of course the increased capacity to collect and order information and to monitor people, processes and transactions through information technology. This too adds to the panoptic vision. Dominique Bessire (2003) connects the panopticon to the current transparency discourse. There too, the costs of transparency are never evaluated, nor are the benefits clearly identified, except for a vague reference to 'market efficiency'. More important however, is Bessire's argumentation that panopticism does not contribute to the moralization of business, but rather to a generalized amorality, stemming from a general distrust and the assumption of calculating and opportunistic individuals. Indeed, how can we at the same time assume opportunism and responsibility? Ponemon (1994) points out that reliable information is more likely to be obtained from an unmotivated[56] whistleblower. Thus, the necessity of designing a whistle-blowing policy is based on the assumption of opportunistic individuals who, given the organizational complexity can not be adequately controlled through supervision, yet the effective functioning of such a policy needs the assumption of responsible, non-opportunistic individuals. Of course, when one contents oneself with the situation in which individuals within organizations act out their discretionary power in such a way that they avoid any decision that might raise doubt or that might create an opportunity for others to blow the whistle on them, there is no contradiction in the assumptions because to act in such a way is not what is meant with responsibility.

The above pertains to internal whistleblowing. The panopticon can be either a management tool, serving as an additional source of information on employee behaviour and performance, or it can create the needed transparency within a corporate governance framework, getting information about the managers to the board or even higher to the shareholders. A different light is shed on the effectiveness and efficiency of whistleblowing as a source of information when external whistleblowing is regarded. Whistleblowing then functions as a source of information about organizational practices for external auditors, NGOs or the media. Whether or not a whistleblowing policy is efficient in terms of the organization concerned is not a concern of those external instances. Rather, the effectiveness of the policy in terms of generating accurate and reliable information is the only important criteria. But that effectiveness is easily attained. The information generated through whistleblowing channels is information they would not be able to get in any other way. Hence, whether the whistleblower is motivated or not is of no concern to them, because the replications on the organization itself of the disclosure of information is not their concern. And whether the information is reliable – are the allegations true? – can be checked with circumstantial evidence

---

[56] It is unmotivated in the sense that the reason for the whistleblowing is grounded solely in an ethical conflict for the whistleblower. Motivated whistleblowing then refers to the reporting of wrongdoing for purposes of personal gain (obtaining economic resources, social power or status) (Ponemon 1994, 120).

or can be a starting point for further forensic research in the case of external auditors. In the case of NGOs and the media, getting the information constitutes the effectiveness of the whistleblowing. Whether or not the disclosed information is reliable can be part of 'bringing the story'. Van Parijs (2002) his 'spotlight and the microphone' mechanisms[57] can be seen in this light.

> The spotlight is the patchwork of organizations and devices that makes visible and assessable what a firm does, directly or indirectly, throughout the world: it includes the NGOs and Trade Unions that detect and document objectionable practices; the media that alert public opinion to what NGOs or Unions denounce or directly echo the complaints of the individuals and communities that suffer from some practices [...] (Van Parijs 2002, 4).

In this sense, information obtained through whistleblowing is a spotlight-application. The microphone then is the way to hold organizations accountable for what became visible through the spotlight. This is the role of the microphone:

> a microphone forcibly pushed before the mouth of the head or spokesperson of a firm that has (or whose suppliers or subcontractors have) allegedly done something objectionable – like injuring, sacking, discriminating, polluting or cheating [...] (Van Parijs 2002, 4).

Sure, the spotlight and the microphone work well to increase the risk of blame for organizations and thereby making the 'soft informative accountability' I discussed in the section on accountability somewhat harder. But while Van Parijs warns that a good spotlight is one that provides correct and reliable information, I see it that the microphone can perform that test. Information is generated by whistleblowers and disclosed to spotlight operators (NGOs, unions, etc.). The microphone is the turning of the disclosed information into allegations, and demanding an 'account' from the organization. If it can be shown that the allegations generated through whistleblowing have no ground, then apparently it was non-accurate and incorrect information. Van Parijs seems to assume that the 'spotlight operators' are mainly interested in correct information. He thereby disregards the possibility that incorrect information might open strategic opportunities and serve the agenda's of the 'spotlight operating' organizations.

Let me position the efficiency construct within the globalization semantic (Figure 3.12). I have argued that globalization in terms of flexibility of law and regulation (avoiding overregulation) and labour organization has created new conditions for organizational efficiency. These new conditions call for decentralization which needs to be controlled through governance. Whistle-blowing policies driven by the efficiency construct exercise this control through a panopticon, which in terms of stakeholders external to the organization takes

---

[57]   Van Parijs too frames them as transparency tools.

the form of an accountability-watchdog, while internally – in terms of corporate governance – it takes the form of transparency.

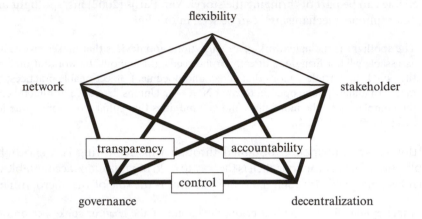

Figure 3.12 Globalization semantic (efficiency)

Drawing Up the Screening Grid

This section consists of drawing up a number of figures and tables, resuming this chapter and preparing the next two chapters. I first summarize the legitimation constructs into a table of 'relevant secondary concepts' and 'line of argument'. In the section after that, I identify the main grounding ethical theories for each normative construct. Up till here, I regard this as summarizing the current chapter. After that, the actor, subject and recipient elements of whistleblowing policies 'as they might be' are derived from the respective legitimation constructs. I then combine the first three subsections into the screening grid which will be used in Chapter 4. Finally, I point out how each legitimation construct denotes movements within the 'diagram of organization enclosure and emphasizing individuality' presented in Chapter 2.

Possible Legitimation of Whistleblowing Policies – Summary

Summarizing sections constructing the different possible legitimation of whistle-blowing policies, Table 3.1 points out the main line of argument and the relevant secondary concepts to each legitimation construct.

Backing Ethical Theories

In this chapter, I have constructed possible normative legitimation for whistle-blowing policies as set out in Chapter 2. This consisted of finding ways to articulate the institutionalization of whistleblowing within the globalization semantic. In

Table 3.1 Possible normative legitimation main lines of argument

Normative legitimation	Other relevant secondary concepts	Main line of argument
Human rights	Truth, self-expression, democracy, human dignity, social responsibility	As protecting and enhancing human rights becomes a social responsibility for all social actors, a whistleblowing policy is needed to ensure freedom of opinion and expression within organizations.
OSR-network	Trust, power balance	Whistleblowing policies ensure power balance within networks, which are made up of interactions. It is through balanced interactions that trust is built up.
OSR-stakeholder	Purpose	Whistleblowing policies allow stakeholders to warn one another when organizational practices differ from the organizational purpose.
Responsibility	Responsibilization, duties, autonomy, moral agency	Whistleblowing policies safeguard individual autonomy and moral agency, both necessary to carry out duties that come with responsibilities, and are suggested in the responsibilization of individuals.
Accountability	Responsibilization, duties, control	Controlling whether or not individuals carry out their duties calls for accountability. Whistleblowing policies ensure accountability is maintained in a wide sense.
Integrity	Self-regulation, accountability, structure. autonomy, control	The demand for integrity points at the impossibility to control through. Therefore, self-regulation by autonomous actors is deemed, as is their accountability. Whistleblowing policies provide the possibility of realizing integrity in that they allow speaking and acting to coincide.
Loyalty	Responsibilization, purpose, control, social responsibility	Both organization and individual carry the responsibility of staying focused on the organizational purpose. Whistleblowing policies allow rational loyalty – loyalty to the organizational purpose – to be manifested.
Efficiency	Control, panopticon, transparency, accountability	Whistleblowing policies install an organizational panopticon. This is the way organizational efficiency can be controlled. Internal whistleblowing ensures organizational transparency for corporate governance, while external whistleblowing serves watchdog accountability.

that sense, each of the normative legitimation constructs is a variation within that semantic, gaining its meaning through increased density of specific semantic links between the primary concepts of the globalization semantic, as shown in Figures 3.5 to 3.12.

But as I am speaking of 'normative' legitimation, it is also interesting to look at what kind of ethical theory backs the normativity of the legitimation. Doing this will help me place the respective legitimation construct within the IOS-diagram. I will consider the three main ethical theories: deontological ethics, consequentialist ethics and virtue ethics.

From a deontological ethics point of view, the normativity of a legitimation rests with the idea that the policy allowing whistleblowing is necessary because the act of disclosing information is valuable in itself. Consequentialist ethics place the normativity of the legitimation of whistleblowing policies in allowing whistleblowing because the disclosure of information contributes to a greater good than when the whistle is not blown. Finally, virtue ethics normatively legitimates whistleblowing policies that allow whistleblowing because the disclosure of information about organizational processes is a constitutive and hence inalienable part of those processes themselves.

Whistleblowing as a human right falls under the header of deontological ethics. Whistleblowing as a human right is built on three rationales: truth, self-expression and democracy. All of those acknowledge human dignity and equality, valuable in themselves. Truth speaking is valuable in itself, and the ability for self-expression is a characteristic of human dignity. As far as democracy is concerned, it acknowledges human autonomy and equality and requires that everyone is recognized a source of ideas and information (truth).

Whistleblowing as organizational social responsibility (OSR) contained two constructions of normative legitimation. The construct around the concept of network is backed by virtue ethics. I have argued that a network is ontologically built up of interactions, and that these interactions are 'good' to the extent that they are characterized by trust. Trust is manifested through subsequent, power-balanced interactions. And a whistleblowing policy is a way to balance power. Hence, a whistleblowing policy is an integral part of network governance, ensuring trust building through interactions. Whistleblowing as OSR, constructed around the stakeholder concept however takes a more consequentialist ethical tone. Here, a whistleblowing leads to more organizational social responsibility because it allows stakeholders to be warned when an organization is shifting its attention from societal purpose to internal goals. However, blowing the whistle is not a purpose itself, nor is it valuable in itself.

Whistleblowing as responsibility has both a deontological and a virtue ethics grounding. It is deontological because it is a safeguard against the suppression of autonomy and moral agency. Within an organizational setting, blowing the whistle is an act of moral agency, valuable in itself. But it also has a virtue ethics turn. Responsibilization of employees is a requirement of organizational flexibility and decentralization. But responsibilization implies autonomy and moral agency. If this implication is realized through a whistleblowing policy – and as I argued, it is – then the ability to blow the whistle forms an integral part of responsibilization.

The construct of whistleblowing around the concept of accountability on the other hand finds it normative grounding both in consequentialist and virtue ethics. Consequentialist ethics, as the ability of individuals within an organization to blow the whistle leads to more accountability. And it is accountability of managers which is valuable within the framework of corporate governance, not whistleblowing itself. The virtue ethics component in this construct is situated in the extent to which a whistleblowing policy succeeds in taking over the functions of the bureaucratic external reference point, as a whistleblowing policy is able to widen the accountability beyond simply whether or not targets have been reached.

The whistleblowing as integrity construct is based on a virtue ethics approach. Organizations within the context of globalization require integrity from their employees. However, the only way in which 'integrity' makes sense is to conceive of it as the unity between discernment, acting and speaking. Whistleblowing policies constitute organizational integrity to the extent that they allow whistleblowing as the coinciding of acting and speaking. Therefore, whistleblowing is an integral part of integrity.

The loyalty construct as a normative legitimation for whistleblowing policies also rests on a virtue ethics approach. The organizational purpose is defined in the explicit corpus of mission and value statements. Organizations need to be able to depend on employee loyalty, but the only kind of loyalty organizations can reciprocate on is what I have called rational loyalty. It is loyalty to the organizational purpose rather than to the physical organization. And, whistleblowing as the signalling of goal-displacement is an integral part of rational loyalty.

Finally, the normative legitimation constructed around organizational efficiency is fully consequentialist. It is to the extent that whistleblowing policies are effective and efficient in generating information – accurate and reliable – that they are valuable. Even though that criteria is somewhat different for internal whistleblowing (management control and corporate governance transparency) than for external whistleblowing (accountability watchdog), it is not the disclosure itself that is valuable but rather the potential usage of the generated information.

Actor, Subject and Recipient Element

Screening the material relevant to whistleblowing policies laid down in legislation will mainly be done by looking in that material for argumentation lines resembling the semantic constructs developed in the previous sections and summarized in Table 3.1. But the screening will be facilitated by looking at the actor, subject and recipient elements as set forth in the advocated or legislated whistleblowing policies. In Chapter 1 I set out a matrix of possible definitions of whistleblowing, based on Jubb (1999). The matrix consisted of seven elements: act, outcome, actor, motive,

Table 3.2   Grounding ethical theories of the legitimation constructs

Legitimation construct	Grounding ethical theory
Human rights	Deontological
OSR-network	Virtue
OSR-stakeholder	Consequentialist
Responsibility	Deontological, virtue
Accountability	Consequentialist, virtue
Integrity	Virtue
Loyalty	Virtue
Efficiency	Consequentialist

subject, target and recipient. However, in Chapter 1, I argued that, as the screening of whistleblowing policies will serve to answer the question whether or not whistle-blowing policies resolve the conflict between organization and society, in terms of what kind of whistleblowing is put forward as legitimate, this required looking at how whistleblowing policies stipulate who can disclose, about what and to whom. Because of this outlook, three elements were considered to be of main interest: the actor element (who can disclose), the subject element (about what can disclosures be made), and the recipient element (to whom should the disclosures be made).

In order to integrate these three elements in the screening grid, I will here derive from the respective legitimation constructs what the content of the actor, subject and recipient elements would be if whistleblowing policies were legitimated by those particular constructs.

I first go over the legitimation constructs one by one, deriving stipulations for the three elements. Because of the just referred to limitation of elements to be looked into, I will not systematically derive other elements' stipulations. However, should any derivable stipulation pertaining to other elements seem relevant, I will also point that out. At the end of this section, I summarize the derived stipulations for the actor, subject and recipient elements according to the legitimation construct they were derived from (Table 3.3).

Human Rights Construct

I argued that whistleblowing policies can be legitimated through the human rights construct by advocating whistleblowing as a manifestation of 'freedom of expression' by referring to the human rights rationales of self-expression, democracy or the argument of truth.

Arguing that whistleblowing ought to be a protected act of 'free speech' as a *human* right, implies the right must pertain to all humans, as the notion of 'human rights' entails the notion of 'equal human worth'. Therefore, whistleblowing policies driven by the human rights construct must stipulate in their actor element that 'any person' can blow the whistle.

The same wideness also applies to the subject element. If whistleblowing is a form of free speech, a whistleblowing policy legitimated as such can not dictate about what opinions can be freely expressed, for that is up to the actor to decide. Therefore, to limit the subject element is contradictive to 'freedom of expression' and hence runs counter the human rights construct.

Stipulations for the recipient element to be derived from the human rights construct, show to be a bit more complicated. In principle, the human right of 'freedom of expression' is the 'freedom to [...] impart information and ideas through any media [...] (Article 19 of the UN Declaration of Human Rights)'. However, the compatibility of the three human rights rationales – self-expression, democracy, truth – might require the qualification of 'freedom of expression' as to how information and ideas are expressed. I have argued that whistleblowing can still be legitimated as a human right even when the whistleblowing policy qualifies that right. Unqualified protection of free speech might be damaging to the public order and the general welfare of a democratic society. The damage of spreading the opinion that someone in an organization or some organization is to blame for this or that, could lie in the opinion being based on unchecked information, or, making accusations through newspapers might make an independent investigation and an eventually the guarantee of a fair trial impossible. Hence, while in principle the human rights construct calls for whistleblowing policies allowing disclosures to any recipient, it might be more appropriate for whistleblowing policies to qualify the 'freedom of expression' with regard to the recipient element. However, if the legitimation of the whistleblowing policy is to be driven by the human rights construct, the recipient element must show extreme wideness at one point or another. A way to do this for a qualified right is to identify a sequential order within the possible recipients – for example first internal, then government, then media. Still, it must be noted that the human rights construct does not necessarily imply a qualified recipient element, rather it is compatible with it.

OSR-Network Construct

I have argued that whistleblowing policies legitimated through the OSR-network construct portray whistleblowing as a way of correcting asymmetry of information, thereby balancing power and building trust between actors within an organizational network. Specific for this construct is the view of organizations as networks and as pertaining to networks – organizational network. The implication is that whistleblowing policies will mirror the desired power constellation within that network. It is possible that this shows in all three elements, but it certainly will be salient in the recipient element.

One way to balance power within an organizational network towards a desired power constellation is by allowing only specific actors to spread information across the network. Hence, whistleblowing policies legitimated through the OSR-network construct can specify the actor element.

Another possibility lies in specifying the subject element. Such a specification would limit the asymmetry of information to be resolved based on what the information is about.

But it is most plausible to find mirroring of the desired power constellation within a network in the recipient element of whistleblowing policies. If power is to be balanced through an enhanced flow of information – which is the crux of the OSR-network legitimation – then it is very likely that those network agents currently deprived of relevant information will be stipulated as recipients. Far more than would be the case by specifying actor or subject element, it is the specification of the recipient element which assigns relevant stakeholders a position within the organizational network. Only in this way the OSR-network construct realizes its potential of balancing power within a network towards the desired power constellation. For, asymmetry of information implies that relevant information is generated, but does not get to the appropriate receiver. By specifying the recipient element, network actors are empowered to receive information which otherwise would not get to them. Moreover, by specifying particular actors in an organizational network as appropriate recipients of information, the OSR-network construct actually channels information to those recipients rather than allowing any random network actor to receive it.

OSR-Stakeholder Construct

I argued that this legitimation construct for whistleblowing policies holds whistle-blowing as a way of warning society about possible negative impact on the prosperity of society, as a guarantee that an organization fulfils its organizational responsibilities, that it stays focussed on its purpose above its goals.

With regard to the actor element, there is no reason why – were the whistle-blowing policy driven only by this legitimation construct – the actor element should have any specification.

Since the purpose of any organization lies in its constitutive aspects towards society, the subject element of whistleblowing policies driven by this construct, must emphasize possible harms to society. It might do so in general or in more specified language.

There are however some important stipulations to be derived from this construct with regard to the recipient element. The crux of the legitimation construct lies in safeguarding organizational purpose. If organizational practice diverts from its purpose, it is displaced within society. The well being of society requires organizational practices coinciding with organizational purpose. Hence, any diversion from that purpose harms society. In this sense, the abstract notion of 'society' can be concretized into stakeholders of an organization. Therefore, any organizational diversion from its purpose harms the interests of the stakeholders. Hence, a whistleblowing policy aimed at warning society of possible negative impact on society's prosperity, must allow information to be disclosed to all stakeholders. This contrasts the OSR-stakeholder construct with the OSR-network construct. Through the latter, a whistleblowing policy identifies which stakeholders are part of the organizational network and assigns them a position and an importance. In contrast to that, whistleblowing policies driven by the OSR-stakeholder construct do not specify which stakeholders are to be regarded as relevant, but instead allows disclosures to be made to a wide range of stakeholders; in the limit to the whole of society.

Responsibility Construct

I based the responsibility construct on the notion of 'ethical distance'. Whistle-blowing policies legitimated through this construct allow organizational members to take 'ethical distance' from organizational practices or outcomes. In the context of decentralized organizations, assigning individual responsibilities becomes highly complex, hence only collective responsibility can be assigned.

The actor element of such whistleblowing policies will be restricted to organizational members. However, given the decentralization process, denoting outsourcing and subcontracting, just which actors are to be regarded as organizational members might vary from people employed by the organization, over people contracted by the organization and volunteers, to employees of a subcontracting organization.

With regard to the subject element, I see no possible stipulations to be derived from the responsibility construct. Stipulations regarding the recipient element can only indirectly be derived. If whistleblowing policies are portrayed as mechanisms for individuals to take 'ethical distance' from organizational practices or outcomes, they will stipulate in detail how one can avoid being implicated in collective responsibility. This can only be done by establishing clear procedures and make them know throughout the organization. Moreover, if disclosures are regarded as acts of taking 'ethical distance', who made the disclosure and when the disclosure was made must be recorded. In order to be able to keep track of disclosures made, specific recipients must be identified.

Another derivable stipulation seems important. If, given the complexity of decentralized organizations, partaking in collective responsibility can only be avoided by using procedures set out by a whistleblowing policy to take 'ethical distance', *not* using those procedures or *not* disclosing about a particular malpractice might automatically lead to being regarded as complicit. In this way, whistleblowing policies legitimated by the responsibility construct are very likely to entail an obligation to blow the whistle.

Accountability Construct

I noted two possible features of the accountability construct. One was that whistleblowing policies can increase the accountability of lower managers to their bosses, the other was that whistleblowing policies might also be a substitute of an 'external reference' point of bureaucracies, hence holding organizations accountable for 'whimsical' management. Hence, what I wrote on the actor element of the responsibility construct also applies here.

If the second feature of the accountability construct is driving the legitimation of a whistleblowing policy, then 'abuse of power' must be included in the subject element in this or other formulation. However, the decisive stipulation with regard to the accountability construct concerns its recipient element. At the heart of the accountability construct lies the notion of 'power hierarchy'. Flexibility and decentralization might have flattened organizational hierarchies, but they still have them. Even to the extent that organizations are perceived as networks, accountability denotes a sense of 'controlling power' – someone is accountable to someone else who is in turn accountable to yet another someone. That is the crux of the accountability construct. A whistleblowing policy driven by that construct is a governance tool in the sense that it aids someone holding someone else accountable. Hence, the recipient element of whistleblowing policies driven by the accountability construct will mirror who is accountable to whom and will do so through a governance approach. Again, I contrast this notion with that of 'government'. In a government approach – based on the assumptions of certainty and effective power – control is centralized, hence everyone is accountable to government. In a governance approach however – based on the inability to control and uncertainty – control is decentralized and accountability is chained – W is accountable to X and Y; X is accountable to Y and Z; Z is possibly accountable to W. This can be called a tiered approach. For example, line managers are accountable to top management, but if top management does not appropriately hold line management accountable, then top management is held accountable for that by the board, and the board is held accountable by the shareholders, who might include some of the line managers' pension funds. Or in another possible way, line management is held accountable by top management, who is held accountable by law enforcement agencies, who are held accountable by Ombudsmen. With regard to whistleblowing policies, this tiered approach can be taken over in the recipient element by stipulating a sequential order of recipients – for example first internal, then board, then government agency. But in any way, the decisive stipulation of an accountability driven legitimation of whistleblowing policies is the tiered approach they take in their recipient element.

Integrity Construct

Given the fact that the term 'integrity' is very often heard in organizational discourses, the aim of constructing a legitimation of whistleblowing policies on that term consisted of finding out what content the concept of 'integrity' could have consistent within the globalization semantic and what implications this particular content would have with regard to whistleblowing. I argued that the only consistent concept of 'integrity' denoted the unity of discernment, action and speaking, and that in whistleblowing, this unity was present.

In this sense, blowing the whistle could be regarded as an act of integrity. Driving the integrity construct as a legitimation of whistleblowing policies is the idea that whistleblowing is 'raising concern' rather than 'making a complaint' or 'making allegations'. Concern needs to be talked through with others, while complaints and allegations require investigation and hence assume evidence. Secondly, these whistleblowing policies are aimed at instigating and sustaining a learning process about appropriate actions and interpretations of values – attuning personal and social value appraisal.

If the communication about actions and values is to be a learning process, the subject element must be kept extremely wide. Complexity and constant change make it impossible to exhaustively sum up about what people can 'raise concern', for we cannot know what is coming and where things can go wrong.

Also, the wider the participation in the learning process, the more qualitative the learning process is, and the larger the number of potential participants, the more chance diverse sets of cognitive biases will interact. However, where organizational learning processes are concerned, raising concern internally is favourable, because the learning process will benefit if all participants can relate to the practice or value 'under concern'. Therefore, a whistleblowing policy driven by the integrity legitimation construct is very likely to limit whistleblowing internally to the organization. However, even within organizational limits, the number of participants must be as high as possible. Therefore, both actor and recipient element of integrity driven whistleblowing policies will favourably be stipulated as 'organizational members'.

Rational Loyalty Construct

This construct pivots on the explicit corpus of mission and value statements of an organization as the object of loyalty. Therefore, the subject element of whistle-blowing policies driven by this construct will include breaches of that corpus as legitimate disclosures.

Since loyalty is bilateral – the agent asking for loyalty must reciprocate that loyalty – the actor element must include all individuals who are asked to be loyal – in other words, all organizational members, whichever way defined – and, the recipient element must include an external recipient to ensure that the organization – asking the loyalty – does not retaliate on loyal individuals who disclose on breaches of the explicit corpus of organizational statements.

Efficiency Construct

I argued that whistleblowing policies legitimated as mechanisms to ensure organizational efficiency are aimed at generating accurate information about organizational inefficiencies caused by the human factor. Therefore, the stipulation of actor, subject and recipient element will be instrumental to that aim. Policies tapping into this legitimation construct will therefore argue that qualifying an element in this or that way will enhance the effectiveness of generating accurate information to counter organizational inefficiency. In this sense, whistleblowing policies advocated as a tool to fight fraud or corruption are very likely to be driven by an efficiency construct. Both these phenomena are hidden by definition and hence require a human factor controlling instrument in order to bring them the surface. In its limit, this construct would offer advantages to those who disclose – promotion or financial reward – over merely protecting against retaliation.

As noted at the outset of this section, Table 3.3 summarizes the stipulations derived from the respective legitimation construct with regard to the actor, subject and recipient elements. Where other relevant derivations were made, they are mentioned under the category 'other'.

Screening Grid

Combining Tables 3.1, 3.2 and 3.3 gives us the grid (Table 3.4) against which whistleblowing policies laid down in legislation or advocated to be laid down in legislation will be screened in Chapter 4.

Placing the Possible Legitimation Constructs within the IOS-Diagram

In this chapter I constructed the possible variations for legitimating whistleblowing policies within the globalization semantic. These legitimation constructs and the actor, subject and recipient elements to be derived from them, form the grid to screen the recent and developing whistleblowing policies against. I will do that in Chapter 4. The result of that screening will be the identification of tendencies in whistleblowing policies laid down in legislation, in other words, tendencies as to what kind of disclosures – made by whom, about what and to whom? – do these policies regard as legitimate.

However, in Chapter 2 I also announced an ethical evaluation of these tendencies, and have developed a diagram to base that ethical evaluation on. The diagram consists of three zones, the individual, the organization and the semantic. As each legitimation construct is a possible variation within the globalization semantic, they will, within the diagram, constitute movements through the three zones of the diagram. As I pointed out, what the diagram visualizes, is whether a legitimation construct either emphasizes difference between the individual and the organizational subject (Touraine) – IS-O and SI-O movements – or encloses the individual within the organizational discourse (Foucault) – OS-I and SO-I movements.

Thus, the ethical evaluation in Chapter 5 will look at the kind of movements the tendencies in whistleblowing policies represent, and draw its conclusions from that. Hence, while the previous sections of this chapter prepare Chapter 4, this section serves as a preparation of Chapter 5. I will be going over the legitimation constructs one by one again, discussion the constructs in terms of the movements they constitute within the diagram.

Human Rights Construct I argued that human rights are individual rights and that globalization has made it necessary to call upon organizations to respect and even

Table 3.3 Actor, subject and recipient elements derived from the legitimation constructs

Legitimation construct	Actor element	Subject element	Recipient element	Other
Human rights	Any person	Unlimited	Not limited (may be qualified, but must show extreme wideness at one point or another	–
OSR-network	Possible specification	Possible specification Emphasize harm to society	Specification in detail	–
OSR-stakeholder	–		Not limited	–
Responsibility	Organizational members	–	Specified in detail	Possible obligation to blow the whistle
Accountability	Organizational members	Mention 'abuse of power'	Tiered approach	–
Integrity	Organizational members	Unlimited	Organizational members	'Raising concerns' rather than 'making complaints or allegations'
Rational loyalty	Organizational members	Mention 'breaches of explicit corpus of mission and value statements of the organization'	Includes at least one external recipient	–
Efficiency	Argued in terms of effectively generating information	Fraud, corruption	Argued in terms of effectively generating information	Possibly offering advantages to those who disclose – promotion, financial rewards

Table 3.4 Screening grid

Legitimation construct	Human rights	OSR-network	OSR-stakeholder	Responsibility	Accountability	Integrity	Loyalty	Efficiency
Other relevant concepts	Truth, self-expression, human dignity, social responsibility	Trust, power balance	Purpose	Responsibilization, duties, autonomy, moral agency	Responsibilization, duties, control	Self-regulation, accountability, control	Responsibilization, purpose, control, social responsibility	Control, panopticon, transparency, accountability
Main line of argument	As protecting and enhancing human rights becomes a social responsibility for all social actors, a whistleblowing policy is needed to ensure the freedom of expression within organizations	Whistleblowing policies ensure power balance within networks, which are made up of interactions; it is through balanced interactions that trust is built up	Whistleblowing policies allow stakeholders to warn one another when organizational practices differ from the organizational purpose	Whistleblowing possibilities safeguard individual autonomy and moral agency, by providing ways to take 'ethical distance	Controlling whether or not individuals carry out their duties calls for accountability; whistleblowing policies ensure accountability is maintained in a wide sense – potentially both upward and downward	The demand for integrity points at the impossibility to control through structure; therefore, self-regulation by autonomous actors is necessary, as is their accountability; whistleblowing policies provide the possibility of realizing integrity in that it allows speaking and acting to coincide	Both organization and individual carry the responsibility of staying focussed on the organizational purpose; whistle-blowing policies allow rational loyalty – loyalty to the organizational purpose – to be manifested	Whistleblowing policies install an organizational panopticon; this is the way organizational efficiency can be controlled; internal whistle-blowing ensures organizational transparency for corporate governance, while external whistleblowing serves watchdog accountability
Grounding ethical theory	Deontological	Virtue	Consequentialist	Deontological, virtue	Consequentialist, virtue	Virtue	Virtue	Consequentialist
Actor-element	Any person	Possible specification	–	Organizational members	Organizational members	Organizational members	Organizational members	Argued in terms of effectively generating information

Table 3.4 cont'd

Legitimation construct	Human rights	OSR-network	OSR-stakeholder	Responsibility	Accountability	Integrity	Loyalty	Efficiency
Subject-element	Unlimited	Possible specification	Emphasize harm to society	–	Mention 'abuse of power'	Unlimited	Mention 'breaches of explicit corpus of mission and value statements of the organization'	Fraud, corruption
Recipient-element	Not limited (may be qualified, but must show extreme wideness at one point or another)	Specification in detail	Not limited	Specified in detail	Tiered approach	Organizational members	Includes at least one external recipient	Argued in terms effectively generating information
Other element related stipulation	–	–	–	Possible obligation to blow the whistle	–	'Raising concerns' rather than 'making complaints or allegations'	–	Possibly offering advantages to those who disclose – promotion, financial rewards

promote human rights. In this sense, the human rights construct sets limits to the organizational discourse and hence to the enclosure of the individual. Therefore, the human rights construct constitutes an IS-O movement (Figure 3.13).

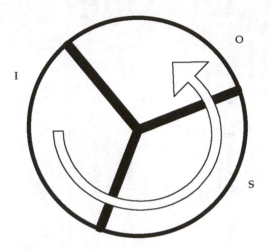

Figure 3.13 Human rights construct in IOS-diagram

OSR-Network Construct This construct entails that organizing takes place through networks. Networks are constituted by interactions and since collaborative interactions are required in an organization, they need to be characterized by trust rather than by imposed regulation. For trust to build up through interactions, power needs to be balanced and whistleblowing policies are such a power balancing mechanism. However, even though 'balancing power' implies that someone is gaining power, the OSR-network construct implies a specification of who the relevant stakeholders are in the organizational network and assigns them a particular position within that network. Hence, the individual gaining power is the individual as positioned within that organizational network. Therefore, speaking of organizations as networks means that the individual gains its identity through the relations it has within the network. As whistleblowing policies driven by the OSR-network construct specify that network, and assign positions in it, the construct limits the individual to its position within the organizational network. In this sense, the OSR-network construct encloses the individual within the organization as an unintended effect of speaking of organizations as networks and hence constitutes a SO-I movement within the diagram (Figure 3.14).

OSR-Stakeholder Construct As I argued earlier on, the OSR-stakeholder construct differs from the OSR-network construct in that it does *not* limit the balancing of power through whistleblowing policies to a specified organizational network, but regards the whole of society as a relevant stakeholder. Here,

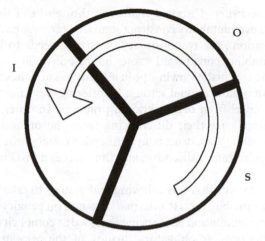

Figure 3.14 OSR-network construct in IOS-diagram

whistleblowing policies aim at stakeholders warning other stakeholders about organizational practices differing from organizational purpose. If an organization was to attain its purpose fully, there would be no alienation of the worker from the purpose of his work within society. Organization and society would fully coincide, as would individual and organizational subject. However, to the extent that this is not the case, stakeholders point out the alienation. Therefore, the OSR-stakeholder construct emphasizes difference between individual and organization and hence constitutes an IS-O movement within the diagram (Figure 3.15).

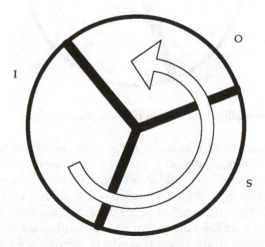

Figure 3.15 OSR-stakeholder construct in IOS-diagram

Responsibility Construct I argued that even though both the responsibility construct and the accountability construct stem from an organizational discourse of 'responsibilization', the responsibility construct needs to be distinguished from the accountability construct. I wrote that responsibility implies autonomy and moral agency. Whistleblowing policies can ensure these otherwise frail notions within an organizational setting, by offering ways for the individual to take 'ethical distance' from organizational practices. In other words, it allows individuals to emphasize their differencing from the organizational subject. Hence, the responsibility construct is an unintended effect of the organizationally intended 'responsibilization' discourse and thus makes a SI-O movement within the diagram.

However, I also wrote that this 'allowing' individuals to take 'ethical distance' can easily flip into an obligation to take that distance, on penalty of taking part in the collective responsibility and hence being regarded as complicit to organizational malpractices. This possible obligatory turning of the responsibility construct constitutes an opposite movement – SO-I – within the diagram (Figure 3.16).

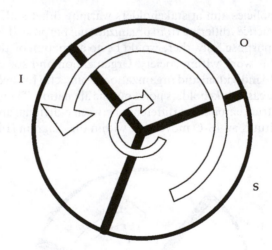

Figure 3.16 Responsibility construct in IOS-diagram

Accountability Construct To the extent the accountability construct implements whistleblowing policies as imposing a causal responsibility for bad results on individuals, the construct designates an attempt to enclose the individual into the organization because in their limit, whistleblowing policies make the individual totally visible to the organization. Therefore, the accountability construct primarily constitutes an OS-I movement within the diagram.

On the other hand, to the extent that whistleblowing policies can substitute the external reference function of bureaucratic regulations, they can safeguard the individual from enclosure into flexible and whimsical organizations. Hence, the accountability construct also constitutes a SI-O movement within the diagram (Figure 3.17).

Figure 3.17 Accountability construct in IOS-diagram

Integrity Construct Placing the integrity construct within the diagram is a special case. The term 'integrity' is very often heard in organizational discourse. In this sense, the instigator of the integrity discourse is the organization, as it is a demand stemming from the impossibility to control through structure. However, the only consistent way of conceptualizing integrity within the globalization semantic, is by stipulating it as the unity of discernment, action and speaking. Hence, the legitimation of whistleblowing policies through the integrity construct is an unintended variation of the organizationally intended integrity discourse, claiming that disclosing information is to be regarded as an act of integrity. Moreover, it emphasizes difference between the individual and the organization, as it is organizational situations and practices the individual discerns and discloses about. The individual 'raises concern' about organizational practices or situations and thereby emphasizes its difference from those situations or practices. Therefore, the construct takes a SI-O movement within the diagram.

However, integrity as the unity of discernment, acting and speaking, picturing whistleblowing as acting coinciding with speaking, favours concerns to be raised internally. It is precisely the internal communication of concerns, dilemmas and doubts that constitutes a learning process through which control is exercised. Therefore, the unintended variation regarding whistleblowing as an act of integrity in turn has an unintended variation, more precisely that of exercizing control through an organizational learning process of communicating concerns, dilemmas and doubts. Hence, the construct also constitutes a SO-I movement within the diagram (Figure 3.18).

Figure 3.18 Integrity construct in IOS-diagram

Rational Loyalty Construct Flexibility and decentralization maintain the organizational need for loyalty, but change the criteria on what kind of loyalty can be reciprocated on. The only way for loyalty to make sense in current organizations is to conceive it as a rational loyalty of both organization and individuals to the explicit corpus of mission and value statements of the organization. But rational loyalty is still loyalty; it clarifies the object of loyalty but that object is no less demanding. Therefore, whistleblowing policies legitimated by the rational loyalty construct are an unintended effect of the organizationally intended need for loyalty. Hence the construct constitutes a SO-I movement within the diagram.

On the other hand, the rational loyalty construct states that within the globalization semantic, organizations can only be identified through their texts, hence the object of rational loyalty is the explicit corpus of mission and value statements of an organization. In other words, the rational loyalty construct equates an organization with its explicit statements. This implies that only legitimate missions and values can be stated as constituting the organization. In this sense, the individual of whom loyalty is demanded, can only be loyal to an object which is accepted by society. Thus, the rational loyalty construct emphasizes a difference between the individual and the organization. Therefore, the construct also constitutes an IS-O movement (Figure 3.19).

Efficiency Construct Finally, the construct of a normative legitimation for whistleblowing policies around the notion of organizational efficiency also has an intended variation as well as an unintended relevant effect. The intended variation is instigated by the organization, designing whistleblowing policies in terms of their effectiveness and efficiency in generating accurate and reliable information about organizational processes and about the behaviour and performance of individuals, with the aim of reducing organizational inefficiency caused by the

Figure 3.19 Rational loyalty construct in IOS-diagram

human factor. In this sense, whistleblowing policies based on organizational efficiency enclose the individual in an organizational panopticon. Therefore, this construct constitutes an OS-I movement within the diagram.

However, transparency within a corporate governance framework might demand the possibility of external whistleblowing in order to be an effective generator of information for its shareholders. In that case, watchdog accountability opens the way for an emphasis of difference between the individual and the organizational subject in the sense that an individual can hold an organization accountable through NGOs or the media. Thus, there is also a SI-O movement to this construct (Figure 3.20).

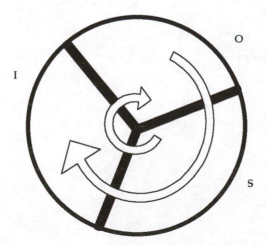

Figure 3.20 Efficiency construct in IOS-diagram

time for public employees simply to be expanded to all employees. Walters spotted new legal trends that whistleblowers 'in private organizations are steadily gaining legal support and may someday enjoy essentially the same rights as employees in government organizations' (Walters 1975, 27). That legal support was to be situated in the US First Amendment's provision that government may not deny citizens freedom of speech. He mentions a number of court rulings that have referred to free speech protection in deciding that a dismissal was wrongful.[4] Arguments used in those rulings include 1) that free and open debate is vital to informed decision making, 2) that it is essential that members of a community most likely to have informed and definite opinions as to how funds are to be spent, are able to speak freely on such questions without fear of retaliatory dismissal, 3) that some critics are engaging in precisely the sort of free and vigorous expression that the First Amendment was designed to protect, and 4) that the First Amendment protects even some speech which could be considered derogatory to the department. All of these arguments use Campell's 'free speech rationales' of truth and of democracy. None refers to free speech as the intrinsic right to self-expression, as an important human need and essential to the flourishing of the individual. Rather, the arguments for free speech are instrumental, as a mechanism for advancing the existence and spread of true belief in society, or as the role of speech and information in a democratic system for making demands and influencing decisions.

Walters explicitly saw First Amendment based arguments as driving the US towards whistleblowing policies. He quotes Emerson, a First Amendment scholar:

> A system of freedom of expression that allowed private bureaucracies to throttle all internal discussion of their affairs would be seriously deficient. There seems to be general agreement that at some point the government must step in. In any event the law is moving steadily in that direction (Emerson 1970, quoted in Walters 1975, 34).

As to the concrete direction this development would take, Walters sees three trends. The first was through collective action, implying a spread of unionism. The second is under the header of 'rights of employment' and consists of a tendency of courts to be willing to take the circumstances surrounding discharges of non-union employees into consideration. This would amount to public policy exceptions to the employment at will doctrine. The third possible development Walters sees is the appearance of specific statutory provisions prohibiting employers from discharging employees who disclose conduct that the statute forbids.

Note that all three of Walters' predictions have come true. Whistleblowing protection has come about in the form of adjunct statutes and public policy decisions. It is also true that legislation has provided specific employee groups

---

[4]   Walters (1975) mentions *Pickering vs. Board of Education, Rafferty vs. Philadelphia Psychiatric Center, Muller vs. Conlisk, Downs vs. Conway School District.*

Chapter 4
Screening Whistleblowing Policies

In this chapter, I screen whistleblowing policies using the grid developed in Chapter 3. As laid out in Chapter 1, I limit the screening to whistleblowing policies laid down in legislation, whistleblowing policies advocated through lobbying activities aimed at legislation, and whistleblowing policies recommended by intergovernmental bodies. Also as indicated in Chapter 1, the screening draws on texts of the Acts and Bills legislating whistleblowing policies, reviews of those Acts and Bills by academics and NGOs, reports of parliamentary readings and discussions on the Bills, reports from official commissions on whistleblowing policies, and position papers from NGOs.

The first sections look at the evolution of legitimation attempts for whistle-blowing in countries that have legislation in force specifically and explicitly aimed at whistleblowing – respectively the US, Australia, New Zealand, the UK, South Africa, Japan and Belgium. The section after those looks at countries with legislations passing through parliament. These include the Netherlands, Ireland, Canada, and India. In another section then I look at Germany and Switzerland where discussions about whistleblowing polices are going on. Finally, I screen whistleblowing policies recommended by intergovernmental bodies – the OECD, the European Commission, and the Council of Europe.

The identification and discussion of tendencies appearing from these screenings will be done in Chapter 5, as will the ethical evaluation of these tendencies.

United States

One cannot discuss whistleblowing policies in the US without putting them into the context of the 'employment at will' principle. Basically, this principle says that an employer can hire and fire employees at his/her own will, without needing to give any reasons for doing so. In legal terms, since the last half of the nineteenth century, employment in each of the United States has been terminable by either employer or employee for any reason or more precisely without the need to give a reason. The employment-at-will doctrine reflected the view the courts held of the relationship between employer and employee as being on equal footing in terms of bargaining power. Since the 1960s however, federal legislative initiatives have identified a number of situations in which such equal footing is not the case. These legislations protect employees from 'wrongful discharge' based on race, religion, sex, age, and national origin (Muhl 2001). These exceptions have been incorporated in common-law or as statutory protections.

An important common-law protection against 'wrongful discharge' is what is referred to as the *public policy exception to employment at will*. Under this exception, an employee is wrongfully discharged if the reason for the termination runs against the public policy of the state, or in other words, if the dismissal is a result of the employers breach of public policy. For example, an employer cannot sack an employee because he/she refuses to break the law at the request of the employer. There is a consensus that public policy can be found in a state constitution, a statute, or an administrative rule. Currently, 43 states accept the public policy exception.[1] The bulk of this development took place in the 1980s (Callahan and Dworkin 2000, Muhl 2001).

According to Muhl (2001), the first case to recognize a public policy exception was *Petermann vs. International Brotherhood of Teamsters*, which occurred in California in 1959. Petermann was employed by the Teamsters Union as a business agent. During his employment, Petermann was subpoenaed to appear before and testify to the Assembly Interim Committee on Governmental Efficiency and Economy, which was investigating into corruption inside the Teamsters Union. Petermann was asked by his employer – the union under investigation – to make false statements to the committee, but he refused and instead truthfully answered all questions. The next day, Petermann was fired. The court found that in this context, California's declared policy against perjury was best effectuated by applying a public policy exception and hence regarded Petermann's firing as a wrongful discharge. It is interesting that Bowers et al. (1999, 249) regard the same case as establishing general whistleblowing protection. Dworkin and Near (1987), in their evaluation of whistleblowing laws, argue that whistleblowing policies are ineffective and that therefore, whistleblowers would rather sue their employer for retaliation under the common law public policy exception. Thus, Dworkin and Near (1987) distinguish whistleblowing laws from public policy exceptions to employment at will. I too would argue that the public policy exception is to be distinguished from a whistleblowing policy. The latter is – as I have put forward in Chapter 1 – an institutionalization of the practice of disclosing dissenting and accusing information by a member of an organization about organizational behaviour. 'Public policy exception' jurisdiction cannot be regarded as such an institutionalization. Rather, what it does is put a legal limit on the amount of employee loyalty an employer can demand. In this sense, referring to my normative legitimation construct on the concept of loyalty, this kind of jurisdiction can be regarded as a rendering explicit of what Corvino called 'some loyalty'. However, it does not qualify for a legitimation on what I have called the only defendable kind of loyalty – rational loyalty – since what is and what is not an employer's breach of public policy is to be found in state constitution, statute or administrative rule (Dworkin and Near 1997, 2; Callahan and Dworkin 2000, 106). It is not to

[1]   The seven states having rejected the public policy exception are: Alabama, Florida, Georgia, Louisiana, Nebraska, New York and Rhode Island (Muhl 2001).

be found in a corporation's code of ethics or value statement, and neither in a professional code of conduct.[2]

Legislative initiatives in the US that do come in reach of being a whistleblowing policy are to be found in what Callahan and Dworkin (2000) have called *adjunct statutes*. These provide protection to whistleblowers through statutes designed to address a particular problem. The protection against retaliation is an adjunct to the statute's principal objectives. The first protections of this type were extended in the Railway Labor Act of 1926 and the National Labor Relations Act (NLRA) of 1935. What these laws do is protect employees from being fired for engaging in union-related activities. Under the NLRA, protection is included for testifying or filing a charge concerning unfair labour practices. Of course, at that time, the practice of disclosing information was not identified as a distinct practice and hence not conceptualized as whistleblowing. Callahan and Dworkin note that such protection was 'merely [...] an incidental means of enforcing employees' organizational rights' (Callahan and Dworkin 2000, 104). Numerous acts were passed by the US Congress that covered the disclosure of wrongful activity only if such reports concerned matters regulated by the specific act or if the discloser was part of the employee group protected by the act.[3]

Statutes specifically targeted at whistleblowing came about at the end of the 1970s at federal level. In the early 1980s, state legislations came about. From the mid 1980s on, new federal whistleblowing legislations were passed, the most recent and remarkable being part of the Sarbanes-Oxley Act in 2002. Therefore, in discussing whistleblowing policies, it makes sense to distinguish pre-legislation period (pre-1980s), the legislative protections at state level, and the federal policies.

Pre-1980s

As I pointed out in Chapter 1, in the early 1970s, the whistleblowing concept was a politico-ethical one. Vogel (1974) saw whistleblowing as one of the tactics of putting pressure on corporations. Walters (1975) too saw an approaching shift in that matters traditionally considered an organization's own business may become the public's as well. But Walters expected the protection measures available at that

[2]   Bowers et al. (1999, 249) mention the case of *Schudolski vs. Michigan Consolidated Gas Co.* in 1982, where an employee blew the whistle on internal accounting procedures, and in doing so relied upon the code of conduct of the Institute of Internal Auditors, but where the court did not accept that this code was public policy.

[3]   For example: Toxic Substances Control Act, Age Discrimination in Employment Act, Occupational Safety and Health Act, Job Training and Partnership Act, Migrant and Seasonal Agricultural Workers Protection Act, Federal Surface Mining Act, Water Pollution Control Act, Safe Drinking Water Act, Title VII of the Civil Rights Act of 1964, Energy Reorganization Act, Solid Waste Disposal Act, Clean Air Act, Comprehensive Environmental Response, Compensation and Liability Act, Surface Transportation Act (Callahan and Dworkin 2000, fn 28).

with protection. Callahan and Dworkin (2000, 113) note that state laws are more likely to cover retaliation for employee harms relating to OSHA or minimum wage, than for disclosures of conduct threatening to the public, for example relating to the environment and child welfare. But what Walters did not foresee were statutory laws aimed specific at whistleblowing. He does hint at private sector corporations to develop whistleblowing policies, but always to avoid external whistleblowing.

In 1977, the GAP (Government Accountability Project) was founded in Washington, DC as a non-profit organization. It became the US leading whistleblower organization, advocating free speech, litigating whistleblower cases, publicizing whistleblower concerns, developing policy and advising legal reforms.[5] What is to be noted is that the GAP too lobbied the whistleblowing issue emphasizing occupational free speech, hence human rights and the US First Amendment. Even today it is still using that discourse (Devine 2004a; 2004b).

What is to be concluded from this short discussion of the pre-legislation period? In terms of screening for normative legitimation constructs, Walter's call for whistleblowing policies is not normative, as it is avoiding whistleblowing which is regarded as in the best interest of the organization.

However, Walter's analysis of the court rulings is interesting. He sees that whistleblowers are being regarded as acting in line with the First Amendment and expects legislation to develop further in that direction in three ways: collective action, public policy exceptions and adjunct protection to specific statutory provisions. However, public policy exceptions have been too narrowly interpreted to count as having a human right normative legitimation. The same goes for the adjunct statutory protections. There, whistleblowing protection finds its legitimation in the importance attached to what the whistle is blown about. Finally, it is hard to see how protection gained through collective action – protecting specific groups of employees – could base itself on the human rights normative legitimation, as the notion that *some* employees ought to be protected runs against the equal worth underpinning human rights.

Therefore, my first conclusion is that the hopes and expectations for whistleblowing policies did tap into a human rights normative legitimation, but that the development of whistleblowing protection in the form of public policy exception and adjunct statutory protection (whether subject based or union based) does not express such a normative legitimation.

My second conclusion is, that the development of a whistleblowing policy was not foreseen. At government level, such a policy consists of legislation specifically aimed at whistleblowing. This kind of legislation first came about in 1978 at federal level and since the early 1980s at state level.

---

[5] See the GAP website: http://www.whistleblower.org.

Legislative Protections at State Level

I will not consider legislation or jurisdiction that does not focus on whistleblowing as such. Since, as I indicated earlier on, these legislations are not to be considered as whistleblowing policies, I believe to have given them already enough attention in this chapter, and they will not figure in the screening.

The early 1980s however saw the passing of the first whistleblowing statutes at state level. Dworkin and Near (1987) include a review of the first five whistleblowing statutes at state level. Micelli and Near (1992, 240–45, 260–73) reviews 34 state legislations protecting whistleblowers. Miethe (1999, 108–32) gives an overview of 44 state legislations. However, Micelli and Near (1992) nor Miethe (1999) depict any evolution in state legislations. The kind of employees they cover varies, but the big majority covers only government employees. A salient constant is the subject element, covering violations of law. Therefore, in a diachronic perspective, the important fact is *that* state legislation came about, and less its gradual spreading across the US. Hence, I will include only the first five state legislations in the screening. The first is the Michigan act,[6] passed in 1981. The motivation was that corporations and government bodies, because of their size, are among the greatest threats to the public welfare when they violate the law (Dworkin and Near 1987, 244–5, quoting House Legislative Analysis Section, Analysis – HBs 5099 and 5089). Protection is offered for employees reporting to a public body on organizational violations or suspected violations of the law. The Connecticut whistleblowing statute[7] does the same. However, in 1983, the Connecticut legislature passed a bill protecting the first amendment rights of employees, stating that the employer is liable to the employee for damages when the employer interferes with an employee's freedoms of speech, religion, press or assembly, and the employee's exercise of these rights does not interfere with his/her job performance or his/her working relationship with the employer. Dworkin and Near (1987, 249–50) argue that the working relationship language requires internal whistleblowing, since this usage of free speech rights interferes the least with the working relationship, and hence conclude that Connecticut's two statutes, if read together, provide protection for both internal and external whistleblowing. Moreover, as far as I see it, the protection for internal whistleblowing would cover a wider subject element than the external whistleblowing which only covers disclosures about violations of the law.

Maine passed a whistleblowing protection statute in 1983[8] which indicates a first step towards a governance approach. The statute explicitly recognized the desirability of internal whistleblowing by providing that the protection only applies when the whistleblower has first brought the violation to the attention of a superior within the organization, and hence has allowed the employer an

---

6   Mich. Comp. Laws Ann. § 15.362.
7   Conn. Gen. Stat. Ann § 31-51m(c).
8   Me. Rev. Stat. Ann. tit. 26, § 832.

opportunity to correct that violation. Therefore, this act encourages organizations to set up ways of dealing with internal problems, although it does not specify any criteria to which these 'ways of dealing with' have to answer.

California and New York passed whistleblowing statutes in 1984.[9] New Jersey passed such a statute in 1986.[10] California followed Michigan in that it only protects disclosure of a violation of a state or federal statute or regulation to a governmental or law enforcement agency. New York and New Jersey followed Maine by requiring the whistleblower to first address superiors within the organization.[11] However, New York's statute is different at the subject element because it does not provide protection for whistleblowing concerning a violation of just any law, rule or regulation, but for whistleblowing concerning violations that create a substantial and specific danger to the public health or safety.

The point I am making here is that the whistleblowing statutes at state level did not – unlike the expectations of the early 1970s (see earlier on my discussion of Walters 1975) – embrace a human rights normative legitimation. The statutes disqualify for such a legitimation because of their restricted subject element.

Moreover, the narrow subject element denotes a mere law compliance outlook. The New York statute is not an exception but rather narrows it down even further, because the protection covers only disclosures about violations of laws and regulations that create a substantial and specific danger. The law compliance outlook is also mirrored in jurisprudence. Callahan and Dworkin (2000, 120) note that 'plaintiffs who were perceived merely to be reporting failures to follow company procedures were generally unsuccessful'. This disqualifies the statutes for a 'rational loyalty' legitimation construct.

More important however is that the state level statutes already at a very early stage – the connected reading of the two Connecticut acts might very well have caused the Maine variation which caught on in New York and New Jersey – show an opening for a normative legitimation based on making organizations accountable for not acting upon internal reports of organizational wrongdoing. But they do not fully take up a normative legitimation on an OSR concept, because in no way are organizations sanctioned if they do not have internal whistleblowing policies.

Civil Service Reform Act – Whistleblower Protection Act

When Jimmy Carter came to office as President of the US in 1977, the Congress had reasserted power over the Executive in response to Watergate and the resignation of Richard Nixon. The scandal had put civil service reform high on the political agenda. The US Senate established a special *Committee on Governmental*

---

[9]   Respectively Cal. Lab. Code § 1102.5 and N.Y Lab. Law § 740.

[10]   N.J. Stat. Ann. § 34: 19–1 to 19–8.

[11]   New Jersey's act differs from New York's and Maine's by requiring that the internal reporting be in writing (Dworkin and Near 1987, fn. 57).

Affairs which had to prepare reforms. In 1978 it issued its report (US Senate 1978, quoted in Parker 1988). The report stated that while Congress was encouraging whistleblowing, the means it provided for its expression were too limited and it failed to provide adequate protection. But the report also expressed why whistleblowing was an important practice. Whistleblowing was described as central to at least two key areas of congressional activity: 1) whistleblowing helps Congress to act vigorously in the elimination of fraud, waste and mismanagement, and 2) whistleblowing is another means of holding the Executive to account. Both of these activities depend upon informed disclosures. A Senator expressed it as follows:

> It is the duty of all Federal employees to make known examples of government waste, misfeasance or malfeasance to which they have been exposed during the course of their employment. These disclosures should be made in a manner which ensures that those in affected policy making positions are held accountable for determining the nature of the problem and bringing about its resolution. Federal employees have a right to fulfil this duty free from harassment or reprisal of any type from their superiors, agency or the Federal government (Senator Leahy, in US Senate 1978, quoted in Parker 1988, 152).

Hence, Congress took action in a number of forms (Parker 1988). The Offices of Inspector General (OIG) were established as a quasi-independent investigation and audit service in 14 of the major executive agencies. One of its duties was to provide a channel for the disclosure of wrongdoing, backed up with investigatory power. It established such a channel in the form of a telephone 'hotline', which can be used to blow the whistle anonymously. In addition to that, the General Accounting Office (GAO) – the congressional accounting agency – also opened a hotline for all federal employees and the public.

Protection against reprisal was included in the *Civil Service Reform Act* of 1978. In that act, civil servants were expected to speak out on issues they believed were a violation of any law, rule or regulation, mismanagement, waste of funds, abuse of authority, or a substantial and specific danger to public health and safety. Also, current and former employees of the federal government who did reveal such information were now formally described as whistleblowers (Parker 1988). However, one could only report matters which had occurred, not on wrongdoing which was about to happen (Bowers et al. 1999). The Civil Service Reform Act created three agencies: the Office of Personnel Management (OPM), the Merit Systems Protection Board (MSPB) and the Office of Special Counsel (OSC), which was a component of the MSPB. The OPM had to administer civil service. The MSPB was charged with the adjudication of appeals of personnel of any matter – including allegations that a personnel action was taken[12] because of

---

[12] §2302(b) of title 5 of the US Code states that it is prohibited personnel practice to take or fail to take, or threaten to take or fail to take, a personnel action because of an individual's legal disclosure of information evidencing wrongdoing ('whistleblowing') (Groeneweg 2001).

whistleblowing activities. The OSC was designed to defend and assist whistle-blowers in raising their concern and in pursuit of redress together with the MSPB. Whistleblowing protection therefore was not entirely in the hands of the OSC, which related to the MSPB as a prosecutor to a judge (OSC 1983, quoted in Parker 1988). For the OSC, whistleblowing is but one of the ten prohibited personnel practices. The OSC has to bring cases of such practices before the MSPB. Hence, both agencies were set up to defend the merit system within the US civil service. With regard to whistleblowing, the OSC serves as a filter for allegations of reprisals for whistleblowing. But there were limitations as to how the OSC could deal with whistleblowing. It could directly investigate reprisals against whistle-blowers, but investigations of the allegations of wrongdoing were to be made by the responsible agency heads of the OIG. Parker (1988) sees the double role of the OSC – investigating reprisals against whistleblowers and assist whistleblowers in making allegations – as one of the reasons for its malfunctioning.

The OSC was severely criticized for its poor performance with regard to defending and assisting whistleblowers (Parker 1988; Bowers et al. 1999; Groeneweg 2001). Apparently, the OSC turned down the vast majority of cases referred to it.[13] Or, in other words, it just did not function. Therefore, the US Congress passed the *Whistleblower Protection Act* (WPA) in 1989, aiming to improve the effectiveness of the OSC and to increase protection for federal whistle-blowers. It did so by allowing whistleblowers to appeal directly to the MSPB if they first complain to the OSC and the OSC does not seek corrective action on their behalf. Furthermore, through the enforcement of the Government Code of Ethics, the WPA ensured that federal agencies encouraged whistleblowing. It also gave employers the duty to permit whistleblowers to return to their job and to remain on the pay roll whilst awaiting the determination of their allegation. As far as the subject element of protected disclosures is concerned, the WPA allowed for threats of illegal acts to be reported on. This was a change from the Civil Service Reform Act from 1978 under which the whistleblower first had to permit the illegal act to occur before he/she could disclose on it.

The WPA was further amended in 1994, in order to change its image and place more emphasis on the OSC as protecting the whistleblower's interests. The OSC became an independent agency away from the MSPB (Bowers et al. 1999, 250; Groeneweg 2001, 9). Its role was defined as to protect federal workers from prohibitive practices. It is still allowed to initiate inquiries and investigate wrongdoing, but such was no longer a task. The double-role confusion mentioned by Parker (1988) was hereby solved. Also, the OSC had to consult more and keep informed those they represented. Another important change in the provision of

---

[13]   Parker (1988, 154) states that 'up to 92% of allegations of reprisals for whistle-blowers were not taken by OSC to the Merit Systems Protection Board'. According to Devine (1997, 119), between 1979 and 1988 the Office of Special Counsel turned down 99 per cent of cases referred to it. For statistics on complaints and allegations received and processed by the OSC, see Parker (1988, 154); Groeneweg (2001, 11).

protection. Up till then, for a claim to be acceptable, the whistleblower had to prove that his/her disclosure was a significant factor causing the reprisal. In the 1994 amendment of the WPA, the onus of proof was not reversed but lowered so that now the federal employee had to show that their disclosure was not a significant but a contributing factor to the retaliation by their employer.

There is a shift in normative legitimation to be noted from the outset of the civil service reform in 1970s to the WPA amendments in 1994. The report of the US Senate special committee on governmental affairs (quoted in Parker 1988), saw whistleblowing as a central feature of the Congress' tasks of holding the Executive to account and eliminating fraud, waste and mismanagement. Whistleblowing was pictured as part of the way a democratic institution such as Congress functions. Holding the Executive branch to account requires a power balance, and it is a perceived power balance between parliamentary and executive institutions which allows society to trust government. Hence, the normative legitimation comes close to the OSR-network construct. Some even went as far as to speak of a personal duty to blow the whistle, thereby calling upon personal responsibility (see supra Senator Leahy). It is Parker's opinion too that Congress, through the whistle-blowing provisions of the Civil Service Reform Act had answered the desire for open decision making and the recognition that civil servants had as individuals a potential for public responsibility (Parker 1988, 157).

Those were the normative appeals of the late 1970s and early 1980s. However, by the 1990s a shift had taken place. Groeneweg (2001) argues that the structure of the internal mechanisms for reporting under the WPA points at a co-option by the US Government of whistleblowing as an efficiency tool rather than provide a mechanism for the protection of government employees who disclose on corrupt practices. By 1993 – at the eve of amending the WPA – this turn in discourse was completed. Groeneweg (2001, 14) cites the opening letter of 1993 MSPB report, in which the chairman and the vice-chairman state their position on whistleblowing, saying that the ideal of whistleblowing is to improve the efficiency and effectiveness of government. The focus of designing or revizing whistleblowing policies then, is not to make protection better, but rather to motivate employees to report:

> Obviously, if meeting current goals to improve Government operations is going to depend significantly on employee reporting of information about fraud, waste and abuse, employees will need to be more willing to do this now than they were in 1983 (MSPB chairman and vice-chairman, quoted in Groeneweg 2001, 14).

This kind of shift is noted by Dworkin and Near (1997). They state that the 'old' model valued motivation over information and viewed whistleblowing as an act of conscience and responsibility. The 'new' model however values information over motivation. Dworkin and Near see the 'new' model as initiated by the revision in 1986 of the False Claims Act, offering rewards for information.

False Claims Act – Qui Tam

The False Claims Act dates from 1863 and is often referred to as the 'Lincoln Law'.[14] It is based on the principle of 'qui tam pro domino rege sequitur quam pro se ipso' or 'he who sues on behalf of the King also sues as well as for himself' (Bowers et al. 1999, 251). The Act establishes that anyone who sues in the name of the US Government in relation to fraud also sues for themselves. Basically, the idea is that the person or organization filing the law suit gets a percentage of the money the government is able to recover. Anyone can file a *qui tam* suit, including employees of the company or agency that is defrauding the government, former employees of the company or agency, competitors, subcontractors, state and local government, federal employees, public interest groups, corporations and private citizens.

Originally, the law was hardly used by individuals because they had to bear the cost of the suit themselves. In 1943, Congress amended the law unfavourably, reducing the reward to the whistleblower who brought the suit, and providing that a person could not file a *qui tam* lawsuit if the government had prior knowledge of the charges.

In 1986 however, Congress once again revised the False Claims Act (FCA), making it a very successful tool in recovering fraud.[15] First, it raised the amount awarded. The whistleblower must bring suit under FCA and go through trial. The government then decides whether or not it joins the suit. If it does and it is able to recover money through the lawsuit, the whistleblower may receive 15–25 per cent of the amount recovered. If the government decides not join, this may increase to 25–30 per cent. Second, the 1986 revision allowed a *qui tam* case to be filed even if the government already knew about the charges. And third, it also included a clause protecting whistleblowers from harassment, demotion and wrongful dismissal.

Micelli and Near (1992, 246–49) and Dworkin and Near (1997) see the FCA revision as a new approach to whistleblowing, moving away from what they call an 'old model' emphasizing motive over information, towards a 'new model' valuing information over motivation. Indeed, one gets a reward if the information is useful and leads to a recovery of fraudulent money. The provisions of the FCA are designed to meet the motivational criteria of a reward system, namely that the reward is sufficiently large to justify the effort, that payout is sufficiently certain

---

[14] It was originally enacted to protect the Union Arms against fraudulent suppliers during the American Civil War, who sold sawdust for gun powder.

[15] Callahan and Dworkin (2000) write that FCA reports of fraud against the government have increased from an average of 6 per year before 1986 to 450 per year in 1998. Saldico (2000) writes that the government's recoveries under the FCA have skyrocketed since its revision, totalling more than $4 billion through more than 3,000 *qui tam* cases, with the majority of those being filed against those who do business in the healthcare industry.

to justify the effort, and that the payout is timely in relation to doing the desired activity.[16] The whole idea is getting the information. Underlying is of course the inability to control, or as Dworkin and Near describe it: 'It encourages citizen enforcement of the laws when the government lacks the resources, information or ability to do it' (Dworkin and Near 1997, 10).

Saldico (2000) also points in that direction. He discusses the position the US Government took in some *qui tam* actions. Some *qui tam* actions are targeted against a whole industry or several companies within an industry. The reason for this is that, when filing a *qui tam* suit, there is a financial interest to state allegations as broadly as possible and to name as many corporate defendants as possible because to do so increases the potential reward paid to the relator – the person taking the *qui tam* action, or the whistleblower. However, Saldico (2000) notes, this is not the kind of 'insider whistleblower' lawsuit that Congress intended to foster. In the paradigm case, the whistleblower transfers inside information to the US Government in exchange for a reward. This arrangement has even been conceptualized by courts as the government purchasing information it might not otherwise acquire. In industry-wide, multi-defendant *qui tam* actions, the person bringing suit is not an employee of 'the' particular defendant – hence is not a whistleblower in a strict sense. It is also typical for this kind of relators that they do not have real inside information. Therefore, Saldico (2000) argues, these actions turn the chief purpose underlying *qui tam* actions on its head. The *qui tam* provisions are supposed to operate as a mechanism under which insiders supply needed information to the US Government and in exchange receive a substantial reward. In industry-wide, multi-defendant *qui tam* actions however, the US receives no useful evidence or information and still must pay a reward. Saldico (2000) then points out how the US Government in two *qui tam* actions in 1997 and 2000[17] took position to undo such a derailment. The courts took up a stricter interpretation of the FCA, requiring that a relator must serve the government with a written disclosure of substantially all material evidence and information in his/her possession.[18] FCA claims have been dismissed where

---

[16]   Dworkin and Near (1987) see opportunities to improve the FCA on the aspect of timeliness. As the whistleblower must bring suit and go through trial, the whole process can be delayed at several stages by the Justice Department or by the most likely well-financed company against whom fraud-allegations have been made, and who has the resources to make the investigation and the discovery of facts a long and expensive process. Recovery time is likely to exceed one year. In this sense, the revision of the FCA that a whistleblower can stay on the pay roll while the process runs, intends to meet this structural demand.

[17]   This concerns two industry-wide *qui tam* actions pending against companies operating in the energy industry. Jack Grynberg alleged that several energy companies had mismeasured gas in calculating the royalties they owe to the federal government, and Glenn Osterhoudt alleged that approximately 25 defendants had underpaid royalties they owe on natural gas. (Natural Gas Royalties Qui Tam Litigation, MDL No. 1293 (D. Wyo. filed July 20, 2000) (Saldico 2000).

[18]   31 USC § 3730(b)(2) (Saldico 2000).

relators did not provide such written disclosure statements, arguing that the disclosure requirement has the primary purpose of providing the US government with enough information on the alleged fraud so that the government is able to make a well reasoned decision on whether it should participate in the filed lawsuit or allow the relator to proceed alone. Hence, the FCA does not give rewards for bare allegations contained in a complaint if these are not supported by evidence, and this evidence must be more substantive than the notion that 'something fishy' is going on.

Now, to base the validity of a relator's status as whistleblower on information he/she provides at the outset of the case, and not on information that the government develops through its investigation, shows that the legitimation of the whistleblowing policies of the FCA – offering a reward for information – is to get information from insiders it would otherwise not be able to obtain. Indeed, as noted at the end of the previous section, it is an absolute focus on whistleblowing as a way to generate information on fraud and the FCA is a whistleblowing policy aiming at an efficient and effective way of generating such information.

The Organizational Sentencing Guidelines

The policies I have discussed so far can be seen as 'government' centred. It is the government who is soliciting for information, who offers protection and who runs the investigations into alleged wrongdoing. The Organizational Sentencing Guidelines (OSG) however, are to be categorized as a 'governance' centred approach. In contrast to the 'government' approaches, the OSG should not be seen as providing an incentive for whistleblowing, but rather as providing an incentive for organizations to implement a whistleblowing policy. Although Callahan et al. (2002) write that the FCA and the tort-based theory of wrongful discharge have also provided an incentive for organizations to provide internal reporting channels, it seems to me that they only implicitly do so while the OSG is explicit in providing such an incentive.

In 1984, Congress passed the Sentencing Reform Act, under which the US Sentencing Commission was established as an ongoing independent agency within the judicial branch. The Sentencing Commission had to reduce disparities and judicial discretion in sentencing.[19] It developed the Sentencing

---

[19] Its principal purposes are: '(1) to establish sentencing policies and practices for the federal courts, including guidelines prescribing the appropriate form and severity of punishment for offenders convicted of federal crimes; (2) to advise and assist Congress and the executive branch in the development of effective and efficient crime policy; (3) to collect, analyze, research, and distribute a broad array of information on federal crime and sentencing issues, serving as an information resource for Congress, the executive branch, the courts, criminal justice practitioners, the academic community, and the public' (Desio s.d., 2).

Guidelines,[20] structuring the previously unfettered sentencing discretion, making the administration of punishment more certain and targeting specific offenders for more serious penalties (Desio s.d.). Even though the first set of guidelines (1987) applied only to individual offenders, the Commission intended to draft organizational guidelines from its outset (Murphy 2002),[21] but decided to undertake research and discussion in advisory working groups before issuing such guidelines. A fundamental limitation in sentencing organizations to be countered was, that fines were often the only useful and authorized form of sanction against corporations and other organizations, but that the:

> practice of punishing corporate crime with fines paid to the United States Treasury has done little to deter corporate crime. Once the payment is made to the Treasury, the public promptly forgets the transgression, and the corporation continues on its way, with its reputation only slightly tarnished by what it usually describes as a 'high technical violation' (Judge Gerald Heaney, quoted in Murphy 2002, 701).

On 1 May 1991, the Commission promulgated a new chapter – chapter 8 (USSC 1991) – to the guidelines, applying specifically to organization offenders. These guidelines apply to corporations, partnerships, labour unions, pension funds, trusts, non-profit entities and governmental units (Desio s.d.). While the guidelines for individuals focus on punishment and incapacitation, the organizational guidelines aim at deterring organizational crime. The approach taken is to significantly increase fines[22] for organizational crimes while at the same time providing sentencing benefits for organizations that have an effective programme to prevent and detect violations of law (Murphy 2002). Such a programme must show that the organization 'exercised due diligence in seeking to prevent and detect criminal conduct by its employees and other agents' (USSC 2002, §8A1.2 note 3). The Commission also described the criteria for what can count as 'due diligence'.[23] These set out a number of steps organizations need to undertake

---

[20]   The original set of guidelines was sent to Congress on 1 May 1987. The Commission has the authority to submit guideline amendments each year to Congress between the beginning of a regular congressional session and 1 May. These amendments automatically take effect 180 days after submission unless a law is enacted to the contrary (Murphy 2002; Desio s.d.).

[21]   Indeed, the US Criminal Code provides for the sentencing of organizations, which are defined simply as persons other than individuals.

[22]   See Murphy (2002: 708) for some statistics comparing fine amounts pre and post OSG.

[23]   According to the OSG, due diligence 'requires at a minimum that the organization must have taken the following types of steps:

(1) The organization must have established compliance standards and procedures to be followed by its employees and other agents that are reasonably capable of reducing the prospect of criminal conduct.

to set up what can be called an effective compliance programme. One of those steps is that:

> the organization must have taken reasonable steps to achieve compliance with its standards, e.g. by utilizing monitoring and auditing systems reasonably designed to detect criminal conduct by its employees and other agents and *by having in place and publicizing a reporting system whereby employees and other agents could report criminal conduct by others within the organization without fear of retribution* (USSC 2002, §8A1.2 note 3, emphasis added).

Hence, the Sentencing Commission considers that it is required of organizations to have a whistleblowing policy, if that organization wants to be regarded as manifesting due diligence in seeking to prevent and detect criminal conduct.

When an organization is sentenced for a crime, a 'culpability score' is calculated based on whether or not the organization had an effective compliance programme in place, and on the size of the organization, the likelihood that certain offences may occur because of the nature of its business, and the prior history of the organization (see USSC 1991, §8C2.5). Other mitigators to the culpability score besides an effective programme to prevent and detect violations of law include self-reporting violations of law, cooperation with authorities and the acceptance of responsibility (Murphy 2002, 706).

---

(2) Specific individual(s) within high-level personnel of the organization must have been assigned overall responsibility to oversee compliance with such standards and procedures.

(3) The organization must have used due care not to delegate substantial discretionary authority to individuals whom the organization knew, or should have known through the exercise of due diligence, had a propensity to engage in illegal activities.

(4) The organization must have taken steps to communicate effectively its standards and procedures to all employees and other agents, e.g., by requiring participation in training programs or by disseminating publications that explain in a practical manner what is required.

(5) The organization must have taken reasonable steps to achieve compliance with its standards, e.g., by utilizing monitoring and auditing systems reasonably designed to detect criminal conduct by its employees and other agents and by having in place and publicizing a reporting system whereby employees and other agents could report criminal conduct by others within the organization without fear of retribution.

(6) The standards must have been consistently enforced through appropriate disciplinary mechanisms, including, as appropriate, discipline of individuals responsible for the failure to detect an offense. Adequate discipline of individuals responsible for an offense is a necessary component of enforcement; however, the form of discipline that will be appropriate will be case specific.

(7) After an offense has been detected, the organization must have taken all reasonable steps to respond appropriately to the offense and to prevent further similar offenses – including any necessary modifications to its program to prevent and detect violations of law' (USSC 2002, §8A1.2 note 3).

Several authors have commented on the OSG, in giving incentive to organizations to take care of compliance programmes, as putting forward a number of broad principles that, taken together, describe a corporate 'good citizen' model (Desio s.d.; Dalton et al. 1999; Swenson 1995; Murphy 2002). If this were so, the OSG could be regarded as using a normative legitimation built around an OSR-concept. It would urge organizations to develop whistleblowing policies as a way to ensure the organizational purpose is safeguarded instead of business goals taking priority. In the section on the OSR-stakeholder legitimation construct, I wrote that such a policy would put emphasis on possible harms to society and allow for wide disclosures. Indeed, given that the OSG accord a fine benefit when self-reporting, cooperation with authorities and acceptance of responsibilities are manifested, organizational whistleblowing policies allowing wide disclosures would qualify for such benefits. The problem however lies with the identified possible harms to society. Currently, the OSG concern violations of law, and do not apply to environmental crimes, food and drug offences, or civil rights violations (Near and Dworkin 1998). Murphy (2002, 717–19) describes ongoing discussions to broaden the scope of the OSG to include provisions for environmental offences. If the OSG would widen its scope to include more types of offences regarded as harmful to society[24] it would strengthen its OSR legitimation. However, since this is not the case, the OSG do not show OSR drivers.

Also documented in Murphy (2002, 714–16) are the suggestions to explicitly include 'ethics' as complementing to mere compliance with the law. The rationale for including 'training in ethics' next to 'training in law' is that:

> a good compliance program must emphasize values and moral responsibility, because this increases the program's effectiveness among employees. A good ethics program must help employees to know and obey the law if it is to have any relevance to the company in its actual environment (Driscoll et al. 1999, quoted in Murphy 2002, 715).

The call for an explicit mentioning of 'ethics' in the OSG is supported by the Ethics Officer Association.[25] If the OSG would explicitly mention ethics training and

---

[24] Organizations have criminalized environmental offences of corporations. In fact, environmental offences are the second most common federal crime committed by organizations after fraud. In 2000, of a total of 304 organizations sentenced, 70 were sentenced for environmental pollution offences, which was the next highest category after fraud with 105 convictions (Federal Sentencing Statistics, quoted in Murphy 2002, footnote 100).

[25] The Ethics Officer Association (EOA) is a non-profit, non-consulting professional association 'for managers of ethics, compliance, and business conduct programs [serving] as a forum for the exchange of information and strategies among individuals responsible for setting the ethics, compliance and business conduct programs in their organizations' (EOA 2001). This job description is fulfilled by the 'Ethics and Compliance Officer', an entirely new organizational post created as a response of organizations to the OSG (Murphy 2002, 710).

ethics programmes, it would tap into the normative construct around the concept of integrity. Developing ways in which ethical dilemmas are discussed and resolved by management and employees will render a compliance programme more effective because this would enhance participation in the further development and implementation of organizational values and standards.

What the OSG as it is now does run on, is the normative legitimation construct around the concept of 'rational loyalty'. This construct stated that blowing the whistle on organizational practices diverging from the organization's explicit corpus of mission, values and codes of conduct is a loyal act. The OSG is saying just that, by summing organizations to have a compliance programme establishing standards and procedures, communicating them to employees, and undertaking steps to achieve compliance including reporting systems with protective safeguards. Dworkin and Near (1997) can also be read as pointing the OSG in the direction of the 'rational loyalty' construct, arguing that when properly implemented, such a scheme is:

> less harmful to employees who complain because they won't be treated as pariahs by employees or the employer [and that this,] in turn, will reduce the likelihood of an atmosphere of suspicion and recrimination (Dworkin and Near 1997, 11).

However, a field research by Near and Dworkin (1998) measuring the extent to which such schemes – whistleblowing policies – are properly implemented, showed disappointing results. The majority of companies included in the research could not be seen as having an effective compliance programme. Most of them had 'open door policies' (81 per cent), while over a third had grievance procedures (44 per cent union-sponsored, 46 per cent non-union, audit committees 56 per cent). Only 14 per cent used an ombudsperson, 12 per cent impartial arbitration and 3 per cent a joint management/employee committee to consider allegations. Near and Dworkin (1998, 1557) argue that 'an open door policy is, in most instances, equivalent to having no policy' because employees do not trust such policies as being effective or protective and hence they have not been successful in encouraging internal reporting.[26] An open door policy lacks the specific high-level involvement and non-retaliatory attitude the OSG require. Moreover, the research showed many companies were inadequate at getting the relevant information – whistleblowing policies, value and mission statements, codes of ethics – communicated to their employees. Nor were the ethics and value statements effectively monitored, trained for, or practiced.

Another approach the OSG currently seems to use is the notion of 'ethical distance' I mentioned when constructing the 'responsibility' legitimation construct.

---

[26] Dworkin and Near (1997) mention research showing a positive correlation between increased internal whistleblowing and having specific, identified routes for whistleblowing, a particular person identified to receive and follow-up the information, and a strong, non-retaliatory policy encouraging whistleblowing.

Under the US Criminal Code, criminal liability can attach to an organization whenever one of its employees commits an illegal act, even if the employee acted directly contrary to organization policy and instruction, and despite the organization's efforts to prevent wrongdoing (Desio s.d.). Seen in that context, the OSG provide the possibility for organizations to create an 'ethical distance' between the organization and the employee committing illegal acts, by having an effective compliance programme, including a whistleblowing policy. If organizations have such a programme and policy, and they can show due diligence (see supra), then their 'culpability score' is reduced, meaning that an ethical distance of the organization from an outcome is created. If the organization does not have such a programme and policy, or it can not show an adequate implementation, then the 'ethical distance' is diminished and the 'culpability score' is increased.

Finally, Murphy (2002, 713–14) writes that an effect of the OSG has been an 'increased potential liability of corporate directors to their shareholders'. Jurisdiction based on OSG[27] held that a corporate director – a member of the board of directors – has a 'good faith duty' to see that adequate information and reporting systems are established within the organization. Directors can avoid liability in shareholder derivative suits by showing a good faith attempt to create such systems. It has even be held a breach of fiduciary duty if directors intentionally or recklessly disregard raised concerns to fraudulent practices within the organization. While this jurisdiction points in the direction of an increase of the board's accountability, it also taps into the OSR-network construct. However, these are perceived effects of the OSG, not part of the policy itself.

Sarbanes-Oxley Act

The first years of the twenty-first century shook the Western world not only with terrorism, but also with corporate failures stemming from lax accounting and corporate governance practices: Enron, WorldCom, Xerox, Swiss Air, Vivendi are perhaps the best known collapses.[28] In response to that, in July 2002, US Congress passed the Sarbanes-Oxley Act[29] – tagged as 'SOX'. According to Paul Atkins (2003), SEC Commissioner, the fact that SOX passed Congress with a vast majority of the votes – only three members opposed – is remarkable and represents a formerly unimaginable incursion of the US Federal Government into the corporate governance arena. Up till then, the individual states had exclusive jurisdiction over corporate governance matters, but the SOX is an attempt to

---

[27] *In re Caremark*, [698 A.2d 959 (Del.Ch. 1996)], *Dellastatious vs. Williams* [242 F.3d 191 (4th Cir. 2001)], *McCall vs. Scott* [239 F.3d 808 (6th Cir. 2001)], quoted in Murphy (2002).

[28] For Flanders, the collapse of Lernout & Hauspie must be included in that list.

[29] Named after two Senators sponsoring the Act, Paul Sarbanes (Democrat) and Michael Oxley (Republican).

provide fundamental mechanisms 'to prevent the misdeeds that led to investor losses'. However, the SOX still represents a governance approach, as it provides corporations to 'disclose aspects and then let the market decide what importance to put on that disclosure'. SOX applies for financial matters, and most of the sections in the Act are implemented by the Securities and Exchange Commission and hence only apply to publicly traded companies.

Basically, with regard to whistleblowing policies, SOX turns the incentive approach of the OSG concerning reporting mechanisms into mandatory requirements. Section 301 of SOX requires that the Audit Committees of publicly-traded companies establish procedures for the receipt, retention and treatment of complaints regarding accounting, internal accounting controls or auditing matters, and the submission by employees of the company of concerns regarding questionable accounting or auditing matters. Sections 806 and 1107 provide for civil and criminal penalties for companies and individuals that retaliate against employees who make covered whistleblowing reports. As Levin (2004) notes, while sections 301 and 806 only apply to publicly-traded companies, the criminal anti-retaliation provisions of section 1107 apply to all businesses, whether publicly traded or not. SOX places the Audit Committee at the centre of the reporting mechanism, seeing as its obligation to establish a whistleblowing policy which meets the requirements of receiving and retaining – a records retention function must be part of the mechanism – complaints. The details of the required whistleblowing policy are left to the companies themselves, leaving flexibility to develop procedures fitting a company's circumstances. Companies can install an internal reporting mechanism by designating an employee of the company to be responsible for receiving, reviewing and transmitting a report to the Audit Committee. Companies can also engage an external hotline provider to assist the company's Audit Committee to meet the requirements, or employees can be allowed to transmit their complaints directly to members of the Audit Committee. However, it is a SOX requirement that the individual making the report remains anonymous and that the report itself is kept confidential from management.

The provision for protection against retaliation puts the onus of proof on the whistleblower, who has to show that the retaliation by the employer was a reaction to a covered report. Also, to be covered, the employee must provide the information either internal to a supervisor or external to a federal regulatory or law enforcement agency, a member of Congress or Congressional committee (Siegel 2002; Gamble 2003; Levin 2004). Civil claims under SOX section 806 regarding retaliation are only possible after filing a complaint with the Federal Department of Labor, who directs the complaints to the Federal Occupational Safety and Health Administration, which commences an investigation and must issue a decision within 180 days of receiving the complaint. If it does not, the employee may file a lawsuit in a federal district court, for example for wrongful discharge under common law public policy exceptions or under statutory whistleblowing protection. SOX section 1107, applying to both public and private companies as well as individuals, provides for criminal penalties, including imprisonment for anyone who retaliates against an employee blowing the whistle to a law enforcement officer regarding the commission or possible commission of any federal offence (Gamble 2003; Levin 2004).

In contrast to OSG, SOX puts the accountability on individuals taking top-positions within companies. It makes CEOs and CFOs personally liable. Sections 306 and 402 stipulate stricter restrictions on employer compensation plans for directors or executive officers, and section 904 increases criminal penalties for wilful violations of the reporting requirements (Gamble 2003).[30] Section 302 requires that the CEO and CFO of an organization:

> certify and assert to stakeholders that SEC disclosures, including the financial statements of the company and all supplemental disclosures, are truthful and reliable, and that management has taken appropriate steps to satisfy themselves that the disclosure processes and controls in the company they oversee are capable of consistently producing financial information stakeholders can rely on (Leech 2003, 5).

The normative legitimation of SOX is quite clear. Although Bush's first speeches on the matter heavily pressed a corporate responsibility discourse, it was also immediately clear that this responsibility was to be attained through increasing the personal accountability of top-functionaries of companies.

> America is ushering in a responsibility era; a culture regaining a sense of personal responsibility, where each of us understands we're responsible for the decisions we make in life. [...] And this new culture must include a renewed sense of corporate responsibility. If you lead a corporation, you have a responsibility to serve your shareholders, to be honest with your employees. You have a responsibility to obey the law and to tell the truth (Bush 2002a).

Basically, the idea was to restore 'trust between a corporation and the investing public, by greater corporate disclosure' (Bush 2002b). Such a restoration could only happen through reform – hence the SOX.

> Reform should begin with accountability, and reform should start at the top. The chief executive officer has a daily duty to oversee the entire enterprise, the entire firm, and therefore, bears a unique responsibility for serving shareholder interests [...] We must also do more to safeguard the rights of investors. America has the best system of corporate disclosure. Yet, the interests of the average investor are sometimes overlooked, especially the need for thorough and timely information about firm performance. And some corporations have used artful and intricate financial arrangements to hide the true risks of the investment (Bush 2002a).

---

[30]   The limitations on criminal fines for individuals is increased from $5,000 to $100,000, the period of potential imprisonment is increased from one year to 10 years (Gamble 2003).

The message is that a crisis in the system of publicly held business, driven by investor capitalism and built on trust, must be *and can be* resolved through a governance approach aimed at better internal control. But since it is a governance approach, the burden of how to install such adequate controls is put on the shoulders of the top executives. It is a duty assigned to them, and if they fail they will be held accountable.

Indeed, SEC Commissioner Atkins (2003) says that SOX strengthens the role of directors as representatives of stockholders and reinforces the role of management as stewards of the stockholders' interest. Being more personally accountable, the desired effect is to make board members more inquisitive. SOX puts an emphasis on a board's oversight function, and 'questions that might have seemed to be "hostile" to management two years ago will now be seen to be in furtherance of a director's function' (Atkins 2003). Here again, just as with the OSG, an appeal is made to the construct of 'rational loyalty': internal reporting is not hostile, it is proof of loyal employees.

Glassman, also a SEC Commissioner, states that in trying to:

> restore investor confidence in our companies and our markets and to enhance investor protection by improving corporate governance and transparency [, the SOX directed the SEC] to adopt rules to increase the accountability of CEOs and CFOs, improve the quality of financial reporting and raise professional, legal and ethical standards for the gatekeeper of our financial system – analysts, auditors, audit committees, boards and attorneys [...] rules requiring securities lawyers to report evidence of fraudulent corporate conduct 'up the ladder' to the chief legal or chief executive officer of the corporation or, if necessary, the board of directors (Glassman 2003).

Thus, the Sarbanes-Oxley Act makes internal whistleblowing policies mandatory for publicly traded companies, and embeds the normative legitimation for doing so in a discourse of corporate governance and transparency, running on the 'accountability' legitimation construct, and drawing nearer to it the line of the 'OSR-network' construct.

Because non-US companies listed on the US exchanges must also comply with SOX and hence have internal whistleblowing procedures in place, the impact of SOX will not be restricted to US companies and employees. In fact, the SOX will force companies and legislators worldwide to deal with the issue of whistle-blower protection and internal whistleblowing procedures. In July 2005, rulings in Germany and France stated that hotlines for anonymous reporting are unlawful. These decisions were arrived at based on privacy regulations and a lack of union consulting (Eversheds 2005; Bond 2005). Obviously, this stalemate needs to be resolved and it is in the attempts to find a solution that the conceptualization and thus meaning-making on whistleblowing will evolve further, and this can be expected especially in Europe.

Screening Conclusions

In the previous sections, I have discussed the several US whistleblowing policies based on the screening grid developed in Chapter 3. Here, I would like to summarize the screening and see what conclusions can be drawn.

Table 4.1 shows how and what elements of whistleblowing are specified in the several policies. The policies differ strongly in their specification of the actor element. State level policies vary from covering only public employees to covering all employees, but according to Callahan and Dworkin (2000), the majority covers only public employees. The Whistleblower Protection Act covers current and former federal employees. The revised False Claims Act and the Organizational Sentencing Guidelines are the widest in actor-scope, respectively aiming at persons with a privileged access to information and personnel of any kind of organization. In principle the FCA is even wider than the OSG, because it does not require of a whistleblower to be a member of the alleged organization. However, as Saldico (2000) has shown, the question is whether a non-member is very likely to have the required 'inside' information. Finally, the Sarbanes-Oxley Act mainly covers employees of publicly traded companies, even though section 1107 also covers employees of private companies.

The subject element shows a tendency to emphasize whistleblowing on financial matters.

Finally, with regard to the motive element, jurisdiction based on state level statutes tends to take motive into account, while the FCA explicitly solicits whistle-blowing for personal gain.

The evolution of normative legitimation constructs used for whistleblowing policies discussed in the previous sections can be visualized as in Figure 4.1. It is the screening placed on a timeline. The thick line shows what legitimation constructs the subsequent policies tap into.

What shows is that the pre-legislature expectations of First Amendment based whistleblowing legitimation did not materialize. What did take place at the end of the 1970s and beginnings of the 1980s were whistleblowing policies embedded in an OSR-networklike argumentation, emphasizing responsibility of the public official. The line of accountability was drawn nearer while the line of 'loyalty' was pushed off. From the mid-1980s on however, the attitude shifted drastically towards the efficiency-construct, offering rewards for information. From the early 1990s on, governance approaches are undertaken – although first steps in that direction are visible in the early 1980s legislations of Maine, New York and New Jersey. The OSG drives on the lines of responsibility and rational loyalty, with a potential in the current discussions of drawing closer the line of the integrity construct. Most recently, the SOX is legitimated through an OSR-network and accountability discourse.

Table 4.1 Whistleblowing elements specified in US policies

Element	State level	WPA	FCA	OSG	SOX
Actor	Varies, but majority covers only public employees	Current and former employees of federal government	Person with privileged access to organization's data or information	Personnel of any kind of organization	Employees of publicly traded companies (except section 1107 covering also employees of private companies)
Subject	Violations or possible violations of law	Fraud, waste and mismanagement of government funds	Fraud	Criminal conduct by personnel	Fraud (Section 1107 covers all federal offences)
Recipient	External (to various government agencies), later internal	OSC, MSPB	Court (personally file lawsuit under FCA), government	Internal	Internal, external to specific law enforcement agencies, but only about retaliations (Section 1107 to law enforcement officers)

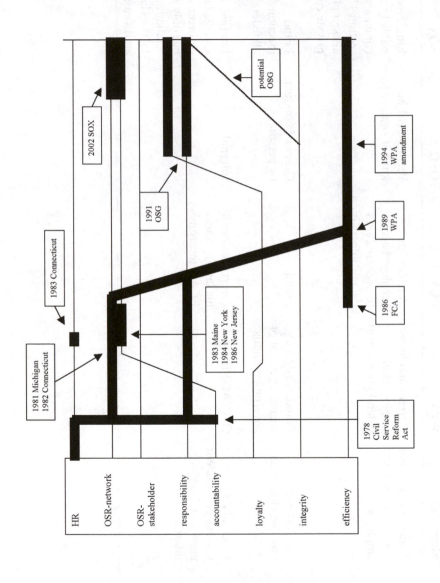

HR

OSR-network

OSR-stakeholder

responsibility

accountability

loyalty

integrity

efficiency

1981 Michigan
1982 Connecticut

1983 Connecticut

2002 SOX

potential OSG

1991 OSG

1983 Maine
1984 New York
1986 New Jersey

1978 Civil Service Reform Act

1986 FCA

1989 WPA

1994 WPA amendment

Figure 4.1   Evolution of legitimation lines (US)

Australia

Australia is a federal state, consisting of six states – New South Wales, Queensland, South Australia, Western Australia, Victoria, and Tasmania – and two self-governing territories – Australian Capital Territory and the Northern Territory. Discussion on the topic of whistleblowing and whistleblowing policies has been going on since the end of the 1980s. Currently, only the Northern Territory has not passed whistleblowing legislation.

I begin the screening of Australian whistleblowing policies by reviewing some early reports, kicking off the discussions before any legislation was passed. After that, I look at the different state legislation on whistleblowing. I then look at how the discussion at the federal level has evolved over the last decade and was bypassed by a Commonwealth legislation covering private sector whistleblowers in June 2004. Finally, I draw up an evolution of argumentation lines for whistleblowing policies in Australia.

Early Reports

Although Australia set up panels and commissions to look into matters related to whistleblowing at the end of the 1980s, the legitimacy of whistleblowing policies in Australia seems to become an issue only from the 1990s on. The early 1990s saw a number of reports recommending whistleblower protection and providing the conditions under which such protection should be offered.[31] The Senate Select Committee on Public Interest Whistleblowing issued a report in August 1994 in which these reports and an academic research report by Paul Finn (Finn 1991) are discussed (SSCOPIW 1994). Table 4.2 offers an overview of the variations between proposed whistleblowing policies prior to any Australian whistleblowing legislation.

The Electoral and Administrative Review Commission (EARC) was established to draw up recommendations to the Queensland government with regard to whistleblowing protection. In its October 1991 report, the EARC spoke of protection for *public interest disclosures*. This concept will linger on in the subsequent name-giving of and discussions on whistleblowing policies. The EARC recommended a whistleblowing policy with very wide actor and subject elements. Remarkable is the proposed three tiered model recommended for the recipient

---

[31] These reports are: 'Report on Protection of Whistleblowers' released by EARC (Electoral and Administrative Review Commission) of Queensland in October 1991, 'Review of the Commonwealth Criminal Law Report' released by the Gibbs Committee in December 1991, Senate Standing Committee on Finance and Public Administration: 'Review of the Office of the Commonwealth Ombudsman' December 1991, and 'Inquiry into the Management and Operations of the Department of Foreign Affairs and Trade (DFAT)' December 1992, House of Representatives Standing Committee on Banking, Finance and Public Administration (aka the Elliott Committee) 'Inquiry into Fraud on the Commonwealth' November 1993 (see SSCOPIW 1994).

element. First, people should raise concern within their organization. A second, external step is provided in reporting to the Ombudsman if internal channels do not work. Should this second step fail to have effect as well, the whistleblower can go 'public', disclosing information to Parliament or even to the media.

Finn, in a research report on integrity in the government, proposed a somewhat restricted three tiered model, taken over by the Commonwealth Ombudsman in his report to the Senate Standing Committee on Finance and Public Administration (F&PA Ombud), the report of an inquiry into the management and operations of the Department of Foreign Affairs and Trade to the same commission (DFAT), and a report on Commonwealth fraud to the House of Representatives Standing Committee on Banking, Finance and Public Administration (Elliot). Finn's three tiered model differs from the EARC model in that the third step includes only disclosure to a Parliamentary committee but not to the media. Also, Finn's proposals limit their focus on government agencies.

The Gibbs Committee, set up to review Commonwealth Criminal Law in February 1987, and releasing its report in 1991, also discussed the possibility of whistleblower protection. The recommendation was made that the official secrecy provisions would be strongly reduced, as they could be used to camouflage government or official wrongdoing. The Gibbs Committee argued that complainants of such wrongdoing ought to be allowed to disclose official information when making the complaint. An exception however would be needed with regard to sensitive defence or foreign affairs material. Although the EARC proposed whistleblower protection to also cover the private sector, the Gibbs Committee decided that the case had not been sufficiently made. Also, whistleblowing legislation did not need to include protection against liability for defamation. The Gibbs Committee does take over the EARC three tiered model, including the provision of disclosure to the media.

The F&PA Ombud report, the DFAT report and the Elliott report raise some technical remarks about whistleblowing policies. The Commonwealth Ombudsman launches the idea that false complaints ought to be made punishable as an 'essential counterbalance to ensure individual privacy rights and official confidentiality are protected' (SSCOPIW 1994, 36). The DFAT argues that 'even whistleblowing which is misconceived or where specific claims are incorrect can expose flaws in management systems' (SSCOPIW 1994, 35). The Elliot report looks at whistleblowing as a means to combat fraud and acknowledges the possibility to 'go public' as a last resort, arguing that if the first two steps work, then the third step will never be used. It also recommends a two year review of whistleblowing policy to 'ensure its operation is effective and efficient [and] to ensure confidence and trust in the new system' (SSCOPIW 1994, 37–8). These remarks are technical in the sense that they concern the efficiency of a whistleblowing policy. This should not surprise us because all three reports were written from a fraud fighting perspective. However, these remarks concerning whistleblowing policies will remain dormant until the early 2000s. Further on, I will discuss Federal whistleblowing bills presented to Parliament in 1991, 1993,

2001 and 2002. The 1991 and 1993 bills have a normative tone quite different from the technically focussed remarks in the F&PA and Elliot reports. By 2001 however, efficiency has become an all pervasive argument and we see the same ideas pop up again.

State Legislation

A second useful overview is that of state legislation concerning whistleblowing policies (Table 4.3). South Australia is regarded as the first state to pass such legislation in 1993 (Trott 2004, 121), although Queensland enacted whistleblowing protection as interim provisions already in 1990.[32] Reacting to incidences of corruption within the Queensland public service, a commission was established to look into illegal activities and police misconduct. The report from that commission, known as the Fitzgerald Report was issued in June 1989 and one of its recommendations was the establishment of the Electoral and Administrative Review Commission (EARC), which had to prepare:

> legislation for protecting any person making public statements bona fide about misconduct, inefficiency or other problems within public instrumentalities, and providing penalties against knowingly making false public statements (Fitzgerald Report, quoted in SSCOPIW 1994).

Meanwhile, in June 1990, interim provisions were enacted, protecting persons providing information to EARC and to the Criminal Justice Commission (CJC) against victimization. The EARC drafted a proposal Bill by October 1991. It strengthened the protection measures of the interim provisions, allowing disclosures to be made to any public sector body, with the CJC as the proper authority to receive disclosures that no other public authority could handle. It also proposed the establishment of a whistleblowers counselling unit within the CJC. When a disclosure would be made to the counselling unit, full protection would be provided regardless of the circumstances.

The CJC did establish such a counselling unit, and also organized training sessions for their staff on dealing with whistleblowers and providing liaison, consultancy and policy advice to other agencies involved in whistleblowers support. But the EARC also proposed to counterbalance the enlarged protection measures by making it a disciplinary and criminal offence to knowingly make a false or misleading disclosure.

The Queensland Parliament took up the EARC draft in 1992, but did not pass the Queensland Whistleblowers Protection Act until 1994. During those two years, the whistleblowing provisions proposed by the EARC were substantially narrowed down: the counselling unit, absolute privilege of disclosures to that unit,

---

[32] In this sense Groeneweg (2001) is right when she writes that Queensland was the first to enact a whistleblowing protection bill. However, she then goes on reviewing the Queensland Whistleblowers Protection Act 1994.

Table 4.2 Early 1990s recommendations (Australia)

Element	EARC 1991	Finn 1991	Gibbs 1991	F&PA Ombud 1991	F&PA DFAT 1992	Elliott 1993
Actor	Any person	Officer or employee of an agency of government (including state-owned companies)	Employee or contractor of the Commonwealth or any Commonwealth agency			Current or former employee or contractor of the Commonwealth or any Commonwealth agency
Subject	Conduct that constitutes an offence under an Act of Queensland	Non-compliance with legislative, governmental or administrative policy	An indictable offence against a law of the Commonwealth, State or Territory			An indictable offence against a law of the Commonwealth, State or Territory
	Substantial and specific danger to public health or safety	Maladministration likely to pose an immediate threat to public health or safety	Substantial and specific danger to public health or safety			Substantial and specific danger to public health or safety
	Official misconduct within the meaning of the Criminal Justice Act, misconduct punishable as a disciplinary breach and conduct which constitutes negligent, incompetent or	Maladministration resulting in fraud or waste and misconduct of an agency official	Gross mismanagement or a gross waste of funds			Gross mismanagement or a gross waste of funds

Table 4.2 con'd

Element	EARC 1991	Finn 1991	Gibbs 1991	F&PA Ombud 1991	F&PA DFAT 1992	Elliott 1993
Subject (cont'd)	inefficient management resulting, or likely to result, directly or indirectly, in a substantial waste of public funds					
Recipient	Three-tiered model: 1 internal 2 ombudsman except for sensitive information on intelligence and security 3 to the public, including media, in cases where information reveals a serious, specific and immediate danger to the public	Three-tiered model: 1 internal 2 ombudsman 3 Parliamentary Committee	Three-tiered model: 1 internal 2 ombudsman except for sensitive information on intelligence and security 3 to the public, including media, providing the action is reasonable in the circumstances	Takes over Finn	Takes over Finn	Takes over Finn

private sector coverage and disclosures to the media were not enacted in 1994. The provisions that got passed are very similar to those of New South Wales, which I will be discussing later on. I will regard the legitimation construct of the whistleblowing Acts of Queensland and New South Wales to be the same.

So even though discussion about State legislation first started in Queensland, the first Australian State to pass whistleblowing legislation through parliament was *South Australia* in 1993. Apparently, the proposed bill drafted by the Queensland EARC did not need to get that hollowed out in South Australia as in Queensland in order to pass parliament. The South Australian Whistleblowers Protection Act 1993 (SA Act) covers both public and private sector whistleblowing. Lewis (2001, 174) notes that the provisions of the SA Act also apply outside the employment field, as the protection is afforded to 'persons' rather than 'employees' or 'workers'. Also, it allows for both internal as well as external whistleblowing, but does not make either mandatory. Instead, it allows the whistle being blown to 'a person to whom it is, in the circumstances of the case, reasonable and appropriate to make the disclosure' (SA Act Section 5(2)(b)).

The SA Act also defines what is to be understood as 'public interest information':

> information that tends to show that an adult person (whether or not a public officer), body corporate or government agency is or has been involved in an illegal activity, or in an irregular and unauthorized use of public money, or in substantial mismanagement of public resources, or in conduct that causes a substantial risk to public health or safety, or to the environment, or that a public officer is guilty of maladministration in or in relation to the performance of official functions (SA Act Section 4).

Defrauding the government is regarded as hindering the public interest, but so are illegal activities of bodies corporate and conduct that causes risk to public health, safety or environment. Section 3 of the Act states that the object of the Act is 'to facilitate the disclosure, in the public interest, of maladministration and waste in the public sector and of corrupt and illegal conduct generally'. Clearly, the subject element is wider than financial fraud. The inclusion of risks to public health, safety and environment makes the subject element covered for the private sector broad, with an emphasis on possible harms to society.

The SA Act did not make it obligatory to make internal reports before disclosing the information to an external agency. Furthermore, there is no obligation upon agencies to set up internal whistleblowing procedures. The SSCOPIW report (1994) writes that the SA Act is intended to deter whistleblowing allegations being sensationalized inappropriately through the media. However, as the Act did not intend to limit existing rights, it does not make access to the media conditional on acting through authorized channels. The idea seems to be the same as the one taken up in the Elliot report, that, given the fact that people prefer to report inside their organization – if they run no risk of retaliation – the possibility of people 'going public' with information will ensure that internal reports will be dealt with appropriately. This points at a governance approach.

However, because the approach is not made explicit – internal procedures are not explicitly encouraged nor is the media as a 'last resort' threat explicitly stated – I would say that the governance approach is underused.

The notion of 'public interest information', together with the broadness of the actor, subject and recipient elements, strongly point in the direction of an OSR-stakeholder type of legitimation construct (see Table 3.4).

Right after the passing of the SA Act, Queensland, Australian Capital Territory and New South Wales passed whistleblowing legislation in 1994. I will first look at the *Australian Capital Territory (ACT)* and then come to the New South Wales legislation. I already discussed the Queensland legislation history. As the legislation which got passed is very similar to that of New South Wales, I will regard the legitimation construct of Queensland and New South Wales to be the same.

The ACT Public Interest Disclosure Act (ACT Act) shows some important differences from the SA Act. Even though the ACT Act also allows 'any person' to make a public interest disclosure, the subject element of the Act narrows the Act down to public sector functions. The ACT Act defines public interest disclosure as a disclosure of information which tends to show:

> (a) that another person has engaged, is engaging, or proposes to engage, in disclosable conduct; (b) public wastage; (c) that a person has engaged, is engaging, or proposes to engage, in an unlawful reprisal, or (d) that a public official has engaged, is engaging or proposes to engage, in conduct that amounts to a substantial and specific danger to the health or safety of the public (ACT Act Section 3).

There are two interesting things about this definition. First, note that (a) to (c) does not specify about whom information can be disclosed – (a) and (c) talk of 'a person', (b) just says 'public wastage' regardless of who is wasting. In (d) however, it is stipulated that a danger to the health or safety of the public caused by a public official can be the subject of a public interest disclosure. Hence, when such a danger is caused by someone other than a public official, the disclosure of that information is not a public interest disclosure. Now, it is true that under 'public official' both employees of governmental agencies as well as government contractors are understood. Nevertheless, this leaves danger to public health or safety caused by a private company which is not a government contractor – selling unsafe cars or dumping toxic waste – out of scope. The second interesting element is the notion of 'disclosable conduct'. Section 4 of the ACT Act defines it as:

> (a) conduct of a person (whether or not a public official) that adversely affects [...] the honest or impartial performance of official functions by a public official or government agency; (b) conduct of a public official which amounts to the performance of any of his or her official functions dishonestly or with partiality; (c) conduct of a public official [...] that amounts to a breach of public trust; (d) conduct of a public official [...] that amounts to the misuse of information or material acquired in the course of the performance of official functions [...].

Disclosable conduct is conduct that distorts governmental functioning as a politically neutral and impartial public service. The legitimation is, just as with the SA Act, of an OSR-construct type, but impoverished compared to the SA Act, because it only concerns public service, not the private sector.

The recipient element is also narrowed down – confirming the impoverishment of the OSR-stakeholder legitimation construct. The media as a last resort recipient is not included in the ACT Act. Disclosures can be made to any government agency. Thus, both internal and external disclosures are covered by the ACT Act, as long as the recipient is a government agency, without the obligation of internal reporting prior to external disclosure.

In contrast to the SA Act, the ACT Act does provide that every government agency establishes an internal whistleblowing procedure. In this sense, the governance approach is strengthened. Yet, since the establishment of internal procedures is an obligation only for government agencies, the governance approach is limited to the public service sector. Of course, this is in line with the subject element. However, taking into account the narrowing of the subject and the recipient element, compared to the SA Act, and the apparent aim of the ACT Act to ensure a trustworthy public service, the ACT Act seems to be driven by a limited OSR-network construct rather than an OSR-stakeholder construct.

The *New South Wales* Protected Disclosures Act (NSW Act) was also passed in 1994. The actor element of the NSW Act is narrow, as it only covers disclosures made by public officials. The subject element too is narrow, allowing disclosures 'in the public interest of corrupt conduct, maladministration and serious and substantial waste *in the public sector*' (NSW Act, Section 3, emphasis added). A motive element is introduced, stipulating that the Act does not cover disclosures made solely to avoid dismissal or disciplinary action. Finally, with regard to the recipient element, disclosures can be made internal or external to an investigating authority. However, if internal procedures are in place, the whistleblowing must report internally first. A third step is also foreseen in allowing disclosures to a member of Parliament or to a journalist, provided that the disclosure had already been made internally or externally.

The narrowness of the actor and subject elements depicts the NSW Act as strictly envisaging the public sector. Furthermore, with regard to the recipient element, the fact that Section 4 of the Act understands 'investigating authorities' to the Auditor General, the Independent Commission Against Corruption, the Ombudsman, the Police Integrity Commission or the Director-General of the Department of Local Government, suggest a whistleblowing policy which is accountability driven, or in other words, as a way to control whether or not public sector departments and their officials carry out their duties assigned to them. This suggestion is strengthened by the explicit provision in the NSW Act that disclosures questioning policy decision of a Cabinet or a Minister are not covered by the Act (Section 17 of the NSW Act).

The second wave of State legislation is situated in the early 2000s. *Victoria* passed the Whistleblowers Protection Act in 2001, *Tasmania* passed the Public

Interest Disclosures Act in 2002, and *Western Australia* passed their Public Interest Disclosure Act in 2003.

All three State legislations cover disclosures about corrupt conduct within the public sector (defined the same way as 'disclosable conduct' in the ACT Act, see supra), mismanagement of public resources, conduct involving risk to public health or safety, conduct involving substantial risk to the environment, if these constitute a criminal offence or would otherwise be grounds for dismissing or dispensing with the services of a public officer. In short, the subject element covers illegal or counter-policy-conduct of public sector organizations and their employees. Tasmania and Western Australia are a bit broader as their respective Acts also cover wrongdoing of pubic sector contractors.

As far as the actor element is concerned, anyone is covered by the Victorian and the Western Australian Acts. Tasmania however, only covers public officials. The recipient element of all three Acts show that by the time they got passed, the governance approach became well understood.[33] In all three states, public bodies (government agencies as well as state-owned corporations) must have internal whistleblowing procedures in place. Moreover, these must be used first before disclosures can be made external to the Ombudsman.

Relevant of those Acts is that none of them has taken up disclosures about private sector wrongdoing, and none allows disclosure to the media as a last resort. This leads me to conclude that these whistleblowing policies are aimed at increasing public officials' accountability. The approach these Acts take fits well with the New Public Management (NPM) approach, acknowledging complexity by turning to a governance type of control, aiming at ensuring trust in the public sector. Thus, here too, I would say the Victorian, the Tasmanian, as well as the Western Australian Act is driven by an accountability construct, limited to the public sector.

This leaves only one Australian State without a whistleblowing legislation, the Northern Territory. Of course, discussions have been going on for some years. There is a report from the Law Reform Committee of the Northern Territory on whistleblowing legislation from 2002 (Asche 2002). The report makes two recommendations. The first is that the provisions of the Victorian and Tasmanian statutes should be adopted as the general model for Northern Territory whistleblower legislation. The second is that the persons to be protected by such legislation:

> should not be in the category of 'public officer' as in the Tasmanian legislation or 'natural persons' as in the Victorian legislation but, rather in the category of 'any person' as in the South Australian legislation (Asche 2002, 2).

---

[33] Barry Perry, the Victorian Ombudsman has issued guidelines for establishing internal procedures, including reporting channels, making the policy known, and investigating procedures (Perry 2001).

This recommendation is repeated twice (Asche 2002, 5 and 7)! The arguments (Asche 2002, 6) used in the report for taking the Victorian and Tasmanian statutes as a model are that the Ombudsman is responsible for dealing with external disclosures. This is regarded as a positive trend because the oversight of the statutory scheme is located within one independent entity whereas the older Acts allowed external disclosure to *any* government agency. Also the recognition of the need to establish internal channels is mentioned – what I have called the enhanced governance approach. As the Northern Territory intends to take the Victorian and Tasmanian statutes as a model, and since I have categorized those as being driven by the accountability construct, I will do the same for the Northern Territory proposals. However, the report seems to indicate that the most important reason for the Northern Territory to have whistleblowing legislation is the fact that all other states have such legislation:

> except for the Northern Territory, all States and the ACT now have the legislation
> [...] and one can only assume that this itself is an acknowledgement by the various
> Parliaments of the need for such legislation and the effectiveness of it (Asche 2002,
> 4).

Federal Bills Since 1991

A third overview to be given before I can proceed with drawing up the evolution of legitimation lines for Australia, is the overview of the discussion about a federal whistleblowing legislation. Discussions about whistleblowing protection at federal level have been going on since 1991, but to this date, a Commonwealth specific whistleblower statute for the public sector still does not exist. Because Australian States have, since 1994 successively confirmed the trend to only cover whistle-blowing on public sector wrongdoing, it must be regarded as a breakthrough that at Commonwealth level, it was private sector whistleblowing that gained protection in June 2004 as part of corporate governance legislation. I will therefore first discuss the discussion at federal level since 1991, and then look at the whistle-blowing provisions in recent corporate governance reforms.

Discussions about whistleblowing protection at federal level have been going on since 1991, when Senator Vallentine introduced his Whistleblowers Protection Bill. However, the Bill was lapsed following federal elections in 1993. Senator Chamarette reintroduced the Bill and the Senate referred the Bill to the Senate Select Committee on Public Interest Whistleblowing. The Bill is discussed in the report of that Committee (SSCOPIW 1994, chapter 12). The 1993 Chamarette Bill is the first one to be discussed. Secondly, the 1994 issue paper (SSCOPIW 1994) also proposes 'legislating in the public interest'. Third, in 2001 a new Public Interest Disclosure Bill was introduced by Senator Murray, reviving discussions about the subject in federal Parliament. Murray replaced his Bill by the Public Interest Disclosure Bill 2002 a year later. I will base my discussion of that bill on the publication in the *Official Hansard* of a discussion and expert hearing in the Finance and Public Administration Legislation Committee of the Senate on 16th

Table 4.3 Australian state legislation on whistleblowing

Element	South Australia	ACT	Queensland	New South Wales	Victoria	Tasmania	Western Australia	Northern Territory
Year	1993	1994	1994	1994	2001	2002	2003	Not yet
Outcome	Anonymous Confidential	Confidential	Anonymous Confidential	Anonymous Confidential	Anonymous Confidential	Anonymous Confidential	Anonymous Confidential	
Actor	Any person	Any person	Public offical	Public offical	Any natural person	Public offical	Any person	Any person
Motive				No protection for disclosure solely made in order to avoid dismissal or disciplinary action				
Subject	Public sector wrongdoing, Private sector illegality	Wrongdoing by public sector officials	Public sector wrongdoing, Danger to health and safety of someone with a disability	Public sector wrongdoing	Improper and corrupt conduct within the public sector	Improper and corrupt conduct within the public sector	Improper and corrupt conduct within the public sector	Improper and corrupt conduct within the public sector
Recipient	To a person who is, in the circumstances of the case, reasonable and appropriate to make the disclosure (including media)	Internal channels must be in place. External to any government agency. No obligation to use internal channels first.	IF internal channels are in place, then these must be used prior to an external disclosure: any government agency. Disclosures to media are not allowed	IF internal channels are in place, then these must be used prior to an external disclosure: any government agency and the media as a last resort	Internal channels must be in place and must be used prior to a disclosure to the Ombudsman	Internal channels must be in place and must be used prior to a disclosure to the Ombudsman	Internal channels must be in place and must be used prior to a disclosure to the Ombudsman	Internal channels must be in place and must be used prior to a disclosure to the Ombudsman

of May, 2002 (Hansard 2002a) and the publication of the Parliamentary debates in the *Official Hansard* (Hansard 2002b).

The Chamarette Bill already talks of 'public interest disclosures' and has as object:

> to promote the ethic of openness and public accountability; and to improve community perception of whistleblowers, in recognition of the fact that they are responsible citizens (SSCOPIW 1994, 231).

It foresees an independent agency reporting to Parliament, created especially for the protection of whistleblowers and the investigation into their allegations. All natural persons would be covered when blowing the whistle on illegalities, waste of public money, abuse of authority, dangers to public health or safety, mismanagement of public money or property, or the suppression of an expert opinion or a document.

The comments on the bill were that it focuses too much on the investigative powers to be given to the independent agency, rather than on providing adequate detail as to what the rights and protections are for people who blow the whistle (SSCOPIW 1994, 234–41). Nevertheless, the 1993 Bill put whistleblowing explicitly within a context of openness, accountability and responsibility.

The 1994 report from the Senate Select Committee on Public Interest Whistleblowing – a Committee set up in response to the 1991 and the 1993 Bills – noted two requirements a whistleblowing policy should meet (SSCOPIW 1994, 77). First, it had to restore a 'loss of faith in "the system"' and secondly there is the need for 'cultural/attitudinal change in the approach to whistleblowers and whistleblowing'. The report argues that rather than 'examining itself for wrong-doing to advance the public interest, ["the system"] moves to protect itself' (SSCOPIW 1994, 77). In general, 'the system' is seen as to be unsympathetic towards accepting and responding to reports of wrongdoing. Where internal whistleblowers were not harassed but taken serious, this was because of 'ethical individuals' and 'people of integrity' at the top of the organization. The report states that:

> An *open, democratic society* should not tolerate the behaviour and resultant effects against members of society which have been described in evidence given to the Committee. All people within 'the system' need to be educated to adopt the attitude and approach currently practised by the few. After all, an organization is only as honest and effective as the integrity of the individuals which constitute that organization (SSCOPIW 1994, 83, emphasis added).

Note the moral tone of that statement. It is used to denounce something regarded as an element of Australian culture. More precisely, antipathy towards 'dobbing'. The concept refers to betraying 'mateship'. The report states a need to develop:

> a greater understanding and acceptance within the community that whistleblowing is an action undertaken in the *public interest*. It needs to be seen in positive terms of *benefiting* not just the organization involved but *society generally*. Legislation alone

would not bring about the cultural and normative changes which are essential if the negativity associated with the dobbing label is to be removed from the *socially necessary act of whistleblowing* (SSCOPIW 1994, 84, emphasis added).

Whistleblowing is portrayed as part of an 'open, democratic society', as benefiting society generally, as being in the public interest instead of being 'dobbing', and even as a 'socially necessary act'. These concepts point at the legitimation constructs of OSR-stakeholder, rational loyalty and responsibility. To phrase whistleblowing as part of an open, democratic society means that whistleblowing safeguards the purpose of governmental agencies to further an open, democratic society. Reaffirming references to responsibility in the 1993 Bill, whistleblowing policies allow citizens to carry out their responsibilities instead of being regarded as a 'dobber'. Where the report describes whistleblowing as a socially necessary act, the rational loyalty construct is activated, making whistleblowing an act of loyalty to an open and democratic society.

However, no legislation was passed. The 2002 Bill still argues that individuals who make disclosures 'serve the public interest by assisting in the elimination of fraud, impropriety and waste [and that] as such, they deserve protection' (Hansard 2002b). By now, the discourse seems to have taken up an 'efficiency' element, portraying whistleblowers as 'assisting' in guarding efficiency. What's more, it is because they are assisting that they 'deserve' protection. Further on in Murray's speech, whistleblowers truly become generators of information:

> Whistleblowers play an important role in ensuring the accountability of government. They are individuals who, by reason of their employment, come across information that reveals corruption, dishonesty or improper conduct at any level of government (Hansard 2002b).

Public officials are best placed to generate information about the agencies they work for and their colleagues. Here, whistleblowing policies are about installing the panopticon, used to hold decentralized government agencies accountable.

Two discussions remain (Hansard 2002a). The first is whether or not disclosure to the media should be allowed or not. Peter Bennett, a whistleblower himself and witnessing to the Committee as member of Whistleblowers Australia, and William De Maria, Lecturer at the University of Queensland are in favour of including the provision on the argument that the public has a right to know about wrongdoing in the public sector. Ronald McLeod, Commonwealth and Defence Force Ombudsman and Andrew Podger, Public Service and Merit Protection Commissioner, are against the idea. McLeod argues that if internal and specific external channels are functioning properly there is no need to blow the whistle to the media. Podger's argument for not allowing disclosures to the media is that it would create wrong incentives for disclosure and would hinder the efficient correction of the wrongdoing.

The second issue is whether or not whistleblowing legislation should cover the private sector. De Maria argues that the Australian public sector has been largely privatized during the 1990s and hence that whistleblower protecting should follow that trend. Otherwise, thousands of people are cut off from protection. Podger and Whitton – who had entered a submission as a private capacity – argue that the issue is not people but rather public interest and that hence the legitimate concern is 'to ensure that we can be confident of the expenditure of public money'. Senator Murray responds to the issue that it would be possible to cover private sector wrongdoing in public service contracts, but covering private sector business in which the government has no link is, following the logic of the constitution, something that must be legislated by the states. However, there is a gap, as only the SA Act provisions are both public sector and private sector provisions. De Maria regards it as:

> a peculiarly Australian thing to not protect private sector whistleblowers [...] Every time administrators and drafters of legislation get to this point in Australia, their knees start to shake and they pull back (Hansard 2002a).

Private Sector Whistleblowing

This 'peculiarly Australian thing' seems to have been bypassed by private sector initiatives. In 2001, Australia had its own Enron-type scandal. HIH, Australia's second largest general insurer, collapsed, causing Australia's largest corporate failure, leaving more than $A5 billion of losses, affecting millions of small investors and policy holders (Rankin 2003). The HIH collapse was avoidable, if only early warnings from an insider and several others to the Australian Prudential Regulatory Authority (APRA) asking to inspect HIH, would have been followed up on, which APRA refused (Rankin 2003; Trott 2004). Following the disaster, Australian media, Transparency International and Whistleblowers Australia, the Australian Securities and Investment Commission (ASIC) and Senator Murray have asked for legislation to extend to the private sector.

In September 2002, a policy proposal paper was issued by the government, which included the proposal to provide protection for company employees who reported a breach of the Corporations Act 2001 – an act stipulating corporate governance regulations – to the Australian Securities and Investments Commission (ASIC) (proposal 35: Commonwealth of Australia 2002, 179). Subsequently, a call for submissions was launched on 'Audit Reform and Corporate Disclosure', which would lead to new legislation under the name of CLERP9, the 9th review of the Corporate Law Economic Reform Program. A number of actors submitted a paper.[34] The Australian Institute of Company Directors (AICD) thought the proposal was not broad enough in the sense that not only company employee whistleblowers ought to be protected but *all* whistleblowers – implying that the actor element should state 'any person' rather than 'employees'. Transparency

---

[34]   The complete list of submissions can be found at http://www.aph.gov.au/Senate/committee/corporations_ctte/clerp9/submissions/sublist.htm (cited October 2004).

International Australia (TIA) criticized the proposal for being too narrow in both its subject and recipient elements (TIA 2002). Whistleblowers ought to be protected not only when disclosing breaches of the Corporations Act, but simply disclosures of breaches of any legislation and any principles of common law that apply to the organization. The Chartered Secretaries of Australia as well as the Finance Sector Union held the same opinion. Moreover, TIA noted that also including breaches of internal codes of practice into the subject element ought to be considered. The AICD was against such broadening, arguing that the ASIC would simply be unable to cope with such broad disclosures. However, TIA stressed the need to include besides ASIC, also regulators (Federal, State and Territory) as well as law enforcement agencies and auditors as appropriate recipients of disclosures. The ASIC itself also commented on it being the only recipient of protected disclosures and proposed to also include directors and auditors of the company. TIA went further in that direction, emphasizing the importance of having internal reporting mechanisms encouraging whistleblowing within the organization.

On 8 October 2003 a draft bill was released. It barely took up the recommendations made. Instead, it proposed a scheme only covering disclosures made to ASIC on the Corporations Act and did not mention internal reporting. The only broadening – although it is an important one – was that protection was extended to cover also officers and subcontractors disclosing information to ASIC. Note however that this still does not mean that the actor element would read 'any person', as for example suppliers are still not covered by the provisions.

A new round of submission was solicited. Again, these criticized the draft bill for stating ASIC as the only recipient and for not including provisions forcing companies to have internal whistleblowing procedures.

In December 2003, a bill – CLERP Bill 2003 – was introduced into Parliament that did contain changes on those issues. The provisions covered whistleblowing to the ASIC, or the company's auditor, a director, a secretary or senior manager of the company, or a person authorized by the company to receive disclosures. Hence, the CLERP Bill allows for internal whistleblowing, but still does not include an obligation on corporations to put in place internal whistleblowing procedures.

In March 2004, the Parliamentary Joint Committee on Corporations and Financial Services,[35] of which Senator Murray is a member, decided to review the CLERP Bill. In June 2004, it issued its report (PJCCFS 2004). In its review report, the Committee writes that:

---

[35] The Parliamentary Joint Committee on Corporations and Financial Services reports to Parliament on the ASIC and on corporations legislation, examines annuals reports under the Australian Securities and Investments Commission ACT 2001, and does follow-up on matters appearing in or arising out of those reports (PJCCFS 2004).

the proposed whistleblower protection scheme is sketchy in detail but that the intention is quite clear [...] Once the proposed whistleblower provisions come into operation, answers to the questions that it poses may become clearer. Indeed the longer term solution may be found in the development of a more comprehensive body of whistle-blower protection law that would constitute a distinct and separate piece of legislation standing outside the Corporations Act and consistent with the public interest disclosure legislation enacted in the various states (PJCCFS 2004, xxii).

Hence, the Committee recognizes that the discussions at federal level – stifled by a reluctance to pass broad whistleblowing legislation – have been bypassed by private sector needs. In its recommendations, the Committee resonates the critiques of the submissions made to the policy proposal paper and the draft bill:

*   it keeps open the question of the subject element. The Committee sees ground in the AICD argument that the ASIC is unable to handle broad disclosures, but counters this argument by the desirability of broadening the recipient element;
*   it recommends the insertion of a provision requiring corporations to establish an internal whistleblowing protection scheme. It refers to the AS 8004-2003 model (see infra).

Perhaps too late, for the CLERP Bill was turned into legislation by 1 June 2004.[36] The CLERP Act includes no extensions in actor, subject or recipient element compared to the December CLERP Bill 2003. The CLERP Act 2004 limits the protection of whistleblowers to company employees or subcontractors (actor element) blowing the whistle on corporations legislation (the corporate governance Corporations Act 2001 – subject element) to the ASIC or internally (recipient element).

Even though one might see similarities with the US SOX – both involve whistle-blowing legislation enacted in response to corporate governance scandals, and both enhance liability of top-functionaries of publicly traded corporations – the differences are important.

The CLERP Act does not make internal whistleblowing procedures an obligation. Hence, it does not apply a tiered approach to the recipient element. This means that the CLERP Act is not driven by the accountability construct as I have constructed it in Chapter 3, although accountability is a concept used in the CLERP-rhetoric (see Costello 2003, iii).

---

[36] The full title of the CLERP Act is: Corporate Law Economic Reform Program (Audit Reform and Corporate Disclosure) Act 2004, No. 103, 2004. An Act to amend the *Corporations Act 2001* and the *Australian Securities and Investments Commission Act 2001*, and for related purposes. Whistleblowing provisions are to be found in Schedule 4 – Enforcement, which inserts into the Corporations Act 2001, after Part 9, the Part 9.4AAA – Protection of Whistleblowers.

The aim of the CLERP Act is, just as that of the US SOX, to restore and maintain investor trust, and both try to do so through corporate governance legislation. Hence both are driven by an OSR-network legitimation, but the CLERP Act does not tap into the OSR-network construct the same way the US SOX does. The message behind SOX is that a crisis in the system of publicly held business, driven by investor capitalism and built on trust, must be and can be resolved through a governance approach aimed at better internal control. The CLERP Act, speaks of:

> promoting transparency, accountability and shareholder activism [through the regulation which] enhances auditor independence, achieve better disclosure outcomes and improve enforcement arrangements for corporate misbehaviour (Costello 2003, iii).

Indeed, both qualify for the OSR-network construct, but the CLERP regards whistleblowing as a means to ensure the control agency ASIC will know when corporate statements are fraudulent. The CLERP Act does not have a tiered recipient, and it has restricted actor and subject elements. Its whistleblower provisions are placed under the header 'Schedule 4 – Enforcement' which means it is a control device aimed at generating information in function of the controlling agency. Thus, the CLERP Act drives on the lines of the OSR-network and the efficiency constructs, but not on the accountability construct.

In the same HIH-momentum, some private sector initiatives have shown an acceptance and embracement of whistleblowing. Deloitte Australia offers a whistleblowing hotline service called 'Tip-offs anonymous', a 'dedicated hotline number and e-mail address for employees to report suspected incidents of misconduct' (Deloitte 2004). The legitimation construct is straightforward 'efficiency'. The website advertizing the service states as reasons for having a whistleblowing hotline policy:

> 1. Fraud detection and prevention is mandatory, 2. Misconduct can destroy a company's reputation, 3. Recommended by governments and regulators, 4. Revenue leakage could be costing millions, 5. Low cost deterrent to misconduct (Deloitte 2004).

Moreover, it is a service offered to organizations and assures them training and confidentiality, which means it is meant to be a purely internal whistleblowing policy. This strengthens the suggestion that the Deloitte service used the efficiency construct as a panopticon.

Standards Australia has issued a whistleblowing policy standard – AS 8400-2003 – as part of their corporate governance services. The standard sets out a number of elements for setting up and managing whistleblowing policies in organizations. These elements regard informing employees about reporting channels, confidentiality, investigation, protection, etc. Interesting is how the necessity of a whistleblowing policy is argued. The foreword states that:

A whistleblower protection program is an important element in detecting corrupt, illegal or other undesirable conduct [...] within an entity, and *as such* is a necessary ingredient in achieving good corporate governance (SA 2003, 4, emphasis added).

The objectives of the standard as stipulated in the section on the scope of the standard include:

(a) encourage the reporting of matters that may cause financial or non-financial loss to the entity or damage to the entity's reputation; (b) enable the entity to effectively deal with reports from whistleblowers in a way that will protect the identity of the whistleblower and provide for the secure storage of the information provided (SA 2003, 5).

In its foreword, the AS 8400-2003 regards a whistleblowing policy to be a necessary part of corporate governance. This implies two possible references. The first is a reference to the OSR-stakeholder construct. Corporate governance in this sense is about ensuring information channels that do not follow the organizational hierarchy. The second possible reference is to the efficiency construct, where whistleblowing policies install an organizational panopticon. In that case, internal whistleblowing ensures organizational transparency for corporate governance, while external whistleblowing serves watchdog accountability.

A stated objective of the standard is to encourage employees to generate information about possible damage to the organization. This opens a third possibility. More precisely, this could mean a reference to the rational loyalty construct. However, the subject and recipient elements can bring more clarity as to which construct underlies the AS 8400-2003. The OSR-stakeholder construct requires a wide recipient element, including the media. The rational loyalty construct requires identified channels, internal and preferably external as well. The efficiency construct can be maintained with only internal channels. As far as the subject element is concerned, the OSR-stakeholder construct implies emphasis on possible harms to society, the rational loyalty construct allows a very wide range of concerns, while the efficiency construct argues its subject element in terms of effectiveness and efficiency.

Now, the AS 8400-2003 standard does not mention the reporting by employees to board, shareholders or media. The policy stipulates that the organization should appoint a Whistleblower Protection Officer and a Whistleblower Investigations Officer to whom concerns can be raised. These people then can report those concerns directly to the CEO and audit, ethics or compliance committee or something equivalent. The standard also states that: 'Entities *may wish* to consider alternative forms of reporting, for example to the internal or external auditor [...] or relevant external agency' (SA 2003, 11, emphasis added). Clearly, the standard concerns an internal whistleblowing policy. It says external channels are a possibility, but not a necessity and it does not offer any guidance as to how a policy could integrate external channels. Therefore, the OSR-stakeholder construct is excluded and strictly spoken, only the efficiency 'panopticon' construct qualifies, although a rational loyalty construct possibility is still open.

Looking at the subject element, the standard mentions as 'reportable conduct':

> Conduct by a person or persons connected with an entity which [...] is—(a) dishonest; (b) fraudulent; (c) corrupt; (d) illegal (including theft, drug sale/use, violence or threatened violence and criminal damage against property); (e) in breach of Commonwealth or state legislation or local authority by-laws [...]; (f) unethical (either representing a breach of the entity's code of conduct or generally); (g) other serious improper conduct; (h) an unsafe work-practice; or (i) any other conduct which may cause financial or non-financial loss to the entity or be otherwise detrimental to the interests of the entity (SA 2003, 6).

The subject element is not phrased in terms of emphasizing harms to society, hence the OSR-stakeholder construct stays out of the picture. Is it phrased in terms of effectiveness and efficiency? Some are, more precisely (a) dishonest, (b) fraudulent, and (i) 'losses' 'detrimental to interests'. Important however is (f) unethical conduct in breach of the entity's code of conduct. This is an explicit referral to the rational loyalty construct. Hence, the AS 8400-2003 standard uses a normative legitimation based on the efficiency and the rational loyalty construct.

Evolution of Argumentation Lines

The change in perspective between the 1994 and 2002 discussions at federal level is drastic. From OSR-stakeholder, rational loyalty and responsibility being the referred to constructs in 1994, by 2002 the efficiency construct seems to be regarded as the most adequate construct to legitimate whistleblowing policies. This is confirmed by the CLERP Act 2004, using lines of argumentation from the OSR-network and efficiency constructs.

Is there a similar change to be noted across the state legislations? No there is not. Rather, one of the argumentation lines activated in the early 1990s is enhanced in the beginning of the 2000s. The 1993 South Australia Act tapped into the OSR-stakeholder construct. The 1994 Act passed in the Australian Capital Territory used a limited OSR-network construct. The Queensland and New South Wales Acts, both from 1994, were driven by an accountability construct. Both were enacted following discussions within a context of fighting corruption. Queensland had interim provisions in place in 1992 following police corruption and the New South Wales discussion was dominated by the Independent Commission Against Corruption. This can explain why both legislations are so similar. State legislations passed in 2001 (Victoria), 2002 (Tasmania), 2003 (Western Australia) and the 2002 discussion in the Northern Territories all further the accountability construct. Remarkable is that the governance approach has been enhanced, making it obligatory (a) for government agencies to have internal channels in place and (b) for whistleblowers to use those internal procedures first before going outside. Also striking is that all provide an external channel to the Ombudsman and that the media is not foreseen as a last resort. The 'three tiered model' introduced in 1991 – EARC, Finn, Gibbs see Table 4.2 – is out of the question, although activists like Bennett and De Maria still try to reintroduce it.

This leaves me with the apparent reluctance to enact whistleblowing legislation which covers both public as well as private sector organizations. Only the first State to pass whistleblowing legislation covers both sectors. All others limit their policy to the public sector. One might argue that the 'dobbing' connotation attached to whistleblowing might be responsible for keeping legislation coverage as limited as possible. If this were true, the attitudinal change wished for in the 1994 report (SSCOPIW 1994) would be appropriate. Moreover, it would explain why the OSR-stakeholder or even the OSR-network constructs used respectively by the SA Act and ACT Act, are not consistently applied also to the private sector. The CLERP Act 2004 covers only the private sector, and in that sense it can be regarded as a breakthrough with regard to what De Maria has called a 'peculiarly Australian thing'. However, it does not establish the broad whistleblowing policy at federal level covering both public and private sector. The scope of the CLERP Act is restricted in all its elements. Comments on the CLERP Bill have called for a broadening on all those elements and in doing so, they have used arguments from the accountability and rational loyalty constructs – respectively the call for obligatory internal procedures and the inclusion in the subject element of breaches of company's code of conduct plus the reference to the AS 8004-2003. This might give new impetus to the discussion at federal level, but as of yet, this impetus is only visible in the report of the Joint Committee (PJCCFS 2004). Therefore, in Figure 4.2, which gives an overview of the evolution of argumentation lines, I have put a question mark behind these outlooks and positioned them on the '2004 momentum'.

New Zealand

The Australian whistleblowing momentum of the early 1990s also instigated discussions in New Zealand about whistleblowing policies. In June 1994, the Whistleblowers Protection Bill (WP Bill) was introduced in the House of Representatives (Bowers et al. 1999, 254). The bill also used the Australian term of 'public interest disclosure' and defined it as conduct or activity in the public or private sector which concerns illegalities, corrupt or unauthorized use of public funds or resources, or otherwise poses a danger to public health, safety, the environment or the maintenance of the law and justice. The broadness of the subject element, covering both public and private sector, suggest this bill was inspired by the South Australian Act of 1993 rather than the ACT, Queensland or New South Wales Acts.

However, the bill did not pass. Actually, it took six years and a rewritten bill for New Zealand to have whistleblowing legislation. Within that process, it is especially the recipient element which underwent drastic changes.

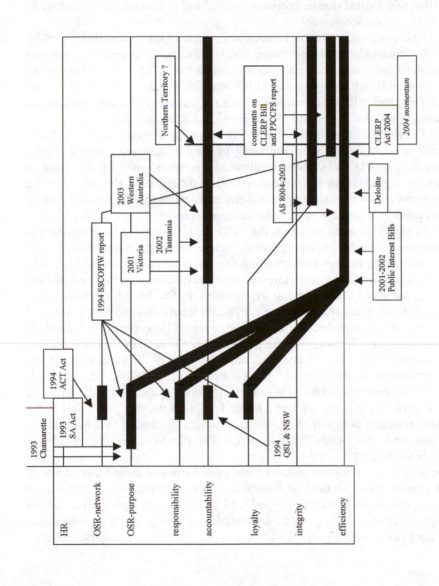

Figure 4.2 Evolution of legitimation lines (Australia)

In 1995, the Privacy Commissioner comments on the WP Bill (Slane 1995). In that comment, he states it is necessary for a whistleblowing legislation to strike a balance between a legitimate 'coming forward in the public benefit' and an 'encouragement of informers in authoritarian regimes', which is to be dissuaded. It is within this context that he proposes the WP Bill to be amended to reduce its scope to the public sector only.

By 1997, a new bill was introduced, the Protected Disclosures Bill (PD Bill). Again, the Privacy Commissioner recommends reducing the scope of the proposed legislation to only cover the public sector (Slane 1997). This time however, the argumentation is that 'an overly broad bill may fail to achieve the objectives set for it [...]' and that 'a far more focused bill, supplemented by focused victimization provisions in relevant legislation, might provide a more effective means'.

The PD Bill differs from the WP Bill in its recipient element. The WP Bill proposed to establish of a Whistleblowing Protection Authority, able to receive disclosures. The PD Bill does not, allowing disclosure to a whole range of government agencies and institutions. Another difference is that the WP Bill does not provide for mandatory internal channels, while the PD Bill does. These changes point at an enhanced governance approach.

Before the Protected Disclosure Act (PD Act) was passed in 2000, the PD Bill underwent some further changes in its recipient element. A four tiered model was adopted, even further strengthening the governance approach. All public sector organizations must have internal procedures for receiving and dealing with concerns about organizational wrongdoing. In the case of a private sector organization, or when the employee has good reasons not to follow internal procedures – for example because the person to report the concerns to is involved in the wrongdoing – the employee can go directly to the head of the organization. In a third step – if the head is involved, does not react or the situation is urgent – information can be disclosed to 'an appropriate authority', including a whole range of government agencies as well as professional bodies but not a Minister of the Crown or a member of Parliament. In the fourth step, accessible if the third step recipient does not react, one can make a disclosure to a Minister of the Crown or to one of the Ombudsmen.[37] The PD Act does not provide for disclosure to the media.

The subject and actor elements have not been narrowed down. Any employee of any organization can disclose information about serious wrongdoing in or by that organization. Under 'employee' is to be understood present and former employees, homeworkers, persons seconded to the organization, individuals under a service contract to do work for the organization, managers, and even

---

[37] New Zealand has three Parliamentary Ombudsmen, besides the Banking Ombudsman and the Insurance and Savings Ombudsman who fulfil a specialist role in the private sector and are not accountable to the Parliamentary Ombudsmen. The Ombudsmen meant here are the Parliamentary Ombudsmen.

members of the Armed Forces. 'Serious wrongdoing' is defined similar to the WP Bill (see supra).

De Maria writes that the New Zealand Act (PD Act) is 'a copy of the South Australian Act' (De Maria 2002, 3). I have a problem with that. As I noted before, it looks like the WP Bill was inspired by the South Australian Act (SA Act). Indeed, both the PD Act and the SA Act cover public and private sector. And in dealing with reprisals against whistleblowers, both Acts provide a link with human rights: the SA Act by stating that reports of reprisals are to be dealt with by the Equal Opportunities Officer and in the PD Act with a provision for an amendment of the Human Rights Act 1993 with the explicit mentioning of the PD Act in its Section 66(1)(a) on victimization. However, the PD Act passed by New Zealand Parliament in 2000 shows some important distinctions from the South Australian one. The first and most important one is the difference in governance approach between both Acts. The SA Act allows disclosures to whatever agency the whistleblowers sees appropriate,[38] without an obligation to use internal channels first. The PD Act is a cascade of four steps, to be followed if a whistleblowers wants to enjoy protection under the Act. The second difference between the Acts also concerns the recipient element. The SA Act allows for disclosures to the media – on the condition that such a disclosure can be proven to have been appropriate. The PD Act does not allow disclosure to the media, not even as a last resort. A third difference is that where the SA Act stipulates the actor element as 'any person', the PD Act only covers actors related to the organization through various kinds of employment. Finally, a fourth difference is that the SA Act – as do the vast majority of whistleblowing legislation – makes the disclosure of information or complaints known to be false an offence. The PD Act – and this is indeed remarkable – does not make it an offence, but only makes such disclosures unprotected.

Table 4.4 gives an overview of the evolution from 1994 to 2000. As I noted at the outset of this discussion, it is the recipient element that has undergone changes, more precisely, an enhanced governance approach. What does this imply for a conclusion regarding the argumentation lines used by the New Zealand whistleblowing policy?

The detailed recipient element, and the clear governance approach expressed in its provisions, suggest the PD Act is hooked on the accountability line. And, because both public and private sector organizations are covered for a wide subject element, the OSR-stakeholder construct is drawn close. Let me explain. The Act leaves it up to the organizations themselves to correct wrongdoing in or by the organization. If it fails to do so, whistleblowers can disclose the wrongdoing to governmental agencies, including police, Auditor-General, Fraud Office, Commissioner for the Environment or the Health and Disability Commissioner. It thereby makes organizations accountable should they not take internal concerns

---

[38] Of course, the whistleblower in the SA Act has to prove the appropriateness of the agencies to which he/she has made the disclosure.

seriously. The suggestion of accountability is confirmed in the first two steps of the four tiered model. Either organizations deal with concerns through their internal channels – if they are public sector organization they are obliged to have them – or employees can go directly to the head of the organization. This means that it is the head of the organization who is responsible for making internal channels work or for dealing with concerns him/herself. If he/she fails to do so, external agencies will be holding the head of the organization accountable for failing to correct or prevent wrongdoing brought to his/her attention.

The OSR-stakeholder construct is also relevant here, because of the usage of the term 'public interest disclosure' combined with the fact that both public and private sector organizations are covered in the actor and subject elements. The subject element contains illegalities and risks to public health, safety and environment. It also contains an:

> act, omissions or course of conduct that constitutes a serious risk to the maintenance of law, including the prevention, investigation, and detection of offences and the right to a fair trial (PD Act, Section 3(c)).

All this should be seen as putting an emphasis on possible harms to society. It does not include breaches of organizational codes of ethics or other specific policies. Therefore, the rational loyalty construct is excluded. Also, the OSR-network construct seems left untouched because there is no specific referral to correcting a power balance in interactions or to trust building.

Hence, drawing up an evolution of argumentation lines used in the New Zealand discussion (Figure 4.3), I would regard it as being – albeit only suggestively – driven by an OSR-stakeholder construct, drawing the accountability line nearer up to the 1997 PD Bill, when the accountability construct becomes the main driver but further enclosing the OSR-stakeholder construct.

United Kingdom

Starting the discussion on whistleblowing in the UK is a report in 1990 from Social Audit, *Minding Your Own Business* (Winfield 1990). The report addressed the issue of self-regulation and showed that people on the work floor know when corners are being cut and things are going wrong. The Social Audit report therefore argued that whistleblowing policies are a vital ingredient of self-regulation. A number of British disasters proved their point, like the 1987 sinking of the Herald of Free Enterprise, the P&O ferry that capsized off the coast of Zeebrugge, killing 193 people, or the Piper Alpha oil platform which exploded in 1988 killing 167 people, or the 1988 train crash at Clapham Junction in London, killing 35 people (Myers 2004). The public inquiries into these cases all showed that staff knew of dangers and problems, but turned a blind eye because they were too scared to speak up, or did try to speak up but with no effect.

Table 4.4 New Zealand Bills and Act

Element	1994 Whistleblowers Protection Bill	1997 Protected Disclosures Bill	2000 Protected Disclosures Act
Actor	Anyone employed by or under contract of an organization	Anyone employed by or under contract of an organization	Anyone employed by or under contract of an organization
Subject	Serious wrongdoing in or by an organization	Serious wrongdoing in or by an organization	Serious wrongdoing in or by an organization
Recipient	Whistleblower Protection Authority	Internal channels to be used first, then external to a whole range of government agencies	Four-tiered model: Internal channels (public sector organizations must have them), head of the organization, government agencies, Minister of Crown, or Ombudsmen

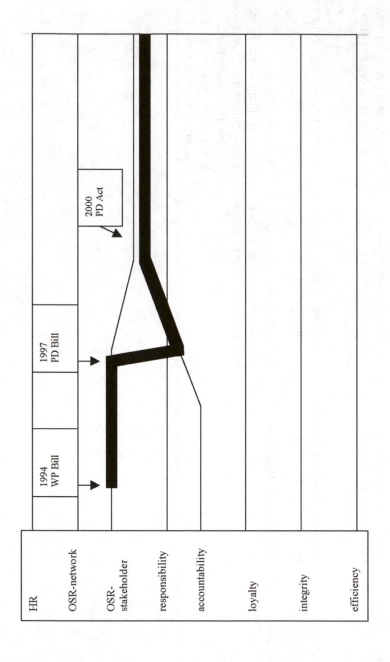

Figure 4.3   Evolution of argumentation lines (New Zealand)

As a result of the Social Audit report, an independent resource centre was set up under the name of *Public Concern At Work* (PCAW), which was launched as a charity in 1993. It had high-profile support from a number of Lords from the House of Commons and MPs. PCAW was set up as a legal advice centre and lobby group, maintaining a telephone 'help line'[39] offering free legal advice to people who wanted to blow the whistle, and writing position papers and reports on the issue of whistleblowing.

In the whole evolution towards whistleblowing legislation in the UK, PCAW plays a crucial role. It is they who draft the Bills and advise organizations on how to set up whistleblowing policies. The fact that PCAW was started up following the Social Audit report, is also important. Social Audit is the publishing arm of Public Interest Research Centre (PIRC), a UK charity founded in 1972, as an offshoot of the Public Citizens network of organizations founded in the US by Ralph Nader. One of the PIRC founders – and still a member of the board of directors of Social Audit – is Charles Medawar, who had collaborated with Ralph Nader at the end of the 1960s, early 1970s – the crucial moment when the whistleblowing concept is explicitly advocated in an organizational context (see Chapter 1). PIRC operates mainly through campaigning organizations such as Health Action International, the Campaign for Freedom of Information, and Public Concern at Work. PIRC's aim is to:

> ask timely questions about the organizations whose decisions and actions shape public life. What, in social terms, do these organizations give to and take from the community, and how do they explain and justify what they do? [...] the issues may differ, but the conclusions always tend to be the same: there is not enough accountability in the major centres of power. There is too much secrecy in the organizations that direct and manage our lives.[40]

If PCAW is to advocate whistleblowing policies on that argument, then besides the accountability construct, they obviously would also tap into the OSR constructs (OSR-network and OSR-stakeholder). The first part of the above quote refers to the OSR-stakeholder construct. Organizations shape public life through their decisions and actions. And, they explain and justify what they do. Whistleblowing policies allow stakeholders to warn one another when organizational practices differ from the organization purpose as expressed in the explanation and justification provided by the organization.

---

[39] Since the enactment of the Public Interest Disclosure Act, the number of people who contacted the PCAW help line with a concern about perceived danger or illegality that they witnessed at work, has increased. In 1994, 386 people called in. In 1999 that was 403, and in 2003 it was 761. (Data provided by Robin van den Hende, case worker at PCAW, on 20 January 2004.)

[40] See http://www.socialaudit.org.uk/1.11.html#1.11%20More%20about%20PIRC/Social%20Audit (cited June 2004).

Also, if whistleblowing policies could lessen the secrecy of power centres, then more balanced interactions with those centres would be possible and hence trust would be built up – an argumentation line based on the OSR-network construct, to be found in the second part of the quote.

Attached to the campaign for Freedom of Information,[41] and at the request of an MP (Tony Wright), PCAW drafted a Whistleblower Protection Bill in 1995. Business, unions, consumer groups and regulatory bodies were consulted, which led to a revised Bill, which was taken up by another MP, Don Touhig (Borrie 1996; PCAW 1997, 12). This Bill – the Public Interest Disclosure Bill, hereafter the 1996 Bill – took a governance approach and it is in this sense that the accountability construct is tapped into. The Bill aimed at encouraging employees to raise their concerns – which they held on reasonable grounds and in good faith – internally. If the matter was not addressed by those in charge, then employees had statutory protection against victimization for reporting the matter outside the organization, hence the accountability (see Borrie 1996, 5).

The Bill received strong support in the 1995/96 session of Parliament by over 100 MPs from all parties. And because of an earlier consultation process, it could also count on support among the societal stakeholder groups. Nevertheless, the Bill did not reach the statute book in 1996 because the then Major Government considered such a protection to be a 'burden on business' (PCAW 1997, 12). Tony Blair made a public pledge that if a Labour government was to be in power, it would introduce whistleblowing provisions.

Meanwhile, the Committee on Standards in Public Life, established in October 1994 and known as the Nolan Committee – Lord Nolan was president of the Committee – issued a number of reports between May 1995 and November 1997, showing its support for PCAW and whistleblowing policies. In its first report – published in May 1995 relating to the quangos[42] NDPB (Non-Departmental Public Bodies) and NHS (National Health Service) bodies – the recommendation is made that departments and agencies should nominate one or more officials entrusted with the duty of investigating staff concerns raised confidentially. A second report – May 1996 and relating to local public spending bodies – argues that it is unsatisfactory for both staff members and for the organization if staff members can only ventilate concerns through the media. Therefore, the report makes the recommendation that local public spending bodies should institute codes of practice on whistleblowing, appropriate to their circumstances and which would enable concerns to be raised confidentially inside and, if necessary, outside the organization. In this recommendation, the Nolan Committee uses a line of argument similar to the one I have used in the responsibility construct, namely that to be able to consistently speak of responsibilization of employees,

---

[41] This concerns the public availability of reports from government meetings and decisions.

[42] A 'quango' is a 'quasi nongovernmental organization', a not-for-profit organization, although taking autonomous decision, is set up and financed by government.

one should provide mechanisms that enable those employees to take up and carry out their responsibility.

In 1997, prior to the election, the Major Government accepted the Nolan recommendations (PCAW 1997, 13). Also in 1997, the Nolan Committee published its third (July) and fourth report (November), stating that the essence of a whistleblowing system is the possibility to by-pass the direct management line if that is the area about which concerns arise. Taking this line of thought further, the report states that staff should be able to go outside the organization if they feel the overall management is engaged in an improper course.

The same year, after the election, another whistleblowers Bill was introduced by Richard Shepherd MP, the Public Interest Disclosure Bill. Apparently, 1997 was the momentum for whistleblowing legislation to be realized in the UK. The political support and recognition for whistleblowing as being in 'the public interest' and as 'raising concerns' was established, data was available through the PCAW 'help line' and PCAW also held the expertise on internal and external whistleblowing procedures through there consultancy work with public and private organizations. The 1997 Bill passed Parliament and got enacted in July 1998 as the Public Interest Disclosure Act 1998 (PIDA). The PIDA operates by inserting sections into the Employment Rights Act 1996 (Sections 43A to 43L).

As I have just argued, in setting up PCAW, the legitimation constructs of OSR-network and OSR-stakeholder are used, and the 1995 Bill already takes a governance approach and taps into the accountability construct. Important however is also that in 1996, the advocated subject element which whistleblowing provisions should be covering includes illegal *and* unethical practices. Borrie – Chairman of the PCAW Trustees from 1993 up to his retirement in 1996 – writes:

> I want it to be clear that I do not share the minimalist view of business ethics that behaving ethically means nothing more than complying with the requirements of the law (Borrie 1996, 2).

This could mean that the rational loyalty construct is also relevant here. And I would say that up till 1996 it was indeed. In the same essay, Borrie (1996, 10-11) writes that PCAW makes a distinction between protest whistleblowing and watchdog whistleblowing. A protest whistleblower objects to a lawful or transparent activity of his employer. A watchdog whistleblower on the other hand discloses information showing an organization is saying one thing but doing something quite different. It is the watchdog whistleblowing that the work of PCAW wants to deal with.

Also, the emphasis PCAW puts on distinguishing whistleblowing procedures from grievance procedures, and on 'employees raising concern' rather than 'making allegations' points in the direction of the integrity construct, as it is speaking up on a discernment of a situation or practice which is to be a protected action, not an allegation with a smoking gun as proof.

Moreover, republished in the same collection of essays the Borrie essay appears in, is a paper by Elaine Sternberg (Sternberg 1996), in which she argues that since the purpose of business is limited and specific, business loyalty is correspondingly limited to 'being true to the proper purpose of the ethical business' (Sternberg 1996, 26–7). The rational loyalty construct I have developed builds on the same line of argument, but goes further in specifying that the purpose of the business must be expressed in its corpus of codes of ethics, mission and value statements, and that this is the external referent to which loyalty is owed. Still, the notion that business loyalty is to be aimed at the purpose of business and not friendships or brands is sufficient for acknowledging Sternberg's argumentation as tapping into the rational loyalty construct.

But there is more in her paper. She talks of whistleblowing policies as 'critical information systems'. Critical information is information which is vital for the business' proper functioning, for example identifying and weighing risk in the production process. A critical information system then, is an organizational mechanism 'intended to encourage the flow of critical information to those responsible for dealing with its consequences' (Sternberg 1996, 33). What Sternberg does is to describe whistleblowing policies as a way of generating information and she thereby uses the efficiency construct. This is even more clear when we look at three functions Sternberg assigns to critical information systems. First, 'they should encourage stakeholder vigilance' (Sternberg 1996, 35). This means as much as 'everyone should be on the outlook' and boils down to advocating the panopticon. The second function is that they 'should encourage those who have critical information to make it available to the business' (Sternberg 1996, 35). The information has to be generated and be useable for the organization, which means that information generated through whistleblowing policies can enhance organizational efficiency. And third, 'information systems should channel the critical information to those responsible for dealing with its consequence (Sternberg 1996, 36). Here, Sternberg alludes to holding people accountable for receiving and processing specific information, and links this with corporate governance: 'Responsible corporate governance includes ensuring that critical information is collected and used to help the business maximize long-term owner value ethically' (Sternberg 1996, 37).

Thus, we see that up till 1996, the legitimation constructs used to argue for whistleblowing policies include OSR-network, OSR-stakeholder, accountability, rational loyalty, and efficiency and in the distance also integrity. As I will be arguing now, the Bill that was enacted in 1998 as the Public Interest Disclosure Act (PIDA), uses only OSR-network, accountability and efficiency as legitimation constructs.

Let me first discuss the constructs that have disappeared. In other words, what are my reasons for saying the PIDA is not legitimated through the OSR-stakeholder and the rational loyalty construct? Let me first handle the rational loyalty construct. Borrie had argued that for him, whistleblowing policies should allow disclosures about illegal *and* unethical conduct, and Sternberg had argued that business loyalty is limited to business purposes. Now, the subject element of the PIDA contains criminal offences, failure to comply with legal obligations, miscarriage of justice, health and safety risks, environmental damages, and 'cover ups', taking place in both public and private sector organizations. Commentating on the act, Bowers et al. (1999) note that the PIDA:

> does not, however, cover a failure to fulfil what might be considered to be a moral (but not legal) obligation of the employer to an outsider. Further, whether disclosure of a breach of a self-regulatory code qualifies for protection will turn upon whether there is a legal obligation to comply with the rule (Bowers et al. 1999, 21).

Thus, if organizational behaviour contradicting the organization's code of conduct or mission statement is not a subject of protected disclosure, the rational loyalty construct cannot be part of the legitimation because this construct argues just the opposite.

And what about the OSR-stakeholder construct? This construct says that whistleblowing policies allow stakeholders to warn one another when organizational practices differ from the organizational purpose. So, the above already makes this construct hard to sustain. However, the subject element does contain harm to society – miscarriage of justice, health and safety risks, environmental damage and 'cover ups'. This would speak in favour of the OSR-stakeholder construct (see the screening grid in Chapter 3). The actor element of the PIDA is very wide, which also leaves the possibility of a OSR-stakeholder construct open. The act protects workers in all sorts of contracts and sectors, including volunteers – provided they have a legal relation with the organization. The only ones not covered are members of the armed forces, police officers, and non-executive directors. Again, this shows the very wide scope of the PIDA.

The crux lies somewhere else. The biggest difference between the 1995 Bill, the 1996 Bill and the 1998 PIDA is to be found in the recipient element (see Table 4.5). The first two Bills did not specify this element, but when we look at the recipient element of the whistleblowing policy as put down in the PIDA, we see what Bowers et al. (1999) have called a two levelled approach. The first level consists of strictly specified disclosure routes, while the second level allows very wide disclosure on the condition that the whistleblower can show that it was reasonable to disclose to that recipient. The second level does not exclude anyone or any organization, hence disclosures to the media are allowed. Now, if this would be the whole story, then this whistleblowing policy would certainly qualify as driven by the OSR-stakeholder construct. However, the PIDA strengthens the conditions for protection for wider disclosures. For a disclosure made to ones employer or in accordance with a procedure authorized by the employer, or made to a regulator (PIDA, Section 43F)[43] to be a protected disclosure, the only conditions are that the

---

[43] I understand a regulator to be a person prescribed by the Secretary of State to deal with specific subjects and issues.

employee is acting in good faith, meaning the whistleblower must have an honest belief that the information disclosed tends to show that one of the subject element specifications is the case. The whistleblower may be mistaken. A disclosure made in the course of obtaining legal advice is also always a protected disclosure.

Note that these provisions put a very low threshold. It even allows disclosures to a regulator without the requirement of making the disclosure to the employer first. On the other hand, even though disclosures to the labour unions are expected to be protected under internal whistleblowing procedures, they are not a statutory right under PIDA (Bowers et al. 1999, 29). Secondly, disclosure to a regulator is only protected if the disclosure is made to the right regulator, meaning the person prescribed by the Secretary of State to receive disclosure about specific issues in the Public Interest Disclosure (Prescribed Persons) Order 1999 (S.I. 1999 No. 1549). This Order prescribes 38 different persons with the respective issues on which disclosures can be made to them.

The point I am trying to make is that, even though the criteria concerning the person making the disclosure are relatively low, the recipient element is extremely detailed, which leads me to regard the recipient element much more driven by the OSR-network construct than the OSR-stakeholder construct. Because of its detailed recipient element, the PIDA identifies nodes in the organizational network between which information interactions are safeguarded. This is a different provision than a OSR-stakeholder legitimation would prescribe. Actually, what Bowers et al. (1999) have called second level disclosures comes in reach of a OSR-stakeholder driven recipient element. However, the criteria for a whistle-blower to be protected in such disclosures are more strict. Just as in first level disclosures, second level disclosure require that the allegations made must be covered by the subject element and it is made in good faith. Moreover, a motive element comes in. The disclosure must *not* be made for purposes of personal gain (PIDA, Section 43G (c)). And, the whistleblower must reasonably believe the allegations are substantially true.

Besides those two stricter criteria regarding the person making the disclosure, one of three further preconditions must be met (Bowers et al. 1999, 35–7). The first is that for a person to be protected when a wider, external disclosure is made:

> at the time he makes the disclosure, the worker reasonable believes that he will be subjected to a detriment by his employer if he makes a disclosure to his employer in accordance with section 43F (PIDA, Section 43G (2)(a)).

This means that it is up to the whistleblower to proof that he would have been victimized by his employer had he made a first level disclosure.

A second precondition is a reasonable belief in a cover-up:

> that, in a case where no person is prescribed for the purposes of section 43F in relation to the relevant failure, the worker reasonably believes that it is likely that evidence

relating to the relevant failure will be concealed or destroyed if he makes a disclosure to his employer (PIDA, Section 43G (2)(b)).

Note that a belief in a cover-up will not be recognized as reasonable when there is a regulator prescribed.

The third precondition is that second level disclosures are protected where the matter has previously been raised in a first level disclosure. What the whistleblower will have to show here is that his employer or the regulator has done nothing to investigate or correct the wrongdoing. The fact that the employer is imperfect and slow in doing that, is not enough for second level disclosures to be protected.

Finally, if the three criteria regarding the person making the disclosure and one of the three preconditions are met, the disclosure must pass the test of reasonableness if it is to be protected. The whistleblower must show that the person to whom the external disclosure is made was, given the situation, reasonable to make the disclosure to. The PIDA does not exclude any person to whom such a disclosure can be made, but protects only disclosure made to a person to whom it can be argued that it was reasonable to make the disclosure to. Criteria for the reasonableness of the disclosure are the seriousness of the perceived failure about which information is disclosed, whether the failure continues, previous disclosures, and whether or not the organization had internal whistleblowing procedures.

Now, even though one could argue that PIDA does protect disclosures made to any person to whom it is reasonable to make the disclosure to, including police, professional bodies, a union official, an MP, relatives of a patient at risk, a website, shareholders, NGOs or the media, the fact that first level disclosure routes are specified in detail and the fact that stricter criteria are held for whistleblowers in second level disclosures, to me seem relevant and make me conclude that the OSR-stakeholder construct is not as firmly embraced as a legitimation construct as earlier argumentations. Indeed, the detail of the PIDA might result in a higher certainty for the whistleblower of protection, but the point I am making is that because of its extremely detailed recipient element, the PIDA is definitely more driven by an OSR-network construct than by an OSR-stakeholder construct.

Another, decisive element for not marking the OSR-stakeholder construct lies not in the PIDA itself, but in the fact that, as Myers (2004, 111) notes, the public has no access to the details of the claims and responses made under PIDA, which means that there is no way of knowing what issues were raised and whether or how serious the malpractice was. PCAW challenged the decision to keep secret the details of these claims, upon which the government decided to make only the names and addresses of the parties available on the public register of claims. Myers regards this as increasing the risk that PIDA will be used 'to trade the public interest in exchange for a favourable out-of-court settlement that agrees that the concern that the malpractice is kept out of the public domain' (Myers 2004, 111, sic). On 27 October (House of Lords)[44] and a day later, on 28 October 2004

---

[44] See Official Report, House of Lords, 27 October 2004, Vol. 665, c. 1388.

(House of Commons)[45], attempts were made to alter the regulations[46] keeping PIDA claims and responses from public access, arguing that the principle of 'open justice' to which government has engaged itself not only means the system of justice is carried on in public but also requires to reveal all documents relevant to the doing of justice. However, the attempts were to no avail. Lord Borrie had to withdraw his motion for the regulations to be annulled in the House of Lords, and in the House of Commons the regulations were approved by nine 'ayes' to five 'noes'. One week earlier, on 18 October 2004, an offer was made to PCAW by Gerry Sutcliffe MP[47] that PCAW would be the only one with access to the PIDA claims and responses forms so that it could monitor the act. However, the condition was that PCAW would enter into a deed of confidentiality. PCAW refused the offer, arguing that the public interest is not served through secrecy (PCAW 2004).

These regulations undermine stakeholders warning each other when organizational practices differ from the organizational purpose, as the OSR-stakeholder construct prescribes. In the figure showing the evolution of argumentation lines (Figure 4.4), I have therefore marked the OSR-network line and have indicated a closeness of the OSR-stakeholder line.

But this still leaves me to show that the PIDA draws on the accountability and the efficiency constructs. The accountability construct is tapped into where the PIDA allows hierarchical steps to be jumped over. Section 43C of the act states that a disclosure is protected when it is made according to internal whistle-blowing procedures, the person of whom the conduct is precisely the subject of the concern, or the employer. Bowers et al. (1999, 27) comment that when the employer is a large organization with many layers of management, disclosure would be protected when they are made to:

> any person senior to the worker, who has been expressly or implicitly authorized by the employer as having management responsibility over the worker.

This means that an employee can disclose wrongdoing by his direct manager to a manager higher in the hierarchy. In this sense, the whistleblowing policy of the PIDA makes line managers accountable to higher managers for what they do and command their workers to do. The third Nolan report (July 1997) regards this as the 'essence of a whistleblowing system' (see supra). And, this approach is maintained for further disclosures. Bowers et al. write that:

---

[45]   House of Commons, First Standing Committee on Delegated Legislation: http://www.publications.parliament.uk/pa/cm200304/cmstand/deleg1/st041028/41028s01.htm (cited November 2004).

[46]   Employment Tribunals (Constitution and Rules of Procedures) Regulations 2004 (S.I. 2004, No. 1861).

[47]   Gerry Sutcliffe MP is the Parliamentary Under-Secretary of State responsible for employment relations matters.

A hierarchy in terms of the desired route for raising concerns might be as follows; internal within the organization – to a regulator with power to redress the concern – to a trade union – to the responsible Minister – to a Secretary of State appointed body – to an MP – to shareholders – to interested third parties e.g. to a concerned citizens group – to the local or trade media – to the national media (Bowers et al. 1999, 38).

My argument for claiming that the PIDA is also legitimated through an efficiency construct is that PIDA has received attention especially within the context of fraud investigation. Anna Myers, Deputy Director of PCAW, proudly writes that already in 1998:

> the Audit Commission – the body regulating local authority and NHS finance and standards – saw the value of promoting whistleblowing as part of its fraud prevention and detection programme (Myers 2004, 112).

Further on, she also writes that:

> In 2002 – prior to the financial scandals at Enron and WorldCom that shook corporate America – the UK's Financial Services Authority (FSA) issued a policy statement recommending that all the companies it regulates implement whistleblowing policies for their staff [and, that] whistleblowing as a means to combat fraud in the public and private sectors has also been understood and promoted as part of counter fraud procedures (Myers 2004, 113).

Myers emphasizes that two regulators are actively promoting the PIDA to combat fraud. And they can rightly do so, because they have a favoured position as a recipient of disclosures. Bowers et al. explain this favoured position on the basis that:

> regulators have a statutory duty to investigate such matters and *they can only perform their role if members of the public are prepared to come to them with information* (Bowers et al. 1999, 31, emphasis added).

Put those two together and it reads that regulators are promoting PIDA because it is a way to generate information necessary to combat fraud and thereby to enhance the efficiency.

South Africa

The South African story on whistleblowing policies cannot disregard the heavy historical weight of the apartheid regime. That regime's repression apparatus included a spy network infiltrated into every sector of society, with monetary rewards for those who reported on others – referred to as *impimpis*. The connotation of *impimpi* attached to reporting wrongdoing still lingers on. Dimba et al. (2004, 143) note that 'one of the key obstacles in fighting corruption is the reluctance of individuals to "speak out" against corrupt activities'. The secrecy

Table 4.5 Subsequent UK whistleblowing Bills

Element	1995 Bill	1996 Bill	PIDA 1998
Actor	Any individual as employee, professional, voluntary worker, member of an organization, contracting worker or office holder	Any individual as an employee	Employees (broadly defined, also covering voluntary workers)
Subject	Offence or breach of statutory requirements or legal obligations, improper or unauthorized use of public or other funds, abuse of authority, miscarriage of justice, maladministration, danger to health and safety of any individual or environment, other misconduct or malpractice	Offence or breach of statutory requirements or legal obligations, improper or unauthorized use of public or other funds, miscarriage of justice, danger to health and safety of any individual or environment	Criminal offence, failure to comply with legal obligations, miscarriage of justice, health or safety of any individual, damage to the environment, cover-ups
Recipient	The wrongdoer, unless this would be ineffective or the matter was too urgent	Internally first
Also covers disclosures made in the course of obtaining legal advice	Internally, or to a regulator first
To another body or person, on the condition that: it is an appropriate recipient, there is no personal gain, and to do so is reasonable, or the matter was exceptionally serious

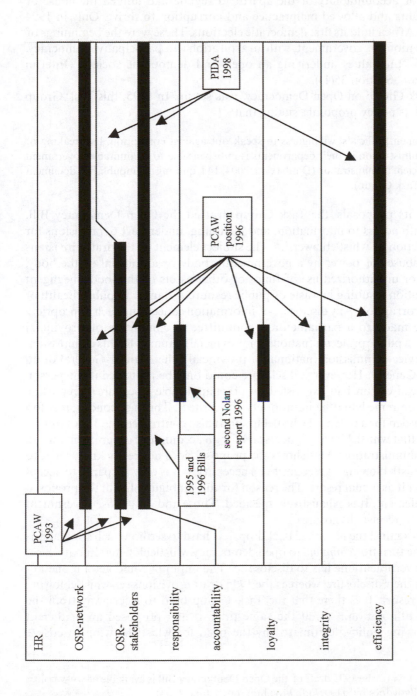

Figure 4.4 Evolution of legitimation lines (UK)

and lack of accountability of the apartheid regime had fanned the abuse of human rights and allowed malpractice and corruption to thrive. Only in 1994 did South Africa hold its first democratic elections. These were the beginnings of transformations of government, with an aspiration to a participative democracy, promoting 'the values underlying an open and democratic society' (Interim Constitution, Section 35(1)).

A 'Task Group on Open Democracy' was set up. In 1995, this Task Group submitted its policy proposals, stating that:

> [government] officials' willingness to speak out against corruption, lawbreaking or maladministration in their departments is indispensable to accountable government and efficient administration (Dimba et al. 2004, 144, quoting an unpublished document of the Task Group).

Based on its proposals, the Task Group drafted the Open Democracy Bill, dealing with access to information, and including, under Part 6, provisions for the 'Protection of whistleblowers'.[48] The subject element of the draft provisions included abuses of power by a governmental body or an official of the body, improper or unauthorized use of funds or other assets of that body, negligent administration resulting in waste of public resources, danger to public health or safety, or corruption. Any disclosure of information concerning such impropriety had to be made to a parliamentary committee, a committee of provincial legislature, a public protector (national or provincial), Human Rights commission, Public Service commission (national or provincial), the Auditor-General or an Attorney-General. However, a disclosure could only be protected if the person making the disclosure had 'exhausted any other applicable procedure for reporting or otherwise remedying the impropriety concerned'. This last condition is too heavy a burden for a potential whistleblower. It also contradicts the Task Group's reasoning that whistleblowing is necessary for an accountable government and an efficient administration. This shows the proposal does not really know what to do with whistleblowing. It recognises its necessity, but is only prepared to accept and protect it as a final resort. The reason for this ambiguity lies in the proposed recipient element. It is exhaustively specified. Those and only those government agencies can receive disclosures.

Viewed against the historical backdrop, it is hard to see how such stipulations embody the turn from *impimpi* to open democracy whistleblowing. In both cases it is the government one has to disclose to. The impimpi could get a monetary reward for their disclosure, whereas the 1995 draft provisions see whistleblowing as a final resort. It is there that the Task Group tried to steer away from the impimpi connotation. Yet, at the same time, it had proposed an inefficient whistleblowing policy, legitimated by the need for whistleblowing to ensure

---

48   The text of the 1995 draft of the Open Democracy Bill is available at www.polity. org.za/html/govdocs/bills/1995/odb9/toc.htm (cited June 2004).

efficient administration. Indeed, a contradiction. The same goes for the aim of accountability. The specified governmental agencies were the only recipients for disclosures about governmental agencies. In another historical context, for example the Australian one, the same recipient element should be interpreted differently. But here in South Africa, one was dealing with a notion of government as one repressive force consisting of a judicial, parliamentary and an executive branch, not a three-independent-powers government. The latter was an aspiration, and the Open Democracy Bill was part of the development towards an open and accountable government. It surely was not a *fait accompli* and therefore, the element specifications of the proposed whistleblowing provisions in the 1995 draft did not meet the intentions of accountability and efficiency.

But the 1995 draft did trigger something. In October 1997, the *Government Gazette* published another draft of the Open Democracy Bill, as it was introduced into parliament. The subject element had remained the same. It was still restricted to the public sector. But the recipient element had changed drastically. It still provided protection for disclosures to the government agencies as specified in the 1995 draft. But the 1997 draft, published in the *Government Gazette* 18381 as general notice 1514, also provided disclosure:

> to one or more news media and on clear and convincing grounds (of which he or she bears the burden of proof) believed at the time of the disclosure [that the] disclosure was necessary to avert an imminent and serious threat to safety or health of an individual or the public, to ensure that the impropriety in question was properly and timeously investigated, or to protect himself or herself against serious or irreparable harm from reprisals, or giving due weight to the importance, of open, accountable, and participatory administration, that the public interest in disclosure of the information clearly outweighed any need for non-disclosure (Open Democracy Bill 1997, Section 63).

Moreover, the 1997 draft did *not* state the condition that other external or internal procedures would be followed prior to disclosure. Hence, the contradiction present in the 1995 draft had been resolved by 1997. The openness and accountability was now ensured by the provision of disclosure to the media. And whistleblowing was no longer a last resort measure, but should be done if there are good reasons to tell society about wrongdoing. This made the accountability aim more solid. However, given the reference to a 'participatory administration' rather than an efficient one, it seems the efficiency drive was substituted by a stakeholder driven legitimation. Also, the wide and non-tiered recipient element points at the OSR-stakeholder construct, allowing stakeholders to warn each other when the safety or health of society or other stakeholders are at risk.

According to Lala Camerer (1999), the 1997 draft was modelled after the New South Wales Act. I have a few remarks on that. The New South Wales Protected Disclosures Act (NSWPDA) from 1994 protects only disclosures made by public officials. The South African 1997 Open Democracy Bill (ODB) protects any person. This is a difference in the actor element. But also the recipient element shows an important difference. The NSWPDA protects media disclosures as a last resort, meaning that one can only blow the whistle to the media when first going through other channels. In fact, the NSWPDA provides that one can only make a media disclosure when the authority to whom a prior disclosure was made decided not to investigate the matter, or did not investigate within six months of the original disclosure (NSWPDA, Section 19). The ODB does not have this '6 months' rule. It protects media disclosures when these can be shown to have been appropriate. Hence, the Australian NSWPDA might have been a model for including media as a possible recipient, but the 1997 ODB is considerably wider in its recipient procedure.

But the subject element of the 1997 Open Democracy Bill only covered the public sector. NGOs – among them Idasa (Institute for Democracy in South Africa) and ISS (Institute for Security Studies) – pointed at the outsourcing process of public services to private sector companies, and started to call for the whistleblowing provisions to be extended to the private sector (Dimba et al. 2004). Two national anti-corruption conferences – November 1998 and April 1999 – created an anti-corruption driven momentum for whistleblowing policies. The November 1998 conference, with delegates from business, faith organizations, NGOs, political parties, academic institutions, media, labour and government, passed a resolution:

> We therefore resolve to implement the following resolution as the basis of a national strategy to fight corruption: To support the speedy enactment of the Open Democracy Bill to foster greater transparency, whistleblowing and accountability in *all* sectors (Resolution taken at the National Anti-Corruption Summit in November 1998, quoted in Dimba et al. 2004, emphasis added in Dimba et al. 2004).

At the summit in April 1999, the concluding text made reference to:

> developing, encouraging and implementing whistle-blowing mechanisms, which include measures to protect persons from victimization where they expose corruption and unethical practices (Resolution taken at the National Anti-Corruption Summit in April 1999, quoted in Camerer 2001).

In June of the same year, Thabo Mbeki became the newly elected president succeeding Nelson Mandela. In his first address to parliament on the 25 June 1999, Mbeki said:

> We will also adopt this same approach of partnership with the people in the fight against corruption. In this regard, we must ensure that we pass the Open Democracy Act and move speedily to ensure the implementation of the provisions relating to the protection of whistleblowers (Mbeki 1999).

In October of the same year, the 9th edition of the bi-annual International Anti-Corruption Conference was held in Durban. There, Guy Dehn, executive director of PCAW, the London-based NGO on whistleblowing, spoke about the UK Public

Interest Disclosure Act and met Johnny de Lange, the Chairperson of the Justice Committee. Impressed by the conceptual approach of the British law, he urged his committee to rewrite the whistleblower protection section of the Open Democracy Bill and triggered agreement in the committee to use the UK law as a central model and hence extend whistleblowing provision to include the private sector (Dimba et al. 2004). But the ISS, and more precisely Lala Camerer, was arguing that the Open Democracy Bill ought to be split up into two bills, one focusing on whistle-blowing, and the other taking up the access to information regulations (Dimba et al. 2004; Camerer 2001). Camerer (1999) argued that one needed to look into the likeliness that public sector management would inspire enough confidence in the effectiveness of whistleblowing legislation. Any doubts about that had to be linked with careful consideration to logistical consequences of the proposed legislation. However, the new Constitution had been called in on 4 February 1997 and specified a constitutional deadline of three years (Section 21 (4)) to enact new legislature prescribing a framework for the government procurement policy for the allocation of contracts and the protection or advancement of persons. Hence, the Open Democracy Bill had to be voted before 4 February 2000. Given the little time left, Camerer succeeded in convincing the Justice Committee to split up the Open Democracy Bill into the Promotion of Access to Information Bill, and the Protected Disclosure Bill. Indeed, the Access to Information Bill got enacted on time, but the Protected Disclosure Bill only passed Parliament in mid 2000. The Protected Disclosure Act 2000 (PDA) redrafted by Richard Calland of Idasa and Lala Camerer of the ISS showed a peculiarity by only covering employer-employee relations. Hence, employees can only disclose about their employer's wrongdoing. Contractors or volunteers are not covered actors. In an era of outsourcing and subcontractors, this indeed is a strange twist, and it is recognized to be a flaw in the South African whistleblowing legislation (Dimba et al. 2004; ODAC 2003).

In its preamble, the PDA[49] makes reference to 'the democratic values of human dignity, equality and freedom' and recognizes that:

> criminal and other irregular conduct in organs of state and private bodies are detrimental to good, effective, accountable and transparent governance in organs of state and open and good corporate governance in private bodies and can endanger the economic stability of the Republic and have the potential to cause social damage.

The PDA also 'bears in mind' that 'every employer and employee has a responsibility to disclose criminal and any other irregular conduct in the workplace'.

To promote awareness of the PDA, Idasa started up the Open Democracy Advice Centre (ODAC) in partnership with the Black Sash Trust and the

---

[49] Protected Disclosures Act, No. 26, 2000, published in the *Government Gazette* on 7 August 2000.

University of Cape Town Public Law Department. Executive director of ODAC is Richard Calland, who had taken the lead in the NGO-call for whistleblowing protection covering the private sector, and had helped to draft the PDA. The ODAC offers training, consultancy and free advice on the two acts coming out of the Open Democracy Bill, the Promotion of Access to Information Act and the Protected Disclosure Act. ODAC sees its mission as to 'promote open and transparent democracy; foster a culture of corporate and government accountability; and assist people in South Africa to realize their human rights' (ODAC website).[50]

Hence, both government enacting the whistleblowing legislation and the NGO driving upon the legislation, encapsulate the PDA in a discourse of openness, transparency, accountability and human rights. Are the elements of the policy, as stipulated in the PDA also pointing in those directions? The actor element clearly states protected disclosures are only related to an employer-employee relationship. The subject element covers both public and private sector criminal offences, failures to comply with legal obligations, miscarriage of justice, endangering the health or safety of an individual, damaging the environment, cover-ups, and unfair discrimination. Here, the UK PIDA was clearly the model for the PDA, with only 'unfair discrimination' added in the PDA – albeit an important addition in the context of South Africa. The same is true even more for the recipient element. What Bowers et al. (1999) have called the first level and second level disclosures are present in the PDA. Most of it is taken over word for word, except for the regulators. Under the PDA, a disclosure is always protected if made in good faith to the Public Protector, the Auditor-General or a person or body prescribed by the administration of Justice. However, South Africa is still waiting for the list of prescribed bodies or person. Still, it is exactly the same mechanism as that of the UK PIDA. And this is the reason why at first sight, the PDA might be regarded as driven by the same constructs as the PCAW: OSR-network, accountability, and efficiency. The argumentation I have used with regard to the OSR-network construct is also applicable to the PDA: the recipient element is too detailed and inserts supplementary conditions for wider disclosures for the OSR-stakeholder construct to be at play here. However, the PDA is more restricted in its actor element than the PCAW. If only disclosures relating to employee-employer relationships are covered, it is hard to maintain the network-concept. The PDA is not about power balance within a network, but rather about power balance within the employer-employee relationship. While that most probably is a relationship to be balanced, the PDA is not driven on a OSR-network construct. Thus, despite the high moral tone, it seems only accountability and efficiency remain as normative legitimation constructs when we look at the elements of the policy as specified in the PDA. Indeed, as an ODAC position paper (ODAC 2003) states, 'the law's central objective is to play a role in the overall fight against corruption'. But what

---

[50] The ODAC mission statement can be found on their website: http://www. opendemocracy.org.za/about.htm (cited June 2004).

about the reference to human rights in the preamble to the PDA, the insertion of 'unfair discrimination' into the subject element, and the ODAC mission statement? I do think that, within the context of the South African history, we should take these references seriously. The human rights rationales used are those of 'truth' and 'democracy' rather than the 'self-expression' rationale, as the whole drive behind the new constitution is a remaking of South African society into a participative and open democracy. Also, the PDA came out of the same Open Democracy Bill as the Promotion of Access to Information Act did. The ODAC deals with precisely these two Acts. Thus, the human right construct should be acknowledged as a legitimation construct driving the PDA. The recipient element matches that construct (see Table 3.4). But the actor element of the PDA is too narrow. The subject element's specifications are too narrow as well. Moreover, because self-expression is not one of the rationales behind the human rights promotion of the PDA, it seems whistleblowing is perceived to be instrumental to the safeguarding of human rights, rather than a strict human right in itself. Therefore, in Figure 4.5, showing the evolution of legitimation lines for whistle-blowing policies in South Africa, I have marked the human rights line, but drawn in between the accountability and the efficiency line.

Since the passing of the PDA in 2000, the need for whistleblowing policies have been taken up by the King Committee on Corporate Governance (King 2002). This committee was formed in 1992, under the auspices of the Institute of Directors, to consider corporate governance in the context of South Africa. It issued a report in 1994, setting standards of corporate governance in South Africa. In 2002, these were reviewed in a new report, which is encouraging compliance with PDA (King 2002). Although the importance of taking up whistleblowing policies as a corporate governance standard should not be underestimated, one should note the affirmation made in the King Report of whistleblowing as an anti-fraud mechanism. Section 3.1.8. of the report states:

> In addition to the company's other compliance and enforcement activities, the board should consider the need for a confidential reporting process (whistleblowing) covering *fraud and other risks* (King 2002, 31, emphasis added).

Fraud is *a* risk, and writing 'fraud and other risks' implies giving fraud a special status as a risk.

In November 2002, the South African Law Reform Commission published an issue paper (SALRC 2002) on the PDA in the form of a questionnaire on which submissions were sought. One of the areas for discussion was whether or not the ambit of the PDA should be extended beyond the strict employer-employee relation, so that persons other than an employee in the strict sense would be able to make protected disclosures. ODAC submitted a position paper (ODAC 2003). An important recommendation made in the paper is the extension of protection for whistleblowers outside the employer-employee relationship to agency workers, independent contractors and the public. If the PDA would be amended in this way, then it would also tap into the OSR-network construct.

ODAC's plea for widening the actor element was supported by the Office of The Director General, Provincial Administration, Western Cape.[51] The Society of Advocates, the Department of Education and Professor Van Jaarsveld of the Department of Mercantile Law, University of South Africa, argued such an extension was not desirable because this would leave the judicial system unable to deal with the resulting increase in whistleblowing matters.

The Congress of South African Trade Unions Parliamentary Office (COSATU) pleaded for an extension of the list of persons or bodies to whom disclosures could be made.

In June 2004, the Law Reform Commission issued a discussion paper on reforming the PDA (SALRC 2004). In that paper, the Commission discusses the current state of the PDA and makes a number of proposals to reform it, based on the submissions it received on its November 2002 issue paper. Its discourse of accountability and curbing corruption is continued. Important however is that the paper proposes to reform the PDA in the direction of widening both the actor and the recipient element.

One of the arguments for extending the actor element raised in the discussion paper is the increase in 'atypical' employment, which is then linked with flexibilization, outsourcing, teleworkers, etc. (SALRC 2004, 29). The paper proposes to change the word 'employee' into 'worker' throughout the Act, so that this would also include independent contractors, consultants, agents and other such workers.

With regard to the recipient element, the discussion paper recognizes that 'there seems no good reason to limit the list to these two particular bodies [Public Protector and the Auditor-General] and "a person or body prescribed for purposes of this section"' (SALRC 2004, 38). The proposal is made to include in the recipient element the 'state institutions supporting constitutional democracy' listed in Chapter 9 of the Constitution: the Human Rights Commission, the Commission for Gender Equality, the Electoral Commission and the Independent Authority to Regulate Broadcasting. Also, the paper proposes to include the South African Ombudsmen, the Speaker of Parliament for matters relating to an MP, the Commissioner of Police for disclosures relating to a member of the South African Police Service, an organ of state, and a Labour Inspectorate. And finally, the proposal is made to also protect disclosures made to a trade union representative and to treat those on equal foot as disclosures made to a legal advisor (SALRC 2004, 73).

The issue of citizen's whistleblowing – actor element is 'any person' – for which the ODAC asked for, is left open. Also, whether a specific duty should be

---

[51] Submissions to the November 2002 issue paper are discussed in SALRC (2004, 28–32).

placed on employers to inform workers of their rights and obligations under the PDA is left open.

Subsequent to the publication of the discussion paper in June 2004, again submissions were called for. ODAC has submitted a paper (ODAC 2004), in which it supports the extension of the ambit of the PDA, but proposes that the definition of worker also includes volunteers, and that the labour broker[52] is covered. With regard to the recipient element, the ODAC agrees with the proposed amendments, but would also like to be included: the permanent chairperson of the National Council of Provinces, the Financial Services Board, the National Nuclear Regulator, the National Electricity Regulator, the speaker of the Legislative Assembly and the speaker of the Legislative Council, the Independent Complaints Directorate and the South African Human Rights Commission.

Further, the ODAC stays firm on its position that anyone should be able to blow the whistle and be protected. It also emphasizes the need to obligate every employer over a certain size to have internal whistleblowing procedures and training (ODAC 2004).

The deadline for entering submissions to the discussion paper was 31 August 2004. Of course, these are all just proposals. Even though it is important that they have been made, the PDA is not amended yet. As I noted earlier on and as I have indicated in Figure 4.5, if the actor element would be extended as in the proposals, then an OSR-network line would be tapped into.

Japan

Even in Japan, with one of the strongest corporatist cultures, the issue of whistle-blowing has gained ground. Organizational loyalty in the old sense of the belief that illegality or malpractice should be overlooked or ignored for the sake of the company, is still very strong, but Japanese corporate culture is nevertheless showing cracks. Lifetime employment is fading, workforce reductions are taking place, a lot of corporations have stopped offering low-price accommodation to their workers. And the last ten years, notions such as 'accountability', 'freedom of information', 'governance', 'business ethics' have been taken up in the language (Miki 2004).

The Global Report by Transparency International mentions that actions of whistleblowers led to a growing demand for introduction of laws to protect them

---

[52] The ODAC gives an example of labour brokerage and its relevance for whistle-blowing protection schemes: 'the security company (business A) who hires out security personnel as security guards to business B. The security guard works every day at B, so on a permanent basis, but A is his employer. If he were to blow the whistle on wrongdoing at B and B informs A that his services are no longer required, A could dismiss him as an operational requirements dismissal if A cannot place him at another business' (ODAC 2004).

Table 4.6 South Africa Bills and Act

Element	ODB 1995 draft	ODB 1997 draft	PDA2000
Actor	Any person	Any person	Employee
Subject	Within public sector: – abuse of power – waste of resources – danger to public health or safety – corruption	Within public sector: – abuse of power – waste of resources – danger to public health or safety – corruption	Pubic and private sector: – criminal offences – non–compliance with legal obligations – miscarriage of justice – danger to health or safety – damage to environment – cover–ups – unfair discrimination
Recipient	– Parliament – public protector – hr commission – public service comm. – auditor-general – attorney-general	– 1995 draft recipients, + media (when necessary)	Internal procedures, employer, public protector, auditor-general, prescribed persons (not yet listed), anyone reasonable

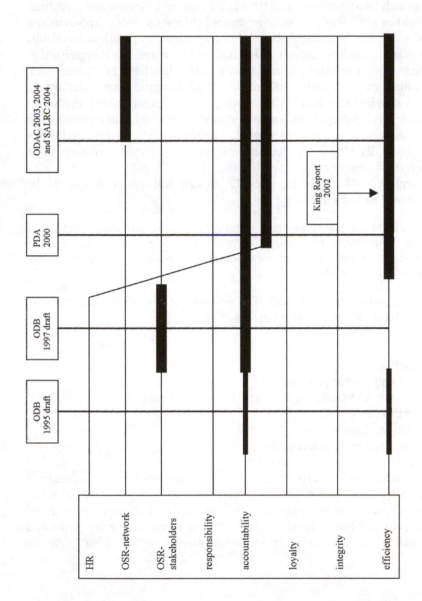

Figure 4.5   Evolution of legitimation lines (South Africa)

(TI 2004, 201). Indeed, it seems the Japanese whistleblowing issue was initiated in 2000, when Mitsubishi employees reported about safety risks and the company recalled two million cars. But the call for whistleblowing legislation gained momentum only two years later, in 2002, when a number of frauds and illegalities came to light in a number of economic sectors (Morioka 2004). Apparently, a number of businesses have established an 'ethics hotline' for employees to report dubious internal practices (Umeda 2004). Kabunushi, a non-profit organization promoting corporate reforms and also known as the shareholders' ombudsman, supported the launch in October 2002 of a legal advice centre for whistleblowers, called PISA (Public Interest Speak-up Advisors). In December 2002, the Social Policy Council issued a report recommending the establishment of a commission to examine a system of protection for people who make public interest disclosures (Morioka 2004). By May 2003, such an examination was underway, targeting a system to protect consumer interests.

On March 9, 2004 a Public Interest Disclosure Bill was submitted to the Japanese Diet. The Bill states that its:

> purpose is [...] to promote compliance with the laws and regulations concerning the protection of the life, health, property, and any other interests of people [...] and to contribute to the stability of people's lives and the sound development of the society and economy in Japan (Article 1).[53]

The actor element covers both public and private sector workers (Article 2 and 7) and the subject element covers breaches of:

- Penal Code,
- Food Sanitation Law,
- Securities and Exchange Law,
- Law Concerning Standardization and Proper Labeling of Agricultural and Forestry Products,
- Air Pollution Control Law,
- Waste Disposal and Cleaning Law,
- Personal Information Protection Act,
- Any laws other than those specified in the preceding Items that are specified in a cabinet order as laws concerning the protection of individuals' lives and health, the protection of consumer interests, the protection of the environment and the protection of fair competition, and other laws concerning the protection of people' lives, health, property and other interests (attached list to Article 2 of the Bill).

---

[53]   An English translation of the Bill is available at http://www1.oecd.org/daf/ASIAcom/countries/japan.htm (cited November 2004). My discussion is based on that translation.

However, protected disclosures are restricted to matters within 'the Entity in Which the Worker Works', or relevant 'to business with regard to an executive, employee, agent, or any other person of the Entity in Which the Worker Works' (Article 2). This not only implies the organization of which one is an employee, but also includes the organization to which a worker is dispatched as an employee of another organization, and also covers 'contract work or any other contract with another business'.

The recipient element allows for internal disclosures, to the 'Entity in Which the Worker Works', or external to 'an Administrative Organ authorized to impose a disposition […] or give a recommendation […]', or even wider to:

> any person to whom such Whistleblowing is considered necessary to be made in order to prevent the occurrence of the Act Subject to Whistleblowing […] (including any person who suffers or might suffer damage from the Act Subject to Whistleblowing, but excluding any person who might damage the competitive position or any other legitimate interests of the Entity in Which the Worker Works (Article 2, section 4).

The Bill was passed unchanged by the House of Representatives on 25 May 2004 and by the House of Councillors on 14 June 2004. It is known as the Whistleblower Protection Act (Law No. 122 of 2004).

As far as legitimation drivers goes, the events and statements leading up to the Bill as well as the stated purpose of the Whistleblower Protection Act (WPA) point at an OSR construct. It is about protecting consumers and society, by regarding a whistleblowing policy as a means to promote compliance with laws and regulations protecting the proper functioning and stability of society. The actor element confirms this: both sectors are covered. The subject element too emphasizes an OSR driver: disclosures to be protected concern individuals' lives and health, consumer interests, environment, and fair competition.

Even the recipient element is wide: internal disclosures, external disclosures to government agencies authorized on the matters concerned, and an open recipient 'to any person considered necessary'.

If that was all that was too it, the WPA would qualify as an OSR-stakeholder driven whistleblowing policy. However, the WPA contains important restrictions to the openness of the open recipient. First of all, the provisions stipulate that 'any person considered necessary' excludes 'any person who might damage the competitive position or any other legitimate interests of the Entity in Which the Worker Works'. Since it is easy to argue that any disclosure to the media or any disclosure that is accessible in any way to competitors, customers, investors, suppliers, etc. 'might' damage the competitive position of an organization on which the whistle gets blown, it is hard to think of any person or body that would fit that restriction of 'any person considered necessary'. Indeed, disclosures made in the course of seeking legal advise still qualifies. Nevertheless, all of a sudden, the open recipient no longer seems open at all.

So, what have we got as a recipient element: 1) internal disclosures; 2) disclosures to an Administrative Organ authorized on the matter; 3) disclosures made in the course of seeking legal advise. This is very similar to what Bowers et al. (1999) have described with regard to the UK PIDA as the first level disclosures. The Japanese WPA has a recipient element with three types of recipients: internal, regulator type of organizations, and others. The recipient element shows a tiered approach, but restricts the open recipient in the sense that a whistleblower can disclose to anyone considered necessary as long as the person or body disclosed to does not harm the competitive position or legitimate interests of the organization.

This is very odd and looks like a compromise text. Nevertheless, it implies that the legitimation construct driving the Japanese WPA cannot be the OSR-stakeholder construct, but rather the OSR-network construct (Figure 4.6).

Apparently, some civil society actors are lobbying for the OSR-stakeholder driver. The Japan Federation of Bar Associations holds the opinion that whistle-blowing to outside watchdogs should be protected (Asahi Shimbun 2004). Also, PISA wants to loosen the restrictions on the open recipient (Morioka 2004). It argues that whistleblowers will not trust the internal channels to be effective because the Japanese corporate culture has only very recently started to diverge from totally enclosing to individual's professional and social life. PISA argues that consumer interests can best be protected if employees as stakeholders can warn other stakeholders like consumers in ways that are appropriate but not necessarily heavily restricted or prescribed, when organizational practices are unacceptable to society. Leon Wolff (Wolff 2004) commented on the WPA by pointing to the stringent conditions on whistleblowers (carrying the burden of proof) before they can enjoy statutory protection. Wolff concludes: 'In its current guise, it is fair to ask: precisely who is protected by the Act – whistleblowers and the general public, or big business and bureaucrats' (Wolff 2004, 213)?

Belgium

The 1999 elections brought a significant shift to Belgian politics. The Greens joined power with the Socialists and the Liberals while the Christian-Democrats went into opposition. In the declaration made by new the government coalition, a chapter is dedicated to the depolitization of the government administration. In that chapter, the intention is made to 'install at every department a channel through which internal dysfunctions or malpractices could be forwarded in confidentiality' (Verhofstadt 1999, 3).[54] The intention fits well within the context of institutional reforms initiated some years before under the name of *Copernicus* and aimed at

---

[54] My translation of 'op elk departement een meldpunt waar op vertrouwelijke basis interne dysfuncties of mistoestanden kunnen worden doorgegeven'.

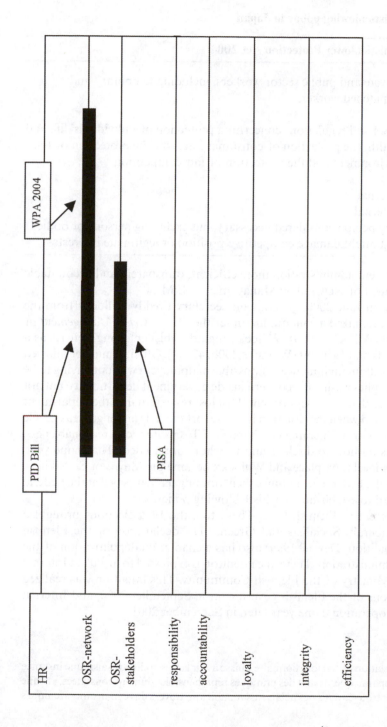

Figure 4.6 Evolution of legitimation lines (Japan)

Table 4.7   Whistleblowing policy in Japan

Element	Whistleblower Protection Act 2004
Actor	Private and public sector workers, including temporary and dispatched workers
Subject	Laws and regulations concerning protection of individuals' life and health, the protection of consumer interests, the protection of the environment and the protection of fair competition
Recipient	Internal External Any person considered necessary, but excluding persons or bodies that might damage competitive position or legitimate interests

making government administration more efficient, transparent and accountable – indeed, a context of New Public Management (NPM).

A year later, in June 2000, government secretary Freddy Willockx from the Socialist Party organized a colloquium under the title of *Crisis Management by the Government* (Willockx 2000). Willockx regards whistleblowing policies as a vital part of crisis management (Willockx 2000, 43–44). Officials must be allowed to raise concern about malpractices or possible malpractices without having to be disloyal. This implies raising the concern inside government departments, but not necessarily inside their own department. Disclosures external to the department ought to be allowed when the situation is of the sort that it is no longer reasonable to go through the normal hierarchical channels.[55] To ensure such a reasonableness, clear guidelines on how to disclose and to whom are needed. That same year, elections at city level took place and Willockx became the Mayor of St-Niklaas, thereby leaving the Federal scene. Since then, nothing has happened at the Federal level with regard to establishing a whistleblowing policy.

This is different at Flemish level. There too, the 1999 elections brought a coalition of Liberals, Socialists and Greens. The declaration of the Flemish government coalition (Dewael 1999) also has a chapter on depolitization of the government administration. There, the intention is expressed to install an Internal Audit for the Ministry of the Flemish Community. This intention was realized through decisions of the Flemish government in September 2000, and Internal Audit became operational one year later, in September 2001.

---

[55]   My translation of 'un fonctionnaire puisse avoir la possibilité de saisir une instance extérieure, s'il apparaît que, devant des pratiques répréhensibles dûment constatées, aucune suite ne peut être trouvée dans des délais raisonnables au travers des canaux hiérarchiques normaux'.

The parallels between the two declarations (Verhofstadt 1999 and Dewael 1999) is no surprise. Both government coalitions were formed at the same time; the Flemish coalition partners were also part of the Federal coalition. Hence, government at both levels was 'in tune' and even though the 'Copernicus' reforms were instigated at Federal level, the whole idea of NPM was also present at Flemish level, where this is known as the BBB-reforms (*Beter Bestuurlijk Beleid* – Better Government Policy).[56]

On 26 January 2001 the Greens issued a press statement urging for a 'Flemish Copernicus' in which they signalled a need for internal democratization and an active idea management. A whistleblowing policy ought to be part of such institutional reforms. In December 2002, Dirk Holemans – member of the Flemish Parliament for the Greens – launched his proposal for legislation. In April 2003, the proposal was introduced into Parliament (nos 1658 (2002–2003)/1 and 1659 (2002–2003)/1) by members of the ruling coalition – Dirk Holemans for the Greens (AGALEV), Marino Keulen for the Liberals (VLD), Leo Peeters and Dirk De Cock for the Socialists (SPA-SPIRIT). In February 2004, the commission for institutional reforms unanimously approved the proposal. On 28 April 2004 the proposal was discussed in a plenary session of parliament, although there was not much of a discussion (see report of plenary session no. 51). There was only a member of the opposition (Vlaams Blok) stating her support for the proposal. The next day, the proposal passed unanimously. It has been published in the *Belgisch Staatsblad* (BS 11 June 2004) and came into force on 1 January 2005.

The provisions have hardly changed from the proposal to the passed legislation. The actor element is limited to personnel of the Flemish government. The subject element defines malpractice as negligence, abuse or crimes, but has been narrowed from malpractice the officials perceive while in function, to the malpractice in their own office perceived while in function. This is a significant difference, however, it seems more a correction rather than a change in vision. The title of Holemans original proposal already pointed at officials disclosing malpractices within their own department.[57]

The recipient element consists of a three tiered approach. The only change was a shortening of the time one had to wait before being allowed to go to the next tier (from three months (Holemans 2002) to 30 days (Holemans et al. 2003)). Holemans argues that the whistleblowing provisions for government personnel is parallel to the possibilities offered to citizens to make complaints (Holemans

---

[56] See the memorandum of the Flemish Government (VR 2001), in which a decentralization of government policy is announced, responsibilising line management of departments.

[57] The title of the original proposal is: 'Legislative proposal – of Mr Holemans – for the protection of officials disclosing irregularities or abuses *within their service* (whistle-blowers)' (Holemans 2002, emphasis added). This is my translation of 'Voorstel van decreet – van de heer Holemans – tot bescherming van de ambtenaren die melding maken van onregelmatigheden of misbruiken binnen hun dienst (klokkenluiders)'.

2002; Holemans et al. 2003). In this sense, the provisions are to be regarded as the application of the principle of transparency in government administration. Holemans states that the provisions do not call for a new logic of governance. He thereby situates the whistleblowing policy in the BBB-context of institutional reforms. A citizen can make a complaint directly to the concerned official. At a second level, a citizen can make a complaint to a specially instance in each government department or organization. Third, a citizen can also take his/her complaint to the Ombudsman, reporting to Parliament and therefore independent from the executive administration. Exactly the same three steps have been taken up in Holemans' whistleblowing policy. First, the government employee can always make a complaint to his/her line manager. When nothing is done about it or the employee has good reasons to expect retaliation, or is experiencing retaliation, then the official can repeat the complaint to the Internal Audit. If the second level complaint has no result either, then the employee can make the complaint to the Ombudsperson.

What the legislation does is expand the tasks of the Internal Audit and the Ombudsperson to allow them to accept complaints by government personnel. The 'Charter of the Internal Audit' from September 2000 allowed only heads of departments to raise matters with Internal Audit; now every government employee can do so and jump the hierarchical step of head of the department. Secondly, the Ombudsperson could only handle complaints by citizens; now, government personnel too can raise matters. Moreover, it is the Ombudsperson who provides protection in the sense that it is the Ombudsperson who decides whether or not a government employee acted in good faith and followed the right procedures.

But what about legitimation? What are the arguments used by Holemans? He cites (Holemans 2002; Holemans et al. 2003) a number of cases in which people who blew the whistle experienced abuse of hierarchical power and sees it only proper that whistleblowers would be protected against retaliations. He adds that if the Flemish Parliament would do so, it would emphasize its pioneering position in institutional reforms (compared to Wallony and the Federal level). In designing such a protection, Holemans sees it necessary to take account of 1) the need to make clear and stable provisions, 2) the fact that in the past whistleblowers had little choice but go to the media, which is unable to solve problems in a satisfying way, and 3) the need to identify an instance able – sufficiently independent – to look into both the complaint – is it done in good faith – and the matter raised by the complaint.

Of course, all three are related. The clear and stable provisions are provided for in the three tiered approach. Whistleblowing to the media is not allowed under the provisions, not even as a final, fourth step. Holemans considers the Ombudsperson as the final, third step under which protection is possible, as 'external enough' to ensure independency. It is true that, since the Ombudsperson reports to Parliament, it constitutes a channel outside of the executive branch of government. So yes, it is external and independent. However, when it comes to investigating the matter, the Ombudsperson still needs to order Internal Audit to start up an investigation. Thus, if I were to make a complaint with Internal Audit and they do not do anything with it, I can take my complaint to the Ombudsperson who will then order Internal Audit – who already refused to take the complaint seriously – to investigate my complaint. One could argue that this creates a short-circuit, however, one could just as well regard this as a governance approach, rendering both line management and Internal Audit accountable. It is line management who has to take complaints seriously. If they fail to do so, Internal Audit can take up the matter and show line management has not carried out their responsibilities. Should Internal Audit fail to hold line management accountable, then the Ombudsperson can force them to do so and even hold Internal Audit accountable when reporting to Parliament. Hence, the recipient element expresses an accountability driven legitimation. The shortening of the term for the line management or the Internal Audit to take up the complaint and start investigating it (from three months to 30 days) – the mere fact that *that* is what they changed – shows that that is what they were attentive for.

What was added in the argumentation for the whistleblowing policy between the original proposal (Holemans 2002) and the enacted text (Holemans et al 2003), is a reference to Bovens' concept of 'institutional citizenship'. As I have discussed in the section on the Netherlands, 'institutional citizenship' emphasizes that government employees, even when in function, are always citizens as well. In Holemans' argumentation, it is used to oppose total hierarchical obeisance. In the construction of the accountability construct, the same reasoning was made: jumping hierarchical steps to raise concerns might compensate for the loss of an objective referent – which a bureaucracy had – to hold orders against. Hence, while Bovens' notion of 'institutional citizenship' was used in the Netherlands to argue within a stakeholder driven legitimation, in Belgium (Flanders) it is used to further the accountability construct.

Table 4.8 Flemish whistleblowing legislation (Belgium)

Element	Flanders 2005
Actor	Government personnel
Subject	Negligence Abuse of power Criminal matters
Recipient	Head of department Internal Audit Ombudsperson

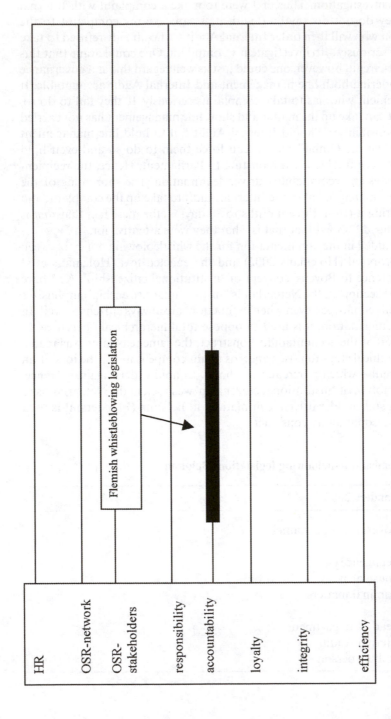

HR

OSR-network

OSR-stakeholders

responsibility

accountability

loyalty

integrity

efficiency

Flemish whistleblowing legislation

Figure 4.7 Evolution of legitimation lines (Belgium)

Whistleblowing Legislations Passing Through Parliaments

The Netherlands

In 1990, Mark Bovens published his PhD on responsibility in organizations (Bovens 1990). He had looked at intellectual and judicial openings for whistle-blower protection. Bovens wrote in Dutch and translated 'whistleblower' into 'klokkenluider' – the person sounding the church-bells. The term 'klokkenluider' found its way into Dutch language, and is still used today in the Netherlands and Flanders (Belgium) as the Dutch translation of 'whistleblower'. This is important, because 'klokkenluider' favours a particular legitimation of whistle-blowing. A person sounding the church-bells is someone calling for the attention of his/her community. A warning, or a summon for help. A church is a refuge, a safe place. It points at the need to protect those who sound the alarm or raise concern.

Indeed, Bovens' translation is very appropriate for the legitimation he had in mind for whistleblowing, which is *institutioneel burgerschap* – institutional citizenship. With this notion, Bovens wanted to emphasize that an official or employee is, also within the context of the organization, always a citizen. Hence, in their actions, organization members should always keep the preservation of their political community and the protection of public interests in mind.

This legitimation places whistleblowing within the early 1970s loyalty dilemma: loyalty to the organization versus loyalty to the community. And just like the politico-ethical stance of that time, loyalty to the community is propagated as primordial. With regard to the constructs I developed in Chapter 3, the notion of 'institutional citizenship' comes closest to that of the OSR-stakeholder construct, in which organization members, as stakeholders, warn fellow stakeholders of organizational goal-displacements. The reader might have expected a link with the 'rational loyalty' construct, but this is not the case. The role of an explicit mission and value statement of the organization as the objective referent of organizational loyalty is crucial to the construct of 'rational loyalty'. Such an objective referent is absent in the notion of 'institutional citizenship'. Hence, it does not approach the 'rational loyalty' construct. 'Institutional citizenship' does not solve the loyalty dilemma, it just takes sides. But besides the introduction of a Dutch term for whistleblower, the work of Bovens on whistleblowing remained on the book shelve for a while.

In 1993, the then Minister of Interior, Mr Dales, instigated the quest for integrity in public services. He did so riding the wave of New Public Management (NPM), aspiring a public service characterized by transparency, client focus, and efficiency. The discussion about public sector governance in the Netherlands today still pivots around the concept of integrity. The issue of whistleblowing gained momentum when Paul Van Buitenen – a Dutch accountant working for the European Commission – had blown the whistle on fraud to the European

Parliament.[58] The issue of whistleblowing was integrated into the integrity discussion. After some questions in parliament concerning loyalty problems of government officials, a report was issued on 'Integrity of Public Governance'[59] in September 1999 (MBZK 1999), making recommendations on how to strengthen integrity in government. The first chapter after the introduction is about *klokkenluiden* or whistleblowing. The report states that external whistleblowing has undesired effects: it undermines trust in the department, and internal relationships are damaged. Yet, it is valuable that officials take up responsibility to make allegations about wrongdoing (MBZK 1999, 6). Therefore, a whistleblowing policy is to be aimed at allowing officials to take that responsibility and at the same time avoid the undesired effects of external whistleblowing. For the specification of the subject element, the report explicitly refers to the UK PIDA, and indeed more or less copies its subject element – criminal matters, violation of regulation, miscarriage of justice, danger to public health, safety, environment, cover-ups (MBZK 1999, 6). The actor element is constrained to public officials and a motive element is introduced in that the official should not have any personal gain in blowing the whistle.

As far as the recipient element is concerned, the UK PIDA is not followed. Rather, how to blow the whistle is framed (MBZK 1999, 7) between loyalty to the Minister and 'institutional citizenship' (the official is a citizen, even as official). But the right to free speech is immediately emptied by referrals to 'fulfilling the duties of the office' and secrecy provisions. The introduction to the proposed procedure (MBZK 1999, 7) ends with a referral to an old duty of the official to report criminal matters to the Officer of Justice. The proposed procedure then (MBZK 1999, 8–10), seems a mere expansion of that duty. Raising concern about 'suspected wrongdoing' is an obligation! Any concern or allegation is to be reported internally first, to the head of the department in which the official works. A second step – only to be taken when internal reporting had no effect or worsened the situation – is raising the concern to an 'independent commission' – *Commissie Integriteit Rijksoverheid* (Commission Integrity National Government). This commission should be made up of retired politicians, judges, or academics, but it is preferred that this commission would have three members: an independent president, a trustee of employees, and a trustee of employers. The task of the commission is to give advise to the relevant Minister. The Minister is not forced to follow that advise, but the advise will be made public.

It is important to note that the externality of the commission in the proposed provisions is fragile. The commission does not belong to any particular department, and in that sense it would be an external channel. Yet, it is not clear who is to appoint the members of the commission. Also, even though the commission's advise is to be made public, this is to be done anonymous. Hence

---

[58]   For an account of Van Buitenen's whistleblowing odyssey, see Van Buitenen (1999).

[59]   My translation of the Dutch title, 'Integriteit van het openbaar bestuur'.

it is not clear how parliament or other institutions might investigate further where necessary.

Amsterdam took the report as a blueprint for her whistleblowing policy. And indeed, as the whistleblowing policy of Amsterdam shows, the independence of the second step recipient is very fragile.

On 20 November 2000, labour unions and the representative body of the city governments signed a collective labour agreement, in which it is stated that city government ought to develop procedures for dealing with concerns about wrongdoing raised by officials. The agreement covers the period October 2000 to February 2002.

Following up to that agreement, in February 2001, the city of Amsterdam installed an integrity office – *Bureau Integriteit*. Its task is to advise and train public sector personnel of the city of Amsterdam on appropriate conduct under the philosophy of new public management. The bureau is also mandated to register and investigate wrongdoing within city departments. The bureau is part of the department of Concern Personnel & Organization, thus its top responsibility rests with the Mayor.

The bureau developed a whistleblowing policy early 2002 (BI 2002a), which became effective at the end of 2002 (Court of Mayor and Aldermen, September 24, 2002). The regulation pertains to city officials and is part of their code of conduct, more precisely the 'line of behaviour with regard to suspected wrongdoing'.[60] The regulation covers city officials blowing the whistle on wrongdoing within their own department. The wrongdoing covered in the subject element are criminal matters, violations of regulation, miscarriage of justice, danger to public health and safety, danger to environment, and cover-ups. Note that this subject element strongly resembles that of the UK PIDA (see section on the UK). The Amsterdam provisions also stipulate (BI 2002a, article 10) that for an official to be protected, he or she should not have any personal gain in the wrongdoing or in blowing the whistle on the wrongdoing.

As far as the recipient element goes, a tiered system is installed. At the first step are internal procedures, head of the department or confidential person if there is such a person appointed in the department. Should the wrongdoing concern the head of the department, then the whistle can be blown directly to the Bureau Integrity. When a concern is not investigated, or in an unsatisfactory way, then the whistleblower can raise the concern with the 'Commission Suspected Wrongdoing'. This commission consists of three members, mandated by the Court of Mayor and Aldermen. Hence, even though the recipient element is tiered, it is important to note that it stays within the scope of the executive branch of city government. Departments, Bureau Integrity and Commission Suspected Wrongdoing are all mandated by and operate under the responsibility of the

---

[60] My translation of 'Gedragslijn vermoeden van misstanden' as it appears in the title of the regulation of the city of Amsterdam (24 September 2002).

Court of Mayor and Aldermen. Recently, at a meeting of Dutch ethicists,[61] Mark Bovens criticized this situation, stating that there is no accountability in such a scheme.

What is also important is that the Amsterdam provisions are not about the *right* to raise concerns, but explicitly talk of the *duty* to raise concerns (BI 2002a, article 2). Hence, in the Amsterdam policy, whistleblowing is obligatory. Obligatory whistleblowing could, according to the screening grid, indicate a legitimation resembling the responsibility construct. The argument was that obligatory whistleblowing decreases the other possibilities of taking ethical distance, or in other words, if one has not blown the whistle, one has not distanced oneself to an organizational outcome and therefore takes part in the collective responsibility for that outcome. The line of argument of the responsibility construct is that whistleblowing policies safeguard individual autonomy and moral agency, both necessary duties that come with responsibilities, and are presupposed in the responsibilization of individuals. Is this the case in the Amsterdam whistleblowing policy? The Bureau Integrity, in its planning reports for 2002–2004 (BI 2002b; BI 2003) writes that it regards the individual moral judgement as the basis of integrity; however, the individual is over-asked. Therefore, judgement power has to be strengthened and backed by debate: others reflect along and bring in arguments. The document also states that basic values and rules can relieve the individual from the strain of individual moral judgement:

> Basic values relieve the judgment power; on the condition that they are suited [...] Rules too can relieve judgment power, time and energy, if they are morally just. It is almost immediately clear what one needs to do. The willpower is relieved by the rules, the control and the sanctions.[62]

The notion of 'integrity' used in the document is described as 'professional responsibility', and is to be understood as trying to capture both the aspect of integrity as compliance and the aspect of integrity as acting on personal discernment. Hence, the argumentation of the 'vision' of the Bureau Integrity makes reference to the responsibility construct – individual morality and structural support for that – and the integrity construct – debate backing individual judgement.

However, the absence of an external channel is a puzzle. Raising concern to the city council – who has the power to control the executive branch of the city government – is not covered in the policy. Everything is to be kept within the executive branch. The mayor looks over both the Bureau Integrity as well as the appeal agency, the Commission Suspected Wrongdoing. In a document explaining

---

[61]   Mark Bovens at the meeting of *Vereniging van Ethici in Nederland*, 16 June 2003, Utrecht.

[62]   My translation of 'Ook de basiswaarden ontlasten de oordeelskracht; mits ze kloppend zijn [...] Regels ontlasten, indien moreel juist, ook de oordeelskracht, tijd en energie. Bijna altijd is direct duidelijk wat je moet doen. De wilskracht wordt ontlast door de regels, de controle en de sancties' (BI 2003, 6).

the whistleblowing provisions, the bureau writes that 'by obliging the official to internally report a wrongdoing, so-called "whistleblowing" is prevented' (BI 2002c, 1).[63] Hence the obligatory character of the provisions and the purely internal reporting are to be linked. Moreover, the emphasis within the integrity policy on rules, control and sanctions make the whistleblowing provisions appear as a control instrument. More precisely, it appears as the instalment of a panopticon which is obliged to generate information on suspected wrongdoing. This, it seems to me, points in the direction of the efficiency construct.

Thus, the Bureau Integrity whistleblowing policy draws close the legitimation lines of responsibility, integrity and efficiency. But I will not mark the integrity line because the Bureau does not show how it is trying to realize the aspirations it makes. The responsibility line seems appropriate to mark: there is the obligatory aspect as well as the reference to individual moral judgement. Linked to that is the panopticon approach to keep everything inside. Prognoses by the Bureau indicate that reporting of wrongdoing should increase in the near future; an extra investigator was added to the bureau's staff; investigations are budgeted 4,500 hours in the bureau's planning, which makes it the most time consuming post (BI 2003). So indeed, the whistleblowing provisions are intended to generate information to start up investigations. Thus, the efficiency line must be marked as well.

In May 2003, national government took up the 'line of behaviour suspected wrongdoing' in an experimental phase, and it is now turned into a law proposal, amending article 125 of the labour law for officials (proposal by Mr. Remkes, sent in on 23 February 2004, article 125 quinquies (1)(f)).

But another demarche must also be noted in the Netherlands. In April 2000, the *Federatie Nederlandse Vakbewegingen* (FNV) – Federation of Dutch Unions – operated a telephone line for whistleblowers, for three days (FNV 2000). In March 1999, the FNV had called for a law proposal for whistleblowing protection, and the telephone line was aimed at generating some substantial data to back that proposal.

The proposal did not include detailed provisions on how to blow the whistle, but it did use a remarkable argumentation. The proposal drives on a human rights approach, emphasizing freedom of expression as an intrinsic right to be respected in the workplace. Workplace free speech furthers the self-realization of the individual (FNV 2000, 7). The proposal also sees workplace free speech as furthering a democratic society. It is in this sense that section 2 of the provision stipulates that public interest overrules any secrecy provision. Here, the old loyalty dilemma on which the politico-ethical whistleblowing activism of the 1970s rested, peeps up again.

In 2003, the Labour Foundation – *Stichting van de arbeid* – issued a paper (SVA 2003) in which it gives its view on how a whistleblowing policy should look like. The paper was issued at the request of the Minister of Social Affairs and

---

[63] My translation of 'Door een ambtenaar te verplichten een misstand intern aan de orde te stellen wordt het zogenaamde 'klokkenluiden' voorkomen'.

Employment. The paper acknowledges the importance of internal procedures, arguing that internal procedures fit very well within an organization regarding itself as a societal activity; it is a way of keeping organizational practice in line with ruling norms and expectations from society.[64] This is in line with the 'rational loyalty' construct. There, internal reporting is praised because it keeps organizational practice in line with organizational purpose – goals as accepted by and in line with societal norms. The paper explicitly states that internal reporting of wrongdoing is to be seen as 'contributing to the improvement of the functioning of the corporation' (SVA 2003, 3).[65] The paper sees an adequate whistleblowing policy as including an actor element covering both private and public sector employees, contractors and volunteers (SVA 2003, 8, footnote 11). The subject element ought to stress the public interest and should be as detailed as possible. As far as the recipient element is concerned, the paper regards a two step approach the best. The first step, the internal channel, should be specified in detail. With regard to the second, external step, the policy ought to emphasize that reasonableness is required, and the policy should specify when the whistle can be blown outside (SVA 2003, 3–4). This double tiered approach indicates an accountability drive.

In July 2003, Ineke Van Gent – Member of Parliament for GroenLinks – introduced a law proposal (Tweede Kamer stuk 28 990) for a 'regulation of the freedom of expression of employees to protect whistleblowers'.[66] The proposal resembles strongly the FNV proposal of 1999. It also drives on a human rights drive. The qualification of freedom of speech stands in sharp contrast to the 1999 report 'Integrity of Public Government'. There, Bovens' institutional citizenship was mentioned but immediately emptied by referral to duties and secrecy provisions. In the introduction to Van Gent's law proposal, the argumentation is turned upside down (Van Gent 2003). The employee has to fulfil his duties and has to respect secrecy provisions, unless to do so would be unreasonable with respect to public interest. The recipient element also turns around reasonableness. Concerns should be raised internally, unless to do so would be unreasonable. If that is the case, then the whistle can be blown externally, to a reasonable and appropriate recipient. The actor element is very wide, covering both public and

---

[64] My paraphrase of 'Een dergelijk instrument past uitstekend binnen een ondernemingsbeleid dat ondernemen beschouwt als een maatschappelijke activiteit Dit vergt immers van de ondernemingsleiding dat zij zich rekenschap geeft van de handelwijze van de onderneming in relatie tot de geldende opvattingen binnen de samenleving over wat hoort en wat niet, alsmede dat zij oog heeft voor de belangen van die samenleving, bijvoorbeeld op het punt van milieu en leefomgeving' (SVA 2003, 2).

[65] My translation of: '[…] dat het intern melden van een misstand gezien wordt als een bijdrage aan het verbeteren van het functioneren van de onderneming' […] (SVA 2003, 3).

[66] The full title of the law proposal is 'Voorstel van wet van het lid Van Gent tot wijziging van het Burgerlijk Wetboek in verband met een regeling van de vrijheid van meningsuiting van werknemers ter bescherming van klokkenluiders'.

private sector workers. And the subject element also takes up a provision regarding the interaction of public and private organizations. Besides criminal matters, violation of regulation, miscarriage of justice, danger to public health and safety, danger to environment, and cover-ups, the subject element also includes waste of public funds and providing public agencies with incorrect information.

Van Gent's law proposal has not passed through parliament yet. The Minister of Social Affairs and Employment has indicated twice (in July and October 2003)[67] that the intention is not to legislate before the initiative by the Labour Foundation (SVA 2003) towards private sector self-regulation has been evaluated. This evaluation is foreseen in 2006. The Minister of Justice has repeated that intention (see Minister Donner in a debate in parliament (Tweede Kamer) on 10 March 2004 (Handelingen Tweede Kamer 56–3705)). Also, in an advice from the *Raad van State* on Van Gent's law proposal, this is reconfirmed.[68] Nevertheless, if Van Gent's proposal would pass parliament, in its current terms and specifications, it would be remarkable as this would be whistleblowing legislation driven by a human rights construct and because of the emphasis put on disclosure in the public interest and the wide recipient element, it is also driven by the accountability construct – because of its double tiered approach – and by the OSR-stakeholder construct – because of its wide open second tier recipient.

There is however, given the latest developments, a potential for the proposal to be amended towards the responsibility line. On 10 March 2004, Halsema and Duyvendak – who belong to GroenLinks, the same political party of Van Gent – sent in a law proposal making it an obligation to report corporate fraud of over €10.000. The website of GroenLinks[69] announced the initiative under the title 'duty to blow the whistle on corporate crime'.[70] The fact that both the human rights driven law proposal as well as the proposal of making it a 'citizen's duty' to blow the whistle come from the same political party, indicates a possible jump from one line to the other.

The advice from the *Raad van State* from 17 September 2004 stands very critical of the human rights driver in Van Gent's proposal. It clearly states that whistleblowing is not about freedom of expression but rather about giving warnings of organizational practices that constitute a breach of law. Hence, not only does the advice steer away from the human rights construct, it also limits the subject element to laws and regulations.

---

[67]   See letters from A.J. de Geus, Minister van Sociale Zaken en Werkgelegenheid, 2 July 2003 (AV/IR/2003/50073) and 24 October 2003 (AV/IR/2003/71688).

[68]   The advice dates from 17 September 2003 and is quoted in Tweede Kamer stuk 28 990 No. 4 from 15 July 2004.

[69]   http://www.groenlinks.nl.

[70]   My translation of 'Plicht tot klokkenluiden bij bedrijfscriminaliteit,' Press release on March 10, 2004.

Also on 10 March 2004, parliament held a debate[71] on the letters from Minister-President Balkenende concerning 'public morality' (see Tweede Kamer stuk 29 454 Nos 1 and 2). In those letters, combating fraud is explicitly mentioned as an exponent of public morality. The proposal of Van Gent's gets wide support, as does the idea of internal whistleblowing procedures. In that debate, mr. Marijnissen – from the Socialist Party (SP) – speaks of an active and participatory citizenship, which he later rephrases with regard to whistleblowing as the 'active mobilization of those involved'[72]. Marijnissen then hands in a list of suggestions from his party towards a better and more effective fight against fraud. One of the suggestions is to offer whistleblowers, besides protection through labour law, a substantial reward! The same move is made by Mr Halsema – from GroenLinks – who calls for a 'whistleblower fund' from which whistleblowers could be paid a financial reward if they come up with hard evidence on big fraud cases. These evolutions in rhetoric and proposals steer further away from the human rights construct and strengthen the legitimation drive of the efficiency construct.

Table 4.9 gives a summary of the proposals and regulations I discussed in this section, and Figure 4.8 shows the operative legitimation lines. It is clear that both Bovens' concept of 'institutional citizenship' as well as the Dales' quest for integrity have rendered the discussion in the Netherlands its peculiarity. All policy proposals have had to deal with those concepts. It is in minimizing Bovens' concept in favour of the other – 1999 report Integrity of Public Governance – or in affirming it – FNV and Van Gent proposals – that the proposals get their content.

The call for private sector self-regulation, initiated by the Labour Foundation (SVA 2003) and widely supported by political actors (both people in government as well as in parliament) indicate a vitality of the accountability driver.

The move of GroenLinks towards an obligation to blow the whistle is to be seen in relation to the operative existence of the Amsterdam obligatory whistleblowing provisions. Furthermore, given the most recent evolutions in rhetoric and proposals, it is very likely that by the time parliament will move towards new legislation – such is foreseen after an evolution in 2006 of the self-regulation process (see supra) – the human rights construct will have vanished from legitimation of whistleblowing in the Netherlands.

Ireland

The Whistleblowers Protection Bill was introduced into Irish Parliament in 1999 (no. 16 of 1999). Its second reading took place on 16 June of that year. It was agreed that the Bill could pass to the Committee stage (it has been referred to the Select Committee on Enterprise and Small Business), where amendments could be made and where public support for the Bill can be sought by consulting

---

[71]   See Handelingen Tweede Kamer 56-3660-3710 and the notes on pages 3735–37.
[72]   My translation of 'actieve inzet van de betrokkenen'.

Table 4.9 Whistleblowing policies proposed in the Netherlands

Element	Amsterdam 2001	SVA 2003	Groenlinks 2003
Actor	City officials	Public and private sector employees, contractors, volunteers	Public and private sector workers
Subject	Criminal matters, violations of regulation, miscarriage of justice, danger to public health and safety, danger to environment, cover-ups	Public interest (details to be specified)	Criminal matters, violations of regulation, miscarriage of justice, danger to public health and safety, danger to environment, cover-ups, waste of public funds, providing public agencies with incorrect information
Recipient	Internal procedures, head of department, Bureau Integrity, Commission Suspected Wrongdoing	Internal channel, another body or person, provided this is appropriate and reasonable	Internal channel, another body or person, provided this is appropriate and reasonable

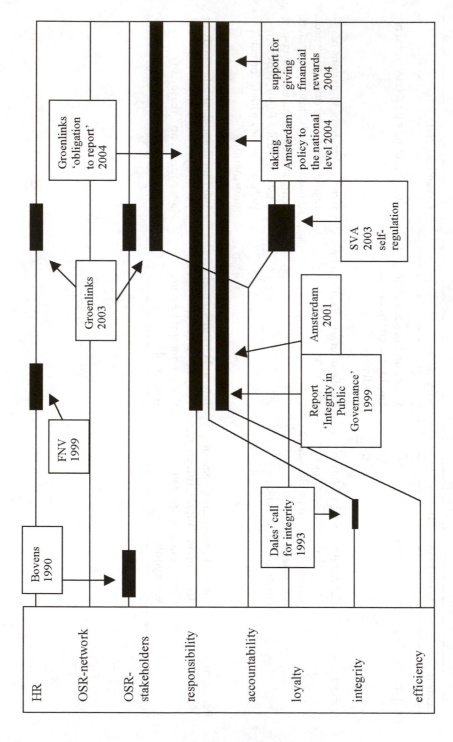

Figure 4.8 Evolution of legitimation lines (the Netherlands)

relevant social partners. But apparently to no result yet. However, the report from the Parliamentary Debates (Houses of the Oireachtas, Dáil and Seanad, 16 June 1999)[73] gives an indication.

The Bill is almost identical to the UK PIDA. The actor element covers both public and private sector employees; the subject element is exactly the same as the UK PIDA, covering crimes and illegalities, miscarriage of justice, danger to health and safety of any individual, damage to the environment, and cover-ups.

Also, the recipient element is very similar to the UK PIDA. One is always covered when disclosing to ones employer, to the person doing the wrongdoing, in the course of obtaining legal advice, or to an officer of a regulating public body. Wider disclosures – 'to some other person' – are protected when reasonable. The criteria for reasonability are the same as the UK PIDA – they disqualify disclosures made for personal gain or made externally prior to an internal disclosure without good reasons to expect retaliation.

Section 1 of the Bill identifies a number of 'appropriate public bodies': the Central Bank, the Comptroller and Auditor General, the Data Protection Commissioner, the Environmental Protection Agency, the Garda Síochána, the Health and Safety Authority, the Information Commissioner, the Ombudsman, the Public Offices Commission, the Revenue Commissioners, and 'any other public body on whom or which regulatory, supervisory or investigative functions, in relation to the matter the subject of a protected disclosure, stand conferred by or under any enactment'. Hence, a public body is an appropriate one for a particular disclosure, if the subject of the disclosure is a matter for which regulatory or supervisory power has been conferred to that body by enactment. Indeed, this is the same principle as in the UK PIDA. In the discussion on the second reading of the Bill, it is asked to specify – in the vain of the UK PIDA – on *who* to disclose *what* to.

Other than that, the second reading is very much an expression of support from both government and opposition, although there are some voices to change the title of the Bill from 'Whistleblowers Protection Bill' to 'Public Interest Disclosure Bill' – again, a change following the UK PIDA.

Based on the current Bill and the second reading discussion in Parliament, the UK PIDA seems to be mirrored in the Irish proposal, which means that the legitimation line figure has to be the same as the UK PIDA: OSR-network, accountability, and efficiency.

Canada

The Canadian government's approach in establishing a whistleblowing policy has so far been very hesitating. At the end of 1996, a NPM-spirit was initiated by the report of a Task Force on Value and Ethics, emphasizing basic values

---

[73] There is a website containing the text of Parliamentary Debates. The text I am referring to can be found at http://www.irlgov.ie/debates-99/16jun99/sect13.htm (cited June 2004).

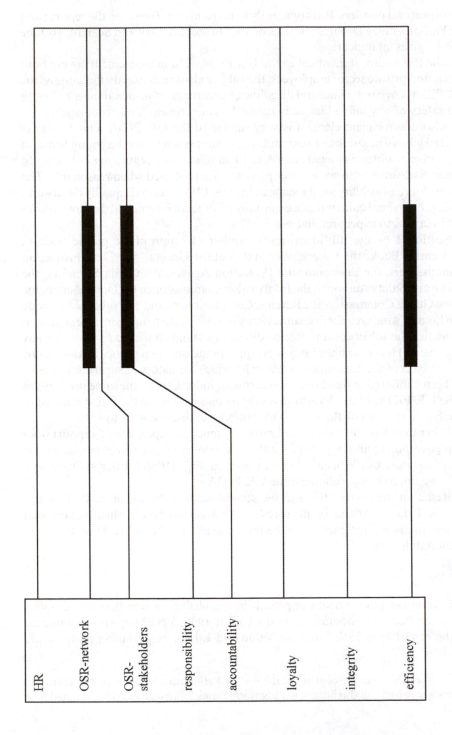

Figure 4.9 Evolution of legitimation lines (Ireland)

HR

OSR-network

OSR-stakeholders

responsibility

accountability

loyalty

integrity

efficiency

Table 4.10 Whistleblowing policies proposed in Ireland

Element	Whistleblowers Protection Bill
Actor	Pubic and private sector employees
Subject	Crimes Failure to comply with legal obligations Miscarriage of justice Danger to health and safety of any individual Danger to environment Cover-ups
Recipient	Internal, or while seeking legal advice, or to a regulato, Other person, provided this is appropriate and reasonable

and commitment of the public service. The development of a draft Statement of principles takes until the end of 2001. Then a consultation period is started, leading to the announcement in June 2003 of a 'Values and Ethics Code for the Public Service'.

Meanwhile, in November 2001, the Treasury Board had adopted an 'Internal Disclosure Policy'. It is applicable only to core public service employees, not employees of Crown corporations – state owned but independent – or separate employees.[74] The subject element is not specified. The policy just states 'wrongdoing'. Recipients for the disclosure of wrongdoing is the senior officer of ones own department designated to do so by the deputy head. The policy also creates a Public Service Integrity Officer as a recipient of disclosures of wrongdoing that an employee believes cannot be raised to the senior officer or have not been dealt with adequately.

In September 2003, the Public Service Integrity Officer issues its first annual report, recommending a legislative regime for disclosures, applicable to the entire federal public sector. Responding to that call, a Working Group on the Disclosure of Wrongdoing is set up, to look into the feasibility of legislating protection.

The report of the Working Group was published in January 2004.[75] The report puts whistleblowing policies into the context of trust and confidence in public institutions. Whistleblowing policies are to be part of a government with 'high ethical standards', based on the principles of transparency, integrity and efficiency. These standards and principles are embodied in civil service codes, value

---

[74] Chronology, and documents such as the 'Internal Disclosure Policy' can be found at http://www.tbs-sct.gc.ca/pshrmac-agrhfpc/announce/0322_e.asp#Chronology (cited July 2004).

[75] The report is available at http://www.tbs-sct.gc.ca/pshrmac-agrhfpc/rep-rap/wgdw-gtdaf_e.asp (cited July 2004).

statements and codes of conduct, but to 'give them 'teeth' and credibility in the eyes of both public servants and the public,' whistleblowing policies are necessary. This is how the Working Group regards the value of a whistleblowing policy. It serves to reassure both public servants and the public that there is a fallback mechanism for exposing and correcting wrongdoing. Whistleblowing policies in themselves do not strengthen ethical government. The Working Group therefore puts a lot of emphasis on making sure 'things go right' by stressing the need to foster within the public sector a good work climate and a supportive organization culture centred around the principles of transparency, integrity and efficiency.

Its recommendations with regard to whistleblowing legislation are that the actor element ought to be expanded to include all employees working in the federal public sector, hence also employees of Crown corporations, separate employees, special contract employees etc. The subject element should be specified as to include 1) violations of any law or regulation, 2) serious breaches of the 'Value and Ethics Code for the Public Service', 3) misuse of public funds or assets, 4) gross mismanagement, 5) substantial and specific danger to life, health and safety of Canadians or the environment. With regard to the recipient element, nothing really changes. The Public Service Integrity Officer is renamed into the Public Service Integrity Commissioner, is to be appointed by the Governor and approved by the Senate and the House of Commons. The Commissioner has to report to parliament, but has to do this 'through a Minister', which implies that there is no direct control from parliament over the recipient of disclosures about malpractice within the executive branch of government. The Commissioner is a second level recipient, the first level being internal procedures at the department or agency. As such, the Commissioner receives and investigates allegations, and ensures the rights of all parties are respected.

On 22 March 2004, the Public Servants Disclosure Protection Bill is tabled in the House of Commons. The bill takes up the recommendations from the Working Group, expanding the actor element, specifying the subject element and fine tuning the recipient element. Important is that the whistleblowing policy set as an administrative regulation in 2001, would be put into legislation – reassuring public servants and public there is a fallback mechanism. Important as well is the discretionary power the Public Service Integrity Commissioner would get to decide which allegations to take up and investigate and which not. It is the Commissioner too who will judge whether or not a disclosure is made in 'good faith', a judgement upon which protection for the whistleblower depends.

On 3 May 2004, the bill was presented to the Government Operations Committee of the House of Commons. The bill is one of several bills aiming at 'modernizing' the public service. Important however – and again, it shows the hesitation on the issue – Minister Coderre, responsible for the Public Service Human Resources Management Agency, talks in his presentation speech about fairness to the persons against whom allegations are made.

Later that month, elections were announced and parliament dissolved. Hence further consideration of the bill was suspended. In October 2004 however, the bill was reintroduced under the same name,[76] the Public Servants Disclosure Protection Bill. The actor element of the October Bill is the same as that of the March Bill. But the October Bill also includes some changes. First of all, the subject element is the same, except that it is not just threats to 'Canadians' that constitute protected disclosures, but threats to 'persons'. Second, the October Bill makes no mention of a Public Service Integrity Commissioner, but allocates that role to the President of the Public Service Commission (PSC), which is a merit commission. Third, the Minister through which the President of the PSC has to report annually to parliament, is the Minister responsible for the Public Service Human Resources Management Agency of Canada (Bill C-11, section 2). However, the President of the PSC is given more power. He or she has the authority to set deadlines for chief executives of departments to respond to recommendations and can submit special reports to parliament (Bill C-11, section 39) at any time if in his/her opinion the matter is urgent and important enough. This would imply more independence of the recipient element from the executive branch of government. But that is not the only change in the recipient element. The October Bill reconfirms that every department must have internal procedures (Bill C-11, section 10). Also very important in the October Bill is section 16, which deals with disclosures made to the public. It stipulates that disclosures to the public will be protected if the situation does not allow sufficient time to follow the procedure and the disclosure concerns a serious offence of an Act under parliament or province legislature or an imminent risk of a substantial and specific danger to the life, health and safety of persons or to the environment.

Thus, the recipient element is set up as follows. Disclosures have to be made through internal procedures. If there is reasonable ground that it would not be appropriate to disclose through internal procedures or the public servant has already disclosed internally but to no avail, then he or she can disclose the matter to the President of the PSC. This two tiered approach is the same as the March Bill. Two additions are made. First, if the matter concerns the PSC, one can raise the issue with the Secretary of the Treasury Board (Bill C-11, section 14). And second, as I just mentioned, urgent matters can be disclosed to the public. Note however, that neither public disclosures nor raising matters concerning the PSC to the Treasury Board constitute a third tier. The bill does not include a provision that allows disclosures to be made to the two additional recipients if both the internal procedures and disclosures to the PSC have any effect – unless of course the matter would have become urgent. Moreover, the subject element for disclosures to the Treasury Board and the public are more restricted than that for internal and PSC disclosures.

---

[76] It was tabled in the House of Commons on 8 October 2004 (38th Parliament, 1st Session, Bill C-11) as the Public Servants Disclosure Protection Bill. Its full title is 'An Act to establish a procedure for the disclosure of wrongdoings in the public sector, including the protection of persons who disclose the wrongdoings'.

In terms of which legitimation construct the Canadian discussion seems to be driven by, I find it hard to say. The difference between the 2001 'Internal Disclosure Policy' and the March 2004 Public Servants Disclosure Bill is that the actor element has been expanded – but remains within the public sector – and the subject element has been specified. Still, these changes do not change the legitimation constructs used.

One could argue it lingers towards the accountability construct, because the Public Service Integrity Commissioner is supposed to report to parliament. However, this is too weak, since the Commissioner has to report 'through a Minister'. Another pointer in the direction of an accountability drive is the emphasis put on whistleblowing policies as an assurance to public servants and public that there is a fallback mechanism to expose and correct malpractice. However, since there is not really an external recipient, the accountability is not from the executive branch towards parliament, but rather stays within the executive branch. Hence, it is only an upwards accountability or, an organizational panopticon. Therefore, the line of the efficiency construct must be drawn. Also, the emphasis put on the importance of the 'Values and Ethics Code for the Public Sector' and the inclusion of breaches of that code into the subject element, points at the rational loyalty construct. An explicit value statement is to be the object of organizational loyalty and any organizational practices that run counter that object must be disclosed.

So, three lines are to be marked – accountability, rational loyalty and efficiency. But since efficiency is not an explicit argument, but merely tapped into because of the internal recipient element, I have drawn it (see Figure 4.10) in between the accountability and the rational loyalty line.

The October Bill causes a minor change in legitimation lines. The two tiered approach, with mandatory internal procedures, is reconfirmed, as is the inclusion of breaches of the code of conduct into the subject element. The broadened recipient element poses a puzzle however. On the one hand, the bill does slightly improve the independence of the second tier recipient (President of the PSC) in the sense that he or she can now report to parliament at any moment. Also, the October Bill provides a possibility for external disclosures to be made to the public. The provisions do not specify that this external disclosure should be made to a person or body of which it is reasonable to assume that these are appropriate recipients. So it remains very wide there. On the other hand however, public disclosures are not a third tier recipient, because its subject element is very restricted – urgent and serious offences or urgent and imminent risks, but not the misuse of public funds, gross mismanagement, breaches of the code of conduct. The non-restrictedness of the public recipient points in the direction of the OSR-stakeholder construct. But the severe restriction of the subject element of public disclosures point towards the OSR-network construct – matters of a specific subject can be disclosed to a particular recipient. Which one should be marked is not clear. It is my expectation however, that in the second reading, the section on public disclosures will be amended or deleted. I have therefore not marked the OSR constructs in Figure 4.10, but have drawn them nearer.

Table 4.11 Whistleblowing policies proposed in Canada

Element	Internal Disclosure Policy 2001	Public Servants Disclosure Bill March 2004	Public Servants Disclosure Bill October 2004
Actor	Core public sector employees	All employees in federal public sector	All employees in federal public sector
Subject	Wrongdoing (not specified)	Violations of laws or regulations, breaches of ethics code, misuse of public funds or assets, gross mismanagement, danger to life, health and safety of Canadians, danger to environment	Violations of laws or regulations, breaches of ethics code, misuse of public funds or assets, gross mismanagement, danger to life, health and safety of persons, danger to environment
Recipient	Internal (appointed senior officer), Public Sector Integrity Officer	Internal channels Public Service Integrity Commissione	Internal channels President of the PSC Secretary of the Treasury Board (on matters concerning PSC) Public (urgent and serious offence or imminent risk)

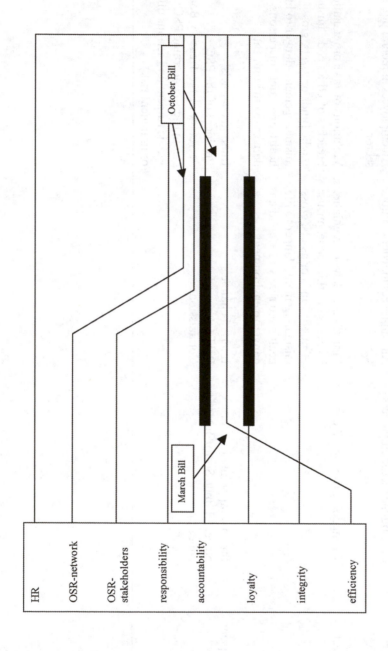

Figure 4.10 Evolution of legitimation lines (Canada)

India

In August 1999, the Chief Vigilance Commissioner of India, Mr Vittal, wrote a letter to the Law Commission, requesting it to draft a bill encouraging to disclose corrupt practices on the part of public functionaries and protecting honest persons from such disclosures. The Law Commission performed a study on the issue and produced a report in December 2001 (LC 2001) which includes a draft of a bill entitled 'The Public Interest Disclosure (Protection of Informers) Bill 2002'.

The report explicitly puts the Bill into an anti-corruption context. It is emphasized that Vittal's request made reference to a speech by the then Prime Minister of India, Mr Vajpayee, in which he condemned 'rampant corruption and highlighting the principle of "Zero tolerance"' (LC 2001, 2). Also, the introduction to the report cites Vittal's letter stressing:

> the need of a statute regarding whistle blowing (meaning thereby disclosure of a conduct averse to the public interest) that might go a long way in strengthening the fight against corruption in the country (LC 2001, 5).

The report opens with a chapter on the phenomenon of corruption, describing it as hindering development (LC 2001, 15), undermining the legitimacy of state institutions and governments (LC 2001, 17), a negative influence on the efforts to deal with the incidence of poverty (LC 2001, 17–18), and a serious threat to democratic institutions and the very existence of social order (LC 2001, 18).

Whistleblowers then, are perceived as playing 'a very important role in *providing information* about corruption and maladministration' (LC 2001, 31, emphasis added). Hence, the whistleblowing policy drafted in the bill here already promises to be driven by the efficiency legitimation construct:

> If adequate statutory protection is granted, there can be no doubt, that the government will be able to get more information regarding corruption and maladministration (LC 2001, 31).

However, three aspects of whistleblowing are considered. First, the 'rule of law' aspect pointing out that 'protection of whistleblowing vindicates important interests supporting the enforcement of criminal and civil laws' (LC 2001, 32). Secondly, the 'public interest' aspect, in which 'whistleblowing can be seen as supporting public interests by encouraging disclosure of certain types of information' (LC 2001, 32). And thirdly, an 'institutional' or 'democratic reform' aspect where whistleblowing 'enables and protects employee participation in the decision making process of public institutions' (LC 2001, 32). Thus, besides an efficiency driven legitimation of a whistleblowing policy, reference is made to the human rights rationale of protecting free speech to further democracy.

Further on in the report (LC 2001, 43–45), the human rights of freedom of speech and expression as well as the right to know are taken up again to come to the recognition that 'while a public servant may be subject to a duty of confidentiality, this duty does not extend to remaining silent regarding corruption of other public servants' (LC 2001, 44). Hence, as to the question of scope of 'free speech', the Law Commission takes the position that a whistleblowing statute should enable 'complaints to be made by public servants, or persons or NGOs against other public servants' (LC 2001, 45).

As far as the subject element goes, the bill defines as 'disclosable conduct' the conduct of a public servant amounting to 1) abuse or misuse of power, 2) an offence under the Prevention of Corruption Act 1988, the Indian Penal Code 1860 or any other law, and 3) maladministration. This latter is defined as: 1) unreasonable, unjust, oppressive or improperly discriminatory use of power; 2) negligence or undue delay; 3) reckless, excessive or unauthorized use of power; 4) breach of trust; 5) wastage of public funds or prejudicial to public interest in any manner; or 6) violations of systems or procedures (LC 2001, 90–92).

The recipient element is clear and restricted to any authority notified by the President in this behalf, or the Central Vigilance Commission, conceived in 1964 as free of control from any executive authority, but still operating under the Ministry of Personnel, Public Grievances and Pensions. There is no governance approach to be found here. The recipient element does not indicate any reference to the accountability or the responsibilization of government departments. Also, the categories of internal/external disclosure do not seem to apply to the Indian bill. There certainly is no possibility to disclose to a recipient external to the executive branch of government. On the other hand, a purely internal disclosure to the department head is not considered in the bill. The only point of the bill seems to be getting information about corrupt public servants to a body authorized by the President or to the Central Vigilance Commission.

Thus, the legitimation construct driving the proposed Indian whistleblowing policy is the efficiency construct. In a sense, the human rights construct is drawn nearer with the promise that fighting corruption is ensuring democracy, development and the reduction of poverty. Yet, if the proposal were also to be driven by the human rights rationale of democracy, it should at least include a recipient under Parliamentary control. Therefore, in Figure 4.11, I have drawn the human rights legitimation line nearing the efficiency line, but only marked the efficiency line.

Strangely enough, while the report of the Law Commission, including a draft bill, was published in 2001, when the Supreme Court asked government on 5 April 2004 to suggest measures to protect whistleblowers,[77] the reply was that this would take at least three weeks (Times of India, 6 April 2004, 5). Nevertheless, government issues an interim resolution (No. 371/12/2002-AVD-III), published

---

[77] The question was raised as a result of an advocate and a NGO (Parivartan) seeking the enactment of a whistleblower act, as well as an investigation into the murder of Satyendra Dubey, an engineer with the Golden Quadrilateral project who had, previous to his death on 27 November 2003, blown the whistle about corruption in the project (*Times of India*, 6 April 2004, 5).

in the official Gazette on 21 April 2004. In that resolution, the Central Vigilance Commission (CVC) is authorized as the sole recipient of written complaints or disclosures on allegations of corruption or misuse of office within the public sector. It is the CVC who will further investigate the issues raised and make recommendations as to initiation of criminal proceedings or corrective measures. The resolution will be in force until parliament passes a law on the subject.

On 17 May 2004, an office order (CVC No. 33/5/2004), a public notice and a press release (GOI 2004) were published further specifying the workings of the resolution. There, it is stipulated that the jurisdiction of the CVC is restricted to Central Government, implying that personnel employed by State Governments or activities of state governments and its corporations are not covered by the resolution.

It is also made clear that the CVC will not take up anonymous or pseudonymous complaints, that all complaints should be in a closed and secured envelope, addressed to the Secretary of the CVC and mention 'Complaint under The Public Interest Disclosure'. The CVC states that it can take 'action against complainants making motivated/vexatious complaints' (GOI 2004). And, the CVC advises whistleblowers not to make contact with CVC after they have sent in their complaint.

Even though the effectiveness of whistleblowing policies is not the topic of this research, I doubt very much whether the policy set by resolution 371/12/2002-AVD-III will create the necessary trustworthiness and guarantees for whistle-blowing to come forward. This is odd, given the legitimation driver, which is the efficiency construct. The whistleblowing scheme is still regarded as an information generating tool. However, the resolution came about as an interim measure following a demand from the Supreme Court which in turn was a response to the murder of a whistleblower. The resolution will remain operative until parliament passes whistleblowing legislation. In that sense, the resolution can be regarded as a 'foot in the door'.

Others

Here, I look at two other countries where discussions about whistleblowing policies are starting up: Germany and Switzerland.

Germany

In Germany, the discussion on whistleblowing is also very new. In September 2003, the INES (International Network of Engineers and Scientists) organized – under the header of '*Ethikschutz Initiative*'[78] – a conference on whistleblowing. The conference took place in Dortmund and was organized as a lobby conference. It

---

[78] http://www.ethikschutz.de/home.html (cited July 2004).

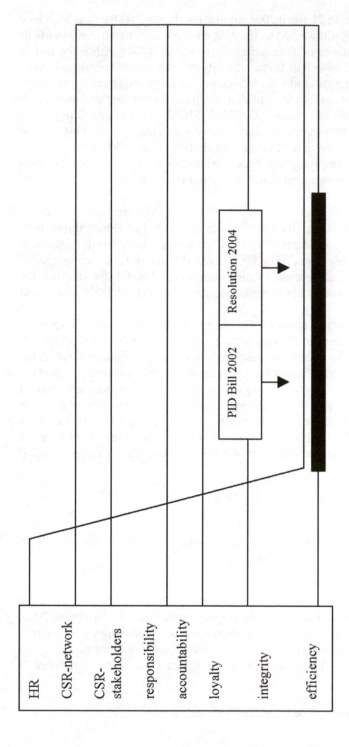

Figure 4.11 Evolution of legitimation lines (India)

Table 4.12 Whistleblowing policies proposed in India

Element	Public Interest Disclosure Bill 2002
Actor	Public servants NGOs
Subject	Abuse or misuse of power: Offences of Prevention of Corruption Act, Penal Code, or any other law Discrimination Negligence Unauthorised use of power Breach of trust Wastage of public funds Prejudicial to public interest in any matter Violations of systems or procedures
Recipient	An authority notified by the President Central Vigilance Commission

staged speakers from the GAP (Government Accountability Project) and PCAW (Public Concern at Work), and a number of testimonies from whistleblowers. The message was that there is a need to protect those who consciously express criticism and who protest against corruption. However, the text announcing the conference argues that flexibility and technological evolutions have made today's worker confront more ethical questions and that hence, it is necessary to create space inside organizations to raise and discuss those questions[79] – albeit an argumentation getting close to the integrity construct of the wholeness of discernment, action and discussing the discernment and the action with others inside the organization.

Leisinger (2003) published *Whistle Blowing und Corporate Reputation Management*, phrasing whistleblowing as a phenomenon of *Zivilcourage*. As far as legitimating constructs are concerned, Leisinger regards whistleblowers as 'internal stakeholders' who's criticism should be given space within the organization. A whistleblowing policy then, can function as a 'sensible internal early-warning-system' (Leisinger 2003, 249)[80] preventing damage to the corporate reputation. Giving employees space to utter criticism as a way to keep the organization 'on track' is an argumentation grasps the 'rational loyalty' construct. It is about keeping the organization focused on its purpose, mission and value statements.

---

[79] My translation of 'Betriekbsintern gehts es dabei im wesentlichen darum, durch Schaffung von Institutionen und Verfahren konkrete Spielräue für Kritik und 'Sinnfragen' in der Arbeit zu schaffen'.

[80] My translation of 'sensibles betriebsinternes Early-Warning-System'.

However, it is not about informing any stakeholder on goal displacement – this would make it more of an OSR-stakeholder type. Rather, it is constricted to the internal space of the organization.

Another construct Leisinger taps into is the responsibility construct, in which blowing the whistle is a means to create ethical distance to the organizational practice: 'Through their actions, whistleblowers want to avoid becoming complicit in illegitimate or illegal organizational practices' (Leisinger 2003, 29).[81]

In a newspaper article, Lübke (2003) also mentions avoiding corporate damage as a good reason for organizations to have whistleblowing policies. But these can also be useful for ethical investors. Lübke hereby points at an OSR-network type of argument: whistleblowing as a correction of informational asymmetry.

Also interesting is that Lübke translates whistleblowing in *den Chef verpfeifen* – to squeal on your boss. The website of the German chapter of Transparency International does not talk of 'verpfeifen' but regards the whistleblower as a loyal employee and translates whistleblower as *Hinweisgeber* – someone giving directions in a search, or someone pointing something out. The website makes reference to 'The Fairness Stiftung'[82] offering consultancy and training on mobbing, and to 'Business Keeper AG'[83] offering an anonymous channel to raise concern. Both talk about *fairness*; they are concerned with 'fair interactions' between organization members. But the Business Keeper website advocates its hotline with the slogan 'Save your company, Save yourself'. Hence, I suspect the Business Keeper hotline to be set up as a fraud detection mechanism, taking allegations from employees and passing them on to top management. It is this suspicion that made me draw the efficiency line.

There are no proposals for whistleblowing legislation yet. Hence, I was unable to draw up a table showing respective actor, subject and recipient elements. However, from the short discussion just presented, some tendencies towards legitimation lines can be seen (see Figure 4.12).

Switzerland

In 1998, Thomas Schwarb writes a discussion paper on whistleblowing (Schwarb 1998) in which he translates it as *verpfeifen*. Schwarb regards the phenomenon of whistleblowing as the expression of an ethical refusal inside business. However, at the time Schwarb wrote the article, whistleblowing was not an issue in German (spoken) Business Ethics – *Unternehmensethik*. Nevertheless, according to Schwarb, the issue of whistleblowing shows that ethical and business considerations have a lot in common. Whistleblowers see themselves as loyal employees and recognizing them as such can enable an organization to correct

---

[81]   My translation of 'Whistle Blower wollen mit ihrem Handeln vermeiden, dass Sie selbst zu Komplizen der illegitim oder illegal handelnden Institution werden'.
[82]   http://www.fairness-stiftung.de/ (cited July 2004).
[83]   http://www.business-keeper.com/bkweb/pages/ger/1 (cited July 2004).

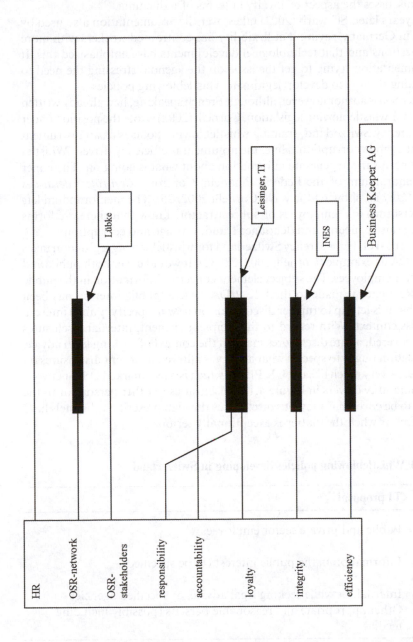

Figure 4.12 Evolution of legitimation lines (Germany)

itself. Hence, ethics and business are not antagonistic (Schwarb 1998, 8–10). This seems an argumentation in the vein of the rational loyalty construct, although Schwarb discusses the aspect of loyalty in terms of a dilemma.

A few years later, Schwarb (2003) takes over the argumentation also used by the INES in Germany, saying that flexibility has confronted workers with more ethical questions and that technological developments have emphasized this. It is an argumentation trying to get the issue on the agenda, stressing the need to start thinking of how to develop legitimate whistleblowing policies.

Another Swiss author however, although French speaking, had already written a proposal for whistleblowing legislation. Cornelli (2002) wrote the position paper of Transparency Switzerland, framing whistleblowing policies as an instrument in the fight against corruption. Here, the argument is efficiency driven. Whistle-blowing is necessary to generate information about what is going on. The paper cites a memorandum of the Federal Financial Control – *Contrôle fédéral des finances (CdF)* as 'showing the way' (Cornelli 2002, 25). The memorandum lets Federal personnel and employees of subcontractors know that there are forms available to raise concerns and denounce fraud, wastage and corruption.

The proposal of Transparency Switzerland for whistleblowing legislation takes the UK PIDA as example (Cornelli 2002, 28–32). It would cover both public and private sector employees. The subject element concerns 'information in the public interest'. Reference is made to the UK PIDA, where 'public interest' has been specified, but it is left up to further discussions on how to specify 'public interest' in the Swiss context. With regard to the recipient element, internal disclosures should be covered, as are disclosures made in the context of seeking legal advice. Also, legislation ought to specify what agency is allowed to accept disclosures on what matters – very much like the UK PIDA, which is why I marked OSR-network and accountability drivers in Figure 4.13. Disclosures to other persons or to the media are to be covered if previous disclosures through prescribed channels have had no effect or when the matter is exceptionally serious.

Table 4.13 Whistleblowing policies developing in Switzerland

Element	TI proposal
Actor	Public and private sector employees
Subject	Information in the public interest (to be specified)
Recipient	Internal, or while seeking legal advice, or specified agencies Other appropriate and reasonable persons (possibly including media)

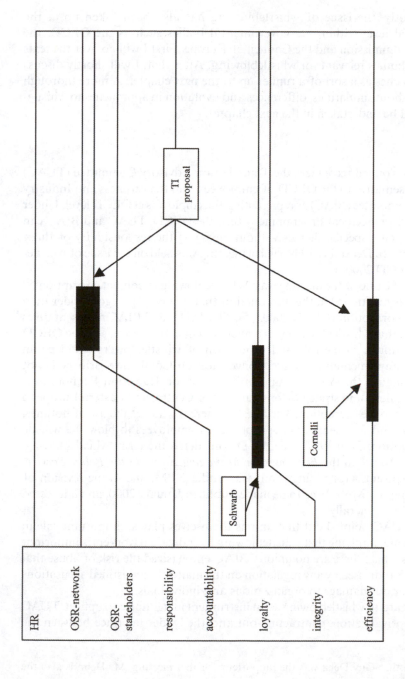

Figure 4.13 Evolution of legitimation lines (Switzerland)

The following labels appear in the figure:

HR

OSR-network

OSR-stakeholders

responsibility

accountability

loyalty

integrity

efficiency

TI proposal

Schwarb

Cornelli

Intergovernmental Bodies and Whistleblowing Policies

Quite recently, the issue of whistleblowing has also been taken up at the international level within intergovernmental bodies such as the OECD, the European Commission and the Council of Europe. First I will go over the texts from these bodies relevant for whistleblowing. After that, I will shortly discuss their approaches as a sort of a runner up to the next chapter. A more thorough discussion about similarities, differences and evolution in approaches to whistleblowing will be undertaken in the next chapter.

OECD

The OECD Council recognizes the Trade Union Advisory Committee (TUAC) as the representative to the OECD of employees, and the Business and Industry Advisory Committee (BIAC) as representing the employers at OECD level. Under the Labour/Management Programme within the OECD, TUAC and BIAC can meet and discuss specific themes without engaging the responsibility of those organizations. In December 1999, such a meeting was held on the issue of whistleblowing (OECD 2000a).

The specific title of the meeting was 'Whistleblowing to combat corruption',[84] although it is mentioned in the introduction that 'the issue [...] goes wider than bribery and corruption' (OECD 2000a, 5). The TUAC and BIAC representatives were briefed that whistleblowing was a relevant issue to four areas of the OECD work programme: 1) the role and protection of whistleblowers could be an area which implementation of the Convention on Combating Bribery is not yet addressing; 2) the Anti-Corruption Network for Transition Economies is looking at policies and strategies for countries of Central and Eastern Europe to address and reduce corruption. The question here is whether the use of hotlines, ombudsmen and the media are appropriate for employees to blow the whistle to on corruption; 3) in 1997, the OECD considered the term 'whistleblowing' too sensitive to use in the *Principles for Managing Ethics in the Public Service*, although exposing wrongdoing is an issue under NPM; and 4) the revision of the Guidelines on MNEs was to be made public in January 2000, and addressed whistleblowing generally.

While TUAC pointed out that unions themselves play an important role in whistleblowing, implying that whistleblowing by individual workers is important in countries where there are no unions, BIAC emphasized the risk of abuse that needed to be addressed by any regulation on the matter, as unjustified accusations can cause serious damage to organizations and individuals.

With regard to whistleblowing as an instrument in fighting corruption, TUAC pointed at privatization, contracting-out and the 'wider interface between the

---

[84] Note that Guy Dehn was the rapporteur for that meeting. Mr Dehn is also the director of Public Concern at Work.

public and private sectors' as the crux of bribery and corruption rather than cultural issues. Hence, the issue of blowing the whistle was a global one, not a national one (OECD 2000a, 7–8). BIAC representatives on their part, recognized the need for employers to create a culture where concerns can be raised internally. To do that, firms have to implement reporting lines as an alternative channel to the line management hierarchy. For BIAC, the principle had to be to protect the least damaging disclosure, and that only disclosures made in good faith ought to be protected (OECD 2000a, 9). TUAC however, stressed the need for an external disclosure option if employees are to have any confidence that their employer will deal with an internal disclosure properly. TUAC also questioned the relevance of taking the motive of the whistleblower into account when providing protection. The reasoning being that:

> as the purpose of a whistleblowing framework is to deter corruption rather than to encourage external disclosures, [labour representatives] were not persuaded that the motive or honesty of the whistleblower should be a critical factor in any new regime (OECD 2000a, 9).

The discussion at the meeting of December 1999 was not ground shaking. Nevertheless, since then, whistleblowing has been used in OECD statements and guidelines and the issue has gained support from both workers and employers representatives. The revised Guidelines for Multinational Enterprises (OECD 2000b) include a provision on whistleblowing policies:

> Refrain from discriminatory or disciplinary action against employees who make *bona fide* reports to management or, as appropriate, to the competent public authorities, on practices that contravene the law, the *Guidelines* or the enterprise's policies (General Policies, provision 9. OECD 2000b, 19, emphasis in original).

In 2003, at the OECD Roundtable on Corporate Responsibility, trade union representatives stressed the importance of protection of whistleblowers (OECD 2003a). The report of the roundtable was figured in the annual report on the Guidelines.

Also, the OECD has introduced the notion of whistleblowing policy in her recommendations to the public sector. In 1998, in its 'Principles for Managing Ethics in the Public Sector', the OECD recommended that 'transparency should be further enhanced by measures such as disclosure systems and recognition of the role of an active and independent media' (OECD 1998, 4). In 2000, in 'Building Public Trust', the OECD mentions a 'growing need to provide protection for whistleblowers in the public service[,] visible across OECD countries' (OECD 2000c, 4). This explicit reference to whistleblower protection is put into the context of legitimating the public sector. Whistleblowing procedures must assist the detection of individual cases of misconduct and to do so is necessary because 'citizens trust public institutions if they know that public offices are used for the public good' (OECD 2000c, 5). In 2003, the need to develop 'procedures for whistleblowing' are mentioned under the more technical header 'monitoring mechanisms' (OECD 2003b, 12).

Another OECD domain in which whistleblowing is mentioned today is the monitoring of the OECD Convention on Combating Bribery of Foreign Public Officials in International Business Transactions. The Convention was signed in 1997 and reached sufficient ratification to come into force by February 1999. Although the Convention itself does not contain any reference to whistleblowing, the monitoring questionnaire of phase 2 – scheduled from 2000 till 2007 – includes two items on whistleblowing. One on public sector measures and one concerning the private sector. Member countries have to report on the implementation of the Convention by responding to the questionnaire, as a sort of multilateral control and monitoring of the Convention.

Finally, also the 2004 revision of the *OECD Principles of Corporate Governance* includes an explicit recommendation for whistleblower protection under the section 'The Role of Stakeholders in Corporate Governance':

> Stakeholders, including individual employees and their representative bodies, should be able to freely communicate their concerns about illegal or unethical practices to the board and their rights should not be compromized for doing this (Principle IV.E, OECD 2004, 21).

In the annotation to the Principles, it is stated that:

> unethical and illegal practices by corporate officers may not only violate the rights of stakeholders but also be to the detriment of the company and its shareholders in terms of reputation effects and an increasing risk of future financial liabilities. It is therefore to the advantage of the company and its shareholders to establish procedures and safe-harbours for complaints by employees, either personally or through their representative bodies, and others outside the company, concerning illegal and unethical behaviour (OECD 200, 47).

The Open Compliance and Ethics Group, a coalition of business leaders, submitted comments to the draft proposal of the revised Corporate Governance Principles (OCEG 2004), in which it recognizes the whistleblowing provisions as necessities, but recommends including the requirement that stakeholders are 'enabled' to blow the whistle, meaning that they should receive training on the existence of whistleblowing procedures and be encouraged to use them when appropriate (OCEG 2004, 2).

European Commission

Whistleblowing became an issue for the European Commission in 1999. When Paul Van Buitenen – an official working in the administration of the European Commission – transferred his allegations and supporting documents about fraudulent practices in EU procurement to members of the European Parliament, some of the allegations became public through press conferences by those MPs.

Van Buitenen's point was that the European Commission was sabotaging its own internal control unit – UCLAF (*Unité pour la Coordination de Lutte Anti-Fraude*). Van Buitenen had tried to raise his concerns internally within the concerned DGs – Directorates General. After five years of such attempts, he took the matters to the European Parliament (Van Buitenen 1999). It was members of that European Parliament who made the allegations public, in an attempt to enforce their controlling power on the executive branch.

In a first instance, the public scandal focused on Edith Cresson and nepotism in contracting out. Later, a 'Committee of Wise Men' was formed to investigate into the failing mechanisms within the administration and make recommendations on reforms. Their work forced the whole Commission-Santer to resign.

The UCLAF was reformed into the OLAF (*Office de Lutte Anti-Fraude*) in April 1999. The OLAF has more investigating powers than the UCLAF had – it can copy documents and request information on personnel. But even though it is supposed to report to the European Parliament, the Council, the Commission and the European Court of Auditors on the findings of its investigations, and even though it has a specific duty to reply to parliamentary questions (Article 197 of the EC Treaty), OLAF is still an 'integral but independent' office of the Commission (Commission Decision L136, 31 May 1999). Hence its independence is still unclear and puzzling (EP 2002). Interesting is that officials have to inform *without delay* their Head of Department, the Director General or OLAF about facts suggesting illegal activity he or she becomes aware of while performing their duties (Regulations 1073/99 and 1074/99). Thus, there is a duty to report!

Recommendations were made concerning whistleblower protection. The white paper on reforms contains a section on 'rules on whistleblowing' (EC 2000, 47) under the chapter concerning Human Resources. It recommends that staff ought to be able to report outside their agency. The recommendation became an adopted Commission Decision on 4 April 2002 (C/2002/845). An official is now able to report concerns to the Presidents of the Commission, Council, Parliament, Court of Auditors or Ombudsman if OLAF and the Commission have had a reasonable time to make the necessary investigations and take appropriate actions with regard to the alleged malpractice.

Except for internal whistleblowing procedures, the European Commission has also issued a Communication in May 2003 on 'what needs to be improved to give fresh impetus to the fight against corruption' (EC 2003, 5). The paper argues that given the hidden nature of corruption and the lack of statistics and crime records on corruption cases:

> the only way to know more is to convince witnesses to report corruption cases. This can only be achieved by the effective protection of whistleblowers [...] Member States should [...] introduce common standards for [...] protection of whistleblowers (EC 2003, 12).

What's more, the paper urges the private sector to do the same with regard to breaking 'the pact of silence' with regard to bribery:

companies should therefore have clear rules on 'whistleblowing' (i.e. procedures to follow if an employee becomes aware of corrupt behaviour inside the company) (EC 2003, 18).

All the recommendations are summarized at the back of the paper, under the title 'Ten principles for improving the fight against corruption in acceding, candidate and other third countries', and principle 7 reads:

> Clear rules should be established in both the public and private sector on whistle blowing (given that corruption is an offence without direct victims who could witness and report it) and reporting (EC 2003, 25).

Council of Europe

Within the Council of Europe, two conventions are of importance: the Criminal Law Convention on Corruption (Treaty No. 173) and the Civil Law Convention on Corruption (Treaty No. 174).[85]

The Criminal Law Convention on Corruption is aimed at improving international cooperation in the fight against corruption and organized crime. It was signed in January 1999 and entered into force after 14 ratifications in July 2002.

The Convention contains under Article 22 provisions for the protection of 'those who report criminal offences or otherwise co-operate with the investigating or prosecuting authorities'. As the Convention is clearly situated in the context of anti-corruption, whistleblower protection might be argued under this article, provided that the subject element is focused on corruption and bribery.

More interesting is the Civil Law Convention on Corruption. This convention was signed in November 1999 and came into force after 14 ratifications in November 2003. Article 9 of the convention reads as follows:

> Each Party shall provide in its internal law for appropriate protection against any unjustified sanction for employees who have reasonable grounds to suspect corruption and who report in good faith their suspicion to responsible persons or authorities.

Whistleblowing legislation would fit perfectly under this article. Far better than under Article 22 of the Criminal Law Convention. However, the articles leave a huge interpretation space open for the ratifying countries. Indeed, the countries who have ratified the convention have no specific whistleblowing legislation.[86]

---

[85] Texts and signatures of both conventions can be found at http://conventions.coe.int.

[86] The countries who have ratified the Civil Law Convention on Corruption are: Albania, Azerbaijan, Bosnia and Herzegovina, Bulgaria, Croatia, Czech Republic, Estonia, Finland, Georgia, Greece, Hungary, Lithuania, Malta, Moldova, Poland, Romania, Slovakia, Slovenia, Sweden, FYROM, and Turkey.

Discussion

As a rule, international conventions, guidelines, or recommendations formulated at an international level leave a lot of room for interpretation. Nevertheless, there are some points to remark about the initiatives at OECD, EC and COE level.

The initiatives at OECD and EC level regard whistleblowing as an issue relevant for both the private and the public sector. The conventions from the Council of Europe are not so clear. There is no explicit distinction made in the respective provisions as is the case in the OECD's Guidelines for MNEs, Principles for Corporate Governance, PUMA policies (regarding the public sector) and the Monitoring of the Convention on Combating Bribery, or as in the EC's 10 Principles to Combat Corruption.

The whistleblowing provision in the OECD Guidelines for MNEs has a subject element including 'the enterprise's policies'. This implies that a 'rational loyalty' driven legitimation would fit under that provision. Provision 9 of the General Policies regard 'competent public authorities' to be the appropriate recipients of external disclosures. This points at an OSR-network driver, because of the limitedness and special positional requirements of the recipients prescribed by the policy.

The OECD Principles of Corporate Governance put the issue of whistle-blowing under the header of the 'role of stakeholders'. There, the role of stakeholders is perceived as informing the board about organizational practices. Indeed, that is precisely the issue of corporate governance: how to make sure owners, board and management are 'in tune'. Or, whistleblowing is a means of correcting an information asymmetry between board and work floor. As such, this hints at the OSR-network construct. But, as the information goes from the work floor to the board – or, as the annotations point out, to shareholders – it is also a way to ensure management's accountability to the board and the board's accountability to the shareholders. Hence, the OECD Principles on Corporate Governance also drive the accountability line.

Although the OECD mentions the role of an active and independent media in disclosure systems (OECD 1998), it remains silent here once the terms 'whistle-blowing' and 'whistleblower' are used. The OECD PUMA policy briefs of 2000 and 2003 express an efficiency drive: detecting individual cases of wrongdoing within the public sector (OECD 2000c; 2003b). Therefore, only the efficiency line will be marked.

The EC call to develop whistleblowing policies in the context of the fight against corruption explicitly legitimates whistleblowing as a way to generate information about otherwise uncontrollable practices such as corruption and bribery. Hence, the legitimation here is clearly driven by the efficiency construct.

The provisions in the COE conventions are extremely broad and vague. The only remark to be made about them is that they are provisions in conventions on fighting corruption, and that hence these provisions are best seen as hinting at ways to generate information and strengthening control.

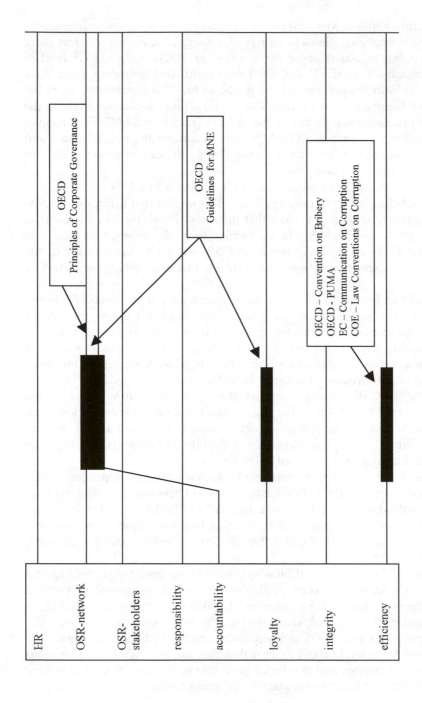

Figure 4.14 Evolution of legitimation lines (intergovernmental bodies)

Even though all of the above provisions leave substantial space for interpretation with regard to specifying whistleblowing elements so that any kind of whistleblowing policy would fit under these provisions, it must be noted that *none* of the discussions at national level mentioned or used the OECD Guidelines, Principles, Convention, the EC Communication or the COE Conventions as an argument.

A possible explanation is that arguing to introduce particular legislation because this has been called for at an intergovernmental level is not a normative legitimation. It is not a 'good reason' but rather 'we have no choice but to do this'. Perhaps politicians proposing the legislation want to position themselves as moral persons arguing for the right things with 'good reasons' rather than technicians legislating directives from an international level. This question lies outside the scope of the research undertaken here.

The EC's Communication, calling on Member States to introduce common standards for the protection of whistleblowers, is peculiar. If there are to be common standards, it is up to the European Institutions to set a limiting framework within which Member States develop their own whistleblowing legislation. The EC Communication does not do that. Perhaps there will be follow-up initiatives taken at that level. Nevertheless, it has to be noted that reference has *not* been made to this call upon Member States by the Netherlands, Belgium or Germany as an extra argument to pass legislation. Given the European Commission's track history on dealing with whistleblowers, to do so would actually weaken one's argumentation rather than make it stronger.

Also to be noted is that none of the countries where the discussion on the whistleblowing issue has started or has already been taken to parliament has ratified the COE Civil Law Convention. The OECD Guidelines apply to the private sector, as do the Principles on Corporate Governance. Most discussions on whistleblowing policies still restrict the issue to the public sector.

Chapter 5

Towards what Legitimation
of Whistleblowing?

In this chapter I evaluate the screening undertaken in the previous chapter. I make an evaluation in two senses of the word. First, I point out what tendencies can be seen in the evolution of legitimation lines. To do that, I concentrate on Figures 4.1 to 4.14 with additional material taken from the screenings summarized in Tables 4.1 to 4.13. I try to look for common and unusual coalitions of argumentation lines, for apparently viable and unfruitful argumentation lines. Or, in other – Luhmann's – terms, which semantic variations are able to stabilize the globalization semantic, and which variations are not.

Secondly, I make an ethical judgement about these tendencies. To do that, I use the diagram developed in Chapter 2. Are the current whistleblowing policies emphasizing the dissociation between individual and organization, or are they enclosing the individual within the organization? It is there that I formulate an answer to the original question my short study of academic literature on whistleblowing (see Chapter 2) had led me to, namely whether the activist whistleblowing concept has survived or whether it has backlashed. In other words, has the 1970s politico-ethical whistleblowing concept solved the conflict between society and organization and how? What are whistleblowing policies doing in terms of the relation between the three categories relevant to whistleblowing, more precisely people blowing the whistle (individual) on organizations operating within (organization) the context of globalization of private capital oriented economy (society)?

In the third section of this chapter, I make some proposals on how whistleblowing policies could be lobbied for. I also formulate recommendations on how to turn the tendencies in the direction of more ethical whistleblowing policies.

Finally, I point at some limitations of this research and raise some future research possibilities with regard to the ethics of whistleblowing policies.

Tendencies in the Legitimation of Whistleblowing Policies

A first observable tendency is that three legitimation constructs seem to be very present today: the efficiency, the accountability and the OSR-network constructs. All countries use at least one of those constructs. I will start the discussion on tendencies in the legitimation of whistleblowing policies with each of these three constructs separately. Then I will look in the second subsection at some combinations of these and other legitimation constructs. Also, legitimation constructs hardly used, or not kept up will be discussed. In a third subsection, the pattern of evolution will be commented on.

Efficiency, Accountability and OSR-Network

Except for countries where the discussion only started at the end of the 1990s, the *efficiency* construct always comes in at a later point, when other argumentation lines are already in use or have already been tried. Striking is however, that when the efficiency line gets tapped into, it stays in use.

The first efficiency marked whistleblowing policy is the 1986 False Claims Act (FCA) in the US (see Figure 4.1). An earlier US federal whistleblower protection, the 1978 Civil Service Reform Act, was amended in 1989 into the Whistleblower Protection Act, thereby changing its legitimation line towards the efficiency construct.

The FCA clearly emphasizes the usefulness of the information over motive, position or function of the whistleblower. The subject element is restricted to financial government fraud.[1] Other efficiency driven policies have also been formulated in a context of combating fraud or fighting corruption: the UK PIDA and the proposal in Ireland, the South-African PDA, the proposal and resolution in India, the Swiss TI proposal, the OECD Convention on Bribery, the OECD PUMA and the COE Conventions on Corruption. In Australia, the discussion on the federal level has focussed on the efficiency argument. Moreover, in a number of countries, accountancy and consultancy firms have started up whistleblowing services aimed at private companies, under the flag of detecting internal fraud.

Formulated within the theoretical framework I developed in Chapter 2, the efficiency construct is one of the possible semantic variations for legitimating whistleblowing policies. Apparently, it is a selectable variation, meaning that the argumentation of whistleblowing policy in terms of efficiency is able to stabilize the globalization semantic. This should not come as a surprise. If we take a look at Figure 3.12, which is a visualization of how the efficiency construct is constituted within the globalization semantic, we see that the semantic density of the efficiency construct is the highest of all constructs. Here, semantic density denotes the extent to which a concept establishes an interconnectedness of the different terms of the globalization semantic – flexibility, governance, decentralization, network, stakeholder. It is a measurement of the relative ties between those terms that render a particular legitimation concept its meaning – the ratio of the number

---

[1]   *Qui tam* procedures, filing suits under the False Claims Act, are still very much used. In May 2004, a whistleblower who had initiated a *qui tam* law suit got a share of $27 million out of the $ 430 million US government recovered from Pfizer, a pharmaceutical giant. Another company in the same sector, GlaxoSmithKline, admitted in February 2004 that investigations had been started up into its operations after allegations had been made by a whistleblower under the False Claims Act (Foley 2004, 9).

of links rendering meaning compared with the total number of possible ties. The higher the density of a semantic construct, the more the construct appears as necessary, as unavoidable.

But exactly how does a whistleblowing policy legitimated through an efficiency argument stabilize the globalization semantic? What is necessary about it? In Chapter 3, I argued with William Greider that efficiency is a capitalistic virtue; it is the ability to yield more from less. Globalization changed the conditions for efficiency. Central planning was replaced by decentralization under the pressure of flexibility – the ability to change and adapt. This shift increased the importance of the human factor in organizational inefficiency. Organizational processes can be designed as very efficient, but if they are not carried out the way they were planned or intended, this causes inefficiency – fraud and corruption. Given that decentralization entails more discretionary power to be dispersed over the organization, there is a bigger risk of processes getting thwarted. At the same time, it becomes more difficult to detect where processes have gone wrong. Hence, governance mechanisms need to be developed leaving enough flexibility whilst at the same time ensure detectability – or in a more euphemistic term, transparency. Efficiency driven whistleblowing policies aim precisely at this and they appear as necessary because it is a way to control – or to govern – the human factor.

Hence, it is whistleblowing policies of which the legitimation does not seem to be driven by the efficiency construct, that require some further attention here. There is one whistleblowing policy I discussed which has fraud as a subject element, yet its argumentation line was not marked as efficiency driven: the US 2002 Sarbanes-Oxley Act (SOX). The reason why I considered SOX as driven by the OSR-network and the accountability constructs is because of the personal liability of top executive officers of publicly traded companies. SOX is all about corporate governance of publicly traded companies. Sure, SOX was an answer to fraud scandals, but the fraud was analysed as a power imbalance within the corporate network: executives misleading investors. A top executive officer who is unable to set up an effective whistleblowing policy – where people trust that the recipient will take concerns seriously – is held accountable through his personal liability should any fraudulent information go out to shareholders. Thus, SOX puts quite some pressure on CEOs and CFOs to make sure their internal control procedures are effective. An effect of this pressure might very well be that the internal whistleblowing procedures developed under SOX pressure are efficiency driven, but we do not know that, and, what is more, these internal procedures would not be part of SOX. So that is why SOX was not marked as efficiency driven; it does not exclude efficiency driven internal policies, but those policies are not part of SOX.

Further, only three countries do *not* have the efficiency line marked: New Zealand, Belgium and Japan. With regard to Japan, the cases instigating the momentum for whistleblowing policies in Japan come from various economic sectors (Morioka 2004) and point at consumer interests in whistleblowing. In

Japan, it seems financial fraud or corruption are not the main preoccupations of those lobbying for whistleblowing legislation.

For Belgium, where the Flemisch Community has passed whistleblowing legislation very recently, I marked the accountability line as driving the legitimation of the whistleblowing policy. The three tiered approach is making heads of department accountable for not taking concerns of their employees seriously or retaliating against them. Furthermore, there is no reference made to fraud detection or fighting corruption. Rather, the argument for the specific provisions are that 'it is nothing new' but merely providing employees with channels already available to citizens. Nevertheless, the proposal was explicitly embedded in a context of institutional reforms – BBB or the Flemish version of New Public Management. Hence, indirectly it must lead to a more efficient government.

For New Zealand too, the tiered model of the Ombudsperson holding heads of department and managers of organizations accountable seems the strongest aspect of the whistleblowing policy. Moreover, the argument made by the Privacy Commissioner in 1997, that the bill then under consideration was too broad to be effective, was an efficiency driven argument to reduce the scope of the proposal to the public sector only. However, the fact that this argument was not taken over – the 2000 Public Disclosure Act still covers private and public sector – indicates that the efficiency of the whistleblowing provisions certainly was not an explicit aim.

Both Belgium and New Zealand are *accountability* driven. So is the US SOX. Others are the UK PIDA, The South-African PDA, legislation in some Australian states and the comments on the Australian CLERP Act, proposals in Ireland, the Netherlands, Switzerland, Canada, and the OECD Principles of Corporate Governance. Why is the accountability construct so much used?

The semantic density of the accountability construct is not that high. Accountability is the governance of decentralized decision-making by autonomous individuals. Whistleblowing policy as an accountability mechanism is assigning a position to particular agents in a chain of accountability. Hence, what made me mark the accountability line in so many cases is this governance approach, this specification of a how stakeholders relate into a network. It is a combination of legitimating the whistleblowing policy by placing it into a context of decentralizing reforms – NPM for the public sector, corporate governance for the private sector – and taking a tiered approach in the provisions of the recipient element – governance by specifying the chain of accountability.

In the US, a first hinge at an accountability driven legitimation was formulated in 1978 with the Civil Service Reform Act, describing whistleblowing as a means of holding the Executive to account. However, this legitimation construct was not fully embraced – hence the line was only 'drawn nearer' – because the recipient element did not mirror a governance approach. It was a special set of agencies that could receive, investigate and protect, not a tiered approach. The accountability line was further emphasized only in 2002 with the enactment of SOX. There again, the recipient element does not really take a tiered approach, but it nevertheless constitutes a governance approach in the sense that top executives are personally liable if they fail to set up adequate internal control mechanisms, including whistleblowing procedures. Hence, the SOX will result in two tiered whistleblowing policies.

In the UK, PCAW shows to be accountability driven from its creation in 1993. Around the same time (1994), the whistleblowing policies of Queensland and New South Wales in Australia also show an accountability driven legitimation. At the end of the 1990s, the South African and the New Zealand whistleblowing legislation drafts use the accountability construct. The legislations passed in Australian states in 2001 (Victoria), 2002 (Tasmania), 2003 (Western Australia) and the one under proposal in Tasmania, are all accountability driven, as is the Belgian legislation, and the Irish and the Canadian proposal. The reason why the accountability line was marked in all those cases is because of the tiered approach in the recipient element, starting of with internal disclosures, and ending with an external recipient – either the media or an agency under parliamentary control. In fact, the only countries still developing discussions about whistleblowing policies that do not use the accountability construct are India and Germany. In the case of India, the whistleblowing provisions in the law proposal, the accompanying report and the resolution from 2004 are clearly anti-corruption focused. Moreover, the recipient element is not tiered at all: one either discloses to the President or to the Central Vigilance Commission. Besides, the aim is more towards investigation than towards accountability. The German discussion is, frankly said, too dispersed yet to have a clear look as to where future legislation might end up, but what we do see is that in the German discussion, just as in the Netherlands, the responsibility construct is tapped into. This indicates an opening for or – as in the Netherlands – an explicit reference to whistleblowing as a duty. I will come back to that in the next subsection and in the ethical evaluation later in this chapter.

Lets get back to my question why the accountability construct is used that much. The overall tendency appearing from Figures 4.1 to 4.14 is that an accountability driven legitimation of whistleblowing policies has become standard since the end of the 1990s. I have just explained that to a large extent, this is because of a tiered recipient element. Therefore, the answer to why the accountability construct is used that much, has to do with the attractiveness of a tiered recipient element. What constitutes this attractiveness? Two answers can be given here. First, a tiered approach serves as a filtering mechanism for the disclosure of organizational wrongdoing. Given that the concept of whistle-blowing was advocated in the early 1970s as a politico-ethical activism opposing organization to society, stating whistleblowing as a dilemma of organization versus public interest, a tiered approach to the recipient element appears as a solution to that dilemma. How? The public interest is specified in the subject element. The tiered recipient element then, allows an organization to bring or keep its organizational practices in line with the public interest as specified in the subject element. Hence, it is not society who takes control over organizational practices. It is only when organizations refuse or are unable to solve problems regarding their own practices, that disclosure can be made to a next-level recipient. At this second level, it is a proxy of society – a governmental control-agency such as law enforcement agency, a specially designed investigation agency, or an agency under parliamentary control such as an ombudsperson – who judges the alleged organizational malpractice – again, relative to the public interest as specified in the subject element. Only in a few cases there is a third level, where society can judge the organizational practice in question when a disclosure is made to the media – the UK, two Australian states (New South Wales and South Australia), South Africa, and the proposals in Ireland, the Netherlands and Switzerland. Hence, the tiered approach allows disclosures in the public interest to be made, but not or only indirectly *to* the public.

Second, the scientific research of the 1980s and 1990s has rendered the tiered approach more than just an option. Through research, it was argued that the perceived seriousness of the malpractice is an important factor on whether or not a person will blow the whistle – the more a practice is perceived as a serious malpractice, the more whistleblowing is likely to occur (Miceli and Near 1985; Near and Micelli 1987, 1995; Near et al. 1993; Callahan and Dworkin 1994). However, Miceli and Near (1992) have shown that even for whistleblowers who disclose outside of the organization, it is very common to have tried internal channels prior to external whistleblowing. Also, the research by Miceli and Near (1992) argued that organizational retaliation against whistleblowers encourages further whistleblowing. Other research argued that having internal whistleblowing procedures encourages internal disclosures but not external whistleblowing (Mathews 1987; Keenan 1990; Barnett et al. 1990). Further, the research by Sims and Keenan (1998) shows that formal policies which support external whistle-blowing are not a significant predictor of external whistleblowing. Informal policies – supervisory support – to do so, however, are!

In short, the accountability construct stabilizes the globalization semantic by conceptualizing whistleblowing in a way that reduces the risk of organizational practices to come under judgement or direct control of society.

The *OSR-network* construct drives the legitimation of whistleblowing policies in the US (SOX), Australian Capital Territory, Australian CLERP Act, the UK, the OECD Principles of Corporate Governance, the OECD Guidelines for MNEs, the proposals in Ireland, Switzerland and Japan, and the discussion in Germany and South Africa. Legitimating whistleblowing policies through the OSR-network construct means that whistleblowing policies are regarded as correcting an information asymmetry between various actors, thereby ensuring a power balance between those actors. What is more, whistleblowing policies driven by the OSR-network construct will specify and delineate who the relevant actors are and position them within a network. Hence, these policies will provide a detailed recipient element in terms of who to disclose to under what circumstances.

The reason why this construct appears to be used so often is similar to the explanation I gave with regard to the accountability construct. It puts restraints on acts of whistleblowing. It constitutes a way out of the initial whistleblowing conflict, that of society versus organization, by containing the conflict in two possible ways. Either by specifying the set of actors: society controls the organization through its proxies – special whistleblowing agencies, law enforcement agencies, regulators, Ombudspersons, and so on – or, by specifying the conditions under which what actor is a valid recipient – a tiered approach. Some whistleblowing policies screened in the previous chapter, use both ways to contain this conflict: the UK PIDA by prescribing in detail who the recipient is for what kind of disclosure and by setting extra criteria for disclosures to other recipients, the Irish proposal because it does exactly the same, the proposals to amend the South African PDA because it lists agencies as prescribed recipients. The Swiss proposal is still too vague to argue the same, however, it is open to the OSR-network construct as it is clearly inspired by the UK PIDA in all its elements.

Moreover, any whistleblowing policy imbedded in corporate governance measures – the US SOX, the Australian CLERP Act and the OECD Principles of Corporate Governance – uses an OSR-network legitimation, because corporate governance is precisely about reducing information asymmetries between certain actors in a corporate network.

Exactly here lies the distinction between the OSR-network construct and the OSR-stakeholder construct. The latter entails no restrictions of whistleblowing recipients. It does not prescribe proxies for society and it does not privilege certain stakeholders over others. In terms of whistleblowing as a dilemma between society and organization, whistleblowing policies legitimated through the OSR-stakeholder construct take more the side of direct societal control over organizational practices. Thus, the tendency of OSR-stakeholder driven whistle-blowing policies evolving into OSR-network legitimated whistleblowing policies – UK PIDA, South Africa and the Japanese discussion – points at a containment also noted with regard to the accountability construct, namely that the OSR-network construct stabilizes the globalization semantic by conceptualizing whistle-blowing in a way that contains the conflict between society and organization by reducing the judgement or direct control of society over organizational practices.

Combinations of Legitimation Lines

Some combinations of argumentation lines appearing in the Figures 4.1 to 4.14 call for comment, as do the breaking off and the absence of certain legitimation constructs as drivers of whistleblowing policies.

From my comments on the stabilizing potential of the most used legitimation constructs, it is no surprise that the *accountability construct and the OSR-network construct* fit well together in the sense that they mutually strengthen one another. The US SOX and the OECD Principles of Corporate Governance actually use that combination. Both calls for whistleblowing policies aim at the private sector. These policies are legitimated as to contain the conflict between society and business by reducing the risk of society taking direct control or making direct judgement over organizational practices.

Some whistleblowing policies add another driver to their legitimation. The UK PIDA, the South African proposals to amend the PDA, the Canadian October Bill, the Irish proposal, and the Swiss proposal are driven by a combination of the *accountability, the OSR-network and the efficiency constructs*. All these whistleblowing policies cover at least the public sector, and most cover both public and private sector organizations. There are efficiency driven whistleblowing policies aiming at the private sector, but these are consultancy firms offering a whistleblowing hotline service to corporations, not legislative initiatives. The Australian CLERP Act is an exception. It is efficiency and OSR-network driven but covers only the private sector. I marked the Act this way because it does not use the accountability driver. That was different with the US SOX, of which I noted earlier on that an effect of the SOX might be efficiency driven internal whistleblowing policies, but since the SOX was clearly accountability driven, the SOX itself did not qualify for the efficiency construct.

Now, why is it that whistleblowing legislation driven by efficiency generally covers at least the public sector, and never only the private sector? I see two reasons. One, it is not government who demands private sector corporations to be efficient, it is 'the market' who does so. Hence, whistleblowing legislation covering only the private sector might lead to corporations developing internal whistleblowing procedures driven by the efficiency construct, but the legislation itself will not be legitimated like that (US SOX). In the case of the Australian CLERP Act it, strangely enough, is a governmental agency (ASIC) that solicits information.

Second, the big legitimator of privatization is the claim that government is inefficient while the market is efficient. Hence, the most legitimate government reforms are those who's argumentation is efficiency driven – see New Public Management discourse. It gives in to the privatization discourse in the sense that it regards government to be only legitimate to the extent that it achieves more efficiency.

The efficiency construct fits very well with the mutually strengthening concepts of accountability and OSR-network. An efficiency driven legitimation makes whistleblowing policies appear as a necessity to ensure detectability of human factor inefficiency – organizational processes are not carried out the way they were intended or designed. Once detected, the human factor can be held accountable. To whom? A proxy of society, or, specified actors in the organizational network.

Four discussions had at one point or another, an argumentation partly driven by the *human rights construct*: US, South Africa, India and the Netherlands. In the US, human rights argumentation – basically in the form of First Amendment referrals – dominates the pre-legislative period (1970–1978). The expectations towards whistleblowing legislation developing as First Amendment driven in legitimation and provisions were not realized, although it is still present in the GAP (Government Accountability Project) discourse. The first enactments of whistleblowing legislation at state level show to be accountability and responsibility driven attempts, with the exception of the 1983 Connecticut legislation which does take a First Amendment approach. This confirms the analysis I made earlier on regarding the stabilizing potential of the accountability construct as reducing risks of direct societal control over organizational practices. Human rights driven argumentation does not have that stabilizing potential. Rather, it points at a power imbalance between society and organization in favour of the latter. A possible explanation of why in the US the human rights line was immediately broken off, is that while both the First Amendment and the employment-at-will doctrine are central to US history, in the context of whistleblowing they contradict each other. To argue for whistleblowing policies through the human rights construct implies rendering employment-at-will totally illegitimate. Hence, the construct is not selectable because it is not stabilizing – the concept of human rights can not be generalized to cover free speech in the workplace. Therefore, whistleblowing policies can only achieve exceptions to the employment-at-will doctrine. Moreover, they can only do so if they are legitimated through constructs that only indirectly allow external control.

In South Africa, the human rights driver enters the discussion in a totally different way. There, whistleblowing legislation was promoted and enacted as part of a democratization process. Initially, the whistleblowing provisions were part of the Open Democracy Bill, which was later split into the Access to Information Bill and the Protected Disclosure Bill. The preamble of the Protected Disclosure Act (PDA) explicitly places the provisions in a context of democratization, referring to human rights values of human dignity, equality and freedom. Moreover, the subject element of the act includes 'unfair discrimination'. Hence, the historical situation of South Africa – dealing with its just ended Apartheid regime – makes the human rights construct a necessity for any legitimation of new government legislation and policy. Here, the human rights construct is selectable because it is able to stabilize the globalization semantic in this particular historical setting. Yet, it is not the only legitimation construct used. I have also marked the PDA as driven by the accountability – the recipient element is tiered – and the efficiency construct – the PDA is quite explicitly aimed at fighting corruption and the King Committee on Corporate Governance advises it to tackle 'fraud and other risks'. Note that I have drawn the human rights line in between the accountability and the efficiency line. The reason for that lies in splitting the Open Democracy Bill into two separate bills. Both bills were enacted in 2000, and both base their legitimation in furthering democracy through human rights, accountability and fighting corruption. However, of the two acts, it is the Access to Information Act which mainly represents the human rights focus – access to information is a human right and it will allow people to exercise their human rights. The Protected Disclosure Act then, emphasizes more the accountability and efficiency lines – organizational practices hindering democracy must be accounted for and corrected.

This is again different for the rationale of the proposal in India. Here, the human rights line is not marked, but only drawn very near the efficiency line. The reason is that the Public Interest Disclosure (PID) Bill is a designed and presented as a tool in the government's fight against corruption. This fight then, is legitimated by describing corruption as blocking the furthering of human rights in terms of democracy, development, and eradication of poverty. Hence, the efficiency construct is not able to stabilize the globalization semantic by itself, but needs the human rights line as a support.

Finally, also the evolution of the whistleblowing discussion in the Netherlands (Figure 5.7) shows two human rights driven legitimation attempts. Both are to be considered one and the same, since the FNV proposal from 1999 was taken over by GroenLinks in 2003. The demarche by the FNV – a federation of labour unions – is quite interesting. It has to be viewed against the developments at government level, and especially the whistleblowing policy installed at city level in Amsterdam. This latter is driven by the efficiency and the responsibility constructs, stipulating a duty to blow the whistle. Therefore, the demarche by the FNV with a human rights driven legitimation of whistleblowing policies, explicitly presenting whistle-blowing as free speech and emphasizing freedom of expression as an intrinsic right, is to be regarded as oppositional to 'the duty of whistleblowing to further efficiency' developments in Amsterdam. The FNV proposal also broadens the actor element to cover both public and private sector.

When in the Netherlands the question of legislating whistleblowing is tilted to the national level, Groenlinks takes over the FNV argumentation. At that time, a detailed proposal is drawn up, broadening the basis of its argumentation by referral to the SVA report offering guidelines for whistleblowing policies. The Amsterdam regulation takes over the UK PIDA subject element, but not the recipient element. The SVA recommendations do not specify the subject element but take over the UK PIDA recipient element. The GroenLinks proposal takes both subject element (and adds some items) and the recipient element from the UK PIDA. Hence, the FNV human rights driven proposal is taken over by GroenLinks in the national parliament, but its gets combined with an accountability drive. Here is a first sign that in the Dutch context, the human rights construct is not a selectable variation by itself. GroenLinks has coupled it with the accountability construct in its proposal. However, the fact that the same GroenLinks has used the term *'klokkenluiden'* in the context of a duty to report, indicates an opening in the direction of the responsibility construct. Such a future development would bring the GroenLinks proposal closer to the second proposal at national level, which is a copy of the Amsterdam regulation. This inclination confirms that the human rights construct is not a selectable variation by itself. What is more, this particular evolution has left the Dutch discussion in an awkward situation. One proposal regards whistleblowing as a duty of government officials with governmental agencies as recipient. The other proposal inclines towards whistleblowing as a 'citizen's duty' to a tiered recipient element, argued as a human right. It is quite logical to combine rights with duties, but not to locate both in the same actor. Hence, it is very unlikely that a 'duty of X to blow the whistle argued as a human right of X', will be regarded as legitimate. Thus, the GroenLinks' legitimation attempt will probably fail if it is maintained.

Looking at Figures 4.1 (US), 4.2 (Australia), 4.3 (New Zealand), 4.4 (UK) and 4.5 (South Africa), it is striking that the *OSR-stakeholder construct* is used at one point in the discussion, but never maintained. Figures 4.6 (Japan) and 4.10 (Canada) show an ongoing discussion about whether whistleblowing policies ought to be OSR-stakeholder driven rather than OSR-network, but in Japan, the proposal laid down in Parliament is OSR-network driven.

This raises the question as to why the OSR-stakeholder line is broken off as a legitimation driver for whistleblowing policies. The distinction I pointed out earlier between the OSR-stakeholder and OSR-network constructs offers an answer to that question. I wrote that while the OSR-network construct contains the conflict between society and organization by specifying relevant actors within the organizational network and by stipulating the conditions under which someone can disclose to a particular actor in that network, the OSR-stakeholder construct entails no such restrictions. Rather, the OSR-stakeholder construct emphasizes the importance of warning stakeholders about possible harms to society. Hence, if the OSR-network driver is being maintained to legitimate whistleblowing policies because it contains the conflict between society and organization – as I argued – then the OSR-stakeholder driver has run into a dead end because it does not contain that conflict. Or, in other words, the OSR-stakeholder construct is a possible but not a selectable or stabilizing variation of the globalization semantic. In New Zealand, the discussion starts with an OSR-stakeholder driven advocacy of whistleblowing policies but gets enacted when the main construct driving the legitimation is shifted toward the accountability construct. In the UK, whistleblowing policy does not get enacted until the OSR-stakeholder line is left. In South Africa, calls are out to further amend the existing whistleblowing legislation away from OSR-stakeholder towards OSR-network, in an attempt to give the PDA more credibility and acceptance. The Irish proposal is a copy of the UK PIDA, but the fact that it is the OSR-network driven UK PIDA which is copied, confirms the selectability of the OSR-network construct, and not of the OSR-stakeholder construct.

Another line that is tapped into, but not sustained, is the line of the *rational loyalty construct*. This construct regards the explicit value and mission statements of an organization as the appropriate object of organizational loyalty, which at the same time constitutes a loyalty to society, because the organizational value and mission statement is a public statement and seeks approval from society for its content. Hence, the subject element of a whistleblowing policy legitimated through the rational loyalty construct includes a reference to organizational policies, values or mission statements.

In the UK, Public Concern at Work maintained the rational loyalty line up till 1996, arguing that the subject element of whistleblowing policies should go beyond compliance to the law. The organization's then Chairman of the Trustees – Lord Borrie – explicitly states that it is the watchdog whistleblower that has to be protected, who discloses information showing an organization is 'saying one thing but doing something different'. And while the 1995 Bill and the 1996

Bill leave room for such interpretation, the Bill that made it to the 1998 PIDA does not.

In Australia, as Table 4.2 shows, the rational loyalty construct was only tapped into by Paul Finn in an academic report from 1991. However, the report and hence its stipulation of a subject element is mentioned in a report from the Senate Select Committee on Public Interest Whistleblowing, in 1994. The report was to initiate a discussion about whistleblowing legislation at the federal level, but had no results. By the time the discussion at federal level is taken up again, the tone has shifted towards an efficiency driven legitimation. Neither of the state legislations had picked up the rational loyalty argumentation.

Others who have taken up the rational loyalty line and have not dropped it yet are countries where the discussion on whistleblowing legislation is still going on. The Netherlands has seen quite some legitimating attempts towards whistleblowing lately – the position of the 'Stichting van de arbeid' (the Labour Foundation) leaves an opening for a rational loyalty driven subject element. The Canadian March and October 2004 bills, explicitly mention 'serious breaches of the Value and Ethics Code for the Public Service' as one of the subjects on which the whistle can be blown. The comments on the Australian CLERP Act call for considering breaches of company policy in the subject element. The German discussion shows usage of the construct, as does the initial Swiss attempt to put the issue of whistleblowing on the agenda. However, none of the whistleblowing policies that have made it into legislation are driven by the rational loyalty construct.

There seem to be two exceptions. The OECD Guidelines for MNEs, issued in 2000, include corporate policies in the subject element. Hence, the rational loyalty line is marked in Figure 4.14. However, two meliorations are in place. First, the commentaries to the Guidelines see it appropriate that the whistle be blown on – in order of importance: 1) breaking the law; 2) bribery and corruption; and 3) other recommendations in the Guidelines. This somehow puts the importance of the rationality loyalty drive into perspective. Still, the Guidelines very clearly recommend MNEs to develop and publish value and mission statements. The second melioration is that the OECD Guidelines for MNEs are not binding. They do not have the same status as legislation. There are no sanctions attached for not following them. Still, these guidelines are presented as 'showing the way'.

The second exception is the US Organizational Sentencing Guidelines (OSG). The OSG summon organizations to have compliance programmes establishing standards and procedures and to communicate them. This points at a rational loyalty driver. However, organizations are not obliged to have them. Rather, the OSG reduce penalties for organizations who have such compliance programmes.

A hardly used line is that of the *responsibility construct*. In Germany it was raised recently, but that is still nothing more as an attempt. In the UK it was tapped into in 1996 at a time when all semantic variations were used. In the Netherlands and the US Organizational Sentencing Guidelines (OSG) the construct is still used. And there is no striking combination with other constructs to be noted. However, in the ethical evaluation, I will come back to this construct because of the radical direction a responsibility driven whistleblowing policy can take. In Germany, Leisinger has described a whistleblowing policy as a means for an employee to take an ethical distance to organizational practices, as does the 1996 Nolan report in the UK and the US OSG. In the Netherlands, to blow the whistle is a duty for officials of the city of Amsterdam. However, the distinction between whistleblowing as a way to increase ethical distance and whistleblowing as a duty is gradual. What if there is a whistleblowing policy in force but an employee who knows about a malpractice does not disclose it? This implies that the employee had the opportunity to take an ethical distance, but chose not to do it. Isn't the next step to hold that employee accountable for *not* disclosing? In other words, is *not* taking an ethical distance to a particular practice any different from approving the practice, hence complicity? Is there, then, still a difference with not fulfilling the duty of blowing the whistle? True, whistleblowing as a means to create an ethical distance is not at the same time whistleblowing as a duty, but it does leave the door towards a duty wide open.

Finally, I would like to raise the attention to the absence of an *integrity* driven legitimation for whistleblowing policies. This is peculiar, as the term 'integrity' is used very often in organizational rhetoric. Still, the concept of integrity as consistently constituted by the globalization semantic, does not seem to be a selectable – in terms of stabilizing potential – variation with regard to whistle-blowing. Schwarb's argumentation in the Swiss discussion taps into the integrity line, as does the INES in the German discussion. However, these are not taken over in any detailed whistleblowing policy proposal. The 1993 call of Dales in the Netherlands for integrity uses an integrity concept that matches the construct, and it is that 'call for integrity' that is still referred to, although the Dutch whistle-blowing policies are not aimed at promoting a unity of discernment, action and speech. Finally, Public Concern at Work includes the integrity construct in their argumentation, but only to the extent that they emphasize the distinction between 'raising concern' and 'grievance procedures' and that they regard the most legitimate whistleblowing to be internally, as soon as possible. But it is not aimed at instigating a collective reflection process on values, regulations, codes of conduct. In fact, currently, it is the US Organization Sentencing Guidelines which shows the most potential of including the integrity construct as a driver. I see this potential – and it is nothing more than a potential – in the discussions to include ethics training and programs to discuss ethical dilemmas in the Guidelines.

Patterns in the Discussion Towards Whistleblowing Policies

What I would like to point out in this subsection are some patterns visible in the evolution of legitimation lines and in content of actor, subject and recipient elements. These patterns do not concern the apparent stabilizing potential of some legitimation constructs or combinations of constructs, nor the unselectable constructs as variations of the globalization semantic. I have discussed that in the previous sections. Rather, of interest here are the apparent evolutions beneath the particular content of legitimation concepts.

Looking at Figures 4.1 (US), 4.2 (Australia) and 4.4 (UK), we can clearly see a diachronic pattern of:

1   raising the issue – the argumentation is based on one or a few constructs;
2   differentiating argumentation – a widening shows; more constructs are mobilized;
3   crystallizing some lines into legislation – some argumentation lines are drawn closer or broken off, some remain.

In terms of Luhmann's semantic evolution, this is a pattern of variation and selection. The globalization semantic is then stabilized, until new realities instigate the formulation of new variations – see in Figure 4.1 (US) the OSG and SOX, Figure 4.5 (South Africa) the comments from the Law Reform Commission. The discussion in the Netherlands (see Figure 4.8) shows an increase in used variations in 2003, with lines drawing closer to each other in 2004 and an expectation of the human rights line broken off.

An explanation for this might be that in order to get whistleblowing accepted and institutionalized into legislation, instead of convincing politicians, the public or relevant social actors of the value of or the need for whistleblowing policies, it is more a question of 'convincing' or amending the concept of whistleblowing to fit a craving opening in the wider semantic constellation of globalization. It is a 'craving opening' in the sense that it 'needs' to be closed. To the extent that it is closed, the globalization semantic is stabilized – it is further maintainable as a semantic for 'meaning making', as constituting our lived experience.

A second pattern concerns the influence the provisions of certain whistleblowing policies have on an international level. As noted earlier, the tiered approach in the recipient element certainly has gained widespread recognition. Nearly all whistleblowing policies prescribe internal channels as the first recipient and several government agencies at a next tier. But the recipient at the final tier in the respective provisions still shows some variation. However, two models can be distinguished. The first is the New Zealand-model, allowing final tier disclosures being made to the Ombudsman. This has been taken over in some Australian state legislations (Victoria, Tasmania, Western Australia, Northern Territory), Belgium and to some extent in the Canadian proposal. The second model is that of the UK PIDA, specifying the final tier recipients as 'any person reasonable'. This has been taken over in South Africa, Japan, Ireland (proposal), the Netherlands (proposal), and Switzerland (proposal). Moreover, UK PIDA's detailed prescription of the second tier recipients is taken over in South Africa (comments by the Law Reform Commission), Ireland, and potentially the Swiss and the Dutch proposals.

Also, in the specifications of the subject element – defining what disclosures are in the public interest – the UK PIDA stipulations seem to have quite some followers. The UK PIDA subject element defines disclosures in the public interest as regarding criminal offences, failures to comply with legal obligations, miscarriage of justice, health and safety of individuals, damages to the environment and cover-ups. These stipulations have been taken over in whistleblowing legislations or proposals in South Africa, Japan, Ireland, the Netherlands, and potentially Switzerland. Neither Australia nor New Zealand specify the subject element of their whistleblowing policies in such detail. However, discussions in Australia, New Zealand, but also India and Canada also make reference to the UK PIDA as an exemplary whistleblowing policy.

What is also striking is the fact that US whistleblowing policies have not been reproduced elsewhere. There is no other country having *qui tam* legislations such as the US False Claims Act – where a percentage of recovered fraud is used as an incentive to blow the whistle. Important to note however are the recent developments in the Netherlands, where two political parties have called for whistleblowing to be given financial rewards.

Neither have the US Organizational Sentencing Guidelines been copied – where corporations get softer sanctions if they have whistleblowing policies in place. Sarbanes-Oxley regulations – holding top executives personally liable – have not been introduced elsewhere, even though corporate governance measures are strengthening worldwide and some (like the Australian CLERP Act) do include provisions for whistleblowers.

This pattern calls for an explanation. As to the New Zealand recipient model, it has to be noted that the legislations that have taken over the Ombudsman as the final recipient, all cover organizational malpractices within the public sector, even though they differ in the actor element. A possible explanation, in my view, has to be sought in the overall success of whistleblowing provisions and legitimation which 'contain' the conflict between society and organization. In that perspective, the Ombudsman – a parliamentary controlled agency dealing with allegations about public sector organizations from citizens and government employees – marks the border of the space in which the conflict is contained. Here, the Ombudsman is the mediator between executive power (public sector organizations) and controlling power (parliament as a proxy of society). Strangely enough, the New Zealand policy covers both public and private sector organizational malpractices. Here, the conflict between society and private sector organizations (business) is also contained by the Ombudsman. This is a wider containment in the sense that it allows a proxy of society to control private sector organizational practices. However, the recommendations of the New Zealand Privacy Commissioner to reduce the scope of the legislation to the public sector only, make it less strange. His argument is that the scope of the policy is too wide to function properly, hence that the containment is inappropriate. In other words, the Ombudsman as a proxy of society leaves society with too much controlling power. Thus, the Ombudsman as the final tier recipient is a legitimate sealer of the containment of conflict between society and public sector organizations, but not of the containment of conflict between society and business.

Yet, the success of the UK PIDA – in terms of its apparent international generalizing potential – seems bigger than that of the New Zealand model. More countries have taken over the recipient provisions and also its subject provisions are being copied. This influence can be explained through the role of Public Concern at Work (PCAW), the London based NGO set up in 1993 as an independent resource centre with government support. PCAW drafted the UK Bills and the UK PIDA and lead negotiations with relevant social actors. It had generated quite some semantic variation trying to legitimate whistleblowing policies – in fact, it produced the most differentiated discussion (see Figure 4.4). It operates a helpline staffed with lawyers offering advice to potential whistleblowers and consulted organizations in establishing internal whistleblowing procedures. It is professionally organized in the sense that it has paid staff. New Zealand has no similar organization to promote its model. Australia does, but the Australian counterpart of PCAW, Whistleblowers Australia does not function as a professionally run NGO focused on whistleblowing. Rather, it is a group of academics and whistleblowers set up to help one another and keep the issue on the public agenda. Hence, the UK PIDA model had much more lobbying possibilities than the New Zealand model. Indeed, PCAW did some consultancy work for the European Commission, and Guy Dehn, the executive director of PCAW, was rapporteur to the discussion session within the OECD. Furthermore, it was the British Council who set up and supported the cooperation between PCAW and the South African Open Democracy Advice Centre (ODAC), and PCAW-staff are willing and eager to travel the world to give lectures and offer advice on whistleblowing policies. Whenever it does so, it introduces a whole set of possible semantic variation to legitimate whistleblowing policies into a new local context 'craving' for a stabilizing 'fit' of the globalization semantic. Moreover, through its work for the OECD, legitimation of whistle-blowing policies based on stabilizing semantic variations – accountability, efficiency, OSR-network – have resonated in a number of normative policy texts.

Thus, because PCAW has generated the most semantic variations to legitimate whistleblowing policies – including the stabilizing 'fits' – and because it has the resources to 'carry out' those semantic variations – including its success story, the UK PIDA – its model is copied more often.

But what about the apparent absence of any influence coming from the US whistleblowing policies? The Government Accountability Project (GAP) has more experience than PCAW, it is run just as professionally, and even has a bigger staff and a bigger budget.[2] However, the GAP deals with several whistle-blowing legislations – 44 states and four policies at federal level (WPA, FCA, OSG, SOX) – whilst PCAW is concentrated on just the UK PIDA. Thus, given

---

2   The GAP has a staff of 30 as well as 50 interns, and a budget of $1.7million, or approximately €1.37 million (Devine 2004b). PCAW has a staff of seven and a budget of £435.000 or approximately € 655.000 (PCAW 2003).

the complexity of the national situation, the US seems to have no NGO able to lobby other national governments.

Adding to that, another element seems important. I have argued that the efficiency construct is a stabilizing construct because it has such a high semantic density. However, the US most famous efficiency driven whistleblowing policy, the False Claims Act (FCA), is not copied outside the US – at least, not yet (see the discussion in Netherlands). Central to the policy is, as just mentioned, the *qui tam* provisions as an incentive to blow the whistle. However, the whistleblower must start up a law suit him/herself and the government might join or not based on the amount of evidence the case shows. Hence, two cultural aspects seem to support the whistleblowing policy of the FCA: a litigation culture – meaning that taking disputes to court as a commonly accepted practice – and a specific employee status – the employment-at-will doctrine central to US labour culture, offering no notion of protection against arbitrary dismissal for whistleblowing policies to hook on. This means that whistleblowing policies legitimated through an efficiency construct in the US, in order to constitute a stabilizing 'fit' for the globalization semantic, aim at offering individual advantages to those who take the risk of getting fired when blowing the whistle. In other countries where whistle-blowing policies have been introduced, this was different. There, the efficiency construct by itself was not enough to drive a legitimate whistleblowing policy. PCAW coupled it to the constructs of accountability and OSR-network, indicating just how conflicts ought to be contained: not through court, but rather through a tiered approach specifying proxies of society.

How Ethical are these Tendencies?

Now that I have identified the tendencies in the development of whistleblowing policies, which was one of the aims of the assessment, I proceed to the second aim: how ethical are these tendencies? I will answer this question in two steps. The first is a very binary approach: they are either ethical or unethical. This is done in the first subsection. After that, I somehow moderate my judgement by speaking of 'the ethical risk of whistleblowing policies' instead of whistleblowing policies being ethical or unethical. This is done in the second subsection. Of course, once formulated in terms of 'risk', the task ahead is merely reducing the risk, not abandoning the work. How to reduce the ethical risks is something I develop further on.

Subjectivation or Subjectaffirmation

At the end of Chapter 2, I started a discussion on the different positions Foucault and Touraine take with regard to the subject. I wrote that whilst Foucault seems to say that we are suffering from integration – coincidence of individual and rationality – Touraine seems to argue that it is disintegration we are suffering from – the rift between economy and society. I noted that these claims are highly relevant to whistleblowing, but that it was only with the results of the assessment of whistleblowing policies that I might be able to say whether or not whistleblowing policies are more Foucauldian or more Tourainean. I then referred to the current chapter for a continuation of that discussion.

Indeed, now the screening has been carried out, and tendencies and patterns have been identified, it is time to round up the assessment by making an ethical evaluation of the way whistleblowing tends to be institutionalized in whistle-blowing policies. As I just mentioned, I hinted in Chapter 2 that this ethical evaluation would be made in terms of the position whistleblowing policies tend to take with regard to the individual – more Foucauldian or more Tourainean?

Let me explain what I mean by this. Foucault's analysis[3] emphasizes *subjectivation*, showing the subject as historically produced. There are two dimensions to such a subjectivity: being subject to someone else by control and dependence, and being tied to ones own identity by conscience or self-knowledge. Both are conterminous. Hence Foucault's term *gouvernementalité* – the subjection of the individual to a mode of government (external control) becomes embodied in the individual as the subject's mentality (internal control or self-governance). *Gouvernementalité* denotes 'technologies of power' turning into 'technologies of self' as the external pressure to 'behave' in a certain way is made an internal pressure to 'be' a certain kind of *individual*.

Touraine's call for the affirmation of the subject[4] on the other hand emphasizes the historical possibility that an individual creates its own mode of being. Touraine also uses the word 'subjectivation' for this. But because I am opposing the Foucauldian subjectivation to Touraine's subjectivation, for reasons of clarity I will use *subjectivation* for the Foucauldian subjectivation, and *subjectaffirmation* for the Tourainean subjectivation.

According to Touraine, what the individual is struggling with today is not a reduction of the subject to a particular knowledge-power constellation, but rather with a de-modernization, a desintegration of rationality and moral individualism. The state is no longer capable of ensuring the fit between the demands of the market and the social demands. The individual is left with the dilemma of choosing between two universes: that of techniques and markets versus that of cultures, or, the universe of instrumental rationality and the universe of the collective memory. Touraine names the two universes as ideologies. The neo-liberalism is an ideology to the extent that it makes the market system appear as the right, the good, as necessary, as freedom. Communitarianism on the other hand is an ideology to the extent that it transforms a culture into an instrument of political mobilization and the rejection of the other.

Today, still according to Touraine, we live in the in-between – *l'entre-deux*. In between what? Touraine's call for the affirmation of the subject implies that he

---

[3]   I refer back to the section on Foucault in Chapter 2.

[4]   I refer back to the section on Touraine in Chapter 2, but take the discussion further here, based on Touraine (1997).

sees the subject taking a central position in a new cultural and social landscape – a new integration of both universes – a position the state used to have. However, that landscape is not yet. Therefore, we live in the in-between of state and subject.

Touraine recognizes that Foucault's esthetical alternative – care of the self, *le souci de soi* – has a liberating power, but he cannot see how this alternative is able to avoid the reduction of the other to a pure object of pleasure. Touraine's affirmation of the subject is not esthetical, but political. Formulated negatively, the subject is the double de-engagement from both market and culture. Positively formulated, the subject is the desire of the individual to be an actor. Hence, subjectaffirmation is the desire of individuation. Touraine's subject is also ethical, driven by a solitary courage – *le courage solitaire* – and the power of collective action. The subject is refusal (*le refus*), self-conscience (*conscience de soi*) and the recognition of the other as subject (*reconnaiscance de l'Autre comme Sujet*). For Touraine, the subject can not be defined as the presence inside the individual of a universal principle, the Truth, Beauty, the Good, which the individual tries to realize. Rather, the subject is nothing more than the resistance, the will and the happiness of the individual trying to defend and affirm its *individuality* against the laws of the market and the laws of the community.

In its extreme form, for Touraine, the subject is the dissident: testifying freedom, not a moralist, not defending dominant values and norms. The task however, is to find and support milder forms of the subject. Recalling Jubb's view (see Chapter 1) that at the heart of whistleblowing lies dissent, the question whether the tendency of whistleblowing policies can be seen as ethical would be whether or not whistleblowing policies support the subject.

It is possible that I am polarizing Foucault and Touraine too much. Indeed, I do see some hinges in the interpretations of Foucault's work which I have used that there might be more convergence than Touraine, truly opposing his work to that of Foucault, is able or willing to see.

As I wrote in Chapter 2, commentators on the work of Foucault distinguish a third phase in his work in which he undertook an investigation into how one could develop techniques to work on one's self, or how one could take care of one's self and thereby construct oneself as a subject, leading to an esthetical ethic – taking care of the relation one has to one's self. The same commentators have also pointed out that this third phase was not really a turn of Foucault's outlook. Rather, the possibility of individuals working on their self was always presupposed in Foucault's earlier writings on subjectivation. Foucault uses the word *assujettissement* to denote the process of subjectivation, which covers both external pressures to a particular 'mode of being' or subjectivity, as well as ways in which individuals themselves participate in the formation of that suggested subjectivity. The article of Barker and Cheney (1994) I mentioned describes a good example of both complementary directions that make up the process of subjectivation. The point is that the Foucauldian subjectivation does presuppose individual freedom and autonomy, for the Foucauldian perspective on power is that it is relational but not within a dualistic scheme of active and passive.

Perhaps Touraine does not recognize that presupposition of the Foucauldian perspective enough. He agrees with the analysis of the reduction of the autonomous subject and thus concludes that we therefore need a reaffirmation of the subject as a resistance to that reduction.[5] Both approaches however imply individuality: in the Foucauldian sense an individual that is subjected and subjects itself, in the Tourainean sense an individual that resists the pressures of subjection and of subjecting oneself.

So, I repeat, it is possible that I am polarizing Foucault and Touraine too much. However, since this research is not about Foucault nor about Touraine – it is about whistleblowing policies – and for the sake of the argument, I will maintain the distinction but make abstraction of the authors. Doing that, another clarification must be made concerning the distinction between subjectivation and subjectaffirmation. One could argue that the term 'subject' always entails the etymological connotation of subjection or submission. Etymologically, it draws on *subiectum*, 'thrown under'. However, there is also a link with *substantia*, derived from *substare*, which means 'standing under' in the sense of supporting something else.[6] This is an ontological meaning of subject; subject as carrier of properties and actions. In a modern sense, subject also denotes the existence of self-consciousness, as that what thinks and at the same time 'thinks itself thinking', as that which is capable of willing and acting.

Thus, the least I can say is that 'subject' has an ambivalent meaning. It denotes a being subjected to an authority posing an undeniable obligation. It also denotes a fundamental being to the forms which we perceive and experience. But even in this latter sense, the subject is ambiguous. The subject as support can be merely passive – supporting the forms imposed on it. But the subject as substance can also be active – causing its own properties.

What I have called subjectivation captures the meaning of subject as a being subjected to undeniable obligations; the subject as 'thrown under'. But, with Foucault, subjectivation also entails the passive notion of the subject as supporting what is imposed on it – the individual works on itself in forming the suggested

---

5   Thus, we might regard the Foucauldian subjectivation as a descriptive notion and the Tourainean subjectaffirmation as a normative notion. Within the context of this research however, to do so would be problematic, since the construction of the idealtypes is based on the presumption that the descriptive is always normative: we describe our organizations in terms of flexibility, decentralization, governance, network and stakeholders, not because our organizations really work that way, but because we believe that such is the way organizations *must* work. Another reason for not making that distinction is that Touraine has identified the descriptive counterpart of the subjectaffirming position in the dissident.

6   This paragraph draws on the articles on '*sujet*' in *Dictionnaire de la langue philosophique* by P. Foulquié (1962, Paris, PUF), '*Subjekt*' in *Historisches Wörterbuch der Philosophie* by J. Ritter (1971, Basel/Darmstadt, Scwabe, Wissenschaftliche Buchgesellschaft), and 'L'éthique comme anthropo-logique' in *Encyclopédie Philosophique Universelle – L'univers philosophique* by A. Jacob (1989, Paris, PUF).

subjectivity. What I have called subjectaffirmation denotes the subject as an active substance – the individual as willing and searching to cause its own properties, or in other words, the individual who wants to be an actor.

Here again, I acknowledge that the distinction Foucault-subjectivation on the one hand and Touraine-subjectaffirmation on the other, is a reduction of Foucault's work because it does not take account of Foucault's third phase, which does call for the subject as an active substance. Nevertheless, as this research is not about Foucault nor Touraine, I maintain the polarization. In Table 5.1, I resume the ambivalence and ambiguity of the notion of subject, subjectivation and subjectaffirmation, and Foucault's and Touraine's position.

Thus, the question which has driven me to do this research, whether or not, given the tendencies in whistleblowing policies, whistleblowing can still be regarded as a politico-ethical concept, can be answered in a normative way. If it is still a politico-ethical concept, then the tendencies in whistleblowing policies will support subjectaffirmation. If, on the other hand, these tendencies point at subjectivation, then the conclusion must be that whistleblowing policies tend to be disciplining.

At the end of Chapter 2 I drew up a diagram consisting of three zones – Individual/Subject, Organization, Semantic. At the end of Chapter 3 I placed the possible semantic variations in the diagram. Every possible legitimation construct for whistleblowing policies was visualized as a movement, either enclosing the individual inside the organization or emphasizing a dissociation between organization and individual. Some constructs were found to offer both possibilities. Hence, what I will do now is look how the tendencies in whistle-blowing policies I pointed out in the previous section describe movements within the diagram, either enclosing the individual within the organization or rather emphasizing the individual as dissociated from the organization. To make the ethical evaluation, these movements will be linked to the subjectivation/subjectaffirmation distinction, in the following way (Table 5.2).

The tendencies in whistleblowing show a high usage of the accountability, efficiency and OSR-network constructs. The constructs of integrity, OSR-stakeholder, and rational loyalty on the other hand appeared unselectable. They were hardly used and until now never sustained. The responsibility was also hardly used, but required more consideration because of its ambiguous potential. The human rights construct was also used a couple of times, and also requires more consideration because it was used in very different combinations. Table 5.3 shows how the type of movements correspond to the tendencies in whistle-blowing policies.

Visualized in the diagram, this shows the following movements (see Figures 5.1 and 5.2). Movements of the highly used legitimation constructs (Figure 5.1) show an enclosing of the individual from two sides (OS-I and SO-I), with an indirect countermovement (SI-O). Movements of the unselectable (not used or broken off) legitimation constructs (Figure 5.2) show a double emphasis of the

Table 5.1 Clarification of the distinction subjectivation/subjectaffirmation

Term used in this research	Foucauldian perspective	Touraine	Notion of subject
Subjectivation	Second phase: asujettissement = process of subjectivation : both external pressure to a particular subjectivity as well as the individual working on itself in forming that suggested subjectivity	Acknowledges only the analytic value	Subject as 'thrown under' Subject as support
Subjectaffirmation	Third phase: esthetical ethic	Political ethic	Subject as active substance, as cause of its own properties

Table 5.2 Distinction subjectivation/subjectaffirmation and IOS-movements

Term used	Relation to individual	Movement in IOS-diagram
Subjectivation	Enclosing the individual	OS-I, SO-I
Subjectaffirmation	Dissociating the individual	IS-O, SI-O

Table 5.3   IOS-movements of current legitimation tendencies

Usage	Construct	Movement
High	Accountability	OS-I, SI-O
	Efficiency	OS-I, SI-O
	OSR-network	SO-I
Low	Rational loyalty	IS-O, SO-I
	OSR-stakeholder	IS-O
	Integrity	SI-O, SO-I
More consideration	Responsibility	SI-O, SO-I
	Human rights	IS-O

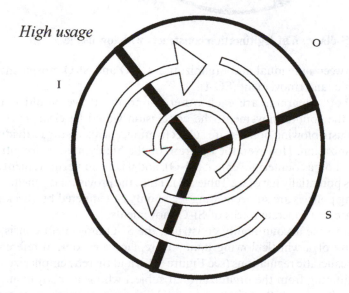

Figure 5.1   IOS-diagram of legitimation constructs with high usage

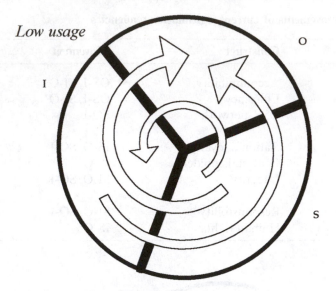

Figure 5.2   IOS-diagram of legitimation constructs with low usage

dissociation between individual and organization (IS-O and SI-O movements), with an indirect countermovement (SO-I).

Note that both diagrams are each others opposite. If we would make abstraction of the countermovement, the conclusion would be clear: current tendencies in whistleblowing policies are subjectivating, enclosing the individual within the organization. However, the diagram of the highly used legitimation constructs does show a countermovement (SI-O), and it is a countermovement all three constructs potentially have (see Table 5.3). Thus, the provisional conclusion – whistleblowing policies are subjectivating – can only be tempered by checking whether there are any concrete traces of SI-O movements.

With regard to the accountability construct, the SI-O movement consisted of the possibility of a whistleblowing policy to replace the external reference function of bureaucratic regulations (see Figure 3.17) and thereby emphasize the individual as differing from the organizational subject who is a subordinate to whimsical bosses. Thus, even though the accountability concept primal movement is to enclose the individual, in the sense that employees are made accountable to power – as Miriam Green points out – the SI-O potential in whistleblowing policies lies in the possibility of employees to hold their superiors accountable for work orders. Hence, in a tiered approach, before disclosing to an external recipient, an employee discloses to his/her direct superior, or, if this direct superior is the subject of the disclosure, then the employee goes a hierarchical step higher, to the superior of his/her direct superior. Although some policies include abuse of power into their subject element, only the comments from the South African Law Reform Commission propose to treat disclosures made to union representatives on equal footing with disclosures made while seeking legal advice. As of yet, none of the legislated whistleblowing policies actually prescribe labour unions as recipients for disclosures. True, internal procedures might include them, but the general absence of the institution of labour unions from whistleblowing policies is striking. Thus, whistleblowing policies are not intended to tackle the problem of whimsical bosses ordering in ways unacceptable for workers, but rather of tackling organizational practices unacceptable for consumers, investors, and societal order.

With regard to the efficiency construct, the SI-O movement consisted of the provision in the whistleblowing policy of watchdog accountability through disclosures to NGOs or the media (see Figure 3.20). The SI-O potential of the efficiency construct is realized to the extent that whistleblowing polices are a spotlight-application – Van Parijs' name for transparency mechanisms alerting the public opinion of individuals and communities 'suffering from some practices'. However, very few whistleblowing policies allow disclosure to the media, and if they do, then only as a final tier recipient, after disclosures have been made internally and to government agencies. Thus, the SI-O movement is only very meagrely present in current whistleblowing policies, and even then much weaker than the OS-I movement.

Thirdly, the SI-O movement brought about by the OSR-network construct is an unintended potential of regarding organizations as networks (Figure 3.14). This emphasizes the importance of the quality of interactions in building trust. Improving the quality of interactions is done by balancing power within networks – network governance. To the extent that whistleblowing policies are a way of balancing power in the sense of giving more power to the individual, the SI-O movement takes place. However, if the organization *is* a network, specified by assigning particular stakeholders a position within the network, power is balanced *within* that network and the individual gains power in so far as the individual takes a specific position within the network – which is an SO-I movement. Hence, the individual gaining power through a whistleblowing policy balancing power within a network, sees its identity restricted within the border and the prescribed interactions of the network. Thus, with regard to the OSR-network construct, the SO-I movement is much stronger and immediate than the SI-O movement.

This means our provisional conclusion holds: whistleblowing policies tend to be subjectivating. Let me reformulate that as follows:

whistleblowing policies as the institutionalization of
people blowing the whistle
on organizations operating within
the context of globalization of private capital oriented economy,
tend to subjectivate,
to discipline,
hence to enclose the individual within the organization.

Institutionalizing the Individual

In Chapter 1, I argued that whereas in the early 1970s whistleblowing was a politico-ethical concept pointing at a conflict between organization and society, by the end of the 1990s the concept was being used to legitimate whistleblowing policies and hence seemed to be presented as a concept able to eliminate conflict between organization and society. Also, I argued that the growing attention for whistleblowing points at a changed societal context in which social actors – business, media, consumers, employees, governments – operate. And the overall term by which we tag this changed societal context is 'globalization'. Hardt and Negri (2001, 261–74) mark the end of the 1960s as the emergence of a new subjectivity and hence of new desires, as shifts triggering globalization in the 1970s – abandoning Bretton Woods, establishing G7 – which in turn prepared the massive privatization and deregulation policies of the 1980s – the reigns of Reagan and Thatcher.

Thus, the concept of whistleblowing arose at the dawn of globalization. Along with the changed societal context comes a particular semantic, which I have named the 'globalization semantic'. From the 1970s through the 1990s into the 2000s – in the terms of Luhmann's theory – this semantic will allow us to make sense of our experiences, only to the extent that the semantic is able to stabilize the crisis which had given birth to the 'globalization semantic' in the first place: the conflict between organization and society.

Therefore, if by the end of the 1990s the concept of whistleblowing is used to legitimate policies pretending to eliminate conflict between organization and society, the 1970s politico-ethical concept pointing at a crisis is used in an attempt to stabilize that crisis. What is that attempt? As I argued in the beginning of this chapter, the accountability construct, the efficiency construct and the OSR-network construct all attempt to stabilize the crisis by containing the conflict between organization and society within the organization or within the limited space of a proxy of society.

In other words, to the extent that whistleblowing policies are able to contain the conflict between organization and society, the semantic constructs used to legitimate those policies – in Luhmann's terms – stabilize the globalization semantic, which implies that the concepts of flexibility, decentralization, governance, network and stakeholder maintain relevance in our meaning-making.

In terms of the Foucauldian perspective, 'power' is the containment of conflict, 'knowledge' is the information and the 'norms' designate the individual subject as generating information to be contained. In Deleuze's terms, containment is the abstract machine of the globalization semantic, whilst whistleblowing polices are the machinic arrangements.

From these perspectives, whistleblowing policies – as they appear to institutionalize whistleblowing, appear as 'necessary'. However, this is different in Touraine's terms. In Touraine's terms, the concept of whistleblowing indeed arises at a moment when the demodernization, the rupture between the economical and the social, or between organization and society becomes undeniable – the turning from the 1960s to the 1970s, or the kick off of the globalization semantic. And indeed, the globalization semantic can be researched in terms of attempts to reintegrate organization and society – as I have done in this research. More precisely, whistleblowing policies can be regarded as an attempt to reintegrate both domains. But, as I have pointed out in the previous section, this attempt is not done through the affirmation of the subject as an actor, as defending its individuality – Touraine's hope. Whistleblowing policies tend to be subjectivating rather than subjectaffirming.

Formulated like that, it is too bold to be a statement about the ethicality of whistleblowing policies. Let me therefore reformulate it in a moderate way. Santoro (2003) has argued that liberalism has distinguished Medieval society from the modern age as the transition from an honour-base society to a dignity-base society:

> in a world of honour, the individual discovers his true identity in his roles, and to turn away from the roles is to turn away from himself […]. In a world of dignity, the individual can only discover his true identity by emancipating himself from his socially imposed roles (Berger et al 1973, quoted in Santoro 2003, 89).

Santoro shows that liberal views claim a shift from moral functionalism to moral individualism, through a shift from a political primacy of duties to a political primacy of rights. Santoro sees common to these views the idea that the advent of rights is the advent of individual subjectivity. Therefore, argues Santoro, what these views hide is 'the difference between entitlement to a domain of freedom or rights and the ability autonomously to express one's individuality' (Santoro 2003, 89–90). It leads Santoro to regard modernity as 'the emergence of the Individual without Individuality' (Santoro 2003, 88). He connects the distinction between individual and individuality to Isaiah Berlin's *Two Concepts of Liberty* (1958), which draws on Mill's distinction between positive and negative liberty – or, respectively 'freedom to' and 'freedom from'. It is positive liberty – or individual autonomy, or Touraine's individuality through subjectaffirmation – which we seek to promote, protect and foster. While negative liberty is a necessary condition for that, it is not a sufficient one. This means that extra attention needs to be paid to make sure positive liberty is achieved.[7] I would like to remind the reader of the usage of the human rights construct supporting the legitimation of whistleblowing policies in India and South Africa, where whistleblowing policy is presented as a way to *free* society *from* fraud and corruption, with the assumption that this negative freedom automatically furthers human rights. From what I have just

---

[7]   An implication of this is that the level of individuality, of positive liberty, of the extent to which individual subjects are actors in the sense that they create their own mode of being, cannot be measured by only looking at the rights bestowed at them.

pointed out, it is clear that such an assumption can only hold if human rights too are perceived as protecting only negative liberties – to be free from poverty or discrimination for example.

In a reasoning analogous to Santoro's, I can rephrase my bold conclusion more moderately as follows:

> Even though whistleblowing policies are necessary, they are ethical only to the extent that they succeed in protecting individuality rather than institutionalizing the individual.

What do I mean with 'institutionalizing the individual'? Paul Du Gay has written in *Consumption and Identity at Work* (Du Gay 1996) about how the concept of consumer has become a central element in discourses on reforms in both the private and public sector. In the hospital, patients have been re-imagined as customers, and so have pupils and parents in the educational system. In a way, the 'sovereign customer provides a novel image for the productive subject' (Du Gay 1996, 77). And it is in that way Du Gay regards the customer as a 'character' in MacIntyre's sense of the term. MacIntyre (1984, 27–9) regards a character not as merely a role or function, but rather as the moral representatives of a culture, because of the way in which moral ideas are embodied through them in the social world. There might still be a distance between role and individual. Doubt, compromize or cynicism can mediate between individual and role – these can give individuality a chance. This is different with regard to a 'character' because its requirements are imposed from outside, from the way others regard it and use it to understand and to evaluate themselves. 'The *character* morally legitimates a mode of social existence' (MacIntyre 1984, 29). Now, to answer my question what whistleblowing policies do when they institutionalize the individual, I would answer that they make the employee into a 'character'. The character of the employee represents the obliteration of the conflict between organization and society precisely in his ability to blow the whistle. The individual is institutionalized into the character of the employee, meaning that every employee must understand and evaluate him/herself in terms of that character. Hence, an employee who fails to blow the whistle, is an employee who fails to safeguard the integration of organization and society, of economic and social concerns.

It is with regard to the risk of whistleblowing policies as institutionalizing the individual that I would like to take up again the discussion on the responsibility construct.

I wrote that the responsibility construct points at the possibility of whistle-blowing policies to be a set of procedures enabling individuals to take ethical distance from organizational practices. As such, the individual is able to express dissent. Earlier I wrote that for Touraine, the extreme form of the subject is the dissident, but that the task is to find milder forms. Jubb regards the expression of dissent to be at the heart of whistleblowing, and indeed, in this sense whistle-blowing policies driven by the responsibility construct – enabling individuals to take ethical distance – could be subjectaffirming, or protecting and furthering individuality. However, I also wrote that the responsibility construct opens the door to 'whistleblowing as a duty'. Given that whistleblowing policies tend to be legitimated by the accountability, the efficiency and the OSR-network constructs, and given that these constructs already show an inclination towards enclosing the individual inside the organization – hence subjectivating and thus institutionalization of the individual into the 'character' of the employee – there is a huge risk that adding the responsibility construct to the legitimation will only strengthen that tendency. As noted earlier in this section, the 'character' of the employee then makes whistleblowing an obligation – an organizational obligation as well as a political obligation – complete with sanctions if the whistle is *not* blown.

And so, the final conclusion of this research reads as follows: the formulation of legitimation constructs for whistleblowing policies as consistent semantic constructions within the globalization semantic, and the screening of recent and developing whistleblowing policies through whistleblowing legislation, has shown these whistleblowing policies:

1) attempt to solve the conflict between organization and society by containing the conflict,
2) tend to institutionalize the individual rather than protect and support individuality,
3) and in this sense entail an ethical risk.

However, the very same legitimation constructs driving whistleblowing policies, as well as the legitimation constructs left untouched or unsustained, can hint us at how to reduce that ethical risk, or in other words, the legitimation constructs can also show us how to make whistleblowing policies more ethical. I will do this in the next section.

Lobbying for Ethical Whistleblowing Policies

I have argued that the ethical risk of whistleblowing policies lies in the tendency to be more subjectivating than subjectaffirming, or, in the tendency to be more an institutionalization of the individual than a support and protection of individuality. Hence, reducing that ethical risk, or, making whistleblowing policies more ethical can be done by strengthening the support and protection of individuality, or emphasizing the subjectaffirming movements in the legitimation constructs.

Earlier I wrote that the subjectaffirming movements are IS-O and SI-O (see Table 5.2). It are these movements in the legitimation constructs that I will take as instructive for reducing the ethical risk of whistleblowing policies (see Table 5.4).

Table 5.4   Subjectaffirming movements in the legitimation constructs

Legitimation construct	IS-O	SI-O
Rational loyalty	X	
OSR-stakeholder	X	
Integrity		X
Accountability		X
Efficiency		X
OSR-network		
Responsibility		X
human rights	X	

The first three constructs are the constructs with low usage – either not used or unsustained. The second block of three constructs are much used, and the last two constructs got more consideration in the previous section. I will review each construct, pointing out what constitutes the IS-O or SI-O movement in each construct, and translate that into concrete lobbying positions. To do so is urgent. As I have shown, whistleblowing policies *are* happening – it is not like they *have* happened or *might* happen. Most of them are new (1990s), brand new (2000s) or are developing (discussions or proposals in parliament). And as I have shown, the tendency of these policies entails an ethical risk. To reduce that ethical risk is therefore not only urgent, but realistic as well, on the condition that alternatives can be concretized. To do so is the aim of this section.

The *rational loyalty* construct has a potential IS-O movement in its stipulation of the object of loyalty as the explicit organizational mission and value statements. This explicit corpus denotes societal control over the organizational practices. Hence, including disclosures on organizational practices running counter corporate policy statements in the subject element of whistleblowing policies strengthens IS-O. At the same time, the SO-I movement of the rational loyalty construct must be avoided. This movement exists to the extent that organizations define the field of collective action, or in other words, the SO-I movement is the extent to which organizations dominate a conception of society, of the goals of society and of societal evolution (see Touraine's 'execution of power' definition of 'political', Chapter 2). Even though this is not a task of whistleblowing policies, it does point at the need for a strong civil society.

In the *OSR-stakeholder* construct, whistleblowing policies allow stakeholders of an organization to warn one another when organizational practices differ from organizational purpose. As I argued (Chapter 3) the organizational purpose is the *telos* of the organization, the place of the organization in the larger whole – society. If purpose and practice of an organization fully coincide, there would be no alienation for those working in the organization. Moreover, there would be no distinction between organization and society. Now, with regard to lobbying for more ethical whistleblowing policies, this implies that 'stakeholders of an organization' must be interpreted very broad. This distinguishes the OSR-stakeholder construct from the *OSR-network* construct. The latter specifies who the relevant stakeholders are and assigns them a position within the organization as network. But the individual gaining power is the individual as positioned within that organizational network. Thus, the recipient element of a whistle-blowing policy driven by the OSR-network construct will tend to be closed. The OSR-stakeholder construct on the other hand, argues that the purpose of an organization is a matter which concerns all of society. Thus, whistleblowing policies driven by that construct will emphasize an openness in the recipient element. This means that lobbying activities should be aimed at a very broad recipient element, avoiding too much specification, yet explicitly including media and civil society organizations.

The *integrity* construct showed what content this much used term can hold consistently within the globalization semantic. I argued in Chapter 3 that it could only mean a unity between discernment, action and speaking, implying that if a situation or practice is discerned as wrongdoing or a malpractice, disclosing information about that is to be regarded as an act of integrity – in whistleblowing, the acting is the speaking. That constituted the SI-O movement coming from the construct. However, the construct also drives a SO-I movement, as the speaking ought to be done internally and it ought to be regarded as instigating a learning process through which control is exercised. Therefore, lobbying for more ethical whistleblowing policies based on the integrity construct remains dubious. If there is any concrete position to take here, it is with regard to the policy discourse, more precisely, to insist that whistleblowing is about raising concern about a situation or an organizational practice rather than an allegation against other persons.

As noted with regard to the *accountability* construct, an OS-I movement is instigated where a causal responsibility for bad results is installed. The potential SI-O movement coming from the construct lies in its possibilities to be a mechanism replacing the 'external reference function' of bureaucratic organizations, as a safeguard against managerial arbitrariness. I see two concrete lobbying positions to be taken to realize that SI-O movement. First, the subject element ought to include 'abuse of power'. In addition to that, replacing the 'external reference function' points at the need for standards of behaviour. Again, civil society organizations can play a role here, especially labour unions and NGOs focussed on labour circumstances advocacy. A second lobbying position then, is to explicitly include these civil society organizations in the recipient element of whistleblowing policies.

The *efficiency* construct founding an internal whistleblowing policy was found to install an organizational panopticon. Hence it took an OS-I movement. However, if the construct would drive a whistleblowing policy including watchdog recipients, such as NGOs and labour unions, it also drew a SI-O movement. Thus, to achieve a more ethical whistleblowing policy, lobbying activities towards an efficiency driven whistleblowing policy must strive to include external watchdogs into the recipient element.

As far as the responsibility construct is concerned, I wrote earlier in this chapter that allowing employees to take an ethical distance (SI-O movement) holds a huge danger to slip into the duty to take an ethical distance, which is the SO-I movement of the construct. Therefore, to prevent this slip from taking place, lobbying activities must be aimed at the explicit mentioning that blowing the whistle is not an organizational obligation.

Finally, I noted that the *human rights* construct, when used in combination with the efficiency construct – in the context of fighting corruption – emphasizes negative liberty (see my remarks about the human rights construct driving whistle-blowing policies in India and South Africa). However, with Santoro I argued that attention must always also be paid to positive liberty. With regard to the human rights construct this implies that whistleblowing policies ought to emphasize the right to and support of self-expression for *all* humans. A concrete lobbying positions to be derived from this is that the actor element of whistleblowing policies ought to cover both public and the private sector workers. In addition to that, both the 'argument for truth' and the 'argument for self-expression' as 'free speech rationales' for whistleblowing as a human right imply a freedom to 'impart information and ideas through any media' as Article 19 of the UN Declaration of Human Rights states. Therefore, highlighting the positive liberty aspects of the human rights construct also calls for a recipient element to include media and civil society organizations.

Summing up the proposed lobbying positions for more ethical whistleblowing policies gives the following table (Table 5.5).

Of course, to effectively lobby the above positions, one needs further argumentation which takes account of possible restraints to the feasibility of these positions. As for the positions regarding the subject element, I cannot see any. However, widening the subject element in the above sense would require labour unions and other civil society organizations to take up those positions, develop the capacity to address the issues involved and provide whistleblowing services to people who want to disclose information about those issues.

The widening of the actor element to include both public and private sector workers can be argued from the blurred line separating the public from the private sector. As I argued in my discussion on the globalization semantic, this blurring is caused by a societal decentralization process, through which private organizations operate public services. Outsourcing and privatization has considerably made organizational practices relevant to the public interest to reach beyond what is left of the public sector. Therefore, if the public interest is at stake, it is hard to see how whistleblowing policies covering only the public sector workers will be of any help. This is even worsened when policies stipulate that only employees at government agencies can blow the whistle about practices inside their own agency, hence not about a malpractice occurring in a subcontracting organization. In fact, the argument of privatization blurring the separation of public and private sector and hence making it untenable to only cover the public sector, has been used in the recent discussion on whistleblowing policies at the Australian federal

Table 5.5 Lobbying positions for more ethical whistleblowing policies

Policy element	Lobbying position	Driving construct
Actor	Public and private sector workers, or even 'any person'	Human rights
Subject	Include disclosures on organizational practices running counter organizational policy statements	Rational loyalty
	Include abuse of power	Accountability
Recipient	Emphasize openness to allow disclosures to media, labour unions and other civil society organizations	OSR-stakeholder Accountability Efficiency Human rights
General attention	Whistleblowing is 'raising concern' rather than 'making allegations' Whistleblowing is not a duty or organizational obligation	Integrity Responsibility

level. However, the mere referral to waves of privatization leaves the argument too sketchy. The argument can be made much stronger by documenting the decentralization process for the geo-political context in which the discussion takes place. In this way, the degree of the blurring can be made tangible. Also, concrete scenarios can be made in which whistleblowing policies covering only the public sector are doomed to fail.

From the discussion on lobbying positions derived from the subjectaffirming movements in the legitimation constructs, it is clear that the recipient element is a very important issue for the reduction of the ethical risk of whistleblowing policies. The lobbying position derived from four legitimation constructs – OSR-stakeholder, accountability, efficiency, human rights – is that emphasis must be put on openness to allow disclosures to media and civil society organizations. In addition, the lobbying position derived from the rational loyalty construct points at a need for a strong civil society.

Two considerations seem to be relevant here. The first is the openness of the recipient element. In its limit, an open recipient element protects disclosure of information about organizational practices to just anybody by whatever means possible. However, problems raised by the economics of information in the theory of asymmetry of information, might force lobbying positions to be moderated. At the centre of its analysis is the problem of imperfect information (Sandmo 1999; Stiglitz 2000). Relevant to the issue of whistleblowing, and especially with regard to the recipient element of a whistleblowing policy, are the following three questions: 1) is the information accurate? 2) is the receiver able to interpret the information?

3) what can the receiver do with it? At first sight, this would favour the restriction of the recipient element to recipients able to interpret the information and to do something with it; it would favour the OSR-network position over the one coming from the OSR-stakeholder construct. Indeed, if the whistleblower's intention is to correct a wrongdoing, it is more adequate to disclose to an organization who has the power to correct the wrongdoing rather than disclose to the media who is only interested in reporting about the wrongdoing, not in correcting it. However, the possibility to disclose to the media as a deterrent to neglecting employee concerns and allegations seems a strong argument to break open the recipient element. Here, combining the OSR-stakeholder position of openness with the accountability driven tiered approach to the recipient element is a way of taking problems of asymmetry of information serious while aiming at more ethical whistleblowing policies. Indeed, the UK PIDA model would be a great example of this, were it not that the extra criteria put on whistleblowers when taking the final recipient tier, and the fact that cases in court are not on public record, make it lapse towards the OSR-network construct. Thus, lobbying for a tiered recipient element is feasible, as such an approach is driven by the accountability construct, but the ethical risk is only avoided when: 1) its final tier is open; 2) there are no extra criteria put on the whistleblower or the information when disclosing to open-tier recipients; 3) cases in court are on public record.

The second relevant consideration regards the huge role civil society needs to play in whistleblowing policies for them to be more ethical. First, civil society organizations can be a perfect midway for the just mentioned consideration, as both addressing the problems of asymmetry of information and providing an openness to the recipient element. NGOs or labour unions can generate the know-how to interpret whistleblowing information. They can put pressure on the organization in question to correct possible malpractice, because they have to power and the freedom to alert the media. Moreover, they can offer independent advice to potential whistleblowers.[8]

NGOs avoid the conflict between organization and society to be contained within the limits of a proxy of society – which is the case when the whistleblowing recipient is restricted to government agencies. NGOs are not proxies but rather 'parcels' of society, constituted by those who care for a particular issue (Fowler 2000; Edwards and Sen 2000; Vandekerckhove 2003). Also, civil society organizations are already playing a major role in 'societal verification' of governmental compliance with international treaties (Dieseroth 2000). Of course, the strength of civil society – NGOs and also media – strongly depends on its independence from the other two societal actors – business and government (Fowler 2000; Edwards and Sen 2000; Vandekerckhove 2003).

Therefore, it seems to me that whereas the early literature on whistleblowing saw a dilemma of loyalties, some 30 years later, solving that dilemma through

---

[8]   The London based NGO Public Concern at Work is to be considered exemplary in this regard.

whistleblowing policies amounts to an ethical paradox (see Figure 5.3). The paradox lies in the fact that openness of the recipient element requires as well as makes a strong civil society.

In order to avoid the ethical risk of institutionalizing the individual rather than protecting and supporting individuality, whistleblowing policies need to apply a broad scope to their actor, subject and recipient elements. However, to make such a broad policy effective – given problems of asymmetry of information – one needs to assume an organizational and societal 'culture' characterized by the absence of abuse of power in highly independent and transparent organizations. However, to assume such a 'culture' annuls the need for whistleblowing.

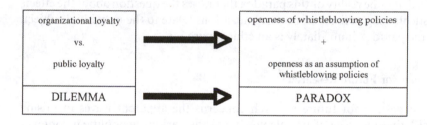

Figure 5.3 Whistleblowing 1970–2000 – from dilemma to paradox

In the Philippines, there are reports about whistleblowing cases which show a 'trial by media' rather than a correction of wrongdoing and protection of individuality (TI 2004). Both whistleblower and alleged wrongdoers are portrayed on television as criminals, even before any investigation took place. Moreover, both the alleged wrongdoers and whistleblowers were sacked. Another example, although less extreme regards the secrecy of court ruling on the UK PIDA. Whistleblowing policies cannot achieve openness, they require openness. At a recent conference, William De Maria has argued that the question about what core infrastructural prerequisites are necessary before enacting whistleblowing statutes is an urgent one. Commenting on the 2001 International Anti-Corruption Conference in Prague, De Maria notes that:

> there was a dangerous sub-text to the whistleblower sales pitch. Why dangerous? Because the messages went out without health warnings on them. Hearing these non-conditional promos were delegates from one-party dictatorships (eg. Singapore), transitional economies (eg. Bulgaria and Slovenia) wobbling out of rights-hating communist rule, parliamentary democracies where dissent is a life threatening condition (eg. Turkey, Zimbabwe) and countries struggling out of yesterdays filled with genocidal horror (eg. Rwanda) (De Maria 2002, 4).

The point De Maria seems to be trying to make is that whistleblowing policies do not create but rather need democracy. I see this paradox at play also in the 'democratic' societies.

If open whistleblowing policies would be common practice in open societies, this would imply that whistleblowing had become an institution without ethical risk. Actually, this would resemble most the SI-O movement of the integrity construct, where people make discernment and speak up on their discernment and act on it. There is no fear for doing so because there is no retaliation against doing so. And, speaking up is genuinely raising concern rather than making allegations. Those presumptions would make legislation redundant. However, since that is not reality – and the neglect of the integrity construct only confirms it is not – explicit policies are necessary, increasing the ethical risk with every specification.

Indeed, it is the reality of this paradox that raises the question about the effects of whistleblowing policies on how organizations relate to the individual subject. Hence the paradox immediately is an ethical paradox.

Suggestions for Future Research

A first suggestion for future research concerns the apparent waves in raising and legislating the issue of whistleblowing at the various geopolitical contexts. The issue was first raised in the US early 1970s and at the end of the 1970s whistleblowing legislations began to appear, with a wave of US state legislations being enacted in the 1980s. A second wave is to be situated from 1993–1995, with legislation being enacted in some Australian states (South Australia, ACT, Queensland, and New South Wales), and discussions starting in New Zealand, the Australian federal level, the UK, and South Africa. Finally, a third wave can be discerned around the turning of the century, with the UK PIDA coming into force in 1999, the South African PDA in 2000, New Zealand PDA in 2000, legislation in other Australian states (Victoria 2001, Tasmania 2002, Western Australia 2003), the Amsterdam policy in 2001 and further evolutions in the Netherlands, Belgium, Germany, Switzerland, Japan, India, Canada and at the OECD level.

However, besides the patterns and the stabilizing legitimation constructs already discussed, the legitimation lines nor the actor, subject and recipient elements show any particular characteristics for each wave. Therefore, future research should be aimed at the exactness of those apparent waves and explanations for their occurrence.

A second suggestion for further research concerns the need to further develop adequate lobbying positions regarding the recipient element. In the previous section I mentioned problems raised by the economics of information and more precisely to asymmetries of information. A framework for analysing case studies, developed from economics of information, could generate adequate knowledge about the effectiveness of a particular recipient constellation and prerequisites of recipient constellations leading to more ethical whistleblowing policies.

A third suggestion for further research concerns the actual and potential role of civil society organizations in whistleblowing policies. Whilst I have argued that these organizations can play a significant role in reducing the ethical risk of whistleblowing policies, they entail a risk themselves. For NGOs are organizations too, hence are also vulnerable to goal displacement and organizational malpractice (Fowler 2000; Vandekerckhove 2003; 2004). Therefore, there is a need to research specific organizational risks of NGOs for goal displacement, for maintaining independency, and for the equilibrium between advocacy and service delivery.

A fourth suggestion for further research builds on the limitations of this research as mentioned in Chapter 1. This research has identified the tendencies at global level in legitimating whistleblowing by looking at whistleblowing policies laid down in legislation. As suggested there, research could be set up with a limited geo-political context or a limited number of organizations, looking for individual and organizational attitudes towards whistleblowing. Data collected through in-depth interviews could be compared with the tendencies identified in this research, which give insight into tendencies of how internal organizational whistleblowing procedures are implemented.

This might be combined with a fifth suggestion for further research, also drawn from the limitations of this research as mentioned. There, a quantitative approach was suggested, counting the number of organizations who have installed internal whistleblowing procedures since the emerging of the concept in the early 1970s. A research in this vein was carried out by Near and Dworkin (1998) measuring the extent to which internal whistleblowing policies were set up under impulse of the US Organizational Sentencing Guidelines. Given the international surge of whistleblowing legislation, it would be interesting to verify the tendencies identified in this qualitative research through such a quantitative approach.

References

Ackoff, R. (1974), *Redesigning the Future* (New York: Wiley).

Amnesty International (1998), *Human Rights Principles for Companies* (Ontario: Amnesty International).

Anderson, R.M., Perrucci, R., Schendel, D.E. and Trachtman, L.E. (1980), *Divided Loyalties: Whistleblowing at BART* (West Lafayette: Purdue University Press).

Andriof, J. and Waddock, S. (2002), 'Unfolding Stakeholder Engagement', in J. Andriof, S. Waddock, B. Husted and S.S. Rahman (eds), *Unfolding Stakeholder Thinking*, Vol. 1, *Theory, Responsibility and Engagement* (Sheffield: Greenleaf Publishing), 19–42.

Andriof, J., Waddock, S., Husted, B. and Rahman, S.S. (2002), 'Introduction', in J. Andriof, S. Waddock, B. Husted and S.S. Rahman (eds), *Unfolding Stakeholder Thinking*, Vol. 1, *Theory, Responsibility and Engagement* (Sheffield: Greenleaf Publishing), 9–16.

Anechiarico, F. and Jacobs, J.B. (1996), *the Pursuit of Absolute Integrity. How Corruption Control Makes Government Ineffective* (Chicago: University of Chicago Press).

Apostel, L. and Walry, J. (1997), *Hopeloos gelukkig. Leven in de postmoderne tijd* (Amsterdam: Meulenhoff).

Arnold, D.F. and Ponemon, L.A. (1991), 'Internal Auditors Perceptions of Whistle-blowing and the Influence of Moral Reasoning. An Experiment', *Auditing* 10:2, 1–15.

Asahi Shimbun (2004), 'A Toothless Protections Bill won't Change Society', *the Asahi Shimbun* 17 May 2004, <http://admin.corisweb.org/index.php?fuse action=news.view&id=113737&src=newdcn> (cited November 2004).

Asche, A. (2002), *Report on Whistleblowers Legislation* (Northern Territory Law Reform Committee Report 26), <http://www.nt.gov.au/justice/docs/lawmake/whistleblowers.pdf> (cited June 2004).

Atkins, P.S. (2003), 'The Sarbanes-Oxley Act of 2002: Goals, Content, and Status of Implementation' (Speech at the International Financial Law Review, March 25, 2003).

Axinn, S. (1997), 'Loyalty', in P.H. Werhane, and R.E. Freeman (eds), *Encyclopedic Dictionary of Business Ethics* (Oxford: Blackwell Publishers), 388–90.

Bailey, J.J. (1997), 'Individual Scapetribing and Responsibility Ascriptions', *Journal of Business Ethics* 16:1, 47–53.

Barker, J.R. and Cheney, G. (1994), 'The Concept and Practices of Discipline in Contemporary Organizational Life', *Communication Monographs* 61:1, 19–43.

Barnett, T. (1992), 'A Preliminary Investigation of the Relationship between Selected Organizational Characteristics and External Whistleblowing by Employees', *Journal of Business Ethics* 11:12, 949–59.

Barnett, T., Cochran, D.S. and Taylor, G.S. (1990), 'The Relationship between Internal Dissent Policies and Employee Whistleblowing: An Exploratory Study' (conference paper – 5th Annual Meeting of the Management, San Francisco).

Barnett, T., Cochran, D.S. and Taylor, G.S. (1993), 'The Internal Disclosure Policies of Private-sector Employers. An Initial Look at their Relationship to Employee Whistleblowing', *Journal of Business Ethics* 12:2, 127–36.

Bendell, J., Concannon, T., Shah, R., Visser, W. and Young, M. (2004), *Lifeworth Annual Review of Corporate Responsibility 2003* (London/Sheffield/Bath: Lifeworth/Greenleaf Publishing/New Academy of Business).

Benson, J.A. and Ross, D.L. (1998), 'Sundstrand: A Case Study in Transformation of Cultural Ethics', *Journal of Business Ethics* 17:14, 1517–27.

Berger, P.L., Berger, B. and Kellner, H. (1973), *the Homeless Mind. Modernization and Consciousness* (Harmondsworth: Penguin Books).

Bessire, D. (2003), 'Exploring Discourses on Transparency' (conference paper – Conference on Corporate Social Responsibility, London Metropolitan University, September 2003).

BLF (2004), 'The BLF in Latin America and the Caribbean', *Corporate Social Responsibility Forum,* <http://www.csrforum.org/csr/csrwebassist.nsf/content/f1c2b3c4.html> (cited March 2004).

Boeser, K. (1977), 'Die Folter das ist die Vernunft. Ein Gespräch mit Michel Foucault', *Literaturmagazin* 8, 60–68.

Bogue, R. (1993), *Deleuze and Guattari* (London: Routledge).

Bok, S. (1980), 'Whistle-Blowing and Professional Responsibilities', in *New York University Education Quarterly* XI, 2–10. [Reprinted in J.C. Callahan (ed.) (1988), *Ethical Issues in Professional Life* (New York: Oxford University Press), 331–40.]

Boltanski, L. and Chiapello, E (1999), *Le nouvel esprit du capitalisme* (Paris: Gallimard).

Bond, R (2005), 'Whistleblowing – a Dutiful Employee or An Informer?', *Current Legal Developments* (August), <http://www.faegre.co.uk/articles/article_1641.aspx> (cited October 2005).

Bordo, M.D. (2002), 'Globalization in Historical Perspective', *Business Economics* (January), 20–29.

Borrie, G. (1996), 'Business Ethics and Accountability', in *Four Windows on Whistleblowing* (London: Public Concern at Work), 1–23.

Bouckaert, L. (2004), 'Politieke filosofie versus bedrijfsethiek. Twee manieren om naar globalisering te kijken', *Ethiek & Maatschappij* 7:2, 66–77.

Bovens, M. (1990), *Verantwoordelijkheid en organisatie. Beschouwingen over aansprakelijkheid, institutioneel burgerschap en ambtelijke ongehoorzaamheid* (Zwolle: Tjeenk Willink).

Bowers, J., Mitchell, J. and Lewis, J. (1999), *Whistleblowing: The New Law* (London: Sweet and Maxwell).

Bowie, N.E. and Duska, R.F. (1990), *Business Ethics* (New Jersey: Prentice Hall).

Brochier, J.J. (1969), 'Michel Foucault explique son dernier livre (entretien)', *Magazine littéraire* 28, 25.

BSR (2003), 'Executive summary CSR leaders meeting September 4–5 2003' (Rüschlikon, Swiss Re Centre for Global Dialogue)<http://www.bsr.org/BSRServices/CSR_Leaders_Meeting-ExecSummary.pdf.> (cited March 2004).

Buchholz, R.A. and Rosenthal, S.B. (2002), 'Technology and Business: Rethinking the Moral Dilemma', *Journal of Business Ethics* 41:1–2, 45–50.

Bureau Integriteit (BI) (2002a), *Gedragslijn vermoeden van misstanden gemeente Amsterdam* (Amsterdam: Bureau Integriteit).

——— (2002b), *Bureau Integriteit – Plan van aanpak 2002–2003* (Amsterdam: Bureau Integriteit).

——— (2002c), *Algemene toelichting gedragslijn vermoeden van misstanden* (Amsterdam: Bureau Integriteit).

——— (2003), *Bureau Integriteit – Plan van aanpak 2003–2004* (Amsterdam: Bureau Integriteit).

Burke, R.J. and Cooper, C.L. (eds) (2000), *the Organisation in Crisis* (Oxford: Blackwell).

Bush, G.W. (2002a), 'President Outlines Plan to Improve Corporate Responsibility' (Washington, DC: Office of the Press Secretary, 7 March 2002) [speech given at Malcolm Baldrige National Quality Award Ceremony, Washington, DC].

——— (2002b), 'Restoring Trust in Corporate America' [speech on Wall Street, 9 July 2002].

Callahan, E.S. and Dworkin, T.M. (1994), 'Who Blows the Whistle to the Media, and Why: Organizational Characteristics of Media Whistleblowers', *American Business Law Journal* 32:2, 151–84.

——— (2000), 'The State of State Whistleblower Protection', *American Business Law Journal* 38:1, 99–175.

Callahan, E.S., Dworkin, T.M., Fort, T.L. and Schipani, C.A. (2002), 'Integrating Trends in Whistleblowing and Corporate Governance: Promoting Organizational Effectiveness, Societal Responsibility, and Employee Empowerment', *American Business Law Journal* 40:1, 177–215.

Calton, J.M. and Lad, L.J. (1995), 'Social Contracting as a Trust-building Process of Network Governance', *Business Ethics Quarterly* 5:2, 275–96.

Camerer, L. (1999), 'Whistle-blowing: An effective anti-corruption tool?', *Nedbank ISS Crime Index* 3:3.

——— (2001), 'Protecting Whistle Blowers in South Africa: The Protected Disclosures Act, no. 26 of 2000', *ISS Occasional Paper* 47–2001 (Pretoria: ISS).

Campbell, T. (2002), 'Workplace Free Speech as a Human Right', *CAPPE Working Papers* 2002/10 (Melbourne/Canberra: Centre for Applied Philosophy and Public Ethics).

Carson, T.L. (1993), 'Does the Stakeholder Theory Constitute a New Kind of Theory of Social Responsibility?', *Business Ethics Quarterly* 3:2, 171–76.

Carter, S.L. (1997), *Integrity* (New York: HarperPerennial).

Castells, M (1996), *the Information Age. Economy, Society and Culture*, Vol. 1, *the Rise of the Network Society* (Oxford: Blackwell).

Chalk, R. and von Hippel, F. (1979), 'Due Process for the Bearers of Ill Tidings: Dealing with Technical Dissent in the Organization', *Technical Review* 81, 49–55.

Chambers, A. (1995), 'Whistleblowing and the Internal Auditor', *Business Ethics: A European Review* 4:4, 192–98.

Chan, A. (2000), 'Redirecting Critique in Postmodern Organization Studies: The Perspective of Foucault', *Organization Studies* 21:6, 1059–75.

Chiasson, M., Johnson, H.G. and Byington, J.R. (1995), 'Blowing the Whistle: Accountants in Industry', *CPA Journal*, February, 24–27.

Christian Aid (2004), *Behind the Mask. The Real Face of Corporate Social Responsibility* (London: Christian Aid).

Clegg, S.R. (1989), 'Radical Revisions: Power, Discipline and Organizations', *Organization Studies* 10:1, 97–115.

Clifton, J., Comin, F. and Fuentes, D.D. (2003), *Privatisation in the European Union. Public Enterprises and Integration* (Dordrecht: Kluwer Academic).

Cohen, J. (2003), 'State of the Union: NGO-business Partnership Stakeholders', in J. Andriof, S. Waddock, B. Husted and S.S. Rahman (eds), *Unfolding Stakeholder Thinking*, Vol. 2, *Relationships, Communication, Reporting and Performance* (Sheffield: Greenleaf Publishing), 106–27.

Commers, M.S.R. (1991), *Het vrije denken. Het ongelijk van een humanisme* (Brussels: VUBPRESS).

—— (1995), *Het semantiekbegrip bij Niklas Luhmann – syllabustekst* (Ghent: Universiteit Ghent).

Commonwealth of Australia (2002), *Corporate Disclosure: Strengthening the Financial Reporting Framework* (Canberra: Commonwealth of Australia).

Conway, J.H. (1977), 'Protecting the Private Sector at Will Employee who "Blows the Whistle": A Cause of Action Based upon Determinants of Public Policy', *Wisconsin Law Review* 77:3, 777–812.

Cornelli, P. (2002), *La protection des whistleblowers: un "nouvel" instrument de lutte contre la corruption* (Bern: Transparency Switzerland).

Corvino, J. (2002), 'Loyalty in Business?', *Journal of Business Ethics* 41:1–2, 179–185.

Costello, P. (2003). *CLERP9 Draft Bill – Introduction* (Parkes: Department of the Treasury).

Courtemanche, G. (1988), 'The Ethics of Whistle Blowing', *Internal Auditor* (February), 36–41.

Cragg, W. (2000), ' Human Rights and Business Ethics: Fashioning a New Social Contract', *Journal of Business Ethics* 27:1–2, 205–14.

Crane, A. and Livesey, S. (2003), 'Are You Talking to Me? Stakeholder Communication and the Risks and Rewards of Dialogue', in J. Andriof, S. Waddock, B. Husted and S.S. Rahman (eds), *Unfolding Stakeholder Thinking*, Vol. 2, *Relationships, Communication, Reporting and Performance* (Sheffield: Greenleaf Publishing), 39–52.

Crowther, D. (2004). 'Limited Liability or Limited Responsibility?', in D. Crowther and L. Rayman-Bacchus (eds), *Perspectives on Corporate Social Responsibility* (Aldershot: Ashgate Publishing), 42–58.

Crowther, D. and Rayman-Bacchus, L. (2004), 'Introduction', in D. Crowther and L. Rayman-Bacchus (eds) *Perspectives on Corporate Social Responsibility* (Aldershot: Ashgate Publishing), 1–17.

Dahrendorf, R. (1998), 'A Precarious Balance: Economic Opportunity, Civil Society and Political Liberty', in A. Etzioni (ed.), *the Essential Communitarian Reader* (Oxford: Rowman and Littlefield), 73–94.

Dalton, D.R., Metzger, M.B. and Hill, J.W. (1999), 'The "New" US Sentencing Commission Guidelines: A Wake-up Call for Corporate America', in T. Donaldson and P.H. Werhane (eds), *Ethical Issues in Business Ethics: A Philosophical Approach* (Englewood Cliff: Prentice Hall), 271–77.

Davis, M. (2002), *Profession, Code and Ethics* (Aldershot: Ashgate Publishing).

De George, R.T. (1980), 'Ethical Responsibilities of Engineers in Large Organizations' (paper presented at the National Conference on Engineering Ethics).

——— (1993), *Competing with Integrity in International Business* (Oxford: Oxford University Press).

De Maria, W. (1992), 'Queensland Whistleblowing. Sterilizing the Lone Crusader', *Australian Journal of Social Issues* 27:4, 248–61.

——— (1994), *Unshielding the Shadow Culture* (Queensland: University of Queensland).

——— (1999), *Deadly Disclosures: Whistleblowing and the Ethical Meltdown of Australia* (Kent Town: Wakefield Press).

——— (2002), 'Common Law – Common Mistakes. The Dismal Failure of Whistleblower Laws in Australia, New Zealand, South Africa, Ireland and the United Kingdom' (paper presented to the International Whistleblowers Conference, University of Indiana, April 2002).

Deleuze, G. and Parnet, C. (1991), *Dialogen* (Kok Agora) [translated from *Dialogues* (Paris: Flammarion 1977) by M. Scheepers].

Deloitte (2004), 'Tip-offs Anonymous', <http://www.deloitte.com/dtt/article/ 0,2297,sid%253D5628%2526cid%253D12609,00.html> (cited May 2004).

Dentchev, N. (2004), 'To What Extent Is Business and Society Literature Idealistic?' (Working Paper 2004/245 – Faculty of Economy and Business Administration) (Ghent: Ghent University).

Desio, P. (s.d.), *An Overview of the Organizational Guidelines* (Washington, DC: United States Sentencing Commission).

Devine, T. (1997), *the Whistleblower's Survival Guide* (Washington, DC: Government Accountability Project).

———— (2004a), 'Whistleblowing in the United States: The Gap between Vision and Lessons Learned', in R. Calland and G. Dehn (eds), *Whistleblowing around the World. Law, Culture and Practice* (Cape Town, London: ODAC, PCAW), 74–100.

———— (2004b), 'The USA: Government Accountability Project', in R. Calland and G. Dehn (eds), *Whistleblowing around the World. Law, Culture and Practice* (Cape Town, London: ODAC, PCAW), 158–68.

Dewael, P. (1999), *Regeringsverklaring Vlaamse Regering – 13 juli 1999* (Brussel: Vlaamse Regering).

Dieseroth, D. (2000), 'Societal Verification: Wave of the Future?', in T. Findlay (ed.) *Verification Yearbook 2000* (London: VERTIC), 265–80.

Dimba, M., Stober, L. and Thomsom, B. (2004), 'The South African Experience', in R. Calland and G. Dehn (eds), *Whistleblowing around the World. Law, Culture and Practice* (Cape Town, London: ODAC, PCAW), 143–52.

Donaldson, T. and Dunfee, T. (1995), 'Integrative Social Contracts Theory: A Communitarian Conception of Economic Ethics', *Economics and Philosophy* 11 (April), 85–112.

———— (1999), *Ties that Bind: A Social Contracts Approach to Business Ethics* (Cambridge MA: Harvard Business School Press).

Donaldson, T. and Preston, L.E. (1995), 'The Stakeholder Theory of the Corporation: Concepts, Evidence and Implications', *Academy of Management Review* 20:1, 65–91.

Doyal, L. and Cannell, H. (1993), 'Whistle Blowing. The Ethics of Revealing Professional Incompetence within Dentistry', *British Dental Journal* 174:3, 95–101.

Dozier, J.B. and Miceli, M.P. (1985), 'Potential Predictors of Whistle-blowing – a Pro-social Behavior Perspective', *Academy of Management Review* 10:4, 823–836.

Driscoll, D., Hoffman, W.M. and Murphy, J.E. (1999), 'Business Ethics and Compliance: What Management Is Doing and Why', *Business and Society Review* 99, 35–51.

Du Gay, P. (1996), *Consumption and Identity at Work* (London: Sage).

Duska, R.F. (1990), 'Whistleblowing and Employee Loyalty', in J.R. Desjardins and J.J. McCall (eds), *Contemporary Issues in Business Ethics* (Belmont CA: Wadsworth), 142–47.

———— (1997), 'Whistleblowing', in P.H. Werhane, and R.E. Freeman (eds), *Encyclopedic Dictionary of Business Ethics* (Oxford: Blackwell Publishers), 654–56.

Dworkin, T.M. and Callahan, E.S. (1991), 'Internal Whistleblowing. Protecting the Interests of the Employee, the Organization, and Society', *American Business Law Journal* 29:2, 265–308.

—— (1998), 'Buying Silence', *American Business Law Journal* 36:1, 151–91.

—— and Near, J.P. (1987), 'Whistleblowing Statutes. Are They Working?', *American Business Law Journal* 25:2, 241–64.

—— (1997), 'A Better Statutory Approach to Whistle-blowing', *Business Ethics Quarterly* 7:1, 1–16.

Edwards, M. and Sen, G. (2000), 'NGOs, Social Change and the Transformation of Human Relationships: A 21st Century Civic Agenda', *Third World Quarterly* 21:4, 605–16.

Elliston, F.A, Keenan, J., Lockhart, P. and van Schaick, J. (1985), *Whistleblowing Research: Methodological and Moral Issues* (New York: Praeger).

Elliston, F.A. (1982a), 'Civil-disobedience and Whistleblowing – a Comparative Appraisal of Two Forms of Dissent', *Journal of Business Ethics* 1:1, 23–28.

—— (1982b), 'Anonymity and Whistleblowing', *Journal of Business Ethics* 1:3, 167–77.

Emerson, T.I. (1970), *the System of Freedom of Expression* (New York: Vintage Books).

Ethics Officer Association (EOA) (2001), 'Mission, Vision, and Values', <http://www.eoa.org> (cited May 2004).

Etzioni, A. (1998), 'Introduction. A matter of balance, rights and responsibilities', in A. Etzioni (ed.), *the Essential Communitarian Reader* (Lanham: Rowman and Littlefield Publishers), ix–xxiv.

European Community (EC) (2000), *Reforming the Commission a White Paper – Part II* (COM(2000)200final) (Brussels: Commission of the European Communities).

—— (2002), *Corporate Social Responsibility. A Business Contribution to Sustainable Development* (Brussels: European Commission DG Employment and Social Affairs).

—— (2003), *Communication from the Commission to the Council, the European Parliament and the European Economic and Social Committee on a comprehensive EU Policy against corruption* (COM(2003)317final) (Brussels: Commission of the European Communities).

European Parliament (EP) (2002), *Background briefing document on combating fraud and corruption in the European Union* (Brussels: European Parliament – Committee on Budgetary Control).

Evan, W.M. and Freeman, R.E. (1988), 'A Stakeholder Theory of the Modern Corporation: Kantian Capitalism', in T. Beauchamp and N. Bowie (eds), *Ethical Theory and Business* (Englewood Cliffs: Prentice Hall), 75–93.

Eversheds (2005), 'Whistleblower Hotlines Ruled Unlawful', *Briefing* (August), <http://www.acca.com/chapters/program/sandiego/whistlebrief.pdf> (cited October 2005).

Feliu, A.G. (1991), 'Legal-rights of Whistleblowing Professionals', *Abstracts of Papers of the American Chemical Society* 202:2, 11.

Finn, P. (1991), 'Integrity in Government' (Interim research report, Australian National University).

Fitzgerald, A.E. (1972), *the High Priests of Waste* (New York: Norton).

FNV (2000), *Meldlijn Klokkenluiders. Eindrapportage* (Amsterdam: FNV).

Foley, S. (2004), '27 miljoen dollar voor klokkenluider in Pfizers marketing-schandaal', *De Morgen* 17 May 2004, 9.

Forrester, V. (1996), *L'horreur économique* (Paris: Fayard).

Foucault, M. (1966), *Les mots et les choses* (Paris: Gallimard).

——— (1975), *Surveiller et punir* (Paris : Gallimard).

——— (1976), *La volonté de savoir* (Paris : Gallimard).

——— (1995), *Breekbare vrijheid: de politieke ethiek van de zorg om zichzelf* (Amsterdam: De Balie) [translated from *Le souci de soi-même* (Krisis/Parrèsia), by Laurens ten Kate].

Fowler, A. (2000), 'NGO Futures – Beyond aid: NGDO Values and the Fourth Position', *Third World Quarterly* 21:4, 589–603.

Frader, J.E. (1992), 'Political and Interpersonal Aspects of Ethics Consultation', *Theoretical Medicine* 13:1, 31–44.

Freeman, R.E. (1984), *Strategic Management: A Stakeholder Approach* (Boston: Pitman).

——— (1994), 'The Politics of Stakeholder Theory: Some Future Directions', *Business Ethics Quarterly* 4:4, 409–30.

——— (1997), 'Stakeholder Theory', in P.H. Werhane and R.E. Freeman (eds), *Encyclopedic Dictionary of Business Ethics* (London: Blackwell), 602–606.

——— (1999), 'Divergent Stakeholder Theory', *Academy of Management Review* 24:2, 233–37.

Freeman, R.E. and Evan, W.M. (1990), 'Corporate Governance: A Stakeholder Interpretation', *Journal of Behavioral Economics* 19, 337–59.

Friedman, M. (1963), *Capitalism and Freedom* (Chicago: University of Chicago Press).

——— (1972), *An Economist's Protest* (Glen Ridge, NJ: Thomas Horton and Daughters).

Gallie, D., White, M., Cheng, Y. and Tomlinson, M. (1998), *Restructuring the Employment Relationship* (Oxford: Oxford University Press).

Gamble, J.G. Jr (2003), 'Interview with the Expert', <http://www.laborlawyers.com> (cited May 2004).

Gaudin, J.P. (2002), *Pourquoi la gouvernance?* (Paris: Presses de Sciences Po -La Bibliothèque du Citoyen).

Glassman, C.A. (2003), *SEC Implementation of Sarbanes-Oxley: The New Corporate Governance* (speech given before the National Economist Club, Washington, DC, 7 April 2003).

Glazer, M.P. and Glazer, P.M. (1986), 'Whistleblowing', *Psychology Today* 20:8, 36.

———— (1989), *the Whistleblowers: Exposing Corruption in Government and Industry* (New York: Basic Books).

Goodchild, P. (1996), *Deleuze and Guattari. An Introduction to the Politics of Desire* (London: Sage).

Goodpaster, K.E. (1991), 'Business Ethics and Stakeholder Analysis', *Business Ethics Quarterly* 1:1, 53–73.

Gordon, K. and Miyake, M. (2001), 'Business Approaches to Combat Bribery: A Study of Codes of Conduct', *Journal of Business Ethics* 34:3–4, 161–73.

Government of India (GOI) (2004), 'Government of India Resolution on Public Interest Disclosure and Protection of Informer – Public Notice and Press Release 17 May 2004' (New Delhi: Central Vigilance Commission).

Grant, C. (2002), 'Whistle Blowers: Saints of a Secular Culture', *Journal of Business Ethics* 39:4, 391–399.

Green, M. (2003), 'Accountability: Discourses and Representations in the Context of New Organizational Structures and Market Ideologies' (paper presented at the Conference on Corporate Social Responsibility, London Metropolitan University, September 2003).

Greider, W. (1997), *One World, Ready or Not. The Manic Logic of Global Capitalism* (London: Penguin Books).

Grisoni, D. (1976), 'Les jeux du pouvoir, entretien avec Michel Foucault', in D. Grisoni (ed.), *Politiques de la philosophie* (Paris: Éditions Grasset et Fasquelle).

Groeneweg, S. (2001), *Three Whistleblower Protection Models: A Comparative Analysis of Whistleblower Legislation in Australia, the United States and the United Kingdom* (Public Service Commission of Canada, Comparative Merit Systems Unit Research Directorate).

Guéhenno, J.M. (1999), *L'avenir de la liberté* (Paris: Flammarion).

Gunsalus, C.K. (1998), 'Preventing the Need for Whistleblowing: Practical Advice for University Administrators', *Science and Engineering Ethics* 4:1, 75–94.

Hamilton, P. (1985), 'Introduction', in B. Smart (ed.), *Michel Foucault* (London: Ellis Horwood and Tavistock), 7–9.

Hansard (2002a), 'Reference: Public Interest Disclosure Bill 2001 [2002]' *Official Committee Hansard, Finance and Public Administration Committee,* Thursday, 16 May 2002 (Canberra: Senate).

———— (2002b), 'Public Interest Disclosure (Protection of Whistleblowers) Bill 2002 – First and Second Reading' *Official Hansard, Commonwealth Parliamentary Debates*, 16, 11 December 2002 (Canberra: Senate), 7751–53.

Hardt, M. and Negri, A. (2001), *Empire* (London: Harvard University Press).

Hartman, E.M. (1996), *Organizational Ethics and the Good Life (*Oxford: Oxford University Press).

Hartmann, D.P. (1971), 'Whistle Blowing', *Computer* 4:4, 34&.

Hill, C.W.L. and Jones, T.M. (1992), 'Stakeholder-agency Theory', *Journal of Management Studies* 29:2, 131–54.

Hipel, K., Yin, X. and Kilgour, D.M. (1995), 'Can a Costly Reporting System Make Environmental Enforcement More Efficient?', *Stochastic Hydrology and Hydraulics* 9:2, 151–70.

Hirschman, A.O. (1970), *Exit, Voice and Loyalty. Responses to Decline in Firms, Organisations and States* (Cambridge, MA: Harvard University Press).

Holemans, D. (2002), 'Voorstel van decreet betreffende de bescherming van ambtenaren die melding maken van onregelmatigheden of misbruiken binnen hun dienst (klokkenluiders)' (Anderlecht: persdienst Agalev, press release 27 December 2002).

Holemans, D., Keulen, M., Peeters, L. and De Cock, D. (2003), 'Voorstel van resolutie betreffende de bescherming van personeelsleden van Vlaamse overheidsdiensten die melding maken van onregelmatigheden of misbruiken binnen deze diensten (klokkenluiders)' (Brussels: Vlaams Parlement – stuk 1659 (2002–2003)/1).

Hooks, K.L., Kaplan, S.E. and Schultz, J.J. (1994), 'Enhancing Communication to Assist in Fraud Prevention and Detection', *Auditing* 13:2, 86–117.

Hunt, G. (ed.) (1994), *Whistleblowing in the Health Service. Accountability, Law and Professional Practice* (Sevenoaks, Kent: Edward Arnold).

Isbell, D.B. (1974), 'Overview of Accountants' Duties and Liabilities under Federal Securities Laws and a Closer Look at Whistle-blowing', *Ohio State Law Journal* 35:2, 261–79.

Jensen, J.V. (1987), 'Ethical Tension Points in Whistleblowing', *Journal of Business Ethics* 6:4, 321–28.

Jeurissen, R. (1997), 'Geen organisatie zonder loyaliteit', *Filosofie & Praktijk* 18:4, 169–82.

Johnson, R.A. and Kraft, M.E. (1990), 'Bureaucratic Whistleblowing and Policy Change', *Western Political Quarterly* 43:4, 849–74.

Johnson-Cramer, M.E., Berman, S.L. and Post, J.E. (2003), 'Re-examining the Concept of Stakeholder-management', in J. Andriof, S. Waddock, B. Husted and S.S. Rahman (eds), *Unfolding Stakeholder Thinking*, Vol. 2, *Relationships, Communication, Reporting and Performance* (Sheffield: Greenleaf Publishing), 145–61.

Jones, T.M. and Wicks, A.C. (1999), 'Convergent Stakeholder Theory', *Academy of Management Review* 24:2, 206–21.

Jubb, P.B. (1999), 'Whistleblowing: A Restrictive Definition and Interpretation', *Journal of Business Ethics* 21:1, 77–94.

Kaler, J. (2002), 'Responsibility, Accountability and Governance', *Business Ethics: A European Review* 11:4, 327–34.

Kaptein, M. (2002), 'Guidelines for the Development of An Ethics Safety Net', *Journal of Business Ethics* 41:3, 217–34.

——— and Wempe, J. (1998), 'Twelve Gordian Knots when Developing An Organizational Code of Ethics', *Journal of Business Ethics* 17:8, 853–69.

Keenan, J.P. (1983), 'A New Perspective on Whistleblowing: Theories and Hypotheses', conference paper (New York: New York State Sociological Association).

——— (1990), 'Upper-level Managers and Whistleblowing: Determinants of Perceptions of Company Encouragement and Information about where to Blow the Whistle', *Journal of Business and Psychology* 5:2, 223–35.

——— (1995), 'Whistleblowing and the First-level Manager: Determinants of Feeling Obliged to Blow the Whistle', *Journal of Social Behavior and Personality* 10:3, 571–84.

Kelly, M. (2001), *the Divine Right of Capital. Dethroning the Corporate Aristocracy* (San Francisco: Berret-Koehler).

——— (2002), 'The Next Step for Csr: Economic Democracy', *Business Ethics Magazine*, <http://www.business-ethics.com/NextStepforCSR.htm> (cited March 2004).

Kerr, C. (1964), *Labor and Management in Industrial Society* (Garden City: Anchor Books).

King, M.E. (2002), *Executive Summary of the King Report 2002* (Parklands: Institute of Directors in Southern Africa).

Knöbl, W. (1999), 'Social Theory From a Sartrean Point of View. Alain Touraine's Theory of Modernity', *European Journal of Social Theory* 2:4, 403–27.

Kooiman, J. (1993), *Modern Governance* (London: Sage).

Koornhof, C. (1998), 'Accounting Information on Flexibility' (Pretoria: University of Pretoria) (Doctoral Thesis).

Lambrechts, M. (1980), 'De struktuur van de verdrukking. Een onderzoek naar de machtsanalyses van Michel Foucault en enkele besluiten voor het strafrecht' (Leuven: Universiteit Leuven) (Masters Thesis).

Lammers, C.J. (1994), *Organisaties vergelijkenderwijs* (Utrecht: Aula).

Lash, S. and Urry, J. (1987), *the End of Organized Capitalism* (Cambridge: Polity Press).

Law Commission (LC) (2001), *the Public Interest Disclosure and Protection of Informers – Report 179* (New Delhi: Law Commission of India).

Lawrence, P.R. (1958), *the Changing of Organizational Behavior Patterns, a Case Study of Decentralization* (Boston: Harvard Business School).

Leavitt, H.J. (1965), 'Applied Organizational Change in Industry', in J.G. March (ed.) *Handbook of Organizations* (Chicago: Rand McNally).

Leech, T.J. (2003), *Sarbanes-Oxley Sections 302 and 404. A White Paper Proposing Practical, Cost Effective Compliance Strategies* (Ontario: Carddecisions Inc.).

Leisinger, K.M. (2003), *Whistle Blowing und Corporate Reputation Management* (München, Merning: Rainer Hampp Verlag).

Lemmen, M.M.W. (1990), *Max Weber's Sociology of Religion. Its Method and Content in the Light of the Concept of Rationality* (Heerlen: Gooi en Sticht).

Levin, M. (2004), 'Update on the Sarbanes-Oxley Act – Complaint Mechanisms and Employee Whistleblowing Provisions', *Advisory*, <http://www.mintz.com> (cited May 2004).

Lewis, D. (2001), 'Whistleblowing at Work: on what Principles should Legislation be Based?', *Industrial Law Journal* 30:2, 169–93.

Liden, R.C., Wayne, S.J. and Kraimer, M.L. (2001), 'Managing Individual Performance in Work Groups', *Human Resource Management* 40:1, 63–72.

Loebbecke, J.K. and Willingham, J.J. (1988), 'Review of SEC Accounting and Auditing Enforcement Released', working paper [cited in Hooks et al. 1994].

Lovell, A. (2002), 'Moral Agency as Victim of the Vulnerability of Autonomy', *Business Ethics: A European Review* 11:1, 62–76.

Lübke, V. (2003), 'Den Chef ruhig verpfeifen', *Die Tageszeitung* 6 October 2003.

Luhmann, N. (1980), *Gesellschaftsstruktur und Semantik. Studien zur Wissenssoziologie der modernen Gesellschaft* (Frankfurt am Main: Suhrkamp).

—— (2000), *Organisation und Entscheidung* (Opladen, Wiesbaden: Westdeutscher Verlag).

MacIntyre, A. (1984), *After Virtue* (Notre Dame: University of Notre Dame).

Maesschalck, J., Biscop, S. and van Vynckt, V. (eds) (2002), *Naar een beter bestuur* (Gent: Academia Press).

Mason, R.O. and Mitroff, I.I. (1981), *Challenging Strategic Planning Assumptions* (New York: Wiley).

Massengill, D. and Petersen, D.J. (1989), 'Whistleblowing: Protected Activity or Not?', *Employee Relations Law Journal* 15:1, 49–56.

Mathews, M.C. (1987), 'Codes of Ethics: Organizational Behavior and Misbehavior', *Research in Corporate Social Performance and Policy* 9, 107–30.

Matten, D., Crane, A. and Chapple, W. (2003), 'Behind the Mask: Revealing the True Face of Corporate Citizenship', *Journal of Business Ethics* 45:1, 109–20.

Mbeki, T. (1999), *President Mbeki's opening address to parliament,* <http://www.polity.org.za/html/govdocs/speeches/1999/sp0625.html> (cited June 2004).

MBZK (1999), *Integriteit van het openbaar bestuur* (Den Haag: Ministerie van Binnenlandse Zaken en Koninkrijksrelaties).

McHoul, A. and Grace, W. (1995), *a Foucault Primer: Discourse, power and the subject* (Melbourne: Melbourne University Press).

Medawar, C. (1976), 'The Social Audit: A Political View', *Accounting, Organizations and Society* 1:4, 389–94.

Mellema, G. (2003), 'Responsibility, Taint, and Ethical Distance in Business Ethics', *Journal of Business Ethics* 47:2, 125–32.

Meyers, R.H. (1999), *Self-Governance and Cooperation* (Oxford: Oxford University Press).

Miceli, M.P. (1988), 'Individual and situational correlates of whistle-blowing', *Personnel Psychology* 41:2, 267–81.

────── and Near, J.P. (1984), 'The Relationships Among Beliefs, Organizational Position, and Whistle-blowing Status. A Discriminant Analysis', *Academy of Management Journal* 27:4, 687–705.

────── (1985), 'Characteristics of Organizational Climate and Perceived Wrongdoing Associated with Whistle-blowing Decisions', *Personnel Psychology* 38:3, 525–44.

────── (1989), 'The Incidence of Wrongdoing, Whistle-blowing, and Retaliation: Results of a Naturally Occurring Field Experiment', *Employee Responsibilities and Rights Journal* 2:2, 91–108.

────── (1991), 'Whistle-blowing as An Organizational Process', *Research in the Sociology of Organizations* 9, 139–200.

────── (1992), *Blowing the Whistle: The Organizational and Legal Implications for Companies and Employees* (New York: Lexington Books).

────── (2002), 'What Makes Whistle-blowers Effective? Three Field Studies', *Human Relations* 55:4, 455–479.

──────, Rehg, M., Near, J.P and Ryan, K.C. (1999), 'Can Laws Protect Whistle-blowers? Results of a Naturally Occurring Field Experiment', *Work and Occupations* 26:1, 129–51.

Miethe, T.D. (1999), *Whistleblowing at Work. Tough Choices in Exposing Fraud, Waste, and Abuse on the Job* (Boulder: Westview Press).

Miki, Y. (2004), 'The Position in Japan', in R. Calland and G. Dehn (eds), *Whistleblowing around the World. Law, Culture and Practice* (Cape Town, London: ODAC, PCAW), 153–56.

Mitchell, R.K., Agle, B.R. and Wood, D.J. (1997), 'Toward a Theory of Stakeholder Identification and Salience: Defining the Principle of who and What Really Counts', *Academy of Management Review* 22:4, 853–86.

Morioka, K. (2004), 'Japan: Public Interest Speak-up Advisers (PISA)', in R. Calland and G. Dehn (eds), *Whistleblowing around the World. Law, Culture and Practice* (Cape Town, London: ODAC, PCAW), 180–86.

Mortier, F. and Raes, K. (1992), *Een kwestie van Behoren* (Gent: Mys & Breesch).

Mowday, R., Steers, R. and Porter, L. (1979), 'The Measurement of Organizational Commitment', *Journal of Vocational Behavior* 14, 224–27.

Mraović, B. (2004), 'The Power of Networks: Organising Versus Organisation', in D. Crowther and L. Rayman-Bacchus (eds) *Perspectives on Corporate Social Responsibility* (Aldershot: Ashgate Publishing), 59–82.

Muhl, C.J. (2001), 'The Employment-at-will Doctrine: Three Major Exceptions', *Monthly Labor Review* 124:1, 3–11.

Murphy, D.E. (2002), 'The Federal Sentencing Guidelines for Organizations: A Decade of Promoting Compliance and Ethics', *Iowa Law Review* 87:2, 697–719.

Myers, A. (2004), 'Whistleblowing – the UK experience, in R. Calland and G. Dehn (eds), *Whistleblowing around the World. Law, Culture and Practice* (Cape Town, London: ODAC, PCAW), 101–18.

Nader, R., Petkas, P.J. and Blackwell, K. (eds) (1972), *Whistle Blowing: The Report of the Conference on Professional Responsibility* (New York: Grossman).

Near, J.P. (1989), 'Whistle-blowing: Encourage It', *Business Horizons* 32:1, 2–6.

———, Baucus, M.S. and Miceli, M.P. (1993a), 'The Relationship between Values and Practice. Organizational Climates for Wrongdoing', *Administration and Society* 25:2, 204–26.

——— and Dworkin, T.M. (1998), 'Responses to Legislative Changes: Corporate Whistleblowing Policies', *Journal of Business Ethics* 17:14, 1551–61.

——— and Jensen, T.C. (1983), 'The Whistleblowing Process – Retaliation and Perceived Effectiveness', *Work and Occupations* 10:1, 3–28.

——— and Miceli, M.P. (1985), 'Organizational Dissidence. The Case of Whistle-blowing', *Journal of Business Ethics* 4:1, 1–16.

——— (1987), 'Whistle-blowers in Organizations: Dissidents or Reformers?', *Research in Organizational Behavior* 9, 321–68.

——— (1995), 'Effective Whistle-blowing', *Academy of Management Review* 20, 679–708.

——— (1996), 'Whistle-blowing. Myth and Reality', *Journal of Management* 22:3, 507–526.

———, Dworkin, T.M. and Miceli, M.P. (1993b), 'Explaining the Whistle-blowing Process. Suggestions From Power Theory and Justice Theory', *Organization Science* 4:3, 392–411.

Nijhof, A., Cludts, S., Fisscher, O. and Laan, A. (2003), 'Measuring the Implementation of Codes of Conduct. An Assessment Method based on a Process Approach of the Responsible Organisation', *Journal of Business Ethics* 45:1, 65–78.

O'Connor, P. (2001), 'A Bird's Eye View. Resistance in Academia', *Irish Journal of Sociology* 10:2, 86–104.

Office of the Special Counsel (OSC) (1983), *Office of Special Counsel Annual Report* (Washington, DC: OSC).

O'Leary, T. (2002), *Foucault and the Art of Ethics* (London: Continuum).

Open Compliance and Ethics Group (OCEG) (2004), 'Comment on OECD Principles of Corporate Governance' – OECD submission, 5 February 2004 (New York: Open Compliance and Ethics Group), <http://www.oceg.org> (cited July 2004).

Open Democracy Advice Centre (ODAC) (2003), 'Blowing the Whistle. in Support of a New Culture of Openness in South Africa', <http://www.opendemocracy. org.za/documents/ODAC%20-%20PDA%20Issue%20Paper%20Response. htm> (cited June 2004).

——— (2004), 'Comments on Discussion Paper 107', <http://www.opendemocracy. org.za/documents/ODAC_COMMENTS_DISCUSSION_107.htm> (cited November 2004).

Organisation for Economic Co-operation and Development (OECD) (1998), *Principles for managing ethics in the public service – PUMA Policy Brief 4* (Paris: OECD).

――――― (2000a), *Whistleblowing to combat corruption – Report on a Meeting of Management and Trade Union Experts Held under the OCED Labour/Management Programme, PAC/AFF/LMP(2000)1* (Paris: OECD).

――――― (2000b), *the OECD Guidelines for Multinational Enterprises – Revision 2000* (Paris: OECD).

――――― (2000c), *Building Public Trust: Ethics Measures in the OECD Countries – PUMA Policy Brief 7* (Paris: OECD).

――――― (2003a), *Annual Report on the OECD Guidelines for Multinational Enterprises: 2003 Edition* (Paris: OECD).

――――― (2003b), *Recommendation of the Council on Guidelines for Managing Conflict of Interest in the Public Service* (Paris: OECD).

――――― (2004), *OECD Principles of Corporate Governance 2004* (Paris: OECD).

Orlin, M. (1973), 'Whistle-blowing', *Social Work* 18:5, 120–21.

Paine, L.S. (1994), 'Managing for organizational integrity', *Harvard Business Review* 72:2, 106–117.

Parker, R.A. (1988), 'Whistleblowing Legislation in the United States: A Preliminary Appraisal', *Parliamentary Affairs* 41:1, 149–58.

Parliamentary Joint Committee on Corporations and Financial Services (PJCCFS) (2004), *CLERP (Audit Reform and Corporate Disclosure) Bill 2003 – Part 1 Enforcement, executive Remuneration, Continuous Disclosure, Shareholder Participation and Related Matters* (Canberra: Parliament House).

Patton, P. (1994), 'Taylor and Foucauldian Power and Freedom', in B. Smart (ed.), *Michel Foucault: Critical Assessments* (London: Routledge), 352–70.

Perry, B. (2001), *Whistleblowers Protection Act 2001. Ombudsman's Guidelines* (Melbourne: The Ombudsman Victoria).

Perry, N. (1998), 'Indecent Exposures: Theorizing Whistleblowing', *Organization Studies* 19:2, 235–57.

Peters, C. and Branch, T. (1972), *Blowing the Whistle: Dissent in the Public Interest* (New York: Praeger).

Petrick, J.A. and Quinn, J.F. (1997), *Management Ethics. Integrity at Work* (London: Sage).

Ponemon, L.A. (1994), 'Whistle-blowing as An Internal Control Mechanism. Individual and Organizational Considerations', *Auditing* 13:2, 118–30.

Presthus, R. (1962), *the Organizational Society* (New York: Vintage Books).

Public Concern at Work (PCAW) (1997), *Public Concern at Work Annual Report 1997* (London: Public Concern at Work).

――――― (2003), *Two Years Back, Three Years Forward* (London: Public Concern at Work).

———— (2004). 'Briefing of 26 October from Public Concern at Work on the Prayer by Richard Shepherd MP', <http://www.pcaw.org.uk/policy_pub/hcbriefing. html> (cited November 2004).

Racic, D. (2002), 'Building a system of corporate governance and its implications for business ethics: The case of Croatia' (paper presented at the EBEN Research Conference, Poznan, June 2002).

Rankin, R. (2003), 'HIH Inquiry Seeks Scapegoats for Australia's Biggest Bankruptcy', *World Socialist Web Site* (published online 10 January, 2003), <http://www.wsws.org/articles/2003/jan2003/hih-j10.shtml> (cited May 2004).

Ravishankar, L. (2003), 'Encouraging Internal Whistleblowing in Organizations' (Report prepared for the Business and Organizational Ethics Partnership at the Markkula Center for Applied Ethics), <http://www.scu.edu/ethics/ publications/submitted/whistleblowing.html> (cited January 2004).

Reichheld, F.F. (1996), *the Loyalty Effect. The Hidden Force Behind Growth, Profits and Lasting Value* (Boston: Harvard Business School Press).

Rhenman, E. (1965), *Industrial Democracy and Industrial Management* (London: Tavistock) [the original publication occurred a year before: Rhenman, E.: 1964, *Företagsdemokrati och företagsorganisation* (Stockholm, SAF/FFI)].

Riesenberg, T.L. (2001), 'Trying to Hear the Whistle Blowing: The Widely Misunderstood "Illegal Act" Reporting Requirements of Exchange Act Section 10A', *Business Lawyer* 56:4, 1417–60.

Ringer, R. (1997), *Max Weber's methodology. The Unification of the Cultural and Social Sciences* (London: Harvard University Press).

Robinson, M. (1998), 'The Business Case for Human Rights', in D. Hart (ed.) *Visions of Ethical Business 1* (London: Financial Times Management), 14–17.

Roche, J. (1971), 'The Competitive System, to Work, to Preserve, and to Protect', *Vital Speeches of the Day*, 1 May 1971, 445.

Roma, G. (1999), *Atypical Forms of Employment* (Rome: Censis).

Rongine, N.M. (1985), 'Toward a Coherent Legal Response to the Public-policy Dilemma Posed by Whistleblowing', *American Business Law Journal* 23:2, 281–97.

Rosecrance, J. (1988), 'Whistleblowing in Probation Departments', *Journal of Criminal Justice* 16:2, 99–109.

Rosenau, J.N. and Czempiel, E. (eds) (1991), *Governance without Government. Order and Change in World Politics* (Cambridge: Cambridge University Press).

Rosenblatt, Z. and Schaeffer, Z. (2000), 'Ethical Problems in Downsizing', in R.J. Burke and C.L. Cooper (eds), *the Organisation in Crisis* (Oxford: Blackwell), 132–50.

Roth, G. (1968), 'Introduction', in M. Weber (1968), *Economy and Society* (New York: Bedminster Press), lxiii–lxiv.

Rothschild, J. (1994), 'The Right to Excess Dissent as Necessary for Organizational Democracy: The Case of Whistleblowers', (conference paper, International Sociological Association).

Rothschild, J. and Miethe, T. (1992), 'Whistleblowing as Occupational Deviance and Dilemma', (conference paper, American Sociological Association).

—— (1999), 'Disclosing Misconduct in Work Organizations: An Empirical Analysis of the Situational Factors That Foster Whistleblowing', in I. Harper and R.L. Simpson (eds), *Research in the Sociology of Work*, Vol. 8 (Ohio: JAI Press), 211–27.

Rowley, T. (1997), 'Moving beyond Dyadic Ties: A Network Theory of Stakeholder Influences', *Academy of Management Review* 22:4, 887–910.

Salcido, R. (2000), 'The Government Declares War on Qui Tam Plaintiffs who Lack Inside Information: The Government's New Policy to Dismiss These Parties in False Claims Act Litigation', <http://www.akingump.com/publication.cfm?publication_id=444> (cited July 2004).

Sandmo, A. (1999), 'Asymmetric information and public economics: The Mirrlees-Vickrey Nobel Prize', *Journal of Economic Perspectives* 13:1, 165–180.

Santoro, E. (2003), *Autonomy, Freedom and Rights. A Critique of Liberal Subjectivity* (Dordrecht: Kluwer Academic Publishers).

Schwarb, T.M. (1998), *Ich verpfeife meine Firma. Einführung in das Phänomen Whistle-Blowing* (Olten: Fachholchshule Solothurn Nordwestschweiz).

—— (2003), 'Reden ist Silber – ist Schweigen Gold?', *HR-Today* (April 2003), <http://www.hrtoday.ch/Artikel_Detail_de.cfm?MsgID=1041> (cited July 2004).

Senate Select Committee on Public Interest Whistleblowing (SSCOPIW) (1994), *in the Public Interest* (Canberra: AGPS).

Sennett, R. (1998), *the Corrosion of Character* (New York: Norton).

Siegel, P.J. (2002), *the Sarbanes-Oxley Act of 2002: Expanded Whistleblower Protection,* <http://www.irmi.com> (cited May 2004).

Sims, R.L. and Keenan, J.P. (1998), 'Predictors of External Whistleblowing: Organizational and Intrapersonel Variables', *Journal of Business Ethics* 17, 411–421.

Slane, B.H. (1995), 'Reports on Proposed Legislation', *Annual Report* (Wellington: Office of the Privacy Commissioner), <http://www.privacy.org.nz/recept/ar1995_2.html> (cited May 2004).

—— (1997), *Report by the Privacy Commissioner to the Minister of Justice on the Protected Disclosures Bill* (Wellington: Office of the Privacy Commissioner), <http://www.privacy.org.nz/people/pdisc.html> (cited May 2004).

Smith, J.M. (1971), 'More on Whistle Blowing', *Computer* 4:6, 13&.

Solomon, R.C (1993), *Business and Excellence. Cooperation and Integrity in Business* (New York: Oxford University Press).

—— (1997), *It's Good Business* (Oxford: Rowman and Littlefield Publishers).

South African Law Reform Commission (SALRC) (2002), *Issue Paper 20 – Project 123 – Protected Disclosures* (Pretoria: South African Law Reform Commission).

——— (2004), *Discussion Paper 107 – Project 123 – Protected Disclosures* (Pretoria: South African Law Reform Commission).

Standards Australia (SA) (2003), *AS 8004–2003. Whistleblower Protection Programs for Entities* (Sydney: Standards Australia).

Sternberg, E. (1996), 'A Vindication of Whistleblowing in Business', in *Four Windows on Whistleblowing (*London: Public Concern at Work), 24–39.

Stewart, L.P. (1980), 'Whistle Blowing – Implications for Organizational Communication', *Journal of Communication* 30:4, 90–101.

Stiglitz, J.E. (2000), 'The Contributions of the Economics of Information to Twentieth Century Economics', *Quarterly Journal of Economics* 115:4, 1441–78.

Stuttard, G. (1992), 'Robert Owen, 1771–1858: A 19th-century Pilgrim's Progress in the World of European Business Ethics', in J. Mahoney and E. Vallance (eds), *Business Ethics in a New Europe* (Dordrecht: Kluwer Academic).

Sullivan, R. (ed.) (2003), *Business and Human Rights. Dilemmas and Solutions* (Sheffield: Greenleaf).

Suzuki, T. (2003), 'The Epistemology of Macroeconomic Reality: The Keynsian Revolution From An Accounting Point of View', *Accounting, Organizations and Society* 28:5, 471–517.

SVA (2003), *Verklaring inzake het omgaan met vermoedens van misstanden in ondernemingen* (Den Haag: Stichting van de Arbeid).

Swanson, D.L. (1995), 'Addressing a Theoretical Problem by Reorienting the Corporate Social Performance Model', *Academy of Management Review* 20:1, 43–64.

Swenson, W. (1995), 'The Organizational Guidelines' "Carrot and Stick" Philosophy, and their Focus on "Effective" Compliance', in *US Sentencing Commission Symposium Proceedings – Corporate Crime in America: Strengthening the 'Good Citizen' Corporation, September 1995, 30–31* (Washington, DC: US Sentencing Commission).

Tengblad, S. (2001), 'Corporate Governance from a Social Movement Perspective: The Case of Sweden' (paper presented at the 16th Nordic Conference on Business Studies, Uppsala Sweden).

Time (2002), 'The Whistleblowers', *Time* 30 (December), 36–62.

Touraine, A. (1969), *La société post-industrielle. Naissance d'une société (*Paris: Denoël).

——— (1997), *Pourrons-nous vivre ensemble ? Égaux et différents (*Paris : Fayard).

———, Perez, C. and Andrade, P. (1995), 'Entretien – la notion de sujet et la modernité', *Atalaia* 1 (Winter), 31–34.

Transparency International (2000), *Transparency International Source Book 2000* (Berlin: Transparency International).

———— (2004), *Global Report* (Berlin: Transparency International).

Transparency International Australia (2002). *Transparency International Australia CLERP 9 submission,* <http://www.aph.gov.au/Senate/committee/ corporations_ctte/clerp9/submissions/sub023a1.doc> (cited October 2004).

Trott, K (2004), 'The Australian Perspective' in R. Calland and G. Dehn (eds), *Whistleblowing around the World. Law, Culture and Practice* (Cape Town, London: ODAC, PCAW), 119–141.

Umeda, T. (2004), 'Japan: Integrity Assessment', <http://www.publicintegrity. org/ga/country.aspx?cc=jp&act=ia> (cited November 2004).

Unilever (2002), *Listening, Learning, Making Progress. Social Review of 2001 Data* (s.l.: Unilever).

United States Senate (1978), *the Whistleblowers: A Report on Federal Employees who Disclosure Acts of Governmental Waste* (Washington, DC: Senate Committee on Governmental Affairs).

United States Sentencing Commission (USSC) (1991), *United States Sentencing Commission Sentencing Guidelines, Chapter Eight – Sentencing of Organizations* (56 Federal Register 22, 786).

———— (2002), *Sentencing Guidelines Manual* (Washington, DC: United States Sentencing Commission).

Van Buitenen, P. (1999). *Strijd voor Europa. Fraude in de Europese Commissie* (Baarn, Leuven: Ten Have, Van Halewyck).

Van de Ven, B. (2004), 'De betrokkenheid van multinationals bij mensenrechten in het licht van de globalisering', *Ethiek & Maatschappij* 7:2, 34–49.

———— (2005), 'Human Rights as a Normative Basis for Stakeholder Legitimacy', *Corporate Governance* 5:2, 48–59.

Van Es, R. and Smit, G. (2003), 'Whistleblowing and Media Logic: A Case Study', *Business Ethics: A European Review* 12:2, 144–50.

Van Gent, I. (2003), 'Memorie van toelichting bij Voorstel van Wet 28 990' (Tweede Kamer stuk 28990 No. 3).

Van Hooland, B. (2003), *Nieuw publiek management. Van bestuurskunde tot Copernicus* (Gent: Academia Press).

Van Hootegem, G. (2000), *De draaglijke traagheid van het management. Tendensen in het productie-en personeelsbeleid* (Leuven: Acco).

Van Parijs, P. (2002), 'The Spotlight and the Microphone. Must Business Be Socially Responsible, and Can It?', working paper of the Chair Hoover No. 92, <http://www.etes.ucl.ac.be/DOCH/DOCH/DOCH%2092%20_PVP_.pdf> (cited April 2004).

Vandekerckhove, W. (1998), *Vergelijkende studie naar de invloed van zingeving bij het oplossen van het probleem van opvolging van charismatisch leiderschap bij twee nieuw religieuze bewegingen: OSHO en ISKCON (*Ghent: Universiteit Ghent) [Masters Thesis].

———— (2002), 'Procedure, Charisma and Whistle Blowing', *Philosophy Today* 16:41, 2–3.

————— (2003), 'Ethische problemen voor en van NGOs in de strijd tegen mensenhandel', in W. Vandekerckhove (ed.), *NGOs in de strijd tegen mensenhandel* (Antwerpen: EPO), 76–97.

————— (2004), 'Health-care Projects and the Risk of NGO Goal Displacement', *Research for Sex Work* 7 (June), 18–20.

Vandekerckhove, W. and Commers, M.S.R. (2000), 'Het onderzoek inzake anticorruptie. Een stand van zaken', *Ethiek & Maatschappij* 3:3, 39–61.

————— (2003), 'Downward Workplace Mobbing: A Sign of the Times?', *Journal of Business Ethics* 45:1–2, 41–50.

————— (2004), 'Whistle blowing and rational loyalty', *Journal of Business Ethics* 53:1–2, 225–233.

————— (2005), 'Beyond Voluntary/Mandatory Juxtaposition. Towards a European Framework on CSR as Network Governance, *Social Responsibility Journal* 1(1/2), 98–103.

Vandekerckhove, W. and Dentchev, N.: 2005, 'Network Perspective on Stakeholder Management: Facilitating Entrepreneurs in the Discovery of Opportunities' *Journal of Business Ethics* 60(3), 221–32.

Verhofstadt, G. (1999), *De brug naar de 21ste eeuw. Regeerakkoord Federale Regering 7 juli 1999* (Brussel: Federale regering).

Vinten, G. (ed.) (1994), *Whistleblowing: Subversion or Corporate Citizenship?* (New York: St Martin's Press).

Vogel, D. (1974), 'The Politicisation of the Corporation', *Social Policy* 5:1, 57–62.

Volberda, H.W. (1998), *Building the Flexible Firm: How to Remain Competitive* (New York: Oxford University Press).

Volvo (2003), *Volvo Group Code of Conduct* (Göteborg: AB Volvo).

VR (2001), *Beter bestuurlijk beleid – reorganisatie van het Vlaamse overheidsapparaat: sectorale invulling van de beleidsdomeinen m.b.t. horizontale beleidsaangelegenheden – nota VR/2001/0106/DOC0444* (Brussel: Vlaamse Regering).

Walters, K.D. (1975), 'Your Employees' Right to Blow the Whistle', *Harvard Business Review* 534, 26–34 cont. 161–62.

Watrick, S.L. and Cochran, P.L. (1985), 'The Evolution of the Corporate Social Performance Model', *Academy of Management Review* 10:4, 758–69.

Weber, J. and Wasieleski, D.M. (2003), 'Managing Corporate Stakeholders', in J. Andriof, S. Waddock, B. Husted and S.S. Rahman (eds), *Unfolding Stakeholder Thinking*, Vol. 2, *Relationships, Communication, Reporting and Performance* (Sheffield: Greenleaf Publishing), 180–201.

Weber, M. (1968), *Economy and Society. An outline of interpretive sociology* (New York: Bedminster Press).

Weick, K.E. (2001), *Making Sense of the Organization* (Oxford: Blackwell Publishers).

Welcomer, S., Cochran, P.L. and Gerde, V.W. (2003), 'Power and Social Behaviour: A Structuration Approach to Stakeholder Networks', in J. Andriof, S.

Waddock, B. Husted and S.S. Rahman (eds), *Unfolding Stakeholder Thinking*, Vol. 2, *Relationships, Communication, Reporting and Performance* (Sheffield: Greenleaf Publishing), 83–105.

Wicks, A.C., Gilbert, D.R. Jr and Freeman, R.E. (1994), 'A Feminist Reinterpretation of the Stakeholder Concept', *Business Ethics Quarterly* 4:4, 475–97.

Willockx, F. (2000), 'Persoonlijke conclusies van het colloquium', in F. Willockx (ed.), *Crisisbeheer door de overheid – Gestion de crise par le gouvernement* (Brussel: Federale Voorlichtingdienst).

Wilson, P.E. (1993), 'The Fiction of Corporate Scapegoating', *Journal of Business Ethics* 12:10, 779–84.

Winfield, M. (1990), *Minding Your Own Business. Self-regulation and Whistleblowing in British Companies* (London: Social Audit).

Wolff, L. (2004), 'New Whistleblower Protection Laws for Japan', *Journal of Japanese Law* 17, 209–13.

Wood, D.J. (1991), 'Corporate Social Performance Revisited', *Academy of Management Review* 16:4, 691–718.

Worral, L., Cooper, C.L., and Campbell, F. (2000), 'The Impact of Organizational Change', in R.J. Burke and C.L. Cooper (eds), *The Organization in Crisis. Downsizing, Restructuring, and Privatization* (Oxford: Blackwell Publishers), 20–43.

Index

accountability
  accountability (in a general sense) 5,
    10, 12, 83, 113–16, 124, 145–6,
    180, 182–4, 194–5, 198–9, 203, 213,
    224–6, 230–31, 238, 246, 253, 258,
    275, 282
  accountability construct 108–10, 113,
    141, 149–50, 158–9, 183–4, 194–6,
    202–3, 205–6, 209–10, 213–6, 220,
    225, 228–9, 241, 248–50, 253, 258,
    262, 268, 275, 279–89, 294–5, 299,
    301–2, 304, 307–9, 311–12
  downward and upward accountability
    115, 150, 220, 275
  responsibility and accountability 75,
    108–10, 158, 262, 291
  to hold accountable 53, 103, 113–14,
    141, 150, 161, 169–70, 183, 199,
    208–10, 216, 220, 224–5, 227, 238,
    241, 281–2, 286, 291, 302
accusation 92, 100, 147, 270
act 8, 13, 22–3, 25, 34, 41–2, 51, 86, 111,
  122–4, 127–8, 132–5, 138–40, 144,
  146, 151, 159, 170, 171–2, 199
action 18, 31, 33 35, 38, 40–46, 52, 55, 60,
  62, 64–6, 69, 77, 79, 83–5, 104, 110,
  112, 122–3, 132, 139, 150, 159, 167,
  170–71, 198, 213, 265, 271, 291, 309,
  320
action theory 45
actor 3, 18–19, 33, 38, 41, 46, 54–5, 59, 62,
  65–6, 70, 82–5, 92, 104, 147–9, 200,
  227, 236, 250, 284–9, 292, 294, 297,
  299, 304–5, 312
actor element 6, 22, 25, 75, 100, 142,
  145–52, 184, 187, 193–5, 201–3,
  208–10, 217, 225, 228–31, 234, 239,
  244, 248, 253, 256–7, 266, 291, 293,
  310, 313–14
allegation 25, 140–41, 151, 170–71, 175,
  179, 198, 215, 218, 244, 256, 263,
  272–30 280, 293, 309, 311–14

anonymous 24, 170, 183, 203, 244, 263,
  266
association 41–4, 47, 59, 103, 178, 236
audit 170, 210, 213, 221, 240–41
audit committee 179, 181, 183, 221
auditing 177, 181
auditor 15, 24, 26, 140, 165, 183, 194, 201,
  203–4, 209, 224, 228, 230, 253, 273
authority 10, 13, 22–3, 43–6, 52, 55, 62,
  83–4, 97, 106, 132–3, 139, 170, 176–7,
  189, 198, 200, 205, 208, 221, 226, 253,
  262, 265, 298
autonomy 14, 53, 62, 80–1, 99, 111–14,
  117–18, 123, 144, 158, 246, 297
autopoietic organization, *see* organization
autopoietic theory 44–5

Bovens, M. 241, 243, 246, 248, 250
bribery 16, 137, 270–75, 280, 290
bureaucracy 11–12, 23, 37, 47–8, 60–61,
  64, 77, 83, 114–15, 135, 137, 149, 158,
  166, 236, 241, 302, 309

capitalism 9, 15, 31, 48, 61–2, 74, 89, 118,
  135, 183, 203, 281
citizen 1, 25, 78, 103, 136, 166, 173–4, 241,
  243–4, 250, 271, 282, 288, 293
citizenship
  corporate citizenship 87, 102–3, 130,
    178, 198–9, 213, 221, 230, 240–41
  institutional citizenship 241, 243–4, 250
Civil Service Reform Act 169–72, 280–82
code of conduct, *see* code of ethics
code of ethics 16, 24, 116, 122–3, 130–33,
  165, 179, 205–6, 210, 216–17, 245,
  255–6, 258, 290
coercion 38–9, 42–3, 53, 89–90, 113
commitment 16, 53, 74, 85, 117, 133, 255
commodity 9, 19, 37
communication 13, 24, 34, 45–6, 81–5, 92,
  97, 104, 123, 133, 135, 138, 151, 159,
  177, 179, 272–3, 277, 290

complaint 16, 23, 87, 141, 151, 171, 175, 179, 181, 188, 209, 231, 239–41, 263, 272
conceptual shift 33
conceptual variation 3, 74, 102
concern 111, 115, 151, 188, 238, 244, 246, 314
confidential 8, 181, 188, 203, 214, 220, 229, 236, 245, 261
conflict 1–3, 8–9, 14–16, 21, 25, 40, 60–64, 69, 84–5, 87, 104–5, 124, 126–7, 138, 140, 146, 279, 285, 289, 293–5, 304, 306–7, 312
consensus 5, 16, 19, 20, 37, 41–3, 70, 81, 98, 104, 113, 164
Cooper, C. 17
corporate governance, *see* governance
corporate misconduct, *see* misconduct
corporate responsibility, *see* corporate social responsibility
corporate social responsibility 75, 87, 101–4, 130, 136–7, 182, 271
corporation 1, 10–11, 15–6, 26, 64, 84–5, 88–9, 95–6, 102–4, 107, 110, 129, 165–8, 176, 181–3, 195, 200–2, 231, 248, 256, 263, 286, 293
corruption 8, 16, 78–9, 118, 137, 139, 152, 164, 172, 189, 192, 194–5, 199, 204–6, 221, 224–8, 230, 261–5, 268, 270–75, 280–83, 287–8, 290, 305, 310, 313
Council of Europe (COE) 6, 20, 163, 270, 274–5, 277, 280
cover-up 217, 218–19, 228, 244–5, 249, 253, 255, 293
criminal
    conduct 176–7, 227
    matters 241, 244–5, 249
    offence 189, 195, 217, 228, 274, 293
CSR, *see* corporate social responsibility

De Maria, W. 14, 16, 21–2, 199, 206, 209, 313–14
democracy 15, 86, 88, 97–103, 113–4, 137, 144–7, 166, 172, 180, 198–9, 224–30, 236, 239, 247, 261–2, 287–8, 294, 313–14
de-modernization, *see* modernization and de-modernization

Dewey, J. 79, 91
dialogue 83, 85, 92, 98, 103–4
discipline
    labour discipline 2, 5, 58, 64
    organizational discipline 48, 53–4, 59, 61, 303
    Weber and discipline, *see* Weber, M.
disclosure
    disclosure of information 1, 8, 22, 92, 97, 113, 139–40, 144, 159, 165, 170, 188, 193, 209, 224
    external disclosure 23, 115, 194, 196, 218, 235, 258, 262, 271, 275
    informed disclosure 170
    internal disclosure 16, 23, 235–6, 253, 255, 262, 268, 271, 283–4
    public disclosure 257–8
    public interest disclosure 187, 193, 206, 210, 218, 234
discourse 2–4, 21, 26, 30, 49–54, 57–8, 64, 69, 71, 74, 85, 91, 98, 109, 113–14, 140, 150, 152, 156–9, 167, 172, 182–4, 228, 230, 286, 306, 309
dissent 5, 15, 19, 22–3, 36, 54, 164, 297, 306, 313
dissociation 30, 59, 66, 279, 299, 302
dobbing 198–9, 206
dominance 3–6, 9, 30, 37, 40–48, 50, 54–5, 57–8, 60, 64, 69, 75, 84, 109, 297
Dubey, S. 262
due diligence 92, 176–7, 180
Dworkin, T.M. 13–4, 16, 22, 164–9, 172–4, 178–9, 184, 284, 315

Electoral and Administrative Review Commission (EARC) 187–9, 192
employment-at-will 12, 163–6, 287, 295
enclosure 59, 59–71, 75, 142, 152, 156, 158, 161, 210, 236, 279, 299, 302–3, 307
enterprise 8, 60–64, 77, 83, 97, 104, 132, 182, 250, 271, 275
ethical distance 110–11, 149, 158, 180, 246, 266, 291, 307, 310
ethics code, *see* code of ethics
European Commission (EC) 20, 103, 136, 163, 243, 270, 272–3, 277, 294

False Claims Act (FCA) 172–5, 184, 280, 293–5

Finn, P. 187–8, 206, 290

Foucauldian 3, 30, 49, 51–8, 61, 64–8, 296–8, 304

Foucault, M. 3, 5, 30, 49–52, 54–6, 58, 62, 66–70, 81, 139, 152, 295–9

fraud 8, 90, 113, 115, 131, 137–9, 152, 170–78, 180, 183, 187–8, 192, 199, 203, 205, 209, 221, 229, 234, 243, 249–50, 266, 268, 272–3, 280–82, 287, 293, 305

Freeman, R.E. 85–8, 90–92, 99

Friedman, M. 83, 89–90, 94–5

Gibbs Committee 187–8

Glazer, M.P. 13, 22

goal-displacement 108, 131–3, 145, 243, 266, 315

Goodpaster, K.E. 88–91

governance
  corporate governance 16, 113, 140, 145, 161, 180, 183, 196, 202–4, 216, 227–9, 272, 275, 277, 281–2, 284–5, 287, 293
  governance approach 150, 168, 181, 183–4, 192–6, 203, 205, 208–9, 214–15, 262, 282–3
  governance and government, *see* government
  network governance 105, 106, 124, 144, 303

government
  government administration 236, 238, 240
  government agency 1, 108, 150, 176, 188, 192–4, 196, 199, 205, 208, 224–5, 284, 286, 288, 292, 303, 312
  government and governance 79–80
  government organization, *see* government agency
  government personnel 12, 239, 240–41

Government Accountability Project (GAP) 167, 265, 286, 294

Greider, W. 135, 281

grievance 16, 98, 179, 215, 262

Guattari, F. 55, 57–8

Hardt, M. 9–10, 19, 48–52, 55, 58

helpline, *see* hotline

Hinweisgeber 266

hotline 170, 181, 183, 203, 213, 234, 247, 266, 270, 286, 294

human rights
  free speech 12, 98–99, 101, 146–7, 166–8, 244, 247, 261–2, 287–8
  freedom of expression 94, 97, 99, 100, 147, 166, 247–9, 288
  freedom of opinion 94, 99
  instrumental right 98
  intrinsic right 98, 166, 247

Idasa (Institute for Democracy in South Africa) 226–7

impimpi 221, 224

information
  disclosure of information, *see* disclosure
  information asymmetry 106, 275, 284–5
  leaking information 18
  source of information 18, 47, 98, 134–40, 144

institution 9, 11, 15, 16, 60–61, 65, 80, 96, 111–12, 128, 172, 266, 303, 314

institutional
  citizenship, *see* citizenship
  level 3, 30, 63–4, 68, 86, 102
  reforms 239–40, 282
  structure 14, 106

institutionalization 5, 14, 20, 25–6, 29, 36, 40, 48, 54, 64, 67–71, 108, 133–4, 139, 142, 164, 292, 296, 303–7, 313

integrity
  concept of integrity 116–24, 188, 243–4, 291
  integrity construct 135, 145, 150–51, 159–60, 184, 215, 246–7, 255–6, 265, 291, 301, 308–9, 311, 314

investigation 110, 139–40, 147, 151, 164, 170–71, 174–5, 181, 194–5, 198, 203–4, 210, 214, 219, 221, 225–6, 240–41, 245, 247, 253, 256, 262–3, 273–4, 280–84, 297, 313

King Committee 229, 287

klokkenluider 239, 243–4, 247–9, 288

labour union 76, 96, 106, 141, 176 ,218,
  221, 230, 245, 270–71, 288, 303, 309,
  311–12
law proposal
  in Canada 253–60
  in Germany 263–7
  in India 261–3
  in Ireland 250–54
  in Switzerland 266–9
  in the Netherlands 243–50
liability 97, 165, 180, 188, 202, 281
loyalty
  absolute loyalty 1, 8, 9, 124–34
  loyalty to the organization 1, 8, 9, 17,
    47, 126, 129, 131, 145, 160, 243
  loyalty to society 9, 199, 243–4, 289
  rational loyalty 126, 130–34, 145, 151,
    160–61, 164, 169, 179, 183–4, 199,
    204–6, 210, 215–17, 243, 248, 258,
    265, 268, 275, 289–90, 299, 301,
    308, 311
Luhmann, N. 2–3, 5, 29–41, 44–58, 62,
  65–6, 68–9, 87, 119, 279, 292, 304

MacIntyre, A. 38, 306
maladministration 192, 194, 224, 261–2
malpractice 25, 139, 149, 158, 219, 224,
  231, 236–9, 256, 258, 284, 291, 293,
  309–12, 315
management
  management structure 50, 53, 63, 77–80,
    85–6, 95, 102, 104, 150, 170, 179,
    215, 220, 239, 241
  management team 8, 16, 77, 113–14,
    133, 181–3, 215, 266, 271, 275
  management tools 16, 85, 138, 140, 145,
    150
  public management, *see* public
  scientific management 9–10, 38, 48, 60
  stakeholder management 85–90, 102
  strategic management 86, 89–90
manager 15–18, 26–7, 53, 62, 78, 82–3,
  86, 88–90, 102, 106, 114–15, 129, 131,
  133, 138, 140, 145, 149–50, 178, 201,
  208, 220, 240, 282, 309
managerial 16, 26–7, 82, 90, 102, 115,
  309

meaning
  meaning-giving 29, 31, 33–5, 38, 40, 45,
    50, 57, 62, 68, 74, 119, 122
  meaning-making 3, 58, 183
  meaning of increased attention for
    whistleblowing 7–21
Miceli, M.P. 8, 10, 13, 21–3, 168, 173, 284
misconduct 17, 113, 189, 203, 271
mission statement 129–32, 179, 217, 228,
  289–90
modernism 49, 66, 305
modernization and de-modernization 9,
  19, 66, 296, 305
motive 22–3, 47, 54, 59, 85, 90, 102, 128,
  133, 138, 140, 145, 172–3, 184, 218,
  244, 263, 271, 280

Nader, R. 1, 8–11, 15, 18, 19, 213
Near, J.P. 8, 10, 13, 21–3, 164, 168–9,
  172–4, 178–9, 247, 284, 315
Negri, A. 9–10, 19, 48–9, 51–2, 55, 58, 304
New Public Management (NPM), *see*
  public
NGO 27, 74, 80, 96, 103–4, 108, 140–41,
  161–3, 219, 226, 228, 262, 265, 294–5,
  303, 309, 312, 315
Nolan Committee 214–15, 220

OECD 6, 20, 163, 270–72, 275, 277, 280,
  282, 284–5, 290, 294
offence 177–8, 182, 189, 195, 209–10, 217,
  228, 257–8, 265, 274, 293
ombudsman 179, 187–8, 194–6, 199, 205,
  208, 230, 234, 240–41, 253, 273, 282,
  284–5, 292–3
Open Democracy Advice Centre (ODAC)
  227–31, 294
opportunity 13, 19, 82, 105, 109, 118–19,
  135, 137, 140–41, 169, 174, 209, 291
organization and society 1, 8, 16, 21, 25,
  29, 40, 49, 58, 66–9, 146, 157, 304–8,
  312
Organizational Sentencing Guidelines
  (OSG) 175, 178–81, 184, 290, 315

panopticon 54, 139–41, 161, 199, 203–4,
  216, 247, 258, 309
Parsons, T. 62, 129

Pashukanis, E. 37
personal gain 140, 184, 245, 253
PISA, *see* Public Interest Speak-Up
    Advisors
postmodern 80–82, 84
power
    abuse of power 150, 241, 309, 311, 313
    discretionary power 77, 109, 111, 123,
        125, 133, 137, 140, 256, 281
    economic power 43, 62–3
    power relation 4, 51–55, 58–9, 64, 88
primary concept 73–4, 101, 144
privatization 19, 78, 80, 136–7, 270, 286,
    304, 310–11
Protected Disclosure Act (New South
    Wales) 194, 225–6
Protected Disclosure Act (New Zealand)
    208–10, 314
Protected Disclosure Act (South Africa)
    227–31, 285, 287, 314
Protection of Officials Disclosing
    Irregularities Act (Belgium) 236–41
public
    new public management (NPM) 80, 195,
        238, 243, 245, 253, 270, 282
    public administration 139, 187–8, 196
    public interest 1, 3, 8, 10, 13, 17, 21–4,
        173, 187, 192–6, 198–200, 202, 206,
        210, 213–20, 225, 234, 243, 247–9,
        253, 261–3, 265, 268, 283–4, 287,
        290, 293, 310
    public management 12, 80
    public opinion 36, 141, 303
Public Concern At Work (PCAW) 213–15,
    219–21, 226, 228, 265, 270, 283, 289,
    291, 294–5, 312
Public Interest Disclosure Act (Australian
    Capital Territory) 193–5, 206
Public Interest Disclosure Act (UK)
    213, 215–21, 228, 236, 244–5, 253,
    268, 280, 282, 285–6, 288–90, 292–4,
    312–14
Public Interest Disclosure Act (Western
    Australia) 194–5, 205, 283, 292, 314
Public Interest Disclosures Act (Tasmania)
    194–6, 205, 283, 292, 314
Public Interest Speak-Up Advisors (PISA)
    234

Qui Tam 173–4, 280, 293

recipient
    external recipient 24, 151, 258, 283, 302
    final recipient 292–3, 303, 312
    internal recipient 24, 238, 255, 258, 268
    recipient element 2, 6, 25, 100, 142,
        145–8, 150–52, 193–5, 201–4, 206,
        208–9, 217–19, 224–5, 228–31,
        235–6, 239, 244–5, 248–9, 253,
        256–8, 262, 266, 268, 282–4, 287–8,
        292, 309–14
    tiered recipient 225, 283, 288, 312
resistance 10, 15, 41, 46, 51, 54–5, 92, 116,
    118, 121, 297, 298
responsibility
    collective responsibility 110–11, 149,
        158, 246
    individual responsibility 85, 149
    responsibility construct 75, 109, 112,
        135, 149–50, 158, 214, 246–7, 249,
        266, 288, 290, 306–7, 310
    responsibilization 53, 77, 109–13, 123,
        125, 133–4, 144–5, 158, 214, 246, 262
Rhenman, E. 86–9, 98
risk
    environmental, health and safety risk
        192, 195, 210, 217, 234
    ethical risk 5, 295, 307–8, 311–15
    risk (other) 13, 19, 22, 53, 61, 77, 90,
        104, 106, 109, 115–16, 119–20, 123,
        133, 137–8, 141, 182, 192, 210, 216,
        219, 225, 229, 257–8, 270, 272, 281,
        284, 286–7, 295, 306–7, 315
Roche, J. 7–8
Rowley, C. 17–8

Sarbanes-Oxley Act (SOX) 165, 180–84,
    202–3, 281–6, 292–4
secondary concept 74–5, 142
semantic
    cared-for semantic 41, 47, 54–5, 57–8, 65
    globalization semantic 2–5, 40, 73–77,
        79–80, 92, 94, 98–9, 101, 106–7,
        109, 112, 115–6, 122–5, 134–6,
        141–5, 144, 150, 152, 159–60,
        279–81, 284–8, 291–2, 295, 304–5,
        307, 309–10

semantic and discourse 50
semantic network 2, 32
semantic variation 62, 71, 279–80, 290,
    294, 299
stakeholder 2, 5, 60, 73–4, 80, 84–92, 95,
    98–99, 101–8, 112–13, 124, 141, 144,
    148,9, 156–7, 182, 213–17, 220, 225,
    236, 241, 243, 265–6, 272, 275, 280,
    285, 289, 298, 303–4, 308–9
Stammler, R. 37, 42
Stuchka, P. 37
subject
    subject of whistleblowing 2, 6, 23–5, 75,
        100, 142, 145–52, 167–9, 171, 184,
        187, 192–6, 201–10, 215, 217–18,
        220, 224–6, 228–9, 234–5, 238–9,
        241, 244–5, 248–9, 253–8, 261–2,
        265–6, 268, 274–5, 281, 283–4,
        287–91, 293–4, 302, 308–14
    whistleblower as a subject 3, 30, 50,
        66–7, 69, 117, 130, 152, 161, 296–9,
        302, 304–6
subjectaffirmation 4, 6, 59, 69, 71, 295–9,
    305, 307–8, 311
subjectivation 4–6, 51, 53–5, 58–9, 62, 66,
    69, 71, 295–9, 302, 303, 305, 307

Touraine, A. 3, 5, 30, 49, 59–71, 77, 83, 86,
    152, 295–9, 304–8
trade union, *see* labour union
Transparency International (TI) 200, 231,
    240, 268, 280

value
    general values 30, 62, 66
    norms and values 62, 297
    societal values 10, 62, 120, 122–3, 151

value appraisal 119–20, 122–3, 151
value creation 62
value reflection 123
Van Buitenen, P. 243–4, 272–3
verpfeifen 266

Walters, K.D. 8–11, 165–7, 169
watchdog 142, 145, 161, 204, 215, 236,
    289, 303, 309
Watkins, S. 17–8
Weber, M.
    bureaucracy 47–8, 60–61, 77, 83
    discipline 41–2, 44, 46–9, 51, 64
    idealism and Marxism 31–2, 37
    idealtype 38–40, 43, 60
    power 40–44, 46–47, 51–2, 54–5, 57, 64,
        81
    Verstehende Soziologie 3, 30, 36–9, 43,
        45, 49–50, 59–60
Whistleblower Protection Act (Japan)
    235–6, 238
Whistleblower Protection Act (US) 169,
    171–2, 184, 294
Whistleblowers Australia 199–200, 294
Whistleblowers Protection Act (SA Act)
    South Australia 192–4, 200, 206, 209
Whistleblowers Protection Act (WPA)
    Queensland 189, 192, 205–6
Whistleblowers Protection Act Victoria
    194
wrongdoing 14, 18, 22–4, 123, 139–40,
    169, 170–71, 175, 180, 188, 195–6,
    198–200, 208–10, 220–21, 225, 227,
    231, 244–8, 253, 255–7, 270, 275, 283,
    309, 312–3

Zivilcourage 265